GODS, GAMES, AND GLOBALIZATION

SPORTS & RELIGION

A SERIES EDITED
BY JOSEPH L. PRICE

Gods, Games, and Globalization

New Perspectives on Religion and Sports

REBECCA ALPERT AND ARTHUR REMILLARD

Editors

MERCER UNIVERSITY PRESS

Macon, Georgia

1979–2019

40 Years of Publishing Excellence

MUP/ P591

© 2019 by Mercer University Press
Published by Mercer University Press
1501 Mercer University Drive
Macon, Georgia 31207
All rights reserved

9 8 7 6 5 4 3 2 1

Books published by Mercer University Press are printed on acid-free paper
that meets the requirements of the American National Standard for
Information Sciences—Permanence of Paper for Printed Library Materials.

Printed and bound in the United States.

This book is set in Adobe Caslon Pro.

ISBN   978-0-88146-722-2
Cataloging-in-Publication Data is available from the Library of Congress

To Joe Price

Scholar, friend, and world-class anthem singer

UNIVERSITY

MERCER UNIVERSITY PRESS

Endowed by

TOM WATSON BROWN

and

THE WATSON-BROWN FOUNDATION, INC.

Contents

Acknowledgments

The origins of this volume trace back to 2011, when I (Art) interviewed Rebecca about her then new book, *Out of Left Field: Jews and Black Baseball*. As an interdisciplinary subfield, the topic of religion and sports had been something of a quirky sideshow in years past. But Rebecca's book along with the work of scholars such as Julie Byrne, William Baker and David Chidester, helped change all of that.

Still, as our conversations continued after this initial contact, we came to agree that in order for this field to truly advance, there would need to be a reconceiving of preexisting narratives, methods, and materials. This guided our decisions as we helped with the founding and development of the American Academy of Religion's "Religion, Sport, and Play" group. In the years since the group started, we witnessed more scholars who shared our interest in broadening the ways in which we think about religion and sports. We also discovered that we worked well together, and that, ultimately, led to this coedited volume.

It is entirely fitting, then, that *Gods, Games, and Globalization* is now part of Mercer University Press's "Sports and Religion" series. For many of us in this field, the series editor Joe Price helped set the terms by which we advance our ideas. We are grateful to Joe not only for his many fine contributions, but also for his editorial assistance with this volume and his excellent article that appears in it. For all of these reasons and more, we have dedicated this volume to him with admiration and gratitude. We also wish to thank Marc Jolley and the Mercer team for taking on this project and seeing it to completion. Of course, none of this would have been possible without the willing participation of our many authors. We knew some of the authors in advance as students and colleagues, but we met others only through this process. It's been a great pleasure working with all of them and learning about the kinds of research that they are doing that we believe will ultimately reshape our field. We appreciate everyone who wrote for this volume, especially as they patiently and thoroughly edited the many drafts of their essays. Maintaining a sense of coherence and conformity in an edited volume such as this is no small task, which makes us particularly thankful for the expert copyediting of Rachael Kamel, who received her PhD in Religion at Temple University and the editorial assistance of Alexandra Leber who did this work as part of Temple's Merit Scholars Program that provides opportunities for undergraduates to work with faculty on their research.

Rebecca wants to acknowledge the community of scholars and administrators at Temple University that has supported and nurtured her work. She is particularly grateful to the graduate students who have chosen to study and teach in the field of religion and sports, and the undergraduates who have studied with her in Honors Sports and Leisure in American Society, all of whom have enhanced her learning many fold and kept her on her toes with their questions and ideas. She accepted Art's invitation to work on this volume while serving in the Dean's Office of the College of Liberal Arts with the hope that co-editing an anthology would be compatible with daily administrative tasks. She is most grateful to her colleagues in the Dean's Office who make coming to work every day a pleasure and who share her belief that administration and scholarship can go hand in hand. She is also grateful for the support she gets at home from family and friends who don't always understand her academic interests but cheer her on nonetheless.

For his part, Art would like to thank his writing circle companions at Saint Francis University, especially Stephen Baker, Grant Julin, Kyle Thomsen, Denise Damico, Sarah Myers, Mike McKale, Kirk Weixel, Brennan Thomas, and Tim Bintrim. He is additionally grateful for the administrative support of Rosemary Bertocci, Tim Whisler, Wayne Powel, and Father Malachi Van Tassell. In encouraging him to pursue his scholarly interests, they have granted him the necessary release time to finish this volume. To my running friends in the Ebensburg Area Running Club, thank you for keeping me fit and sane: Kevin Doyle, Mike Bradley, Pedro Muíño, and John Balouris are the most reliable running partners a person could hope for. Finally, to his wife, Kate, Art is eternally grateful for her unending and abundant love and support. When he is deep in the weeds and short on perspective, she is there with the helpful reminder to breathe deeply and look at the sky.

Contributors

Rebecca Alpert, Professor of Religion, Temple University, Philadelphia, Pennsylvania, USA

Jennifer Baldwin, Director of the Grounding Flight Wellness Center, Founder of the Center for Trauma-Sensitive Faith Leadership, Woodstock, Georgia, USA

Annie Blazer, Associate Professor of Religious Studies, College of William & Mary, Williamsburg, Virginia, USA

Linda J. Borish, Associate Professor of History and Gender and Women's Studies, Western Michigan University, Kalamazoo, Michigan, USA

Stuart Braye, Senior Lecturers in Sports Studies, School of Health and Social Care, Teesside University, Middlesbrough, TS1 3BX, UK

Nick DeLuca, Information Science and Technology Major ('19), Temple University, Philadelphia, Pennsylvania, USA

Seth Dowland, Associate Professor of Religion and Chair of the Women's and Gender Studies Program, Pacific Lutheran University, Tacoma, Washington, USA

Tom Gibbons, Senior Lecturers in Sports Studies, School of Health and Social Care, Teesside University, Middlesbrough, TS1 3BX, UK

Kevin Hargaden, Social Theologian at the Jesuit Centre for Faith and Justice, Dublin, Ireland

Carmen Nanko-Fernández, Professor of Hispanic Theology and Ministry, Catholic Theological Union, Chicago, Illinois, USA

Janelle Peters, Independent Scholar, Los Angeles, California, USA

Joseph L. Price, Emeritus Professor of Religious Studies, Whittier College, Whittier, California, USA

Arthur Remillard, Associate Professor of Religious Studies, Saint Francis University, Loretto, Pennsylvania, USA

Duncan Reyburn, School of the Arts, University of Pretoria, South Africa

Scott D. Strednak Singer, Religion Department, St. Stephen's and St. Agnes School, Alexandria, Virginia, USA

Roberto Sirvent, Professor of Political and Social Ethics, Hope International University, Fullerton, California, USA

Tracy J. Trothen, Professor of Ethics, School of Religion and School of Rehabilitation Therapy, Queen's University, Kingston, Ontario, Canada

Dries Vanysacker, Faculty of Theology and Religious Studies, KU Leuven (Catholic University Leuven), Leuven, Belgium

Introduction

By Rebecca Alpert and Arthur Remillard

As the 1994 World Cup neared, the people of Zambia had lofty expectations for their soccer team. Many of the players had participated in the 1988 Olympics, where they finished tied for fifth place. Now, however, a more experienced team entered the Cup qualifiers, carrying with them the collective enthusiasm of their homeland. No other country this far south in Africa had ever made it to the Cup finals; Zambia appeared poised to make history. Playing in the World Cup would send a message to the world that Zambia was no longer to be colonized or pitied, but rather admired and respected.

Then on 27 April 1993 everything changed. A plane carrying the team to a World Cup qualifier crashed off the coast of Gabon. Eighteen teammates died, as did twelve of their support crew. A stunned and grieving nation responded to the news with disbelief, shock, and frustration. Their dream had also died in that plane crash. A funeral service was held shortly after at Independence Stadium, the largest structure of its kind in Zambia. This was the place where fans had come to cheer on their team. Tragedy, though, transformed it to a site of mourning. Approximately 30,000 attendees packed inside for the service, while roughly 100,000 more lingered outside. All of them witnessed the deceased being buried along the periphery of the stadium, making what was a special place even more significant. "This is sacred ground. These are our national heroes," remarked one security guard at the stadium.

Remarkably, a decision was made to reconstitute a team and forge ahead with the Cup's qualifying games. Win or lose, playing was the only way the country could redeem the deaths of its fallen comrades. Fortunately, Zambia would play a home match against Morocco. Once again, Independence Stadium became the center of national attention, but this time the focus was on soccer. By any reasonable measure, however, the makeshift home team had little chance of victory. Morocco was the more experienced and prepared team. Once the game began, things looked bleak as Morocco took a 1-0 lead into the halftime break. The Zambian players seemed hopelessly outmatched.

When the game resumed, the momentum inexplicably—or perhaps supernaturally— shifted. One fan described it this way:

> We Africans, we are Christian, most of us, but we also are believers in the spiritual. Morocco took a 1-0 lead in the first half, and you could see people standing, down at the end of the stadium that is near the graves. They were turned in the direction of the graves. They were shouting to the departed players, calling their names, asking for help. Where are you now that we need your help? What are you going to do about this? We need your help now. I was shouting along with everyone else. Then Kalusha scored on a direct kick and then we scored again.... I don't know about spirits. I just say what happened.

The word "miracle" was in no short supply in describing this victory. More miracles were on the way. The team proceeded to have a remarkable run of games, beating South Africa and shooting a tie with Zimbabwe. "Chipolopolo, yo! Chipolopolo, yo!," became the team's slogan, which translates to "strong, impervious, unbeatable." Zambia's last test, played in Casablanca, was a losing effort against the Moroccan team. The loss was heartbreaking. The role of the Zambian team in repairing the identity and dignity of a nation, however, cannot be understated. "There have been no psychiatrists involved, no grief counselors to help with pain," explained one journalist. "The national psychiatrist, the national grief counselor, has seemingly been this new soccer team as much as anyone or anything."[1]

More than a Game

The account of the rise, fall, and redemption of the Zambian soccer team offers a window into the ways that religion and sports interact on the global stage. At a surface level, we see a mix of Christian and indigenous religions punctuating the highs and lows of this account. "From the ashes of disaster, our soccer program is headed for glory, glory hallelujah," pro-

---

[1] Leigh Montville, "Triumph on Sacred Ground," *Sports Illustrated*, 18 October 1993, http://www.si.com/vault/1993/10/18/129564/triumph-on-sacred-ground-after-the-zambian-soccer-team-perished-in-a-plane-crash-a-new-team-rose-to-bring-hope-to-a-troubled-nation. See also Arthur Remillard, "Playing on Sacred Ground: Uncovering the Religious Dimensions of Athletic Venues around the World," in *The Changing World Religion Map*, ed. Stanley D. Brunn (New York: Springer, 2014).

claimed one Zambian sports announcer.[2] Fans and followers called upon their various faith traditions to provide a language for expressing their hopes, dreams, and aspirations. Additionally, soccer itself seemed to have a certain religious sensibility about it. Independence Stadium was not just a physical structure for sports matches; it was a sacred place—a location for grieving, for celebrating, for remembering, and for connecting with the living and the dead. To picture the crowd on the day they defeated Morocco, we see a nearly perfect description of what Emile Durkheim called "collective effervescence." In Durkheim's formulation, religion has its foundation in moments like these, when individuals feel "swept up into a world entirely different from the one they have before their eyes."[3]

In Zambia, soccer—both then and now— is far more than *just* a game. It is, instead, a deeply meaningful activity, a location for reveling in the collective ideas of Zambia and Zambians. Soccer is also a place where this single national identity comes to interact with broader global forces. Significantly, soccer arrived in Zambia by way of the British, who had colonized what was then known as Northern Rhodesia in 1911. When Zambia gained independence in 1964, the British left, but soccer remained.[4] By 1993, the Zambian team was playing games throughout the continent, aspiring to compete in a World Cup held in the United States. As news of their tragic circumstance spread, a global audience watched in admiration as this beleaguered team labored away on the pitch. The story of soccer in Zambia is also the story of globalization. It reveals how local identities shape, and are shaped by, an international flow of people, goods, ideas, technology, and culture.[5]

This is one of an untold number of stories of its kind. Accordingly, the focus of this volume is on the varieties of religious experiences in sports on the global stage. The scholarly conversation on religion and sports is vibrant and growing. It needs a new phase, however. The first phase of scholarship offered us a point of departure for thinking theoretically and historically about this topic. The first generation of authors de-

---

[2] Montville, "Triumph on Sacred Ground."

[3] Emile Durkheim, *The Elementary Forms of Religious Life*, trans. Karen E. Fields (New York: The Free Press, [1912] 1995), 228.

[4] Paul Darby, "A Context of Vulnerability: The Zambian Air Disaster, 1993," in *Soccer and Disaster: International Perspectives*, ed. Paul Darby et al., (New York: Routledge, 2005).

[5] Roland Robertson, *Globalization: Social Theory and Global Culture* (Thousand Oaks, CA: SAGE, 1992), 8.

bated the ways in which sports intersected with, or even replaced, traditional religions. Our task here is to expand, revise and complicate this conversation. The articles in this volume accomplish this by looking both within and beyond such conventional frames in order to shine a light on the many dark corners of this compelling topic.

Theory and History

Mircea Eliade looms large in the theoretical conversations on religion and sports. In the concluding pages of his classic text, *The Sacred and the Profane*, the author ruminates on the condition of modern humans and their "desacralized" world. To the "nonreligious" person of this era, he asserts, the rhythms of daily life have their foundation in science and reason. For Eliade, however, the craving for mythic experiences persists, as evidenced by a growing attraction to popular culture. "A whole volume could well be written on the myths of modern man," Eliade exclaims, "on the mythologies camouflaged in the plays that he enjoys, in the books that he reads."[6]

With this, Eliade gestures toward thinking differently about where religious frames of reference are situated and how they work. Modernity had placed religion in a box associated with private piety, formal structures, and official hierarchies. For the theorist, however, the phenomenon that we call "religion" has much deeper roots in the human quest to make life meaningful. Eliade, therefore, advises a method of comparison, of placing the symbolic stories of modernity side-by-side with their ancient precursors. Being both a novelist and historian of religions, Eliade identifies film and literature as places where people seek transcendent experiences. Since then, scholars have transferred this insight to the realm of sports—a realm, undoubtedly filled with heroes and villains, triumphs and tragedies, rivalries and friendships. Put simply, playing fields are another place where powerful myths and symbols lurk amid the camouflage of modernity.

Joseph Price's *From Season to Season* drew deeply from Eliade's methodological well. In his introduction the author writes, "Eliade's recognition that many forms of contemporary secular rituals manifest fundamental religious proclivities of human beings and reflect the sacred rites and myths of previous, religiously oriented cultures." For his own

---

[6] Mircea Eliade, *The Sacred and the Profane: The Nature of Religion*, trans. Willard R. Trask (New York: Harcourt, Brace, and Co., 1959), 97, 205.

part, Price references Eliade's ponderings on the "myth of the center"—
the recurring account of a mountain that connects the heavens and the
earth—to interpret the pitcher's mound. "As the mythical center of the
field," Price suggests, "the pitcher's mound is the point at which creation
of the game begins."[7]

Price is one of a handful of scholars and theologians who launched a
serious conversation on religion and sports.[8] For this crowd, Eliade and
similar theorists provide a language for thinking through their topic.[9]
Some have even begun making the case that sports in the modern world
are "a religion."[10] This prompted one pair of scholars to pen an extensive
denunciation of these "sports apologists."[11] A more productive approach
to theorizing about sports, however, has come from David Chidester,
who emphasizes that the attentive eye might detect "traces of transcendence, the sacred, and the ultimate" in sports as it does in other manifesta-

---

[7] Joseph L. Price, ed. *From Season to Season: Sports as American Religion*
(Macon, GA: Mercer University Press, 2001), 8, 67. See also, Joseph L. Price,
Rounding the Bases: Baseball and Religion in America (Macon, GA: Mercer
University Press, 2006). Eliade is also featured prominently in John Sexton,
Baseball as a Road to God: Seeing Beyond the Game (New York: Penguin, 2014).

[8] See also Michael Novak, *The Joy of Sport: End Zones, Bases, Baskets, Balls,
and the Consecration of the American Spirit* (New York: Basic Books, 1976);
Charles S. Prebish, ed. *Religion and Sport: The Meeting of the Sacred and the
Profane* (Westport, CT: Greenwood Press, 1993).

[9] In addition to Eliade, other common theoretical sources include: Ninian
Smart, *Worldviews: Crosscultural Explorations of Human Beliefs* (New York:
Charles Scribner's Sons, 1983); Robert N. Bellah, "Civil Religion in America,"
Daedalus: Journal of the American Academy of Arts and Sciences 96 (1967);
Durkheim, *The Elementary Forms of Religious Life*; Clifford Geertz, "Religion as
a Cultural System," in *The Interpretations of Cultures: Selected Essays by Clifford
Geertz*, ed. Clifford Geertz (New York: Basic Books, 1973).

[10] See, for example Craig Forney, *The Holy Trinity of American Sports: Civil
Religion in Football, Baseball, and Basketball* (Macon, GA: Mercer University
Press, 2012); Eric Bain-Selbo, *Game Day and God: Football, Faith, and Politics in
the American South* (Macon, GA: Mercer University Press, 2009); Eric Bain-
Selbo and D. Gregory Sapp, *Understanding Sport as a Religious Phenomenon: An
Introduction* (New York: Bloomsbury, 2016).

[11] Robert J. Higgs and Michael Braswell, *An Unholy Alliance: The Sacred
and Modern Sports* (Macon, GA: Mercer University Press, 2004).

tions of secular popular culture.[12] In other words, sports are not religions in the same way as Christianity, Islam, Judaism, or Buddhism; however, they can do real religious work—binding together communities, elevating heroes, producing sacred objects, and manufacturing mythical stories and memories.[13] Other scholars have noted that the distinction between the secular and the religious makes no sense in the contemporary world where these realms continuously intertwine.[14]

While some scholars have focused on the general ways in which sports can be interpreted in religious terms, others have documented how institutional religions have made use of sports throughout history. William Baker's *Playing with God* is a comprehensive synthesis of religion and sports in America. His narrative, therefore, reflects the main focus of the literature, which tends to place heavy emphasis on the origins, development, and legacy of "muscular Christianity." This unique packaging of muscles and morals began in England and traveled to the United States after the Civil War. In the following decades, an emerging breed of "body as temple" theologians sought to glorify the body and make health a scriptural mandate, while at the same time glorifying masculinity for an audience of men challenged by the changing social and gender norms created by the industrial revolution.[15]

Muscular Christianity has certainly lived on in Protestant circles, both in the United States and beyond. Other religious groups have also been at work mixing playing and praying, including Catholics, Jews, Mormons, Muslims, Buddhists, and an array of smaller religious communities. These stories are beginning to find a place in the historiog-

---

[12] David Chidester, *Authentic Fakes: Religion and American Popular Culture* (Berkeley: University of California Press, 2005), 10.

[13] Gary Laderman, *Sacred Matters: Celebrity Worship, Sexual Ecstasies, the Living Dead, and Other Signs of Religious Life in the United States* (New York: The New Press, 2009), 43–62. As a popular culture parallel, see also, Kathryn Lofton, *Oprah: The Gospel of an Icon* (Berkeley: University of California Press, 2011).

[14] Jeffrey Scholes and Raphael Sassower, *Religion and Sports in American Culture* (New York: Routledge, 2014) and Daniel A. Grano, *The Eternal Present of Sport: Rethinking Sport and Religion* (Philadelphia: Temple University Press, 2017).

[15] William J. Baker, *Playing with God: Religion and Modern Sport* (Cambridge, MA: Harvard University Press, 2007).

raphy of religion and sports.[16] Additionally, scholars have begun to look more closely within Protestant circles, paying attention to themes of race, gender, and class. In her ethnographic study of women and sports, Annie Blazer offers a ground-level examination of what she calls "sports ministry." What Blazer discovered was female athletes who, through engaging with their sport, came to question and wrestle with matters of moral authority, gender, and sexuality.[17]

Part of Blazer's research focus was on a women's soccer team. For scholars in the United States, this game has been woefully under-examined, despite its worldwide appeal. Scanning the literature on religion and sports, we find no shortage of attention given to basketball, football, and baseball—the "holy trinity" of American sports, as theologian Michael Novak calls it.[18] In such discussions, the focus has been primarily on Britain and the United States, but scholars are now beginning to look outward at the world, and examining a broader range of sports in a global context. It is our goal in this volume to collect different visions of the new global perspectives on religion and sports.

Tugging at the Edges

As we have seen, the initial wave of scholarship on religion and sports went in two directions: One addressed the religious dimension of sports themselves, while the other investigated self-identified religious adherents and institutions that have used sports in traditional religious contexts, often to their own ends. The essays of this volume aim to advance both of these efforts, tugging at the edges of an established discussion on religion and sports. The following sections are not meant to be neatly divided; instead, there is a healthy amount of thematic overlap

---

[16] Julie Byrne, *O God of Players: The Story of the Immaculata Mighty Macs* (New York: Columbia University Press, 2003); Richard Ian Kimball, *Sports in Zion: Mormon Recreation, 1890–1940* (Urbana: University of Illinois Press, 2003); Michael J. Zogry, *Anetso, the Cherokee Ball Game: At the Center of Ceremony and Identity* (Chapel Hill: University of North Carolina Press, 2010); Rebeccca T. Alpert, *Out of Left Field: Jews and Black Baseball* (New York: Oxford University Press, 2011).

[17] Annie Blazer, *Playing for God: Evangelical Women and the Unintended Consequences of Sports Ministry* (New York: NYU Press, 2015).

[18] Novak, *The Joy of Sport*, 34.

between them. From this we find both fascinating new stories and potential for future inquiry.

In section 1, "A Global Perspective," articles are set in many countries around the globe, particularly in relation to the "muscular Christian" movement. These essays extend out to the far corners of the world, to developed and developing nations, and from urban to rural landscapes.

To begin, Kevin Hargaden focuses on soccer and ethics, using soccer as a lens to bring into view the relationship between its Christian origins and its current role in the global economy. Hargaden traces the history of soccer from its roots in the nineteenth-century Anglican Church to its current status as an essential part of the global neoliberal economy. Positing that Christian theology is inherently anti-capitalist, Hargaden suggests that finding new ways to experience soccer—as a game to play communally rather than a sport to worship, for example— might lead to new challenges to neoliberalism.

Keith Vanysacker is also interested in the connections among sports, religion, ethics, and political economy. His essay takes us back to the European colonial and Catholic missionary roots of sports in the Belgian Congo, where the Catholic Church established the first sports association on the continent of Africa in the early twentieth century, and demonstrates the ways in which the church used sports as a colonial project to bring Christian and western values to the native population.

Seth Dowland considers the theme of Christian masculinity, telling the story of the failures of the planned 1919 Inter-Allied Games that were envisioned by the YMCA as a means to heal the world from the horrors of war. Dowland argues that the effort failed because it was (and continues to be) impossible to separate sports from the military and therefore impossible to use sports as a vehicle to promote the Christian value of peace.

Finishing this section, Janelle Peters takes us to the Vatican to introduce us to its official soccer tournament—the Clericus Cup—a "World Cup" for clergy and seminarians. Peters shows how sports and ethical values are often but not always compatible, informing us about conflicts the Catholic Church faces when difficult choices need to be made, and raising important questions about the relationship between sports and ethics.

"Beyond the Holy Trinity" is the title of section 2. In it, articles examine mixed martial arts, fly fishing, pole dancing, hockey, and track and field—sports with devoted followings that are underrepresented in conversations on religion and sports. What can these games tell us about the creative ways people have inscribed sacred meaning onto their favorite games?

Jennifer Baldwin's essay shows how the sport of pole dancing has been defined through a lens of Christian ethics. Pole is a relatively new competitive sport, emerging first in Australia in the early twenty-first century. The first World Pole Sports Championships did not take place until 2012. Because pole emerged from the sensuous world of the strip club, questions about its "sinful nature" have been raised by Christian thinkers. Baldwin counters those claims, creating what she calls a soteriology of restoration that she has discovered in the pole dance world.

Joe Price examines another sport that is not commonly the subject of religious analysis: fly fishing. He examines its culture through the lenses of both nature and lived religion as well as through its roots in Christian fish and fishing stories, as expressed in two works of memoir and fiction. Through his literary analysis, Price illuminates the deep Christian and mythical values inherent in the sport.

Annie Blazer and Scott Singer take different approaches to the world of Christian mixed martial arts. Blazer spent time observing activities of the Power Team, an evangelical group that performs feats of strength at Christian meetings and assemblies. Blazer contends that the Power Team's power lies in their combining physical strength with the vulnerability and weakness of the believer. It is this aspect that allows them to successfully encourage audience members to commit to the evangelical life.

Singer pursues the question of the challenge to religious values created by the violent nature of mixed martial arts when performed by Christian athletes who assert their skills are part of their faith. Tracing the commitment to violent sport throughout Christian history, Singer argues that violent sport has been a common strategy to masculinize Christian communities, which is seen as necessary especially today in the face of feminist threats to Christian masculine identity.

Linda Borish tells the little-known story of Syd Koff, a Jewish track-and-field star during the mid-twentieth century. She examines how Koff overcame gender bias while also integrating her Jewish commitments into her track and field career both through her boycott of the 1936 Olympics and through her outstanding performances in the Maccabiah games in Palestine in 1932 and 1935.

In the final section, "Emerging Theoretical Insights," articles look beyond the standard canon of thinkers in the conversation about religion and sports. Instead, this section focuses on scholars of religious studies who have developed new methodologies and who reveal U.S. and European connectedness the broader global forces of capitalism, education, philanthropy, and international conflict.

Tom Gibbons and Stuart Braye are interested in the relationship between Christian values as professed by elite Christian athletes and test out a new socio-theological paradigm. They explore the motivations of a small group of athletes who consider themselves born-again, with the goal of understanding the nature and authenticity of these athletes' faith commitment in relation to their athletic accomplishments.

Roberto Sirvent and Duncan Reyburn question the oft-cited link between religious fervor (labeled as "fanaticism" in the case of sports) and violence that overlooks other political dimensions related to sports and violence. Their goal is to question the assumption that religious belief is irrational and therefore easily marginalized.

Carmen Nanko-Fernández looks at the role religion played the mythic encounter between Brooklyn Dodger president Branch Rickey and Jackie Robinson, the first African-American player in organized baseball, who is credited with initiating what Rickey termed "the great experiment." Nanko-Fernández argues that Rickey constructed a strategy of racial martyrdom as part of his orchestrating the re-integration of baseball. He grounded that strategy in the Christian dictum "turn the other cheek." This approach had, and continues to have, consequences for black and brown players.

Tracy Trothen's essay returns to the perennial question of the connection between religion and sport. Trothen suggests that spirituality rather than religion should be the mechanism through which we understand why sports are so powerful for fans and athletes. Sports provide a medium for a spiritual "search for the sacred" because sports are a critical arena where people experience hope and transcendence.

The final essay stands alone in a section that we have called "Overtime." Similar to a game that extends past regulation, this essay adds something extra, unique, and unconventional to our volume. Nick DeLuca is an undergraduate at Temple University interested in the interplay between Canadian hockey and the Christian tradition. Specifically, he focuses on the role of violence in hockey and its apparent contradiction of the Christian values of peacemaking and nonviolence.

10

Contrary to this assumption, DeLuca argues that there is warrant to view the violence in hockey as part and parcel of Christian and Canadian tradition. By concluding *Gods, Games, and Globalization* with this essay, we aspire to punctuate one of this volume's central purposes: to identify and create a new future for the study of religion and sports. Indeed, we believe this future is very promising.

"Possessed by a Deity"

It is a common understanding that the word "fan" derives from the Latin *fanaticus*, or "possessed by a deity." The etymology here is far from accidental. The possessed person is acting in an uncharacteristic way, controlled by an outside force and made to do unusual things. Sports fans scream, twitch, and gesticulate madly. They dress in absurd costumes and commit obscene amounts of money and resources toward adorning their homes and bodies in their favorite sports colors.

Sports make ordinary people act in extraordinarily strange ways. But this strangeness is a signal that tells us about the importance of people's pastimes. Sports are engaging. Sports are exciting. And sports are fun. Indeed, the articles in this collection are not here to "suck the fun" out of sports. Most of us are fans in our own right. Our hope, instead, is that readers will develop a deeper appreciation for this curious human activity. Because whether it's a soccer game in Africa or a baseball game in New York City, we all have a great deal to learn about the games that people play and love.

PART I

A GLOBAL PERSPECTIVE

A Very Serious Game
Soccer as a Window into
the Theology of Capitalism

Kevin Hargaden

When we think of money and sports, our thoughts quickly turn to the stratospheric wages earned by elite athletes. We may think, for example, of the players in the Premier League—the pinnacle of England's club football system. The teams are followed by millions of supporters both around the country and the globe, and their star players are exalted as heroes and rewarded with wages that would inspire Croesus to jealousy. The Premier League is a uniquely attractive marketing vehicle, which means that television rights to the games are extraordinarily valuable. Between 2016 and 2019 the clubs competing in this league will share a domestic television-rights deal worth £5.136 billion ($6.5 billion). The salaries of top-rated players track with this television largesse, leaving plenty of examples of ostentatious spending to be reported by tabloid newspapers. While playing for Manchester City, the Italian forward Mario Balotelli was the source of many such stories, receiving coverage for his collection of custom sports cars and motorbikes, and for running up £10,000 in parking fines over a three-year period.

While we may be scandalized by these flagrant displays of excess, such superficial reporting obscures the structural ways in which elite sports synchronize with global capitalism. This chapter will examine sports' complicity with capitalism on a deeper level than personalized Ferraris or tasteless mansion renovations. A long tradition of criticism has considered sports an extension of hyper-competitive capitalism. In sports, the body is disciplined for physical competition while the self is conditioned for the wider competition of the marketplace. A "structural osmosis"[1] tethers together sports and capitalism both on the field of play and in the offices beneath the stadium's stands. A sports economy exists

---

[1] A term used by one of the key figures in this tradition, Jean Marie Brohm in *Sport: A Prison of Measured Time* (London: Ink Links, 1978), 116.

where the match or game is the nexus around which a range of industries find their focus. Sporting events become the excuse for infrastructure spending, a catalyst for tourism initiatives, and a means for marketing a baffling array of products. This is to say nothing of the necessity of sports in sustaining the gambling industry.[2] The interlocking of sports and capitalism is revealed with almost comedic clarity when we remember that the ideal of the Olympian spirit is now expressed through means of a partnership with McDonalds. Embrace the champion within! And on your way out, pick up some chicken nuggets.

The interactions between sports and capitalism in this chapter are best examined through the relationship between English soccer, neoliberal governmental policies, and the role of Christian churches in society.[3] Historically, organized sports in England owe much to the contributions of churches, which strongly encouraged sporting competition and established many of today's prominent sporting clubs. As these clubs thrived, their ecclesial origins typically retreated into the background. The first part of this essay will tell this story.

These sports clubs are now major international brands and multi-million dollar businesses. This transition, however, represents a transformation that demands more attention. The creation of the Premier League in 1993 can best be understood as a classic example of neoliberal government policy at work, whereby public goods are privatized, and

---

[2] David Forrest and Robert Simmons's article, "Sport and Gambling," is a relevant touchstone here. They argue that many sports have historically been actively shaped by gambling (p. 598), but they consider the issue from the perspective of economic policy. Critically, they frame the context of the discussion in terms of the provision of huge increases in funding for sports at both the grassroots and the elite levels by means of a state-sanctioned National Lottery. "The sports sector was entitled to 5.6 pence for each lottery ticket sold. This is implicitly a "sports tax" imposed on the purchasers of National Lottery products" (p. 599). One of the robust externalities of such investment is a boon to the gambling industry, since the media for their product (sporting infrastructure) has been so solidly improved. As they summarize it, "[g]ambling is a complementary good with many sports" (p. 602). "More interest in the game," they add, "is, indeed, likely to translate into more interest in betting on the game" (p. 603). David Forrest and Robert Simmons, "Sport and Gambling," *Oxford Review of Economic Policy* 19, no. 4 (1 December 2003): 598–611.

[3] In this paper, the terms soccer and football are synonymous, as is typical in Britain.

where profit becomes the decisive factor that determines viability. The second part of this essay will address this transformation.

When we consider these two trajectories—the role of churches in the beginning of organized sports and the role of capitalism in the beginning of contemporary sports—it becomes clear that Christianity can engage with capitalism. As surely as sports are embedded in our shared lives, Christians find themselves embedded in capitalism. Christian communities have cause to critique sports, but they cannot evade them. Their stance toward capitalism must be similar, rejecting the fantasy of separatism while engaging the imperative to critique. Sports can serve as a window into the theology of capitalism: As the seductive draw of competition between our favorite athletes and teams becomes subordinated to the competition of globalized capitalism, Christian communities are offered an opportunity to reconsider and respond to the excesses of the market in new ways.

When placed side-by-side, the two narratives—ecclesial involvement in sports' beginning and neoliberal manipulation in its present—can offer an approach to discussing how the inextricable connection of sports to capitalism is reflected in the lives of Christians in Britain (and by extension, nations in the West generally). In light of this reflection, we see that soccer is a very serious game, as well as an enjoyable one.

The Role of Churches in the Emergence of English Soccer

Christianity's relationship with sports is historically ambivalent. I grew up in Ireland in the 1990s where the homily at summer mass would often make reference to the Gaelic games to be played later in the afternoon, and prayers would sometimes be offered for our county's success. (God was not swayed by such petitions. In my lifetime my home county of Kildare has never been victorious.) Sports enjoyed the uncomplicated approval of the church.[4]

The early Christians took a decisively different line. The religious significance of Roman sports meant that the church viewed the empire's games with profound suspicion. Competitors swore sacred oaths, and priests led the athletes into the arenas to the acclaim of spectators who

---

[4] Kevin O'Gorman discusses the historical reasons for this stance in his *Saving Sport* (Dublin: Columbia, 2010), especially pp. 38–41.

typically offered sacrifices before attending.[5] Noting that the games were instituted in honor of Jupiter or Hercules or the departed, Tertullian declared, "[w]hat wonder, then, if idolatry pollutes the combat-parade with profane crowns, with sacerdotal chiefs, with attendants belonging to the various colleges, last of all with the blood of its sacrifices?"[6] He was unequivocal in his opinion on the games: "We may hold it as a thing beyond all doubt, that for us who have twice renounced all idols, they are utterly unsuitable."[7]

Between the modern era, when sports are so comfortably ensconced in the life of the church that the Vatican has established a "Church and Sport" office within the Pontifical Council for the Laity, and the ancient era, when sport was widely condemned by early Christians, lies a long period in the church's history where the ecclesial attitude towards games was much more ambivalent.[8] In France, local parishes pitched themselves against their neighbors in the riotous twelfth-century game known as *la soule*, but bishops opposed these tremendous mauls so enthusiastically embraced by the common people.[9] After the Reformation, while there was some allowance for the bodily benefits of exercise, Puritans often opposed sports, going so far in some cases as to outlaw it through legislation.[10]

It was during the Victorian era that attitudes toward sports in the British church took on the positive hue that persists today. The starting point for that transition may seem surprising: In 1857, the British MP and social reformer Thomas Hughes wrote what might be termed today a "Young Adult Novel." A Victorian moral fable, *Tom Brown's School Days* became a phenomenally influential book that sought to inculcate in the gentry of British society a form of robust masculinity that allied Christianity with competitive verve. The novel tells the story of young

---

[5] Shirl James Hoffman, *Good Game* (Waco, TX: Baylor University Press, 2010), 26–29.

[6] Tertullian, *The Shows*, XI.2.

[7] Ibid., XIII.1.

[8] As is so often the case, it seems that the congregations may have listened politely to the denunciations from the pulpit and then continued to go watch the games nevertheless. See Lincoln Harvey, *A Brief Theology of Sport* (London: SCM Press, 2014), 30–31.

[9] Edward Brooke-Hitching, *Fox Tossing: And Other Forgotten and Dangerous Sports, Pastimes, and Games* (New York: Touchstone, 2015), 151.

[10] See Harvey, 49–53.

Tom Brown's adolescence at the elite Rugby School, the friendships he makes, and the path he takes to prepare himself for an admirable adulthood. In the novel, team sports are the crucible in which virtue is forged. In one scene, Tom's teacher presents a philosophy of life informed by cricket: "The discipline and reliance on one another which it teaches is so valuable," because both the sport and life "ought to be such an unselfish game. It merges the individual in the eleven; he doesn't play that he may win, but that his side may."[11]

Contemporary readers may be discomfited by the blatant classist and nationalistic themes within the novel. When one of Tom's friends joins the British army in India and another is dispatched by his family to deal with business in the "South Seas," we glimpse the reality of the career paths open to the English middle classes in the middle of the nineteenth century. We also glimpse how the reality of the brutality of the British Empire and its colonial undertakings around the globe were both normalized and professionalized.

Tom Brown's School Days can thus be interpreted along a spectrum that stretches from sentimental Victorian *bildungsroman* to a testimony of the violence implicit in nineteenth-century British life. Regardless of the reader's conclusions, however, it would be hard to avoid the central role played by the development of Tom Brown's faith within the novel. Woven within the tales of soccer matches and cricket games, heart-to-heart talks with kind-but-fair masters, and fistfights over Latin homework, is a sustained account of religious conversion. Brown becomes a devout Christian at school. More to the point, it is within the community of sports teams that Brown finds Christianity to be true. The duties to one's teammates are just one facet of a person's responsibility to God, which took expression in service to nation, loyalty to clan, and perseverance on the field of play. Tom was raised to believe that "the powers which be were ordained of God and that loyalty and steadfast obedience were men's first duties."[12] It is during *Tom Brown's School Days* that he comes to understand this for himself.

This novel and others like it came to be known as the Victorian "muscular literature" genre, and in their reading, British Christians made their peace with sports. Writers such as Hughes, F.D. Maurice, Charles

---

[11] Thomas Hughes, *Tom Brown's School Days* (London: Wordsworth, 1993), 328.

[12] Ibid., 62–63.

Kingsley, and movements such as the newly founded YMCA (which built its first gymnasium in Britain in 1876) sketched a vision of the faithful life that resonated with the desires of their society. The muscular Christian "combined physical strength, religious certainty, and the ability to shape and control the world around oneself."[13] Christians and their churches found this account compelling. Team sports came to be seen as a crucible for Christian virtue and were enthusiastically embraced by pastors and parents alike.

This embrace soon found expression in ministry. Sports became a central outreach device, especially in the booming industrial cities of northern England. Clergy created sports clubs to channel the energies of youth. How much better was it for young men to be diverted from a path of vice and temptation to one of Christian health and camaraderie? The extent of this outreach can be affirmed by the fact that of the forty-seven clubs that have participated in the Premier League, fourteen of them owe their original existence to some form of Christian ministry.[14] These institutionalized sporting bodies are legacies of a more pervasive Christian commitment to sports as a means of forming virtue and encouraging discipleship. Parish bulletins of the time are replete with news articles about games played at church outings or small sporting initiatives started by this parish committee or that activist youth worker.

The game of soccer was codified by the Football Association in 1863, followed by a period of development where the elite level of the sport became more popular as a spectator event. Organized soccer was notionally amateur, but clubs engaged in a complex system of expenses, compensation for lost wages, and financial incentives to secure the finest players.[15] A battle ensued between the largely aristocratic leadership of the football bureaucracies that wanted to maintain the amateur ideal, and the largely working-class leadership of northern football clubs that want-

---

[13] Donald E. Hall, "Muscular Christianity: Reading and Writing the Male Social Body," in *Muscular Christianity: Embodying the Victorian Age*, ed. Donald E. Hall (Cambridge: Cambridge University Press, 1994), 7.

[14] They are: Aston Villa, Barnsley, Birmingham, Blackpool, Bolton Wanderers, Bournemouth, Charlton Athletic, Everton, Fulham, Liverpool, Manchester City, Southampton, Swindon, and Tottenham Hotspurs. Leeds United was established in a church hall, albeit via a public meeting, and Queens Park Rangers was formed by the union of two prior clubs, one of which, St. Jude's, was formed under the approval of the local clergyman Rev. Gordon Young.

[15] Barry Smart, *The Sports Star* (London: Sage, 2005), 45.

ed to pay people for their work. The battle reflected the wider tensions within British society, as industrialization disrupted class divisions.

Advocates of amateurism appealed to the arguments of lofty virtue that *Tom Brown's School Days* had made familiar. From this perspective, to be paid to compete was to debase the appeal of the game. The argument did not prevail. As Robert Ellis wrote, "amateurism was never really about money as such: but about control and social separation."[16] As the reality of the demand for the sport became apparent, the control rested in the hands of those who were able to capitalize on the market opportunity.

Professionalization may have been strongly resisted by the founding fathers of English football, but they were unable to prevent the pull towards increased monetization.[17] Now that clubs were responsible for wage bills, the need for predictable cash flow and liquidity meant that the league system, which scheduled matches across an entire season, became central to the business and operation of football. To meet that need, and at the behest of a board member of Aston Villa (a club originally established by the Villa Cross Wesleyan Chapel), the Football League was born in 1888. From that point forward, the initial ecclesial involvement in founding the clubs receded.

Professionalization of English soccer was regulated with strict restraints on the transfer of players between clubs and a hard maximum weekly wage of £4. The wage restrictions were finally lifted in 1961 following a campaign led by one of the leading players of the day, Jimmy Hill. Regulations that limited the remuneration of board members, known as Rule 34, were also slowly eroded, especially after clubs began to float on the stock market in 1983. The transfer system was largely deregulated by a 1995 European Court of Justice verdict known as the Bosman ruling, after the Belgian player Jean-Marc Bosman who brought the case.

The "club" terminology that persists in English football is trace evidence of the earliest era of organized soccer, which predated the concern for profit. Of the hundreds of clubs established across the country, many were formed by congregations or as a vehicle for parish church ministry. The successful football teams that emerged were most commonly pri-

---

[16] Robert Ellis, *The Games People Play* (Cambridge: Lutterworth, 2014), 28.

[17] John Beech, "England," in *Managing Football: An International Perspective*, ed. Sean Hamill and Simon Chadwick (Oxford: Butterworth-Heinemann, 2010), 240.

vately owned businesses, and their influence on soccer remains one of the most striking legacies of the now largely forgotten muscular Christian movement.

Today it is common for clubs to have official chaplains; in the case of Everton, there is even a chapel built into the stadium. Having considered the transition of early football clubs from community and church groups into small-scale sporting entertainment enterprises, we now turn to examine how those clubs came to be such highly prized expressions of global capitalism.

The Neoliberal Transformation of English Soccer

In 1985, at the mid-point of Margaret Thatcher's government, soccer in England seemed moribund. Hooliganism among fans was widespread, and attendance at matches was diminishing. On the field, English soccer tactics were increasingly seen as regressive and ineffective in comparison to those of its continental neighbors.[18]

In May of that year, Bradford City hosted Lincoln City in an end-of-season match. The largest crowd of the campaign showed up, since Bradford had won the Third Division and were due to be awarded the trophy. At the end of the first half, a fire broke out in a wooden grandstand. Fire extinguishers had been removed from the spectator area because of fears that hooligans might use them as weapons. The fire spread rapidly, devouring the stand within four minutes. Fifty-six people died and 265 were injured.[19] Two weeks later, crowds clashed at the European Cup final between Liverpool and their Italian rival Juventus. English fans initiated the conflict, and the ensuing riot led to the collapse of a perimeter wall. As thousands of people sought to escape the violence through

---

[18] After a remarkable period of domination, when English teams from relatively small cities such as Nottingham, Ipswich and Birmingham joined the world-renowned Liverpool to win major European tournaments, the mid-1980s saw a tactical shift from a patient focus on passing to what came to be known as "long-ball football." English football "went in the opposite direction, and favored a high-octane style readily dismissed as kick-and-rush." Jonathan Wilson, *Inverting the Pyramid: The History of Football Tactics* (London: Orion, 2009), 282.

[19] A striking first-person account is provided in Martin Fletcher's book *Fifty-Six: The Story of the Bradford Fire* (London: Bloomsbury Sport, 2015), 45–67.

the ruins of the wall, thirty-nine people were killed and 600 were injured.[20]

These tragic events exposed both the dire condition of the English football infrastructure and the apparently intractable problem of fan-led violence. In the aftermath of the Bradford fire, inquiries and legal inquests were held, but little was done to address the dangerous condition of many of the stadiums around the country. Construction of new wooden grandstands was banned, and smoking in existing wooden grandstands was outlawed.[21] The problem of precarious stadiums persisted. In response to the Heysel disaster, the European football authorities banned all English teams from competing in continental competition.[22] This restriction was gradually lifted after 1990. The British government passed laws to make it easier to exclude fans who had committed violent acts from future matches, but the problem of hooliganism persisted.[23]

In 1989, an FA Cup semi-final match between Liverpool and Nottingham Forest was due to be held at the Hillsborough stadium in Sheffield. High metal fences had been erected in the stadium to protect the pitch from fan invasions. These steel fences proved to be a crush risk, and various incidents through the 1980s showed the stadium to be unsafe and prone to overcrowding.[24] Minutes before the game was due to start, the turnstiles became blocked by the large number of fans seeking entrance. To relieve the crowds, police opened gates into the stadium, and thou-

---

[20] One of the rare academic treatments of this disaster was written by Fabio Chisari based on the testimonies of Juventus supporters who were present in the stadium that night. Fabio Chisari, "'The Cursed Cup': Italian Responses to the 1985 Heysel Disaster," in *Soccer and Disaster: International Perspective*, ed. Paul Darby et al., (Abingdon: Routledge, 2005), 77–94.

[21] David Eves, *Disasters: Learning the Lessons for a Safer World* (Abingdon: Routledge, 2015), 168. See also Megan O'Neill, *Policing Football: Social Interaction and Negotiated Disorder* (Basingstoke: Palgrave Macmillan, 2005), 48.

[22] Clemens Kech, "Heysel and Its Symbolic Value in Europe's Collective Memory," in *European Football and Collective Memory*, ed. Wolfram Pyta and Nils Havemann (Basingstoke: Palgrave Macmillan, 2015), 159–60.

[23] It is of interest that there were no major efforts made by churches to combat hooliganism in England. Contemporary parachurch ministries do explore the potential of transforming the soccer spectator culture by means of prayer. An example is the Raw Faith initiative (http://cvm.org.uk/rawfaith/).

[24] Hillsborough Independent Panel, "The Report of the Hillsborough Independent Panel" (London: The Stationery Office, 2012), 61–66.

sands of fans entered the spectating area. A crush began as those already in that sector of the grandstand were pressed against the steel barriers. The numbers involved meant that safety officials, and even the players on the pitch, were initially unaware of the crisis unfolding. The tragedy unfolded during a live television broadcast on the BBC, and the match was stopped after six minutes when some desperate fans found a way to climb over the fence onto the pitch. That day, ninety-six people were crushed to death and 766 people injured.[25]

Initially, a false account of this disaster laid the blame at the feet of fans. By 1989, this tale of aggressive working-class football louts was a narrative with which the British public were familiar,[26] and the acceptance of the official lie by the general public can perhaps be seen as a classic expression of "residual class-based prejudice" in British life.[27] A twenty-seven-year campaign to reveal the truth of the events and expose the fact that the police, the emergency services, and the dangerous design of the stadium were to blame was finally triumphant in 2016 after the longest jury trial in British history exonerated the crowd from any responsibility.[28] That the demonization of the victims would take decades to undo indicates the ways in which football was culturally and politically isolated. Stadiums were death-traps; lawlessness was expected. Disasters continued to occur, and very little was done to remedy these fundamental problems.

Churches may have played a central role in the origins of English football, but that relationship had grown distant by 1989 as evidenced by the long struggle of those who had been injured or bereaved to be heard

---

[25] Phil Scraton, a professor of criminology at Queens University Belfast, is one of the experts on the Hillsborough Disaster. His account is remarkable. Phil Scraton, *Hillsboroug—The Truth* (Edinburgh: Mainstream, 2009), 41–96.

[26] Phil Scraton gathers a chilling collection of responses from close to the event, ranging from columns in nationally distributed broadsheet newspapers, prominent television stars, football managers, and even MPs, all of whom laid the blame unambiguously with the alleged "thuggishness and ignorance" of football fans. Phil Scraton, "4 Death on the Terraces: The Contexts and Injustices of the 1989 Hillsborough Disaster," *Soccer & Society* 5, no. 2 (January 2004): 195–96.

[27] Michael Brennan, *Mourning and Disaster: Finding Meaning in the Mourning for Hillsborough and Diana* (Newcastle: Cambridge Scholars Publishing, 2008), 161.

[28] "The Hillsborough Inquest; Justice for the 96," *The Economist*, 30 April 2016, 29.

by wider society. "The collective 'view from below'"[29] was exactly the kind of voice that churches are called to advocate for; yet apart from a few notable exceptions,[30] ecclesial influence has been absent from this discussion.

Today, English professional football is typically played in world-class sporting arenas. Every stadium is seated and designed with safe evacuation in mind, and many feature an increasing range of accessory attractions such as restaurants, corporate hospitality zones, museums, hotels, and club shops selling memorabilia and merchandise. Lawless hooliganism exists now largely as a memory. When flare-ups do occur between fans, it is rare, and extensive legal measures have been introduced to ensure that fans involved in organized violence are banned from attending any kind of future match. The figures from the 2014-15 season (the most recent to be released) are notable for the extent to which matches were conducted peaceably. Total football-related arrests per 100,000 attendees stood at fewer than five.[31] English football today is a family-friendly activity.

This transformation in how soccer is viewed is most clearly demonstrated when we consider the cultural and political status of the game. Soccer is a preoccupation of the British media, consuming pages of every newspaper, being discussed hourly in televised news broadcasts, and winning the widespread support of political authorities. Former Prime Minister David Cameron was commonly derided after it was revealed that he was posturing as a "real fan." Cameron claimed on one occasion to support Aston Villa, a team based near his home in the Midlands. Years later, having apparently forgotten this lifelong devotion, he sought to ingratiate himself with an audience of Londoners by declaring himself an avid fan of their local team, West Ham.

How do we account for this transformation? It is my contention that the shift from the low point of 1985 to the complete renewal of

---

[29] Phil Scraton, "The Legacy of Hillsborough: Liberating Truth, Challenging Power," *Race & Class* 55, no. 2 (1 October 2013): 25.

[30] The former Bishop of Liverpool, Rt. Revd. James Jones, chaired the Hillsborough Independent Panel, which was instrumental in the eventual achievement of justice.

[31] "Statistical News Release: Football-Related Arrests and Banning Orders, England and Wales, Season 2014–15" (London: Home Office, 26 November 2015), 2.

2015 cannot be explained without factoring in the role of neoliberal economic policies.

Neoliberalism is the political movement that came to prominence with the elections of Ronald Reagan in the United States and Margaret Thatcher in the United Kingdom. Neoliberals sought to reduce the size of government, minimize government's interaction with the market, encourage the individualization of workers (at the expense of trade unions), and emphasize the importance of business interests in policy concerns. It is a political philosophy dedicated to implementing a particular form of capitalism across all sectors of society.

A brief definition is provided by [university professor] David Harvey, who describes neoliberalism as:

> [A] theory of political economic practices that proposes that human well-being can best be advanced by liberating individual entrepreneurial freedoms and skills within an institutional framework characterized by strong private property rights, free markets, and free trade.[32]

After the collapse of the Soviet Union, this approach to politics and economics became the norm across western democracies. In Britain, which since World War II had developed a multilayered social security system, neoliberalism was preoccupied with privatizing common goods held in public trust. For much of the twentieth century, Britain was committed to large-scale construction of public housing, which was later sold off in tranches by Thatcher and subsequent governments. The railways, electrical utilities, water supply, and British Airways were some of the state enterprises that were privatized and deregulated. One can tell the story of the British economy during these years as the attempt to enrich society by enriching individuals through the sale of social assets for individual profit.

In the aftermath of the Hillsborough tragedy, the UK government commissioned an investigative report into the state of British soccer stadiums. The resultant Taylor Report was published in January 1990. It begins with the "depressing and chastening fact" that its publication is the ninth such report published in the modern era.[33] Taylor made eighteen specific recommendations about how to ensure crowd safety in the

---

[32] David Harvey, *A Brief History of Neoliberalism* (Oxford: Oxford University Press, 2005), 2.

[33] Lord Chief Justice Peter Taylor, "The Hillsborough Stadium Disaster" (London: Home Office, January 1990), 4.

future, centered on the removal of standing terraces from each stadium and a total conversion of stadiums to an all-seated format.

The initial capital for these developments came from a government levy on gambling, which passed directly to a "Football Trust." What happened varied from city to city, but the majority of stadium upgrades took place with active subsidies from national or local government. In some instances, annual lump sums were paid by local governments to help renovate or maintain stadiums. In other cases, local governments provided credit at favorable terms for new stadiums.[34] Within a year of the Taylor Report, leading clubs such as Manchester United and Liverpool had begun the process of overhauling their stadiums. Every other club followed suit.

The new stadiums were thus erected in an economic climate poised to fit with the demands of neoliberalism. It is no coincidence that their design allowed for television cameras and often included media suites. Revenue from selling the rights to televise games had risen three-fold in the years between 1986 and 1988, and the deregulation of the television market allowed the two largest satellite broadcasters to merge into British Sky Broadcasting in 1989. This was a commercial opportunity soccer clubs could not afford to miss, and club owners were aware that the next round of television deals had the potential to be hugely lucrative. Rebuilt stadiums positioned the elite clubs to capitalize on this new market opportunity. In 1991, the clubs that made up the First Division offered their resignations and formed a new "Premier League." Television rights were sold to British Sky Broadcasting for £304 million, which represent-

---

[34] Manchester City and West Ham are two notable examples of the continued public participation in the renovation of stadiums. Both clubs had made modifications to their arenas to comply with the Taylor Report. Years later, both came to occupy brand new, state-of-the-art stadiums built entirely with public money. In the case of Manchester City, they took ownership for a nominal fee of a stadium built initially to house the Commonwealth Games. West Ham agreed a deal to rent the London 2012 Olympic stadium at favorable terms. West Ham is owned by David Gold and David Sullivan, two businessmen who made their fortunes in the adult entertainment industry. Manchester City is owned by Sheikh Mansour, a member of the ruling family of Abu Dhabi. Hundreds of millions of pounds of public spending was appropriated by private interests without any significant political discussion, never mind popular unrest.

ed an immediate 60 percent increase in the revenue available to these clubs.

While millions of fans attend games throughout the season in England, the phenomenal rise in the attention paid to the game in public discourse is owed largely to television rights. Almost a million tourists visit England every year with the primary intention of watching a Premier League game; the vast majority of global fans follow their teams on TV. Many economists have concluded that this television market is the source of the economic inflation enjoyed by English clubs.[35] A central assumption of this business model is the existence of safe arenas full of boisterous, festive fans. Only after this guaranteed through the commitment of public funds following the implementation of the Taylor Report could the transformation wrought by television revenue be countenanced.

Public investment became an asset for the privately owned clubs and directly contributed to revenue generation since ticket prices rose with the increased quality of the setting provided by the new stadiums. The real transformation in value caused by television can thus only be understood in the light of neoliberal policy. Tax revenues were committed to assist private companies (football clubs) to deliver a common good (sport), instead of following the common European practice of either building municipal stadiums to be rented out to the clubs (as modeled in France) or of converting the club structures to community ownership (as modeled in Germany).

The English Premier League is a global media phenomenon, accessed primarily by television screens in the living rooms of suburban Birmingham as well as the pubs of Bremen, Boston, or Bangkok. The owners of the clubs made fortunes from this dynamic, with the annual turnover of each elite club now standing at hundreds of millions of pounds.[36] Such a scenario is not explained by the natural enthusiasm of the fans (however energetic they may be!). Instead, a long-term business

---

[35] Such a view is propounded in Simon Kuper and Stefan Szymanski's altogether excellent and eminently readable introduction to the role of money in contemporary global soccer, *Soccernomics* (New York: Nation Books, 2009), 79–80.

[36] As an example, the English businessman Doug Ellis invested £500,000 in Aston Villa in 1982. He paid himself a salary as the club's director each year, made millions when the club was floated on the stock market in 1997, and then sold his shares to the American billionaire Randy Lerner in 2006 for £23 million.

strategy aided by government policy has created the context for this to occur. The transformation in football's fortunes from 1985 to 2015 was sparked by a series of tragedies, but it is a critical conviction of neoliberalism to never let a crisis go to waste. As the British sociologist David Goldblatt argues, football was "steered down a particular path of development by the hand of the state; and a good chunk of the investment costs was paid by the taxpayer."[37] The profits were collected by the private investors.

This nexus between sports and capitalism is not tangential to Christian ethical reflection. In his discussion of the influence of capitalism—what he referred to as the "lordless power of Mammon"[38]—Karl Barth cites sports as one expression of this ideology. "Sport," he argues, "seems to have become the playground of a particular earth-spirit," rising in the twentieth century to "a public matter of first rank."[39] The enthusiasm for sports is set within the capitalist system, and it is this context that renders it "a special form of derangement."[40] The fan's enthusiasm in victory, or disconsolation in loss, and their obsessive interest through each team's ups and downs is of a part with the "palpably lordless chthonic power" of capitalism.[41] It is to this intersection that we now turn.

Soccer, the Theology of Capitalism, and how to be a Christian in Britain

Soccer as it exists today is part of the globalization of culture. The U.S. journalist Franklin Foer can, thus, confidently declare that soccer "explains the world."[42] The game's appeal is global even while maintaining its roots in local communities. Children grow up in sub-Saharan Africa dreaming of playing for Chelsea (a leafy, wealthy district of London) and middle-aged men gather north of the Arctic circle to follow the travails of Newcastle United. The specific argument made here is that the Eng-

---

[37] David Goldblatt, *The Game of Our Lives* (London: Viking, 2014), 15.

[38] Karl Barth, *The Christian Life* (Grand Rapids, MI: Eerdmans, 1981), 213–33.

[39] Ibid., 229.

[40] Ibid., 230.

[41] Ibid., 232.

[42] Franklin Foer, *How Football Explains the World* (London: Arrow Books, 2004).

lish Premier League represents a case study in how the political policies of neoliberalism affect economic activity and in turn serve globalization. National taxes and local councils pay to develop infrastructure that is owned and traded privately. Through the use of new media technology, it is projected into marketplaces far from the mansions of Chelsea or the terraced houses of Newcastle-upon-Tyne.

Taking English soccer as our example, a connection between capitalism and sport can be seen that goes deeper than moralistic opinion pieces about the shocking size of salaries or endorsement deals signed by elite stars. Christian theology has deep resources for critiquing the excesses of capitalism, most notably in Jesus of Nazareth's antipathy towards money. Warnings about the risks of affluence occur throughout the Hebrew Scriptures. For example, in the Pentateuch we find repeated prohibitions on charging interest (Exod. 22:25-27, Lev. 25:35-37, Deut. 23:19-20). Among the historical books such as Ruth we find an entire text dedicated to telling the story of two marginalized female laborers. The Psalms repeatedly remind the reader of their responsibility to the poor (Ps. 82:3-4), and in the Wisdom literature we find a fascinating, multi-layered ambivalence to wealth in the writings of Qoheleth. Barely a prophet can be read without encountering warnings of the risk of material prosperity as an inducement to idolatry (Amos 6:4-6 is a particularly apt example).

This skepticism is heightened in the New Testament. Beyond Jesus' warning that a camel can fit through the eye of a needle more easily than a rich person may enter into heaven or his admonition that one cannot serve two masters, Paul's letters offer repeated exhortations to radical generosity (2 Cor. 8 is one such extended argument). The Epistle of James also famously excoriates of the rich, "Now listen, you rich people, weep and wail because of the misery that is coming on you..." (James 5:1).

Early Christians did not ignore these seams within their scriptures. *The Shepherd of Hermas* was a widely read Christian text from the second century CE. It offered financial advice for the rich: "Instead of fields buy souls that are in distress, as anyone is able, and visit widows and orphans, and do not neglect them; and spend your wealth and all your possessions, which you received from God, on fields and houses of this kind."[43] This commitment to economic redistribution persists in different ways

---

[43] *Shepherd of Hermas* 1:8.

through the Christian traditions. One example is the voluntary embrace of poverty. The Desert Fathers, Francis of Assisi, and twentieth-century figures such as Dorothy Day and Peter Maurin have exhibited this form of Christian witness based around the renunciation of wealth.

These sources and countless others like them constitute a rich tradition of thinking that can be brought to bear against the excesses of capitalism. The core of Christian skepticism towards systems of wealth can be found in the Sermon on the Mount, where Jesus promises, "[w]here your money is, there too is your heart" (Matt. 6:21). Reflection on the numerous claims of this kind made by Jesus prompted Christians to characterize the temptation toward greed as a form of idolatry. The heart is captured by the promise of wealth, but when greed occurs, justice suffers.[44]

Early Christian communities were thus suspicious of trading.[45] This skepticism carried into the medieval era as the church sought to find ways to limit interest-bearing loans and other economic devices.[46] The European Reformation is considered the point of divergence in this narrative. After the arrival of Luther and Calvin, Christians came to a sort of peace with the marketplace. In Max Weber's famous formulation, Protestantism widened the language of vocation to apply to all work, and

---

[44] In a very earthy illustration of this, the contemporary American theologian Phyllis Tickle recounts the childhood catechesis of her son-in-law, who was raised in Italy and was taught, "when the devil tempts you, he uses money. After he has consumed your soul, he defecates more money." Phyllis A. Tickle, *Greed* (Oxford: Oxford University Press, 2004), 63.

[45] Helen Rhee goes so far as to suggest that "the extant [early] Christian texts are almost unanimous in disapproving and warning of the dangers of business affairs because they were thought to obscure Christian identity and responsibilities." Helen Rhee, *Loving the Poor, Saving the Rich: Wealth, Poverty, and Early Christian Formation* (Grand Rapids, MI: Baker Academic, 2012), 160.

[46] R. H. Tawney writes of "the innumerable fables of the usurer who was prematurely carried to hell, or whose money turned to withered leaves in his strongbox, or who (as the scrupulous recorder remarks), about the year 1240, on entering a church to be married, was crushed by a stone figure falling from the porch, which proved by the grace of God to be a carving of another usurer and his money-bags being carried off by the devil." These ghoulish morality tales were, Tawney proposes, "more illuminating than the refinements of lawyers" in the Christian quest to domesticate the marketplace. R.H. Tawney, *Religion and the Rise of Capitalism* (New York: Mentor Books, 1954), 27.

through the various formulations of the doctrine of predestination, destabilized the assurance of the individual believer with respect to their salvation. This double impetus—to work in the secular world as if for God and to seek signs of God's blessing wherever they could be found—created a collective culture suited to capitalist competition.[47] Yet the Reformers themselves were not proto-capitalists, eager to turn their congregations into bustling community of entrepreneurs.[48] Calvin, for example, opposed merchants whose power grew too great, insisting that demand could never drive prices beyond the reach of ordinary people, In line with many early Puritans, Calvin saw interest rates as a matter requiring strict regulation.[49]

Contemporary theological discourse continues this complicated compromise with the economic order of our day. Mainstream Christian discourse across Protestant denominations is often quick to distance itself from a position that baptizes capitalism, while also being slow to wholeheartedly reject it. Doug Bandow both asks and answers the question: "Is capitalism Christian? No."[50] That answer, however, follows from his writing earlier in the same essay that [capitalism] is a system that "rewards honesty and trustworthiness"[51] and that that "one of the hallmarks

---

[47] This Christianity was still ascetic, but "now it strode into the marketplace of life, slammed the door of the monastery behind it, and undertook to penetrate just that daily routine of life with its methodicalness, to fashion it into a life in the world, but neither of not for this world." Max Weber, *The Protestant Ethic and the Spirit of Capitalism* (London: Routledge Classics, 2001), 101.

[48] George Thomas reminds us that "it would be a mistake to speak of Calvin or his early followers as defenders of economic individualism in the modern sense." George Thomas, *Christian Ethics and Moral Philosophy* (New York: Scribners, 1956), 309.

[49] When it came to just prices, interest-bearing loans, and the other contentious economic questions of the Reformation era, "Calvin was much concerned with all these matters in his sermons and commentaries, and in keeping with his prophetic stance he was unstinting in his condemnation of the luxurious, the hard-hearted, the idle and those in any way lacking in *humanitas* towards their neighbour." Harro Höpfl, *The Christian Polity of John Calvin* (Cambridge: Cambridge University Press, 1985), 195.

[50] Doug Bandow, "The Conundrum of Capitalism and Christianity," in *Wealth, Poverty and Human Destiny*, ed. Doug Bandow and David L. Schindler (Wilmington, DE: ISI Books, 2003), 345.

[51] Ibid., 327.

of a relatively unregulated market is the abundance of goods."[52] Capitalism can encourage good work,[53] cooperation[54] and a host of other values that Christians wish to affirm.[55]

A theological account of capitalism remains critical, however. For example, capitalism raises profound doctrinal challenges to the Christian account of creation. Capitalism assumes scarcity, whereas Christianity "has long proclaimed that God has given and continues to give abundantly; there is enough."[56] Capitalism posits an anthropology that is troubling to the Christian account of the person. Capitalism imagines the human in the mode of the *homo economicus*, who engages in rational decision-making driven by self-interest.[57] Christianity conceives of the human being as a creature, in solidarity with other creatures in the cosmos and in relation to a creator. [French sociologist] Jacques Ellul summarizes this difficulty when he comments that "one of the results of capitalism that we see developing throughout the nineteenth century is the subservience of *being* to *having*. This result makes allegiance to capitalism virtually impossible for the Christian."[58] Furthermore, capitalism conceives of a politics that is in tension with Christian conceptions of how to arrange communal life. It has become a central tenet of capitalism that markets have priority over politics.

In describing contemporary capitalism, Karl Polanyi writes that "instead of economy being embedded in social relations, social relations are

---

[52] Ibid., 330.

[53] One might think here of Pope John Paul II's description of a "neocapitalism," which offers a "clearer and more committed realization" of workers' rights. *Laborem Exercens*, 8.

[54] William F. May, "The Virtues of the Business Leader," in *On Moral Business*, ed. Max L. Stackhouse et al., with Preston N. Williams (Grand Rapids, MI: Eerdmans, 1995), 697.

[55] Donald A. Hay, "Introduction: The Role of Values n a Market Economy," in *Christianity and the Culture of Economics*, ed. Donald A. Hay and Alan Kreider (Cardiff: University of Wales Press, 2001), 1-11.

[56] Daniel M. Bell, *The Economy of Desire* (Grand Rapids, MI: Baker Academic, 2012), 179.

[57] Andy Hartropp, "Why Is Engagement between Christian Economists and Theologians Difficult?" in *Theology and Economics*, ed. Jeremy Kidwell and Sean Doherty (Basingstoke: Palgrave Macmillan, 2015), 16.

[58] Jacques Ellul, *Money and Power* (Eugene, OR: Wipf & Stock, 2009), 20.

embedded in the economic system."[59] Against this supposition, Christianity insists that economy exists for society, not the other way around. This claim can take different forms, but its most developed expression is in the central pillar of Catholic social teaching: the universal destination of goods. This is the claim that "God wishes every human being to have at least a basic sufficiency of this world's goods," which is regularly extended to explicitly state that "markets alone, however, do not assure this outcome."[60]

In a context where market considerations begin to shape and influence games, any Christian engagement with sport will have to draw upon a theological analysis of capitalism. This is the case with English soccer. The particular form of neoliberal capitalism that holds sway in contemporary British society is subject to all of these critiques. Neoliberalism's political project seeks to erode communal goods in pursuit of private profit. We are no longer exhorted to be solid and dependable laborers in a collective trade union, but to be flexible and adaptive entrepreneurs of the self, mobile and willing to serve the market.[61] Margaret Thatcher famously claimed that there was no such thing as society, only individuals—which is as close to a slogan of neoliberalism as one can hope to find. The Christian suspicion of wealth is grounded in scripture, tradition, and practice. It is a corollary of its commitment to community. For Jesus, the concrete need of one's neighbor undoes any ownership rights one might claim (Luke 6:30). Theologically, then, Christianity is at the very least primed to identify those "palpably lordless" political and social movements that seek to inculcate corrosive individualism that destroys the sharing of the abundant goods of this world.

If it is true that English soccer's structural organization has been shaped by neoliberal policy for the sake of profit, then it becomes a field of profound importance for Christians wrestling with the injustices that accompany capitalism. What appears on the surface to be a communal activity—spectators attending matches with friends and joining the crowd to form a sort of temporary community—may nonetheless be shaping and molding us to be rampantly individualistic economic actors.

---

[59] Karl Polanyi, *The Great Transformation* (Boston: Beacon Press, 2001), 60.

[60] Angus Sibley, *Catholic Economics* (Collegeville, MN: Liturgical Press, 2015), 9.

[61] Michel Foucault, *The Birth of Biopolitics*, ed. Michel Senellart (Basingstoke: Palgrave Macmillan, 2008), 226.

Contemporary English soccer enjoins its supporters to endorse a form of competition that mimics the new politics of neoliberalism. The winner takes all. The rich get richer. The connection between the grassroots joy of the game and the televised spectacle of elite matches becomes ever more tenuous. The many subsidize the enrichment of the few.

It is in this light that soccer makes capitalism susceptible to theological critique. That our hearts are swayed by sports is often taken as a given. In Shirl James Hoffman's words, it is a meeting point where the "unquestioned belief in the character-enhancing properties of sport, belief in the inherent goodness of mass consumerism, and faith in competitiveness and confrontation leads to growth."[62] We can conceive of sports as being religiously charged. If sports are a business, surely this means that we can think of business in the same terms? The window that sports provides for the theology of capitalism is unusually transparent because neoliberalism's capture of soccer represents the monetization of a domain that is entirely nonessential. Theological interrogation of economy is complicated by the necessity of markets. Theologians could spend their entire careers concerning themselves with the theological implications of fossil fuels, but they most likely still use internal combustion engines to get to speaking engagements.

Sports, however, are at their base impractical. They need not be construed as profit-generating devices. Unlike other forms of entertainment, sports do not require recording studios, sound-stages, or other expensive inputs. The trope of "jumpers for goalposts" (the practice whereby players use their sweatshirts to mark out an ad-hoc football pitch) is common in British culture and speaks to the inherent freedom of the game of football. That even soccer is prone to such a transformation suggests that the theological task of analyzing capitalism requires a marked sensitivity and attunement to the temptations of wealth. Jesus talked about this temptation in the terms of a personification: *Mammon*. Mammon's seduction is not straightforward. It rarely appeals to base desires. Instead, it hides itself inside other goods. If it propagates its rampant individualism in the context of a harmonious crowd cheering as athletes chase a ball around a field, then an opposition to it calls for strategies more oblique than simple denunciation.

---

[62] Hoffmann, *Good Game*, 263.

Jacques Ellul approaches the pull of power and money in this fashion when he argues that "all we have to do to be lost in riches is to follow our own heart."[63] The neoliberal conceit is one that prioritizes personal autonomy over communal concern and emphasizes private profit over collective investment. In encouraging us to allow our hearts be captured by our favorite soccer teams, the market trains us to be people who think in terms of winners and losers, who stand in adoration of those sports stars presented as our superiors and who value efficient competition as a good in itself. We invest our hearts in the competition of these soccer teams during our recreation time and are renewed in our readiness to compete in the marketplace for our corporations.

How can Christians who live in such a system reconcile it with their religious commitments? Capitalism is inescapable. There is no noneconomic refuge to which Christians can retreat. Most of us must earn wages to pay rent and put food on the table. Jesus, meanwhile, preached against wealth, emptied the temple courts of traders, and was ultimately sold for a handful of coins. How, then, can a member of a parish church in England avoid being implicated in the global financial system, with its unstoppable appetite for natural resources? They cannot. Secession is not an option. Retreat is not possible. Compromise is inevitable. Implication is irresistible.

For Christian communities where these problems are real issues, the sincere love of sports may be one way to probe such dilemmas without creating total resignation. Experimenting with new ways to be sporting may create space to imagine new ways to live with economics. In communities where people's hearts have been given to the heroism and tragedy of supporting an elite football club, theological exploration may offer fresh purchase on the problem of religious devotion within contemporary capitalism. Soccer emerged in institutional form in England through communal commitments, led by trade unions, town councils, and churches. Its co-option by neoliberalism should be named and described, as uncomfortable as the implications may be for those involved. Reflection on the ways in which sports train us to be consumers and competitors may prompt Christians to cease supporting the professional clubs they have backed for years. For Christians, however, the question of where loyalties lie is always a question of deep theological significance. Breaking with neoliberalized sports need not mean breaking with sports

---

[63] Ellul, *Money and Power*, 80.

36

altogether; inspired by historical commitments, it could, instead, involve a return to soccer as a shared good, a game to be played with friends for fun.

This call to grassroots sports echoes earlier commitments. Today's experiments arise from different motivations than those that drove Victorian Christians. Nonetheless, the exchange of adoration of elite, professional, heavily marketed sports stars with dedication to neighborhood teams may prove to be analogically fertile for how Christians can subversively engage in market activity in a fashion that undercuts the claims of capitalist individualism. There is a coherency connecting, say, a localism dedicated to fostering sports among neighbors and a localism that rejects industrial agriculture through the direct support of farmers. The establishment of many of England's football clubs stemmed, at least in part, from a religious commitment to serving the common good.[64] These goods held in common and the social fabric that supported them has been corroded by decades of neoliberalism. A renewed appreciation of sport on this level may help to undo individualism so that alternative forms of enterprise can be conceived and explored.[65]

---

[64] It is important to remember the connections between muscular Christianity, Christian socialism, and the emerging labor movement in Britain. In his essay "On the Making and Unmaking of Monsters," Donald Hall examines a muscular Christian newspaper, *Politics for the People*, and finds there an "emphasis on cooperation between classes and individuals [which] hinges on reciprocal responsibilities." It should be noted that Hall also writes in that same essay of the muscular Christian ability to bend and form rhetoric so as "to repudiate demands that they found uncomfortable and irreconcilable with their own class-bound view of the proper constitution of the body of the nation." The argument we are making here holds that contemporary Christians may be called to redescribe their relationship to sport, recommitting to grassroots organizations in a way that echoes the Victorian era, but for reasons that would subvert the particular form of common good (specifically classist and nationalist assumptions) held dear by our forebears. Donald E. Hall, "On the Making and Unmaking of Monsters: Christian Socialism, Muscular Christianity, and the Metaphorization of Class Conflict," in *Muscular Christianity: Embodying the Victorian Age*, ed. Donald E. Hall (Cambridge, Cambridge University Press, 1994), 50, 64.

[65] An example of a thinker who has already beaten a trail in this direction is the Catholic moral theologian William Cavanaugh, whose *Being Consumed* explores how Christian worship can inspire new modes of economic engagement.

Soccer's promise of moments of sporting transcendence wins our allegiance. Capitalism also seeks to win our allegiance. The claim of Christianity is that God's love alone has the rights to our allegiance. As Ellul puts it, "love, in the Bible, is utterly totalitarian."[66] Soccer is a globalized game, but in England specifically it is a colonized game taken over by neoliberalism. For many, this transformation may be cause for lament. (It should be recalled that lament itself is a biblical category.) There are voices from many directions that protest at the gradual but dramatic marketization of football. Christian churches are well placed to go beyond protest, proposing constructive alternatives through a renewed commitment to the benefits of the game as a source of fun and fellowship. Considering neoliberalism through the lens of soccer might lead to considering the public good of churches in the light of pluralist, multicultural twenty-first-century Britain.

Conclusion

Sports can tempt us to sentimentality. The argument here has sought to resist that temptation. Two aspects of English footballing history have been drawn upon as a basis from which to reflect theologically on the meaning of capitalism and to consider the social and political possibilities of religious communities.

English soccer was not invented by churches, even if many of its clubs were. What ecclesial influence existed quickly retreated as the game gained popularity and became a profitable activity. It is important to limit the claim made in the first part of this essay: that as clubs thrived, their ecclesial origins typically retreated into the background. To whatever extent parishes were involved in the formation of clubs, it is taken to demonstrate how the emergence of soccer as the most popular game in England was a grassroots and community-driven phenomenon, albeit informed by the values of the era and driven by the priorities and emphases of muscular Christianity.[67] It is equally important not to overstate the

---

William T. Cavanaugh, *Being Consumed* (Grand Rapids, MI: Eerdmans, 2008), especially 27–28.

[66] Ellul, *Money and Power*, 83.

[67] For example, Watson and his collaborators state that one of the "less publicized" commitments running behind muscular Christianity was "the need to protect the British Empire and produce leaders that were well educated and 'manly'." This is another important reminder that what is being proposed here,

claims being made in the second part of this essay: that the transition of clubs into private enterprises was entirely driven by neoliberal government policy. To whatever extent the economic growth surrounding the game in the past generation is an outcome of neoliberal politics, it is taken to be a continuation of a process that has been in play since before professionalization. There is neither a pristine past of local community gamesmanship, nor a pristine past when the profit motive was not chiefly determinant of how and why the elite game was played.

That English soccer began as a grassroots and community-driven phenomenon is significant because it largely remains that way. More people participate in the game as players, coaches, and referees in local parks and on school pitches each week than attend professional games as spectators.[68] That the accelerated revenue-generation of the recent era can be tied to the wider neoliberal transformation of the economy is significant because it is a political movement that threatens the very form of community activity that sustains the grassroots game. The market is a disciplining force that valorizes competition and encourages individualism. Elite commercialized sport is an expression of this dynamic. As it attracts our desire, we come to see in microcosm how neoliberal capitalism operates on us at the macro level. It is seductive because it offers good things. It is to be resisted not because its promises are empty but because they come at too high a cost: our conversion into competitive, individualized entrepreneurs of the self.

This theological insight demands some response from church communities. The path proposed here is just one of many that could be imagined. Returning to the community engagement that was so fruitful in the late nineteenth century is not to retread old ground. Rather, it in-

---

when grassroots sporting involvement is encouraged, is not a rejuvenation of muscular Christianity for a twenty-first century context. Nick J. Watson et al., "The Development of Muscular Christianity in Victorian Britain and Beyond," *Journal of Religion and Society* 7 (2005): 2.

[68] In this domain, it quickly becomes clear that the sort of reorientation toward the grassroots advocated in this essay does not require wholesale innovation but rather renewed attention to what is already happening. Among the thousands of amateur and friendly soccer leagues active in England, there is a thriving "church leagues" tradition. UK Sports Ministries have a database of more than thirty currently running (http://uksportsministries.org/category/ organisations-list/football/churchleagues).

volves exploring a new space located between the claims of the market and the claims of a community's religious convictions. The regime of Christendom that Victorian churches assumed and actively sustained is gone. Many British church communities rejoice at this fact and the liberation it brings.[69] They are freed to no longer be relevant. By redirecting their enthusiasms from the business of Premier League fandom, these churches might find the time and space to engage in the serious business of football for fun at the local level.

By repairing their social fabric worn thin through decades of neoliberal policies, churches can find renewed relevance for their congregations at the center of their local communities. This promises to be a scenario where everyone wins.

---

[69] This dislocation from centers of influence means that churches have more distance from economic power, which permits a different form of critique. This liberation can be seen in the robust critiques of neoliberalism offered by the Argentinian (hence, economically and culturally peripheral, from the perspective of globalization) Pope Francis or in the many British churches responding to post-2008 austerity with invitations to engage in new economic or environmental experiments. See, respectively: Pope Francis, *Evangelii Gaudium* (Dublin: Veritas, 2013) and Peter Selby, *An Idol Unmasked: A Faith Perspective on Money* (London: Dartman, Longman and Todd, 2014), 129.

"Sport with a Mission":
Sport as a Means of Renewed Catholic Apostolate among Indigenous People in former Belgian Congo (1919–59)

Dries Vanysacker

In response to changing views on apostolate after the First World War, several Catholic missionary congregations adopted new missionary methods within their territories. In what was then known as the Belgian Congo (now Democratic Republic of the Congo), Catholic missionaries (along with missionaries of other faith groups) took a new interest in social apostolate among the indigenous people living in increasingly urbanized areas. Along with other social activities such as establishing youth movements or creating cultural centers (libraries, theaters, cinemas), sport took on a very important role. During the interwar period, several missionary congregations, working in close collaboration with colonial representatives in the cities of Leopoldville (modern-day Kinshasa) and Elisabethville (modern-day Lubumbashi), focused on creating sports organisations and building sports stadiums for the benefit of indigenous people. Sport was, of course, no new phenomenon in the Belgian Congo, but it had been practiced exclusively by European colonials, be it in a military context[1], or as representatives of mostly commercial and industrial companies.[2] Black people, until then, were only allowed to attend as spectators.

---

[1] Victor Boin, "Les Sports, facteur de civilisation et de cordiale collaboration," in V. Boin, *Le livre d'or jubilaire de l'U.R.B.S.F.A. 1895–1945* (Brussels: Les éditions Leclercq and De Haas, 1946), 499; Roger Vanmeerbeek and Pacal Delheye, "Military Sport in the Belgian Congo: From Physical Training and Leisure to Belgian-Congolese Records in Track and Field, 1945–1960, *"The International Journal of the History of Sport* 30 no. 16 (2013): 1929–1946.

[2] Bénédicte Van Peel, "Aux débuts du football congolais," in Jean-Luc Vellut (dir.), *Itinéraires croisés de la modernité Congo belge (1920–950)* (Cahiers Africains, no. 43–44) (Tervuren: Institut Africain-CEDAF, 2001), 141–187; Béné-

Drawing on archival material (correspondence, diaries, photographs and films)[3], contemporary studies and sport-related archaeological evidence that I observed during my research stay in the modern Congo, I will explore several initiatives taken by Catholic missionaries to include sport in their social apostolate. I will show that congregations such as the Scheut Fathers, the Brothers of the Christian Schools in Leopoldville-Kinshas, the Benedictine Fathers of the Abbey of Saint-Andrew of Bruges, and the Xaverian Brothers in Elisabethville-Lubumbashi—within the context of their missionary work in the field of education and culture during the period from 1919 to 1959—opened the door to indigenous people to discover a new active sporting life. The two privileged sports disciplines that the missionaries transferred from their home country of Belgium were soccer and cycling. The missionaries concentrated on male Congolese, and sporting activities were organized independently from those of the European colonials. It is good to notice that the Catholic Church, the colonial government, and the industrial powers worked together to make sport a tool to create a disciplined, efficient, moral, and healthy population of African students and working-class people. As a historian, I tried to stay as close as possible to the facts. The language used during that period was also very "colonial."

Leopoldville-Kinshasa

In Leopoldville-Kinshasa, it was the Congregation of the Immaculate Heart of Mary (also known as the CICM or Scheut Fathers, a congregation established in Belgium in 1862 to focus exclusively on missionary work in, at that time, Inner Mongolia, China, and the Congo)[4] that took the lead in the person of Raphaël de la Kethulle de Ryhove (1890–1956),

---

dicte Van Peel, *"Le Sport à Léopoldville-Kinshasa et à Élisabethville, 1910–1940. Aux débuts d'une culture urbaine moderne au Congo,"* (Louvain-la-Neuve: Université catholique de Louvain [UCL]), 1997.

[3] See, for example, *Le rêve d'un grand Roi* by Yves de Brouwer (1951), http://www.filmarchives-online.eu/viewDetailForm?FilmworkID=be5ba2527-c7c21a81bfd73c39a867c4d and http://www.europeana.eu/portal/en/record/08623/6293.html.

[4] On this congregation, see, for example, Daniël Verhelst and Nestor Pycke (eds), *C.I.C.M. Missionaries, Past and Present 1862–1987: History of the Congregation of the Immaculate Heart of Mary (Scheut/Missionhurst)* (Leuven, Leuven University Press, 1995).

known informally as Tata Raphaël.[5] His initiative and later activities must be seen in the context of the general approach of the Catholic Church to sport and the human body, as well as with his own upbringing. Sporting and youth movements played a prominent role within Catholic Action, an initiative taken by Pope Pius XI to reach as many young people as possible in contemporary society in both Europe and the mission territories. Sports—particularly athletics, gymnastics, and soccer—were encouraged as part of the Catholic education systems (if mostly outside of school hours). The motivation behind this was the pursuit of the familiar ideal of "Christian knighthood," in connection with ideas on the internal hierarchy between spirit and body, the healthy body being the servant of the Christian spirit.[6] On a personal level, the young La Kethulle, born in Bruges in 1890 to a noble family, experienced the openness that the Xaverian Brothers adopted with regard to English sports. The athletic and intellectual education he received from the Brothers was fundamental to his later missionary work as a Scheut Father in the Belgian Congo. In his (very colonial) eyes, sports—and soccer in particular—were a crucial means to counteract what he called the "deleterious temptations of the immoral dances, the obscene songs and the orgies of the natives within the colony."[7]

Arriving in Leopoldville in 1917, La Kethulle established a primary school at Saint-Anne, the eventual Saint-Joseph's school (Elikya). Two years later, in 1919, he created the Association Sportive Congolaise (ASC), the very first sporting association for indigenous people. Sports that were promoted included soccer (1919), gymnastics (1920), athletics (1927), swimming and water polo (1935), basketball (1946), and tennis

---

[5] Emmanuel Coppieters, *L'audacieux "Tata Raphael" de la Kethulle, éducateur, créateur d'écoles et de stades à Kinshasa, de 1917 à 1956* (Kinshasa-Bruxelles: Afrique Editions, 1990); Roland Renson and Chr. Peeters, "Sport als missie: Raphaël de la Kethulle de Ryhove (1890–1956)," in Mark D'hoker et al. (eds.), *Voor lichaam and geest. Katholieken, lichamelijke opvoeding en sport in de 19de en 20ste eeuw* (Leuven: Leuven University Press, 1994), 200-215.

[6] Dries Vanysacker, "The Attitude of the Holy See Toward Sport During the Interwar Period (1919–39)," *The Catholic Historical Review* 101 no. 4 (2015): 794–808; Idem, "The Catholic Church and Sport: A Burgeoning Territory within Historical Research," *Revue d'histoire ecclésiastique Louvain Journal of Church History* 108 no. 1 (2013): 344–356.

[7] Coppieters, *L'audacieux "Tata Raphael,"* 21–35.

(1947).[8] In 1927 the association became affiliated with the Comité Sportif Européen de Léopoldville, under the patronage of the Governor General of the colony.[9] In 1930, the soccer section of the ASC obtained its affiliation with the Royal Belgian Football Union. Their funding allowed the first official Congolese soccer pitch to be installed at Parc Saint-Pierre in 1931.[10] The first soccer games of the Congolese students took place in front of Saint-Anna's church. Typical for the Catholic view at that time, there was total separation between boys and girls with the opinion that girls should practice only gymnastics and always indoors or behind walls.[11] Track and field remained closed to girls until 1955.

Along with other initiatives, such as the Congolese Boy Scouts Saint-Norbert (including a brass band) (1922) and a theater group (1926), all sporting activities were made possible in connection with the growth of Saint-Joseph's school and with new educational achievements, such as the establishment of a technical school in 1925 and the first complete secondary school in 1945.[12] In 1931, La Kethulle invited General Paul-Charles Ermens (1884–1957),[13] Vice Governor of the Congo-Kasai Province, to inaugurate Parc Saint-Pierre, which was situated next to the church of the Scheut mission of Saint-Pierre. Here was located the first Stade de la plaine Saint-Pierre with a soccer pitch and a stand taking the place of what had been swampy and unhealthy ground.

The first athletics competitions were organized in this stadium in 1933 and 1934. On the same site, Scheut built a hall to organize theater performances, to show films, and to hold school parties. In 1933, the Scheut Missions edited the first journal for the indigenous Congolese

---

[8] For more information, see the Diocesan Archives of Leopoldville/Kinshasa, preserved in the General Archives of C.I.C.M. situated at Leuven, KADOC, BE/942855/1262/5016, Dossier "Association Sportive Congolaise" (1936–1953) http://abs.lias.be/Query/detail.aspx?ID=851584.

[9] "L'association royale sportive congolaise, "*Le Bulletin des Missions* 51 no. 1 (1950): 91–92.

[10] J. Daubresse, "Le football au Congo Belge. L'U.R.B.S.F.A. aide efficacement à son épanouissement," in V. Boin, *Le livre d'or jubilaire de l'U.R.B.S.F.A. 1895–1945*, 491–495.

[11] This was a universal idea of the Catholic Church. See, for example, Vanysacker, "The Attitude of the Holy See toward Sport during the Interwar Period (1919–39)," 800–805.

[12] Coppieters, *L'audacieux "Tata Raphael*," 39–42.

[13] L.A. Pétillon, "Ermens (Paul-Charles)," in *Biographie Belge d'Outre-Mer* (Brussels: Académie Royale des Sciences d'Outre-Mer, 1973), 7A: 1217–222.

people, *La Croix du Congo*, a weekly magazine published by secretariat of the Catholic and Social Action, which aimed at educating and training indigenous people. *La Croix du Congo* reported regularly on the activities of the ASC.[14] By 1935–36, Parc Saint-Pierre had a swimming pool more than 4,000 square meters in size.[15] Unfortunately, it was destroyed in 1942 after a member of a U.S. military unit was infected with malaria while swimming. Due to the growing success of the Association Sportive Congolaise, and the ever-expanding indigenous population of Leopoldville, La Kethulle sought to have the sports complex extended and modernized. In 1936, the parish of Saint-Pierre had a new, multi-functional stadium constructed that was named after Queen Astrid of Belgium and which contained a velodrome (a track for cycling) as well as a soccer pitch. In 1947 the stadium was equipped with electricity, allowing sports activities to be held at night.[16]

The velodrome at Saint-Pierre was not the first in Leopoldville. As early as December 1935, the Institute of the Brothers of the Christian Schools had built the first stadium with a soccer pitch and a velodrome in the Kintambo district of the city, some 5.6 kms away. In 1911, after their first mission in Boma (1909), the Brothers had settled in the eastern corner of Leopoldville (the district named Léo II), and focused on education and extracurricular sports activities as a "means to instil discipline in the children." In the Congo the Brothers replicated their Belgian educational and sports apostolate,[17] and when they opened the vocational school of Saint-Georges in 1936 near their primary school "de la Montagne," their instruction in gymnastics, soccer, and especially cycling be-

---

[14] Van Peel, "Aux débuts du football congolais," 163–179.

[15] Coppieters, *L'audacieux "Tata Raphael,"* 44–47.

[16] Ibid., 52–55.

[17] See, for example, the illustrated article "À l'Exposition Internationale de Bruxelles; Démonstration de gymnastique éducative," published in *Signum fidei: organe des anciens élèves des Frères des écoles chrétiennes au Congo* 6 no. 8 (1935). On the sports initiatives by the Brothers of the Christian Schools, see the articles "Het turnfeest van de Katholieke Scholen van Brussel," *Bode van de Christelijke Scholen* 8 (1935): 291–214; "Turnfeest te Laken," *Bode van de Christelijke Scholen* 9 (1936): 284–288; "Sint Amandusinstituut te Gent. Drie kwart eeuws opvoeding en onderwijs," *Bode van de Christelijke Scholen* 11 (1938): 247–248.

came a benchmark.[18] The support from the director of the school, Brother Damien, from a certain M. Fichefet (secretary of the cycling club and of the association of former students of the Brothers—l'Association des Anciens Élèves—founded in 1927), cannot be overlooked.[19] The velodrome had been a realization of the brother-architect August Driesen (Brother Herman).

On 6 December 1935, the Kintambo Bicycle Club (Vélo-Club) was set up. On 4 October 1936, the club organised the first real cycling competition in celebration of the twenty-fifth anniversary of the Brothers' arrival. The race was held on the streets of Leopoldville and finished at the velodrome of Kintambo. The forty-eight African cyclists were welcomed by the *beau monde* sitting in the grandstand: Governor General Pierre Ryckmans, Vice Governor General Ermens, Head of the Province Maquet, Commander in Chief of the Colonial Armies Hennequin, Chief Engineer Devroey, and Commissar of the Urban District Léon Morel.[20] Only a few months later, several journals of the Brothers reported that the velodrome's rectangular form and its construction of tamped earth surrounding the soccer pitch had quickly been developed into a modern, concrete, oval track, with a width of eight meters. The edges of the velodrome were protected by sheet metal, and speakers blasted music. On the anniversary of the bicycle club's establishment, several races were organized, such as speed, pursuit, Madison (*course à l'americaine*), and races behind a motorbike, in the presence of a segregated crowd of Congolese and white people, among whom the Governor General, the Vice Governor General, and Mgr. Six, Apostolic Vicar of Leopoldville. The stands had a capacity of a thousand European and five thousand African spectators.[21]

---

[18] "Frères des écoles chrétiennes au Congo," *Signum fidei: organe des anciens élèves des Frères des écoles chrétiennes au Congo (ASSANEF)*, numéro spécial 11, 12 (February 1962). See also "Chronique de Léopoldville. Journée Jubilaire (4 October 1936)," *Signum fidei: organe des anciens élèves des Frères des écoles chrétiennes au Congo* 8 no. 1 (1936): 8–15.

[19] "Les Œuvres post-scolaires de Léo II," *Signum fidei: organe des anciens élèves des Frères des écoles chrétiennes au Congo* 7 no. 8 (1936).

[20] "Léopoldville a assisté à une magnifique compétition due à des initiatives dévouées," *Signum fidei: organe des anciens élèves des Frères des écoles chrétiennes au Congo* 7 no. 4 (1936): 103–106.

[21] "Chronique de Léopoldville. Premier anniversaire de la fondation du Vélo-Club," *Signum fidei: organe des anciens élèves des Frères des écoles chrétiennes au*

A point of interest during this time is the growing popularity of soccer competitions for indigenous teams. As Bénédicte Van Peel has shown for Leopoldville, until the 1920s there existed at most an organized competition for European representatives of industrial or business firms looking for a healthy Sunday distraction. The Congolese were only permitted to attend as spectators and were kept well apart from the white elite.[22] The Scheut Fathers and the Brothers of the Christian Schools acquainted the African children with soccer by introducing the sport at their schools' recreation grounds. Soon after La Kethulle had founded his extracurricular Association Sportive Congolaise in 1919, the Association counted four indigenous soccer teams. Regular championships were organised from 1924 onwards, and by 1931 there were already sixteen teams. In 1936, the Association des Anciens Élèves, founded in 1927 by the Brothers in Kintambo could boast four different teams.[23] After a crisis in 1933, the competition restarted in 1935 with seventeen teams spread over four divisions. In 1939, there were no fewer than fifty-three teams spread over six divisions, for a total of 815 effective members. Depending on their level of play, teams were further divided into *bottés* and *non-bottés*: those who could field players with or without soccer boots. Meanwhile, several tournaments were organized, including the Coupe de La Croix du Congo (1934), Coupe du Bas-Congo (1935), and Coupe Belga (1936).[24]

The multitude of photographs and reports in the contemporary press and in journals of the involved congregations are the best evidence of the growing popularity of soccer in Belgian Congo. This popularity was not limited to Leopoldville and Elisabethville but extended to the congregations' other mission stations. The Brothers of the Christian Schools, for example, were also active in Tumba, where, from 1921 on-

---

Congo 8 no. 3 (1937):68–70; "Les Courses cyclistes au Vélodrome," *Signum fidei: organe des anciens élèves des Frères des écoles chrétiennes au Congo* 8 no. 8 (1937):240–242; "Vélodrome de Léo-Ouest. Courses du dimanche 1ᵉʳ août 1937," *Signum fidei: organe des anciens élèves des Frères des écoles chrétiennes au Congo* 8 no. 10 (1937): 294–295.

[22] Van Peel, "Aux débuts du football congolais," 146–157.

[23] "Les Œuvres post-scolaires de Léo II," *Signum fidei: organe des anciens élèves des Frères des écoles chrétiennes au Congo*, 7 no. 8 (1936).

[24] Daubresse, "Le football au Congo Belge. L'U.R.B.S.F.A. aide efficacement à son épanouissement," 491–495.

wards, they had set up their Teachers' Training College (*école normale*),[25] as well as in Boma, home to their *Colonie Scolaire*.[26] In Coquilhatville (modern-day Mbandaka), a pitch for games, soccer, and gymnastics was opened in 1936.[27] Meanwhile, by 1934, the Benedictines and the Xaverian Brothers had established soccer teams in their respective missions and schools at Jadotville (modern-day Likasi).[28]

What Van Peel does not mention, is that the Reine Astrid stadium (known after 1966 as Stade du 24 Novembre, in reference to Gen. Mobutu's coup d'état, but then renamed to Stade du Cardinal-Malula in 1992) served from 1936 onward as home for two teams, both founded by La Kethulle and composed of several former scholars of Saint-Anna's primary school and Saint-Joseph's secondary school. The first club, FC Renaissance, was founded in 1935 but changed its name in 1939 to Diables Rouges (Red Devils) and in 1942 to Victoria Club. In 1973, this Association Sportive Victoria Club, known by then as the Dauphins Noirs ("Black Dolphins"), changed its name once more to Vita Club. Since 1990, this omnisport association for basketball, nantei (soft tennis), volleyball, and cycling, has been called Association Sportive Victoria Club.[29] On 22 February 1936, La Kethulle created a second team: Daring Faucon (Daring Falcon), nicknamed "the Immaculates" in reference to the official name of the Scheut Fathers: the Congregation of the Immaculate Heart of Mary, known today as Daring Club Motema Pembe Imana.[30] One of the other teams of Leopoldville, the Dragons (FC

---

[25] "Jubilé. Le Cher Frère Médard, Directeur de l'École Normale de Tumba, fête ses vingt-cinq années de vie missionnaire au Congo." *Signum fidei: organe des anciens élèves des Frères des écoles chrétiennes au Congo* 9 no. 1 (1937): 1–15.

[26] "Boma: L'équipe des 'Boy-Scouts' (Colonie scolaire)," *Signum fidei: organe des anciens élèves des Frères des écoles chrétiennes au Congo*, 6 no. 8 (1936) : 279.

[27] "Inauguration de la plaine des jeux à Coquilhatville," *Signum fidei: organe des anciens élèves des Frères des écoles chrétiennes au Congo* 7 no. 9 (1936); "Chronique du Coq," *Signum fidei: organe des anciens élèves des Frères des écoles chrétiennes au Congo* 9 no. 1 (1937): 269–270; "Chronique de Coquilhatville," *Signum fidei: organe des anciens élèves des Frères des écoles chrétiennes au Congo* 9 no. 3 (1938): 70.

[28] *La Croix du Congo*, 7 June 1934, 15 July 1934, and 23 September 1934, cited by B. Van Peel, "Aux débuts du football congolais," 182, note 185.

[29] See https://fr.wikipedia.org/wiki/Association_Sportive_Vitoria_Club; http://www.rdcfoot.net/category/equipes/as-v-club/#.V2VA60lf1f4; http://www.banavea.com/

[30] See https://fr.wikipedia.org/wiki/Daring_Club_Motema_Pembe; http://www.imana-dcmp.com/

Dragons Du Sang et du Monde), currently Amicale Sportive Dragons-Bilima, was established in 1938 by the Brothers of the Christian Schools and had their ground at the stadium of Kintambo.[31]

During the Second World War, a cooperation between La Kethulle and the above-mentioned Vice Governor General Ermens led to the construction of the Parc des Sports Général Ermens, a public area of about thirty hectares that included five large and small soccer fields, basketball courts, nine tennis courts, and a new outdoor swimming pool in cement, ninety-one meters by thirty-three meters (at which races with canoes were organized). This sports area was open to all native Congolese, whatever their religious background.[32] The complex was built with support from local firms, led by Joseph Rhodius, delegate administrator of Texaf, a Belgian textile company.[33] At the inauguration of the complex on Easter Sunday in 1946, Governor General Pierre Ryckmans (1891–1959) called for similar efforts to improve the lives of indigenous people. According to a contemporary article by the Belgian journalist Pierre de Vos, published 14 April 1946 in *Pourquoi Pas?*, the aim of this sports complex was to offer indigenous people a healthy way of spending their leisure time. Vos believed the combination of physical and moral education would keep them out of bars and discourage similar distractions. The finishing touch was the completion of an electricity network that permitted the indigenous working class to come and play sports after work in the evening.[34]

La Kethulle's activities and his open-mindedness towards other faith traditions (such as the YMCA, Salvation Army, and other Protestants), were not always welcomed by his superiors nor by some local white people. His tolerance *avant la lettre* of the Scheut missionary toward Protestants ("heretics!") and "heathens" was, for missionaries of all kind of backgrounds, unacceptable. La Kethulle's superiors and Scheut *confrères* were uneasy with his individualistic style of working and fundraising and looked warily on his friendship network, which included administrators of all sorts. Some qualified his work as too profane and superficial, while others wondered why the stadiums were clustered so close together. Still others, envious colonizers in particular, complained

---

[31] See http://www.as-dragons-bilima.com/las-dragons-devient-as-dragons-bilima/

[32] Coppieters, *L'audacieux "Tata Raphael,"* 52-55.

[33] See http://www.texaf.be/fr/a-propos-denous/histoire.html

[34] Coppieters, *L'audacieux "Tata Raphael,"* 52-53.

that their swimming pool's water at the exclusive Funa Club was being polluted by the water of the natives' sports center.[35]

The dreams La Kethulle's, however, did not end here. Realizing that the continuous growth of the indigenous population in Leopoldville (3,000 in 1917; 30,000 in 1931; 120,000 in 1947) increased the need for urban and social infrastructure, La Kethulle argued that the stadium Reine Astrid was too small to host the ever-expanding group of spectators of soccer games and athletics events. Sports were no longer a mere pastime; they had become a social phenomenon that attracted thousands of spectators.[36]

Between 1948 and 1952, Tata achieved his magnum opus, the then-called Stade Roi Baudouin. With a capacity of 70,000, it was the biggest sports stadium in Africa at that time and was bigger than any stadium in Belgium. Its educational, symbolic, and nationalist value was immense. The first stone was laid 4 July 1948 by the Governor General of the Belgian Congo, Eugène Jungers, and blessed by Cardinal Jozef Van Roey (1874–1961), Archbishop of Malines. The timing, which coincided with the fiftieth anniversary of the completion of the railway Matadi-Leopoldville, was the perfect occasion to request the assistance of the president of the Otraco (the Association of Transport in Belgian Congo) in transporting the necessary cement to the construction site. Thousands of teachers from schools in Leopoldville helped by carrying stones on their heads for the construction of "their" stadium. Four years later, on 1 July 1952, the stadium's inauguration took place.[37] Journalist Pierre Davister published his personal observations in the *Courrier d'Afrique* on 2 July 1952:

> It was a magnificently colorful spectacle with enthusiastic blacks and whites united for one and the same feast. All had come spontaneously to applaud the indigenous boy gymnasts and the girls wearing white robes with the emblem of the Olympic rings... [A]t the end of this ceremony, Governor General Pétillon made an admirable gesture towards Tata Raphaël: he took him in his convertible and made the tour of the stadium. A frenetic ovation saluted the one who had endeavoured years

---

[35] Ibid., 44-47.
[36] Ibid., 63
[37] Ibid., 63–65

on end to finalize this magnificent work. It was the coronation of his oeuvre![38]

Nonetheless, the hunger of La Kethulle was anything but stilled. From 1953 on, he provided classrooms under the bleachers of the Stade Roi Baudouin for teachers of physical education at the first Higher Institute in Congo. This institute for physical education was modeled on the Institute of Physical Education at the Catholic University of Leuven and was intended to train indigenous physical education teachers as a way to disseminate sports knowledge throughout the territory. Jef Ghesquiere, a Leuven graduate in physical education, was recruited to develop the sports infrastructure within the stadium, to organize a large sport festival for its inauguration, and to shape the curriculum of the future institute. Together with André Flour, doctor of philosophy, collaborator at the Institute of Physical Education at Leuven, and director of the Brewery of Bralima at Stanleyville (Kisangani), Ghesquiere also provided courses in gymnastics to the students of Saint-Anne's College and the Saint-Raphael School of Commerce.[39]

Falling ill in 1954, La Kethulle was forced to return to Belgium, where he died on 25 June 1956. His body was transferred to Leopoldville and buried on 29 July 1956. A mausoleum and stele were erected near the Stadium Roi Baudouin, which was rebaptized Stade Tata Raphaël in the context of the Grand Naturalization by President Mobutu on 23 June 1966. One year later, the stadium's name was changed again to Stade du 20 Mai, this time in reference to the Manifeste de la N'Sele that created the Movement of the Revolution—the only political party then permitted. Since 1997, the stadium is once again known as the Stade Tata Raphaël, in honour of the Scheut Father.[40]

Elisabethville-Lubumbashi

In the meantime, the Benedictine Fathers of the Abbey of Saint-Andrew of Bruges—active in the Katanga Province since 1910—had launched a parallel sport apostolate among the indigenous people of the city of Elisabethville-Lubumbashi. Elisabethville had grown up in the middle of one of the richest provinces, thriving on copper, tin, and cobalt mines.

---

[38] Ibid., 65–71.

[39] Ibid., 60–62, 74–77, 86; Vanmeerbeek and Delheye, "Military Sport in the Belgian Congo," 1932.

[40] Coppieters, *L'audacieux "Tata Raphael,"* 91–137.

The Africans who left their villages to settle in the urbanized districts, separated from the Europeans, were all employed at big companies, such as the copper giant Union Minière du Haute Katanga or the Railway of Katanga. It was here that the Benedictine Monsignor Jean-Félix de Hemptinne (1876–1958), Apostolic Vicar of Katanga, created a parish devoted to Saint John in the midst of the *cité indigene* with an indigenous Christian population of 15,000–20,000.[41] Here also, in 1925, Dom Grégoire Coussement (1895–1957)[42] founded the Société des Sports et Attractions together with Jean-Guillaume Derriks (1901–61),[43] at the time a lawyer at the service of the Union Minière du Haut Katanga and with the support of Paul Alsteen, founder-director of the Brewery of Katanga (Brasimba). This association was later known as the Fédération Royale des Associations Sportives Indigènes (FRASI). In 1933, this social initiative became, among others, part of the Secretariat of Catholic Action, while in 1933 and 1934, it was slotted in with the Foyer Social Indigène, a Benedictine project consisting of seven services: documentation, information, educational assistance, family assistance, recreation assistance, a female section, and extracurricular works.[44] Two different school soccer teams of the Benedictines were part of this Association: FC Prince Charles (founded in 1926 and currently known as Lubumbashi-Sport[45]) and FC Prince Léopold (later changed into FC Vaticano and today known as FC Vijana Katuba).

Writing for the journal of the Benedictines of the Abbey of Saint-Andrew, *Le Bulletin des Missions*, Dom Grégoire Coussement underlined several times the role of the Sport Association within the urban apostolate. In 1933, he voiced the opinion that his association had an important role to play in the general education of the indigenous people, in adherence to the adage *mens sana in corpore sano* (a healthy spirit in a healthy body). In his mind, the games and many other forms of entertainment provided members of this association with many advantages. Sports, according to Coussement, was a remarkable tool for the physical and moral improvement of indigenous people. Rather than spending their Sunday

---

[41] Legrand and Thoreau, *Les Bénédictins au Katanga: Vingt-cinq ans d'apostolat (1910–1935)* (Lophem-lez-Bruges: Abbaye de Saint-André, 1935).

[42] Van Peel, "Aux débuts du football congolais," 178–184.

[43] R.J. Cornet, "Derriks (Jean-Guillaume)," in *Biographie Belge d'Outre-Mer* (Brussels: Académie Royale des Sciences d'Outre-Mer, 1968), 6: 314–316.

[44] Legrand and Thoreau, *Les Bénédictins au Katanga*, 255–261.

[45] See http://republic.pink/lubumbashi-sport_2769442.html.

afternoons in an unhealthy hut, drinking the local beer *pombé* or getting drunk in bars in the company of women or girls of easy virtue, they were giving themselves wholeheartedly over to outdoor sports: soccer, push-ball, running, jumping, and even tennis. He was proud that his Société des sports et d'Attractions, the first to have been set up among the Africans of Elisabethville, had brightened up the local festivities. What was more beautiful, he thought, than two teams battling fiercely for victory in a praiseworthy display of discipline and respect for the referee and the rules of the game?

The society's undeniable social importance urged Coussement on to develop it further.[46] In 1935, the missionary reiterated how essential a role sports played within the Service of Recreational Assistance (*Service d'assistance récréative*), in particular within the project of the Foyer Social Indigène of Elisabethville. The eternal question was how to give the urban dwellers a decent alternative to spending their free time attending European dances, such as the "immoral" Malinga. Apart from the theater and the cinema, with its educational and entertaining scope, sports were the most important and attractive alternative, at least for the boys and men. The favorite sport was soccer, and as many as eight teams were established that played every week on the pitch near the Foyer. Tennis, gymnastics, and athletics also attracted many Africans. A large gymnastics hall was built near the Foyer. For swimming enthusiasts, the construction of a swimming pool, some 500 meters from the Foyer, was underway. Indoor games were not neglected: those who preferred quieter entertainment could play table tennis, billiards, darts, and checkers. In the eyes of Coussement, the work of the Foyer Social Indigène was the only possible answer to the changing times and the challenge for a new apostolate in the increasingly urbanized cities of the Congo, where Africans were rubbing shoulders with the colonizing Europeans, sharing their way of living and their leisure habits.[47]

In 1939, the parish of Saint-John opened a sports stadium named after King Leopold II. It was seen as the culmination of the collaboration between the Benedictines and civil authorities, among whom were the Head of the Province and diverse commercial enterprises, particularly Union Minière. At the inauguration, Monsignor de Hemptinne conse-

---

[46] Coussement, "Les réalisations," *Le Bulletin des Missions* 9 no. 2 (1933): 131–136.

[47] Coussement, "Le Foyer Social Indigène d'Elisabethville," *Le Bulletin des Missions. Le courrier de l'apostolat monastique* 14 suppl. no. 2 (1935): 68*–80*.

crated the stadium, expressing his hope "that it would bring health to the spirit and the body." The Leopold II stadium was adjacent to the Benedictine mission post of Saint-John, itself strategically located on the southeastern border between the cité indigène—the segregated residential area for urban Africans established in 1921—and the "white" city of Elisabethville.[48]

The collaboration between the Service de la Main-d'Oeuvre Indigène of the Union Minière—established to take care of the accommodation, schools, and hospitals, as well as to organize leisure activities for indigenous workers and employees—and the Benedictine missionaries was very close. In 1939, the missionaries of the Saint-Boniface School (providing a ten-year curriculum for 700 students) set up a proper soccer team, FC Saint-Georges (patron of the Boy Scouts), which was immediately affiliated with the FRASI. The team finished third in its first season, behind the teams Prince-Léopold and Prince-Charles. In 1944, FC Saint-Georges became Saint Paul FC and when, some years later, the missionaries left the teams' management, the name was changed to that of the sponsor: FC Englebert—the direct precursor of the current Tout Puissant Mazembe.[49]

This collaboration was not always a success story, as was made clear during the Second World War when labor protests eventually forced the Union Minière du Haut Katanga to expand its sporting and recreational opportunities in mining compounds. The initial failure of its industrial sports policy was tragically exposed in December 1941 when troops armed with machine guns massacred almost 100 striking mineworkers on the soccer field at the Elisabethville compound.[50] According to Peter C. Alegi, the usefulness of what he calls "political athleticism" in Katanga—the public display of "corporealized nation-states" that replicated the racial and economic hierarchies found in the mineral zone of Congo—

---

[48] Th. Nève, "Deux capitales spirituelles du Congo Belge, "*Le Bulletin des Missions* 18 no. 3 (1939): 193–204 (especially 201).

[49] See http://englebertmazembe.unblog.fr/historique-du-tp-mazembe/; http://www.tpmazembe.com/fr/actualite/5767/mazembe-n-a-pas-perdu-sa-foi-des-benedictins; http://www.memoireonline.com/08/11/4648/m_La-problematique-de-la-multiplicite-des-sponsors-autour-dune-equipe-de-football-cas-du-TP-Maz24.html

[50] John Higginson, *A Working Class in the Making: Belgian Colonial Labor Policy, Private Enterprise, and the African Mineworker, 1907–1951* (Madison: University of Wisconsin Press, 1989), 192–194.

grew significantly when the colonial trinity (Union Minière, the colonial government, and the Catholic Church) tightened its control in 1945:

> After the war, colonial administrators, Catholic missionaries and industrial capitalists reinvigorated the 'good health, good spirits and high productivity' strategy to defuse the political tensions of a rapidly expanding African population in Elisabethville.[51]

Between 1945 and 1957 there was a yearly population increase of eight percent (with 70,000 born and arriving in 1945, growing to 170,000 in 1957). In 1950, the FRASI counted more than thirty affiliated clubs who competed in four leagues spread over three divisions. Soccer's low-level violence, teamwork, and mass appeal suited a colonial agenda aimed at keeping the bodies and social forces of African athletes in check. An added bonus was its very low organizational cost, its adaptability to any sort of playing ground, and its instant popularity among the African population.

Soccer's success as a social pacifier and as a display of "political athleticism" reached its apex with the Double Triangular Tournament held on the National Day of Belgium on 21 and 23 July 1950 in the King Leopold II stadium. The three participating teams were Katanga (a home team composed of players from Englebert, Vaticano, Lubumbashi, and Kipushi), a team from Broken Hill (a Northern Rhodesian industrial town, home to some of the oldest lead and zinc mines of the copper belt), and an assembled team from Johannesburg. It was a grandiose colonial showcase staged in front of a segregated crowd of 30,000 black and white spectators at a packed Leopold II stadium. All the players were black, while the referee and the linesmen leading the game were white.[52] According to Alegi, this was because "for the white-minority regimes, such as Belgian Congo and South Africa, black athletes were subordinated cultural ambassadors who would improve the domestic and international image of both Belgian and South African totalitarian rule."[53]

In the anniversary book of the Belgian Soccer Federation of 1945, a special chapter by Victor Boin was devoted to soccer and other sports in the colony of Congo. Its very title. *Le Sport, facteur de civilization et de cordiale collaboration*, along with the author's overall approach, bring to

---

[51] Peter C. Alegi, "Katanga versus Johannesburg: a history of the first sub-Saharan African football championship, 1949–50," *Kleio* 31 (1999): 57.

[52] Ibid., 55–74.

[53] Ibid., 56.

light just how much sports, as organized by both the Belgian civil administration and the Catholic mission congregations, aimed to "civilize" the
indigenous[54].

Conclusion

This overview of missionary activities among the urbanized African population of the former Belgian Congo serves to clarify the motivation behind the sports apostolate of several Catholic mission congregations after
the First World War. Catholic missionaries did not take an interest in
sports just for their own sake. Instead, by continuously stressing the adage *mens sana in corpore sano*, these missionaries molded sport into a remarkable tool for the physical, hygienic, and moral improvement of indigenous people.[55] Sport, with its intrinsic rules, offered an excellent
means to acquaint Africans with discipline and hierarchy. We can argue,
while paraphrasing Jean-Luc Vellut and Alegi, that since the 1920s, the
"colonial trinity" that ruled the two biggest cities of the former Belgian
Congo—the Catholic Church, the colonial government, and the industrial powers—had devised a means to create a disciplined, efficient, moral, and healthy African student and working-class population.[56]

We find a significant example of this strategy in the edition of 30
September 1934 *La Croix du Congo* magazine. The issue published the
ten commandments of the sportsman:

> (1) do not cheat, always play honestly; (2) learn the rules of the game
> and follow them to the letter; (3) try your hardest and be an excellent
> team mate; (4) be modest at all times, for pride comes before a fall; (5)
> when the game goes against you, turn away, but do not leave in a cow-
> ardly way; (6) take defeat with a smile, accept it cheerfully; (7) do the
> same with victory, accept it graciously; (8) do not ever say an insulting

---

[54] Boin, "Les Sports, facteur de civilisation et de cordiale collaboration,"
497–501.

[55] Lies Van Rompaey, "Mission et Education Physique dans le Congo
Belge (1908–1960)," in *Education, Physical Activities and Sport in a Historical
Perspective. Fourteenth ISCHE conference, 1992. Conference working papers / materials del congrés / materiales del Congreso. 14è Congrés International. Internal Standing Conference for the History of Educatio* (Impremta Barcelona, S.A., 1992): 307–
312.

[56] Alegi, "Katanga versus Johannesburg," 57; Vellut, "Mining in the Belgian Congo," in D. Birmingham and P. Martin (eds), *History of Central Africa*
(London and New York, 1983), 2:153.

word, speak courteously at all times; (9) when situations in the game are debatable, favor the other side; (10) in short, play sports for fun and never think of what is at stake.[57]

In a sense, sport was part of the general pursuit of civilization, in which the Church collaborated with the Belgian state, a collaboration based on funds from industrial giants. Sports in the Belgian Congo seemed to be a privileged place of affirmation, self-development, and social promotion for Africans. Nonetheless, they remained for many years a male-only activity under the guidance of male European missionaries since girls were only prepared to be good housewives. Girls only gained access to public sporting events after 1955, with the exception of their "ornamental" presence at feasts, at the openings of new stadiums, or as spectators at male competitions. Sports were, furthermore, organized independently from the sport and leisure activities of the colonial elite. Sport, as organized by the Catholic missionaries for the urbanized Africans in the former Belgian Congo, was without doubt "sport with a mission."

---

[57] Quoted by Van Peel, "Aux débuts du football congolais," 176.

Kinshasa, Stadium Kintambo.
Above, the stadium in 1937 and below as seen in 2014.
Courtesy Dries Vanysacker

Kinshasa, Stadium Reine Astrid, 1936.
Courtesy Dries Vanysacker

Kinshasa, statue of Tata Raphaël at the Stade Tata Raphaël.
Courtesy Dries Vanysacker

Kinshasa, Parc Ermens.
Above, aerial view of the stadium in 1946;
below, present-day ruins of the Grand Stand at the stadium.
Courtesy Dries Vanysacker

Kinshasa, Stadium Cardinal Malula, 2014.
Courtesy Dries Vanysacker

The Paradox of Christian Masculinity:
Sports, War, and Internationalism at the
1919 Inter-Allied Games

Seth Dowland

Muscular Christianity rippled across the religious landscape of the United States in the late nineteenth century. Imported from Britain, the movement taught that the perils of modernity demanded "manly Christians" who could provide strength of character and body. The perception of a feminized Christianity compelled muscular Christians to construct gymnasiums and athletic fields to support U.S. imperialism in the Spanish-American War and to recast Jesus as fearless and confident. At the onset of the Great War in 1914, leaders in the Young Men's Christian Association (YMCA) had convinced U.S. policymakers that muscular Christianity could play a critical role in "beating the Hun," and YMCA secretaries enjoyed both the blessing of President Woodrow Wilson and a presidential order allowing them unprecedented access to U.S. troops during the war. In this "war to end all wars," muscular Christians saw the potential for their masculine faith to engender international peace and brotherhood.

No event better epitomized these convictions than the 1919 Inter-Allied Games, a postwar competition among veterans of the Allied forces sponsored by the YMCA. Modeled on the modern Olympics—which Pierre de Coubertin had launched just twenty-three years earlier—the Inter-Allied Games featured competitions in twenty-six sports and participants from twenty-nine countries, all of whom were veterans of the Great War. Organizers hoped that "the practice of athletic sports" would "repair the cruel ravages of war."[1] E.C. Carter, the Chief Secretary of the

---

[1] *The Inter-Allied Games* (Paris: The Games Committee, 1919), 4. Various editions of this publication exist, including an abridged, bilingual (English and French) (see http://babel.hathitrust.org/cgi/pt?id=njp.32101063695132;view=1up;seq=32). The page numbers cited here refer to the print edition held in the Kautz Family YMCA Archives, University of Minnesota.

American Expeditionary Forces-YMCA, compared the hastily constructed Pershing Stadium, home of the games, to the Statue of Liberty.
Just as France had once built a "monument to liberty" in the United
States, the U.S. population had returned the favor by offering France a
monument to another "aspect of liberty—the right to play."[2] By channel-
ing masculine energy and promoting competition, fairness, and sportsmanship, the Inter-Allied Games hoped to promote peace through an
athletic program shot through with ideals of U.S. democracy, virtuous
manhood, and Christianity.

The hopes of muscular Christians to promote eternal and lasting
peace through sports, however, fell apart even more quickly than Pershing Stadium itself, which closed in 1960. Global depression and another world war chastened the optimistic theological rhetoric of the Pro-
gressive Era. This essay investigates a particular facet of that rhetoric: the
convictions of muscular Christians that their program linking mind,
body, and spirit held the key for unlocking international cooperation in
the modern age. Muscular Christianity contained competing ideals. On
the one hand, muscular Christians believed that their vision provided a
template for international unity through broadmindedness, charity, and
Christian values. On the other hand, muscular Christians celebrated
masculine ideals of competition, struggle, and conquest, which undermined their rhetoric of cooperation. Moreover, muscular Christians understood themselves as the elite, which facilitated their unprecedented
access to Allied soldiers but also limited the reach of their message to
those who shared their racial identity as white people and their socioeco-
nomic standing. When muscular Christians talked about manly Christianity, they almost always envisioned white, upper-and middle-class men
engaging in the struggle to save society. The vision of Christian manhood put forward by early twentieth-century muscular Christians contained incompatible ideals that fell apart in the wake of the Great War.

Many studies have established the white, upper class character of
muscular Christianity—particularly the form of muscular Christianity
championed in U. S. YMCAs.[3] This essay builds on those studies by
demonstrating how muscular Christians' failed internationalism unveiled
the paradox in their vision of Christian masculinity. Muscular Christians

---

[2] Ibid., 175.

[3] For example, see Clifford Putney, *Muscular Christianity: Manhood and
Sports in Protestant America, 1880–1920* (Cambridge, MA: Harvard University
Press, 2001).

believed that the Inter-Allied Games could offer the world a vision of international cooperation. This vision, however, demanded winners and losers. Elite American muscular Christians would not relinquish their privileged position, and their vision of sports as a competitive struggle demanded all-out effort against one's adversary. Sports, in other words, resembled war more than peacemaking. Muscular Christians wanted the world to celebrate the power of sports to build character and promote camaraderie, but they also needed to win. The Inter-Allied Games revealed that paradox by featuring sports that favored U.S. residents and emphasized militarism. Nationalism was central to the competition. Muscular Christians believed that sports could sponsor peace, but themes of struggle and conquest remained endemic to their games.

Muscular Christianity and Sports

When muscular Christianity came to the United States in the 1860s and 1870s, it faced an uphill battle in convincing U.S. Christians of the salutary effects of sports. Early YMCAs in the United States—those built in the first two decades after the Civil War—featured large reading rooms, auditoriums for revivals, and classrooms for Bible instruction. These were likely modeled on the London YMCA, which in 1854 advertised its 500-seat lecture hall and the spacious dimensions of its reading room, reference library, and parlor, but featured no gymnasium.[4] As late as the 1880s, YMCAs gave comparatively little room to gymnasiums, which were seen simply as prophylactic—places for young men to blow off some steam more wholesomely than they could at the local brothel.[5] This negative view of athletics emanated from the worries of many U.S. Protestants, who knew all too well the deleterious effects sports could bring. Prizefights attracted shady bookies; duels and cockfights bred violence.[6] The growth of baseball as a popular form of entertainment frightened many Christians, who worried that Sunday games would encourage Sabbath-breaking.

---

[4] Paula Lupkin, *Manhood Factories: YMCA Architecture and the Making of Modern Urban Culture* (Minneapolis: University of Minnesota Press, 2010), 4.

[5] Ibid., 37–72.

[6] Ted Ownby, *Subduing Satan: Religion, Recreation, and Manhood in the Rural South, 1865–1920* (Chapel Hill: University of North Carolina Press, 1990).

1919 Inter-Allied Games poster.

Courtesy Wikicommons

Muscular Christians were convinced, however, that sports could play a critical role in men's spiritual development. The YMCA shepherded an important shift in the understanding of sports in the late nineteenth century. Whereas mid-nineteenth century evangelicals had largely thought of sports as custodial—occupying boys to prevent them from indulging in sin—late-nineteenth century Protestants increasingly focused on the "character building" aspect of athletics.[7] In 1888 Luther Halsey Gulick, the director of the International YMCA Training School's Physical Department and most prominent writer in the American YMCA movement, argued that earlier generations had mistakenly thought of the gymnasium as "simply a trap to catch young men." Gulick insisted, however, "[t]he whole man for Christ is our aim. The gymnasium and athletic field then have an important place to fill; they must not only build up as perfect bodies as possible, but...we may expect even more from them in direct spiritual results than we are able to secure in physical results."[8] An 1892 *Boston Globe* article noted, "[i]t would have astonished the early church fathers and those of the Middle Ages, who believed in long fastings, penances and the sort for keeping the body under, to see the modern Young Men's Christian Association giving men as vigorous a physical training as did the old Greeks."[9] In the 1860s and 1870s, the YMCA seemed embarrassed about its athletic facilities. Beginning in the late 1880s, however, the YMCA placed physical activity on a pedestal, convinced that bodily fitness played an essential role in salvation.

Throughout the 1880s, 1890s, and 1900s, Gulick made the case that physical activity and spiritual vigor went hand in hand. In an 1890 letter he wrote that it did not make a man "any less worthy a Christian that he was acknowledged leader of athletic sports in his college, nor did it interfere at all with his good playing that he was a devout Christian.

---

[7] Putney, *Muscular Christianity*, 67.

[8] Gulick, "Fundamental Basis of the Young Men's Christian Association," 1888. Luther Halsey Gulick Papers, Series 4, Box 9, Folder 16, Springfield College Archives and Special Collections.

[9] A.C. Merritt, "Gospel of Muscle: Bible and Dumbbells the Instruments," *Boston Daily Globe*, 25 January 1892. Amos Alonzo Stagg Papers, Box 275, Folder 5, Special Collections Research Center, University of Chicago. This article unintentionally confirmed why some church fathers worried about obsessions with physical fitness by noting in a subhead, "Stagg an Instructor—Pretty Women Send Him Their Pictures."

On the contrary there is little doubt but that the development of each side of his character was a help to the other."[10] This connection depended on a sense that healthy bodies were necessary to build up the kingdom, and that healthy souls were the only guarantors of good conduct—whether on the playing field or in the business of daily life. In an 1894 address to Massachusetts legislators, Gulick declared, "[t]he building up of healthy, erect, symmetrical, enduring, and graceful bodies we regard as of direct relation to the great aim of Association work."[11] By "association work," he meant the YMCA's activity in spiritual development and urban social reform. Only the strong could survive in these realms.

As a result of this attitude towards physical fitness, the YMCA buildings constructed between 1890 and 1915 gave comparatively greater space to gymnasiums, which began to crowd out reading rooms and revival halls in urban YMCAs. When asked why they came to the YMCA, young men overwhelmingly cited the availability of physical fitness facilities. The YMCA responded to popularity of gyms by devoting more square footage to them, and ensuring that they contained the best equipment for physical training.[12] Books like William Blaikie's *How to Get Strong and Stay So* (1879) began appearing on young men's shelves, as the new sport of bodybuilding took hold in northern cities. The fear of flabbiness—often associated with the rise of cities and their attendant sedentary lifestyles—animated a widespread pursuit of physical fitness.

Muscular Christians, however, did not view physical training for its own sake as an unmitigated good. Sports needed supervision; gyms needed physical directors to organize the games; athletes needed leagues where Christian character would be cultivated. Gulick admitted that "athletic sports [were] conducted in such a way in many, if not most, cases as to be of direct unwholesome influence on the contestants." He worried about "discourteous, ungentlemanly, unfair, or even dishonorable acts" and spent much time cataloguing the proper attitude with which men ought to engage in sports. He also wrote a lot of rules for the games

---

[10] Gulick, "Letter from Luther Gulick to Amos Alonzo Stagg," 8 March 1890, Amos Alonzo Stagg Papers, Box 273, Folder 3, Special Collections Research Center, University of Chicago.

[11] Gulick, "Legitimate Place of Athletics in the Young Men's Christian Association" (Massachusetts State Convention, 1894). Luther Halsey Gulick Papers, Series 4, Box 9, Folder 16, Springfield College Archives and Special Collections.

[12] Lupkin, *Manhood Factories*, 111–135.

he supervised. The rise of YMCA athletics in the 1890s coincided with the development of athletic leagues, which set down lengthy lists of rules for competitors. Gulick urged athletes "to regard rules not as laws which are being imposed by some other body contrary to the wish of the contestants…but as a mutual agreement which one would no sooner think of taking advantage of…than one would think of lying in any other direction for personal advantage."[13] Gulick was determined to stamp out sports' reputation as a free-for-all. Proper participation required playing by the rules.

The obsession with rules and leagues meant that certain sports were taboo. Chief among these was prizefighting, which muscular Christians believed corrupted men's bodies and souls. In assessing boxer John L. Sullivan, columnist Philip Poindexter wrote that while "his shoulders and arms and chest are certainly splendidly developed ..he still has what is called a paunch. From his waist down he is in no sense a fine man. His thighs are not nearly so large as they should be in keeping with his shoulders and arms." Such lack of physical development coincided with moral depravity. Sullivan, wrote Poindexter, "is as ignorant a man as ever broke a rock for a living, or thrashed his wife for diversion. He is a bully and a blackguard from the top of his head to the sole of his feet."[14] Muscular Christians assumed that athletics ought to develop the whole body proportionally, and they disdained professional boxers' deformed physiques, developed in pursuit of knock-out blows and lucrative paydays.

Muscular Christians also sneered at professionalism. The overwhelming majority of Christians involved with the movement preferred amateur sports, convinced that amateurism was essential to preserving the Christian character of their games. In an 1889 "Address on Manliness," the Earl of Mulgrave (Manchester, England) declared, "there is, I believe a great danger in the present day of athletics being made a business in life, and not the recreation of life."[15] Of course, it was comparatively easy for a British peer to make athletics a leisurely diversion; many

---

[13] Gulick, "The Athletic League," 189, Luther Halsey Gulick Papers, Series 2, Box 2, Folder 1, Springfield College Archives and Special Collections.

[14] Philip Poindexter, "The Modern Gladiators," *Frank Leslie's Weekly*, 1 September 1892, Amos Alonzo Stagg Papers, Box 275, Folder 5, Special Collections Research Center, University of Chicago.

[15] Rev. the Earl of Mulgrave, "Address on Manliness" (pamphlet, Manchester, England, 1889), Y.USA.52 Box 6, Social Hygiene Pamphlets, Kautz Family YMCA Archives, University of Minnesota.

workers in the growing cities of the industrial era hardly had time for such games. Nonetheless, muscular Christians remained convinced that amateurism was essential in athletics. In 1923, University of Chicago football coach Amos Alonzo Stagg declared, "The amateur principle and amateur spirit can produce such great character building elements...no other basis than this will be constructive."[16] Stagg's assertion depended on the assumption that any professional athlete was a mercenary and thus could never offer the type of sacrifice and loyalty Stagg demanded of his players.

The importance of amateurism to muscular Christianity, alongside its focus on college sports, underscored the elite character of the movement. At the turn of the twentieth century, about 2 percent of 18- to 24-year-olds in the U.S. were enrolled in colleges and universities.[17] A majority of U.S. residents never made it to high school, much less college. Focusing their efforts on colleges and universities meant that muscular Christians targeted the U.S. elite. Occasionally they commented on this reality. Gulick wrote, "athletics represent the chief interest and form the ethical and social relations of the men who in the future are going to dominate this country." While only 2 percent of U.S. residents attended college, he noted, "these two per cent are going to hold fifty per cent of the positions involving the greatest leadership in the public opinion of America."[18] Given the movement's strategic outreach to elites, muscular Christianity contained cues about manliness that corresponded to particular racial and class markers.

In particular, muscular Christians were convinced that they had responsibility for redeeming society, both domestically and abroad. According to muscular Christians, playing sports well gave athletes extraordinary power over themselves and the broader culture. "What greater thing is there than to be masters of ourselves? If we were our complete masters, we would be supermen," wrote Stagg. "Something has got to sweep over this country to reach our boys and girls if we are to have a

---

[16] Amos Alonzo Stagg, "Amateurism in Athletics Produces Character," 1923, Amos Alonzo Stagg Papers, Box 109, Folder 11, Special Collections Research Center, University of Chicago.

[17] "120 Years of American Education: A Statistical Portrait" (National Center for Education Statistics, 1993), 64, http://nces.ed.gov/pubs93/93442.pdf.

[18] L.H. Gulick, "Amateurism," *American Physical Education Review* 13, no. 2 (February 1908): 2.

sound citizenship. Athletics will be an important agency of this revolution."[19] Stagg, like his fellow muscular Christians, understood athletes (particularly college athletes) as catalysts of social reform, who would learn in sports the power of teamwork and the necessity of sacrifice. Along the way they would develop well-proportioned, strong bodies that could fight wars and promote peace with equal vigor. This was a view of sports as socially redemptive, and it depended on both a high view of physical activity and an elitism forged in the era of the "white man's burden."

Muscular Christianity, then, reflected a vision of masculinity that contained markers of both race and class. Photographs of American YMCA teams in the early twentieth century reveal no racial diversity, and the rhetoric surrounding muscular Christianity assumed a white audience. When Gulick and Stagg told their charges that "we" have a responsibility to master ourselves and redeem society, they were speaking to young white men. Further, they spoke to executives. In a 1904 speech, Gulick declared, "[m]en who work in cities work at desks....He plays the typewriter; he adds columns, making little figures; and the work on the brain has been increased tenfold, and the work of the muscles has decreased tenfold."[20] He could hardly say the same about immigrant laborers on the docks or in factories, but those were not the men Gulick had in mind. Like other muscular Christians, Gulick spoke to and for elite white men. That inherent bias pervaded muscular Christianity, even as YMCA secretaries began carrying the movement to every corner of the globe.

Games and Internationalism

Muscular Christians in the YMCA took their gospel of sports abroad early in the twentieth century. The Inter-Allied Games' official yearbook identified the introduction of volleyball to the Philippines in 1910 as the event that convinced the YMCA of the power of sport to bring nations together. Ellwood Brown, who would later become director of the

---

[19] Stagg, "Moral Value of Athletics," 8 August 1922, Amos Alonzo Stagg Papers, Box 109, Folder 7, Special Collections Research Center, University of Chicago.

[20] Gulick, "The Making of a Life: Dangers of a Sedentary Life," 24 February 1904, Luther Halsey Gulick Papers, Series 4, Box 10, Folder 4, Springfield College Archives and Special Collections.

YMCA's Department of Athletics, served then as Physical Director of the YMCA in Manila, which U.S. troops had occupied since defeating the Filipino insurgency in 1902. Brown reported that Filipinos could not make heads or tails of the Americans' favorite pastime, baseball, but that he had greater success engaging the natives with volleyball, which did not require as much skill as baseball did. Brown's narrative about Filipinos embrace of volleyball reads like a tale of conversion: "The sport interested them; very soon it enthused them." After showing casual interest at first, the Filipinos soon hungered for volleyball, setting up games of their own that pitted rival neighborhoods against one another. Brown described the Filipinos' "enthusiastic" participation in "mass play." Brown, in short, was a missionary spreading the gospel of sport.[21]

According to this missionary account, the sport of volleyball was instrumental in forging ties of brotherhood across the Far East. By 1913 the YMCA had staged a mini-olympiad called the Far Eastern Games in Manila; subsequent Far Eastern Games occurred in Shanghai in 1915 and in Tokyo in 1917. The President of China requested an audience with the YMCA delegation to Shanghai in 1915, when he marveled at how "the medium of athletics had induced Chinese from such politically hostile districts as Canton, Shanghai, and Peking, to stand shoulder to shoulder as champions of a common China."[22] Further, YMCA leaders thought the introduction of athletics helped nations move into modern society. "It may be noted," said Iowa YMCA stalwart John L. Griffith, "that the backward nations of the world are in no sense of the word athletic nations."[23] Not only had sports broken down barriers between formerly hostile Asian states, they had moved these nations close to the ranks of "civilization."

As the YMCA's celebration of the Far Eastern Games demonstrated, one of the most urgent social problems facing twentieth-century Christians was international hostility. During the late nineteenth century, the United States had gradually abandoned isolationism in foreign policy, replacing it with the conviction that the U.S. had to play an integral role in international affairs. This conviction on the part of U.S. poli-

---

[21] *The Inter-Allied Games*, 12.

[22] Ibid., 13.

[23] John L Griffith, "Education for Character and World Peace," Address before the State Teachers Association (Rapid City, SD, 26 November 1929), Amos Alonzo Stagg Papers, Box 104, Folder 3, Special Collections Research Center, University of Chicago.

cy makers had huge implications for liberal Protestants. In his famous book *A Theology for the Social Gospel*, Walter Rauschenbusch described the Apostle Paul as the "chief exponent of international religion," whose life's mission was "to make an international religion of Christianity." Like Paul, Rauschenbusch wanted to spread Christianity abroad in order to bring God's peaceable kingdom to the nations. Rauschenbusch held perhaps even more ambitious goals than Paul. He intended to abolish war as well as most forms of private property, replacing capitalism with a form of Christian socialism that he believed more faithful to gospel teaching.[24]

While Rauschenbusch's views veered left of the political mainstream, he nonetheless voiced a common refrain among U.S. Christian elites: the United States had a duty to project its power around the world. Social gospel leaders such as John R. Mott and Josiah Strong "did not see a contradiction between empire and progress."[25] These men believed that Protestantism had bestowed upon the United States the mantle of a redeemer nation. Muscular Christians, with their belief in the character-building quality of physical struggle, were eager to join the imperial march. Most notably, former President Theodore Roosevelt railed against isolationists and pacifists in the debate over America's involvement in World War I. "A flabby cosmopolitanism, especially if it expresses itself through a flabby pacifism, is not only silly, but degrading," Roosevelt wrote. "It represents national emasculation."[26] Real men—and true Christians—needed to accept that now was the time to fight. The advance of the American cause meant the advance of Christian civilization.

As the Great War intensified in 1915 and 1916, more and more U.S. Christians fell in line with Roosevelt, abandoning or modifying the strong pacifist stances many had taken in the first two decades of the twentieth century. At the same time, the steadfast belief in U.S. righteousness forced muscular Christians to refine their understanding of the

---

[24] Walter Rauschenbusch, *A Theology for the Social Gospel* (New York: Macmillan, 1917), 13, 217; Markku Ruotsila, *The Origins of Christian Anti-Internationalism: Conservative Evangelicals and the League of Nations* (Washington, DC: Georgetown University Press, 2008), 23.

[25] Andrew Preston, *Sword of the Spirit, Shield of Faith: Religion in American War and Diplomacy* (New York: Anchor Books, 2012), 224.

[26] Theodore Roosevelt, *Fear God and Take Your Own Part* (New York: George H. Doran & Co., 1916), 18.

connection between battle and manhood. In his fascinating study *Faith in the Fight*, historian Jonathan H. Ebel showed how modern weaponry undermined Progressive-era notions of masculinity. Whereas late-nineteenth-century men believed it possible to exert mastery and control, soldiers in WWI came to understand their survival as a matter of fate. "The Great War," wrote Ebel, "forced men to reconsider the mythic millennial efficacy of the masculine man with which they were so familiar....According to a great many, strength, skill, goodness, wisdom, pluck, vigor, and industry played no part" in determining who would survive."[27] The destructive machinery that dominated the Western Front compelled men to acknowledge their dependence on a divine ordering beyond their control.

Even so, there were plenty of soldiers and civilians who saw the exertion of battle as a crucible of manhood and faith. U.S. soldier Amos Wilder wrote, "we men are the tools with which greater beings fight each other." Marine Walter Poague described the Great War as "the most wonderful war in the world...which means the real salvation of the world."[28] While the capriciousness and totality of modern war pushed some to reconsider the religious valences of war, most U.S. soldiers and citizens thought their cause was just and worthy. The Wilsonian vision of American involvement in the war viewed the U.S. armed forces as redemptive, suffering on behalf of the world just as their savior had done.[29]

If the war was to fulfill its redemptive ends, the soldiers fighting it needed to reflect U.S. righteousness. In his wartime book *With Our Soldiers in France*, YMCA leader Sherwood Eddy remarked that the exigencies of war had revealed soldiers' courage, brotherliness, generosity, straightforwardness, and cheerfulness. It also placed them outside the moral constraints of their homes and in danger of temptation. Fortunately, from Eddy's perspective, the YMCA was there to shepherd U.S. soldiers away from evil. Eddy praised the "unconscious virtues" of Allied soldiers, who only needed to be shown the truth of the gospel to understand the source of their morality.[30] The YMCA had placed itself in Allied camps across Europe in order to minister to these unconsciously vir-

---

[27] Jonathan H. Ebel, *Faith in the Fight: Religion and the American Soldier in the Great War* (Princeton, NJ: Princeton University Press, 2010), 67.

[28] Ibid., 29, 37.

[29] Preston, *Sword of the Spirit, Shield of Faith*, 252.

[30] Sherwood Eddy, *With Our Soldiers in France* (New York: Association Press, 1917), 133–135.

tuous soldiers. Eddy said the Association was "at once the soldier's club, his home, his church, his school, his place of rest, his entertainment bureau, his bank and post office, his tourist guide, and the friend that stands by him."[31] That was only a slight exaggeration. Woodrow Wilson himself issued a presidential order permitting the YMCA access to U.S. Army camps around the globe, and Allied commanders had placed the Y in charge of base canteens during the war. Alongside the organization's role in providing recreation to soldiers, presidential and military endorsement of the YMCA meant that the Y's Red Triangle symbol was ubiquitous in army camps across Europe.

As the war neared its ending, then, the YMCA was uniquely positioned—both logistically and philosophically—to cater to U.S. and Allied soldiers after the armistice. U.S. Protestants had embraced the visions of Rauschenbusch, Strong, and Roosevelt, who saw Jesus as a manly social reformer and the Christian civilization of the United States as a model for the rest of the world.[32] Allied forces were about to supervise the largest reconstruction project in human history. The Great War had caused unprecedented casualties and unimaginable damage in Europe. It was time for U.S. Christians to come to the aid of their beleaguered European counterparts.

The Inter-Allied Games

The Inter-Allied Games became a central way for the YMCA to promote international amity. The Far Eastern Games had demonstrated to key YMCA leaders the possibility of sport to heal wartime rifts. The ravages of the Great War simply demanded a bigger effort. So YMCA secretaries began organizing a massive Olympiad for the summer of 1919, even before Armistice Day in November 1918. The Y sought and received the blessing of the French government to host the Games in France, and General John Pershing sent invitations requesting soldier-participants in the Games to leaders of all of the Allied armies. From January to May 1919, the YMCA organized mass Games on an unprecedented scale. Secretaries staged competitions in soccer, rugby, baseball, and volleyball, alongside Games of tug-of-war and sit-up drills. Organizers ensured that even "unskilled men" had a chance to participate in these

---

[31] Ibid., 71.

[32] Stephen Prothero, *American Jesus: How the Son of God Became a National Icon* (New York: Farrar, Strauss, and Giroux, 2003), 87–123.

Games (hence the sit-up drills), while the YMCA also ensured the best sportsmen would rise to the top through a series of championships in a half-dozen major sports. The U.S. YMCA believed in the ability of sports to promote international cooperation, but it also wanted to win big at the Inter-Allied Games.

This desire for victory undermined the YMCA's attempt to make the Inter-Allied Games an agent of cooperation and international amity. Gulick, for one, was occasionally dismissive of Britain, the nation that had launched muscular Christianity in the first place. "I am not an advocate of the easy loser. I think the primary difference between sport in America and in England is a distinction of this kind," he wrote. "They say we go into athletics with the desperate earnestness with which one goes into a battle. I think that is right. The ability to do a thing tremendously, to take hold, to expend all of one's power, to go to the limit, that is the quality that is making America what it is."[33] Even more damning, in 1915 Gulick condemned British squabbles during the war as reflective of its inferiority to Germany. Germany is "a nation doing team work on an unprecedented scale," he declared. "The controversies in the British Empire sound like the rows in a small boys' baseball team as compared with the swift, powerful obedience, cooperation, and hence freedom, of a team from a major baseball league."[34] Gulick reflected American muscular Christians' sense of superiority over their wartime Allies.

The disconnect between the U.S. rhetoric of cooperation and superiority did not slow the progress towards the Games. During the winter, the YMCA approved plans for the construction of a stadium on land donated by France for that purpose. Set in a working class neighborhood, the stadium was designed by a French engineering firm and built by civil contractors. When labor unrest halted construction around the first of May, the YMCA marshaled U.S. soldiers to work around the clock in order to finish the project before the Games' June opening. The 25,000-seat reinforced concrete stadium, christened Pershing Stadium after the Allied commander, opened to dazzling reviews. It featured a state-of-the-art cinder track and a large football field. Flags from the Allied nations—including that of the newly formed state of Czechoslovakia—ringed the track. The YMCA saw the stadium as both a majestic setting

---

[33] Gulick, "Amateurism," 4.

[34] Luther H. Gulick, "Benefits of This War," 10 Dec. 1915, 6, Luther Halsey Gulick Papers, Series 4, Box 9, Folder 10, Springfield College Archives and Special Collections.

for the Games and as a pledge towards peacetime reconstruction. General Pershing ceded the stadium to France at the end of the Games. The YMCA suggested that "no parting gift that America could have made to her ally would have better attested to her deep desire for the speedy rehabilitation of France, or have offered greater possibilities for aiding to that end." Here again, the YMCA showed its faith in the power of sports to heal wartime wounds.

By June, the forthcoming Games were the talk of the town. The YMCA reported that English-language newspapers in Paris "devoted more space to the Games than to the Peace conference" going on simultaneously at Versailles. U.S. residents held several advantages in the run-up to the event. From a field of more than five thousand U.S. servicemen, 80 athletes had won places in the U.S. delegation to the Games. Other countries, the YMCA conceded, faced "formidable difficulties" in assembling similarly competitive delegations, given that so many more Europeans than U.S. soldiers had died in the Great War. Moreover, U.S. sports predominated in the Games. The Italian basketball team had only recently learned the sport, and they "entered for the purpose of competition only and not with any idea of winning the meet against the admittedly superior American team."[35] The U.S. delegation featured a raft of YMCA-sponsored coaches and a strength and conditioning trainer. Soldiers who had not made it to the front before Armistice Day arrived from the United States, occasionally for the express purpose of participating in the Games. Organizers did allow Allied nations to petition for their favorite sports to be included in the Games. England sponsored a cricket competition (and determined the rules), while France supported and regulated the fencing contests. The YMCA yearbook does not record which nation was responsible for the introduction of hand-grenade throwing as an official sport in the Games.[36]

The Games opened on 22 June 1919, with a large number of track and field competitions. France and the United States dominated the winner's circle throughout the two-week olympiad, as those two nations featured the largest and most competitive delegations. Czechoslovakia upset the French in the soccer competition, while New Zealand and Australia turned in strong performances in the wrestling and boxing events. The United States swept all three medal spots in the hand-grenade competition and edged out the Belgians in tug-of-war. The

---

[35] *The Inter-Allied Games*, 88.
[36] Ibid., 78–83.

Games' official yearbook listed the top three finishers for each sport; results filled eighteen pages.

Participants in the Inter-Allied Games suggested that the competition spoke volumes about the superior character of the Allied nations. "That an athletic tournament of any sort could have been held after fifty-two months of devastating war," contended one YMCA leader, "was in itself a remarkable exhibition of the sportsmanlike spirit which had distinguished the peoples leagued against the Central Powers."[37] The yearbook for the Games detailed the preparations with painstaking detail; organizers saw everything from the decoration of the stadium to the selection of the Belgian wrestling team as examples of the power of the Games to bring forth fraternal spirit. "Although the meet was directly the outgrowth of the war," the YMCA suggested, the Games "in no way reflected the gigantic contests fought out on the battlefields of the Western front."[38] In the wake of the Great War, the Games had come to symbolize the role of sports in international reconciliation. U.S. Protestants hoped everything from the construction of Pershing Stadium to the introduction of U.S. sports would promote peace and brotherhood.

Sports failed to bring the nations together, however, in the years after the Inter-Allied Games. Adolf Hitler infamously used the 1936 Munich Games not as a testament to world peace, but as a way to trumpet Nazis' superior technological and athletic prowess. The massive fascist rallies that swept across Europe in the 1930s bore a resemblance to the growing spectacle of team sports. Hitler viewed German boxer Max Schmeling's heavyweight title in 1930 as a validation of Aryan supremacy; the United States was jubilant when their hero Joe Louis proved otherwise with a one-round knockout of Schmeling in 1938. Professional sports leagues grew in popularity, crowding the amateurs off the sports pages—particularly those playing the national pastime, baseball. Sports contests were a form of struggle, and manliness demanded victory. Games and leagues required winners and losers, and the white American missionaries of sport were not about to lose at their own games.

Imperialism was encoded in muscular Christianity's DNA. Born in England during the heyday of the British Empire, muscular Christianity took up residence in the United States at the dawn of the American Century. The muscular Christians of the late nineteenth century had seen America's imperial adventures as exciting the souls of men; liberal

---

[37] Ibid., 3.
[38] Ibid., 48.

Protestants' increasing pacifism in the wake of the Great War could not overcome the lingering sentiment among many in the United States that battle tested men's characters. The YMCA's hyperbolic commentary on the transcendent nature of sports in general and the Inter-Allied Games in particular ignored the ways in which U.S. control over the event demanded other nations submit to U.S. customs. While the battles of the Great War bore little resemblance to the athletic competitions staged in its wake, the combination of liberal internationalism and muscular Christianity was tenuous at best. Muscular Christianity could not quickly abandon its longstanding belief in war as a character-building exercise, even among a growing pacifist movement. Wilsonian hopes for international alliances—built in this case through the power of friendly competition—ignored that the competitive nature of sports themselves always encouraged some type of hostility. Even the Games showed "a striking illustration of the place of athletics in the military training of the Allied Armies," according to the YMCA.[39] The YMCA hoped the Inter-Allied Games could sate the appetite of soldiers accustomed to the rigors of battle with strenuous but amicable competition. In reality, however, the two pursuits went hand in hand.

It is no accident that contemporary discussions of sport continue to feature military metaphors—many of them drawn from the era of the Great War. NFL games always feature blitzes, bombs, and battles in the trenches. These metaphors speak to football's martial character. While the significance of metaphors can easily be overstated—no soldier, after all, lost his life in the Inter-Allied games—they reflect the ways in which sports and imperialism overlap. Coaches preach military discipline, even as generals commend timing and teamwork. U.S. Christians frequently support the military in their athletic arenas, with little thought given to the ways imperialism and sports intersect. The Inter-Allied Games showed that sports could indeed excite the souls of soldiers. Still, the YMCA organizers—like many early-twentieth-century U.S. Protestants—overestimated the power of Christian character-building to eradicate the world of war.

---

[39] Ibid., 23.

The Clericus Cup

Janelle Peters

The Vatican has recently embarked on several formal ventures into the world of competitive sports. Some of these ventures, such as the Vatican cricket team, involve playing against teams from other religions and traveling to international locations. Vatican involvements in sports have also included both the purchase of a professional Italian soccer team and the inauguration of a soccer tournament for priests, called the Clericus Cup. Occasionally billed by the Vatican and the media as the Catholic version of the FIFA World Cup, the Clericus Cup is nonetheless understood to be on a more spiritual plane than secular soccer competitions. This intramural soccer tournament, hosted by the Vatican every year since 2007, is held by seminarians from the Vatican colleges who are joined by a few Swiss Guards. The name "Clericus Cup" anticipated the later Clericus Chess Tournament, a chess competition that has been open to all religions and priests of both sexes. Both tournaments are under the supervision of Monsignor Claudio Paganini.[1]

Under the present form of the rules, only seminarians and priests enrolled at the pontifical institutes of Rome are allowed to participate in the Clericus Cup. These institutions may educate women religious, monks, and laypeople, but only those on the priesthood track may participate in the tournament. The Catholic hierarchical and Vatican agencies sponsoring the tournament are those with ties to the Italian bishops and culture, as well as the laity. The precise agencies have fluctuated during the course of the tournament, but at present three agencies—the Conferenza Episcopale Italiana, the Pontificium Consilium de Cultura, and the Pontificio Consiglio dei Laici—are prominently featured on the first

---

[1] The Clericus Chess tournament differs somewhat in having parallel events at primary and secondary schools in the Lazio region. See "La Clericus Chess Attende La Prima Mossa," http://www.csi-net.it/index.php?action=pspagina&idPSPagina=1208.

page of the Clericus Cup website.[2] Much grander in scale than most intramural competitions, the tournament operates as a bridge between the spheres of sport and church for seminarians and priests from around the world who are studying at the Vatican.[3] The Clericus Cup is a representation of the Vatican City as a political state with a moral theology. It allows for priests' development by participating in sports that the Vatican maintains are necessary for human growth and education. Priests learn how to make a "gift of self" by playing for the shared goals of their teams.

The venue for these games is Columbus Pius XI Field within Vatican City: a field with artificial turf, a grandstand, and hilltop views of St. Peter's Basilica. Teams play from February to the end of June in Rome, which can coincide with Lent and Easter—a schedule more liturgically significant than the fall.

The Rules and Purpose of the Clericus Cup

The first Clericus Cup was announced in 2007 by Cardinal Tarcisio Bertone, the Vatican's Secretary of State. The spiritual advisor of the Centro Sportivo Italiano (CSI), Monsignor Claudio Paganini, has served as the president of the Clericus Cup since the Cup's inception.[4] Although the tournament is organized every year in the same format of sixteen teams from pontifical institutes, Bertone originally suggested that the tournament teams might be expanded to include players from across Italy, or that the Vatican might have a Serie A team playing in the yellow and white of the Vatican flag.[5]

---

[2] Carol Glatz, "Vatican's Offices Switch Sponsorship of Seminarian Soccer Series," *Catholic News Service*, 15 March 2012, (http://www.catholicnews.com/services/englishnews/2012/vatican-s-offices-switch-sponsorship-of-seminarian-soccer-series.cfm. Clericus Cup, http://www.clericuscup.it/Index.aspx?idmenu=3592.

[3] According to the CSI's Edio Constantini, "We want to raise the awareness of current and future leaders of parishes and Church communities of the educational and pastoral importance of sport." See also "Italy Holds Priestly 'World Cup,'" *BBC*, 21 February 2007, http://news.bbc.co.uk/2/hi/europe/6382055.stm.

[4] Edward Pentin, "The Clericus Cup," *National Catholic Register*, 27 February 2007, http://www.ncregister.com/site/article/the_clericus_cup.

[5] Malcolm Moore, "Vatican Wants to Play Priests in Serie A," *Telegraph*, 16 December 2006, http://www.telegraph.co.uk/news/worldnews/1537367/Vatican-wants-to-play-priests-in-Serie-A.html. There are other athletic compe-

Potential players from the pontifical colleges at the Vatican and from the Swiss Guard nominate themselves for the team associated with their institution. When teams are choosing their players, players take it as a point of pride at being a first-choice selection for a particular position, and while some players are in their fifties, others have recently left budding professional soccer careers.[6]

The articles of the tournament establish the parameters of the game: The Clericus Cup accepts the applications of sixteen teams that are submitted by the end of the preceding year. Each team can have a maximum of twenty-four athletes and four managers. Athletes must have physical confirmation that they are fit to play in the tournament. The athletes must be prepared for the rigors of going through a group and knockout phase, meaning the sixteen teams compete on multiple occasions during the same year of play. Teams that advance to the knockout stage face single elimination at the quarterfinals. Then, the top four teams play both semifinals and finals to determine first, second, third, and fourth rankings. The top team receives the coveted *saturno* trophy. Matches pit eleven players from one team against eleven players of another. Each match has two periods of thirty minutes each. During a match, both teams are allowed a timeout of two minutes. Ties at the end of play are settled by five penalty kicks.[7]

Penalties are a feature of the tournament.[8] A player who is shown a blue card, christened "sin cards" by the media, receives a five-minute sus-

---

titions for priests in Italy and around the world Annual athletic matches within a diocese or at a seminary between priests and seminarians are fairly common Vocations are a recurring theme of these events Cf. Daniel Meloy, "Seminarians defeat priests in inaugural soccer match at seminary," *Michigan Catholic*, 27 October 2016, http://www.themichigancatholic.org/2016/10/seminarians-defeat-priests-inaugural-soccer-match-seminary/.

[6] Janelle Peters, "The Vatican Soccer Tournament You've Never Heard Of," *Busted Halo*, 8 May 2017, https://bustedhalo.com/life-culture/vatican-soccer-tournament-youve-never-heard.

[7] Regolamento, Clericus Cup, http://www.clericuscup.it/Index.aspx?id-menu=3595.

[8] The emphasis on penalties in the Cup has not been lost on the media. As journalist Giovanna Pasqualin noted in a tweet (28 May 2016), the most recent Cup in 2016 was decided by penalties, http://www.twitter.com/GiovannaPasq/status/736671846356115460.

pension.[9] The blue cards bear a color distinct from the red and yellow cards of FIFA that are known from U.S. indoor youth soccer. These temporary suspensions penalize players who have tripped an opponent or touched the ball with their hands. Warnings carry over from the group phase to the knockout phase, with three warnings requiring a player to be disqualified from a match. Expulsions entail penalties that have details determined by one referee the next day. Moreover, the points assigned to teams for wins vary depending on the penalty. There are three points for a win, two points for a win on penalties, one point for a defeat on penalties, and zero points for a defeat.

Just as important as the rules are the customs that have evolved around the Clericus Cup. Cardinal Pio Laghi reminded players before the first match between Collegio Mater Ecclesiae and Gregorian University, "You are playing in view of St. Peter's Cupola, so behave well."[10] Priestly formation, according to Monsignor Melchor Sanchez de Toca y Alameda, undersecretary of the Pontifical Council for Culture, is a chief objective of the Clericus Cup. Priests and seminarians play each other, learning about themselves as they try to win for their respective teams. When Pope John Paul II was beatified, he was named the captain of the team by Paganini. For the Cup president, the athletic pontiff exemplified the qualities that priests should strive to acquire and develop.[11] Because the Clericus Cup sponsors those studying for or ordained into the priesthood, its trophy reinforces this fact by featuring a soccer ball wearing a priestly *saturno*—a wide-brimmed hat. The winning team receives the *saturno* trophy "des mains de" Monsignor Claudio Paganini in his role as Cup president.[12]

---

[9] "Vatican Tournament to Use 'Sin Bin' Card," *BBC*, 19 Feb 2009, http://news.bbc.co.uk/sport2/hi/football/7900177.stm.

[10] "Vatican Cup Lifts Spirits in Rome," FIFA, 13 March 2007, http://websites.sportstg.com/assoc_page.cgi?c=0-996-0-0-0&sID=12633&&news_task=DETAIL&articleID=3638386.

[11] Orazio La Rocca, "Calcio, Riparte la Clericus Cuppapa Wojtyla Capitano Unico," *Repubblica*, 23 March 2011, http://roma.repubblica.it/cronaca/2011/03/23/news/vaticano-14003997/.

[12] Nicolas Senèze, "Les séminaristes de la Grégorienne remportent la Clericus Cup," *La Croix*, 31 May 2011, www.la-croix.com/Urbi-et-Orbi/Vatican/Les-seminaristes-de-la-Gregorienne-remportent-la-Clericus-Cup-2011-05-31-620595.

Like other sports in which communal identity features prominently, the Clericus Cup allows participants to play in a way that can be used to shape a positive self-image. When sporting events are run by leagues with constitutions and rules that are semiautonomous from other religious and civic structures, they can create critical distance from other social identities for players and spectators. As such, participation often outweighs winning—suggesting that the tournament functions like the Olympics in promoting a social and cultural ideal more than physical excellence.

For those involved in the Clericus Cup through competition or spectatorship, the pitting of men of the cloth against one another results in a situation of not only fair play, but "fair pray." The adherence of players to both the constitution of the event and the ideals of athletics demonstrates that good sportsmanship should be the ultimate goal of sports. The organization overseeing the Clericus Cup, the CSI (Italian Sports Center), has been consistently described by the papacy as an instrument essential for the integration of the individual into society, particularly in Italy after the rise of Nazism and World War II.[13] Cheating or aggressive behavior do not belong in sports, and the outcome of the game is not determined by one side's superior morality or relationship with the divine. It might be necessary to give up strenuous exertion for the greater good of bodily preservation, particularly when one is a priest who expects to genuflect frequently. Sports shows that humans of all cul-

---

[13] John Paul II's address to the members of the CSI characterizes it: "The Italian Sports Center came into existence sixty years ago with this goal: to propose to young people, then marked by the appalling consequences of the Second World War, the practice of sports, not only as a source of physical well-being but as an ideal of life, courageous, positive, optimistic and a means for the integral renewal of the individual person and of society. My venerable Predecessor, the Servant of God Pius XII, then asked your Sodality to be the leaven of Christianity in stadiums, on roads, on mountains, at sea, wherever your banner is raised with honour (cf. *Address to the Italian Sports Center*, 1955)." John Paul II, *Address of John Paul II to the Members of the Italian Sports Center*, Saturday, 26 June 2004, http://w2.vatican.va/content/john-paul-ii/en/speeches/2004/june/documents/hf_jp-ii_spe_20040626_csi.html. However, as Benedict XVI has noted, the more general Catholic recognition of sports as part of the moral development of individuals is found in the publications of Vatican II: "The Second Vatican Council listed sports among the educational resources which belong to the common patrimony of humanity and facilitate moral development and human formation (cf. Gravissimum Educationis, n. 4)."

tures and religious traditions can compete physically and create emotional bonds with their own team and the opposing ones.

The Clericus Cup and the "Gift of Self"

According to John Paul II in 1979, the "Church has always been interested in the problem of sport, because she prizes everything that contributes constructively to the harmonious and complete development of man, body, and soul."[14] His predecessor Pius XII made a similar point by asking the rhetorical question: "How can the Church not be interested in sport?[15] Bishop Carlo Mazza, who led the ministry of Leisure, Tourism, and Sport of the Italian Bishops Conference from 1988 to 2010, has characterized sports as involving the same "gift of self" essential to other identity-shaping activities in which humans engage.[16] German Cardinal Joseph Ratzinger, who was promoted to head of the influential Roman Curia department the Congregation for Doctrine of the Faith (1981–2005) and who was later elected pope, gave an interview on the Bavarian Radio program *Zum Sonntag* on 1 June 1978 that characterized athletic events as a desire for a lost paradise.[17]

When Mazza used the term "gift of self," he invoked a concept defined by Pope John Paul II. In his 1992 *Pastores Dabo Vobis*, Pope John Paul II claimed that the "gift of self" for a priest was a priest's efforts on behalf of his community. Mazza connected this understanding of the gift of self to those playing sports by saying that players who choose to participate in sports give their whole person to the unity of the team and to the greater good of the team. This gift of self can be made by seminarians as future priests or by Swiss Guards. The Vatican sponsors the Cleri-

---

[14] "Sport as Training Ground for Virtue and Instrument of Union among People," 20 December 1979, in *A Catholic Perspective: Physical Exercise and Sport*, ed. R. Feeney (Minneapolis: Aquinas Press, 1995), 59–62.

[15] Pius XII, Address to Roman Athletes, 20 May 1945. English translation found in R. Feeney, *A Catholic Perspective: Physical Exercise and Sport* (Minneapolis: Aquinas Press, 1995), 28. Original Italian text found in "Discorsi e Radiomessaggi di Pio XII" 7 (1945), 56.

[16] Carlo Mazza, "Sport in the Magisterium of John Paul II," in *Sport and Christianity: A Sign of the Times in the Light of Faith*, ed. Kevin Lixey (Washington, DC: Catholic University of America Press, 2012), 134.

[17] Michael Rasmus Schernikau, *La partita non è solo quello che vedi in campo: Fußball im kritischen Blick der italienschen Gegenwartsliteratur* (Berlin: Lit Verlag, 2012), 10.

cus Cup to allow priests and seminarians, both men and women, to demonstrate how to make this gift of self. Martin Rodriguez, a seminarian from the Archdiocese of Indianapolis, talks about pushing the body to its physical limit and compensating for injured members of the team: "When I felt that my legs were about to collapse, I thought about my teammates who were injured and needed me to step up for them."[18] Here, competition is reframed from individual achievement to team mission. From this seminarian's perspective, the point of his participation is the opportunity to give his own talents and efforts for other individuals on the team.

By affirming the gift of self in this way, the Vatican underscores the ability everyone has to act as a priest and access this aspect of spirituality. As undersecretary of the Vatican Council for Culture Monsignor Melchor Sanchez de Toca y Alameda told me, this universal aspect of the gift of self is reflected by the interfaith cricket matches played by the Vatican's cricket team in locations both outside the Vatican City and Rome and around the globe.[19] Sport takes us beyond the priesthood of all believers to the spirituality of all players.

Women and the Gift of Self

The "gift of self" is a Catholic concept that applies to both sexes in the context of human relationships. Women religious can also be included in the Clericus Cup as there is no prohibition on women's participation in competitive sports within Catholic sports theology. Sports are very clearly included within the Catechism as a basic right that is not restricted to one sex or the other. To date, no Catholic or secular media source has reported any seminarian, priest, cardinal, or pope as intentionally excluding women from this tournament in order to develop seminarians' masculinity. Women religious already study at the same universities as seminarians. Thus, if the gift of self is a characteristic of sport as well as of the priesthood, and if athletic participation allows for human development, then why not create a soccer tournament for women studying at the pontifical universities? Popes and cardinals have already praised women lead-

---

[18] Sean Gallagher, "Seminarian is a Member of a Championship Clericus Cup Team," *Criterion*, 18 May 2012, http://www.archindy.org/criterion/local/2012/05-18/clericuscup.html.

[19] Peters, "The Vatican Soccer Tournament You've Never Heard Of," 8 May 2017.

ers of interfaith movements, such as Chiara Lubich of the Focolare Movement, so an interfaith women's cricket tournament could be in the foreseeable future.[20]

Fair Play and Competition

At the heart of the Clericus Cup are the meaning of sports and the need for ethical conduct. Fair play typically refers to morals that are larger than the rules of the game. Researchers of sports ethics have distinguished between two kinds of fair play—with formal fair play adhering to the established rulebook. Such rules range from the bounds of the playing field to the physical actions one takes toward another player. Informal fair play centers on the interaction of a player with officials, fellow players, and the ideas of the game and sports more generally. At the Vatican, Pope Pius XII defined fair play as forbidding "resorting to subterfuges." Pius's *Address to the Italian Sports Centre,* given on 5 October 1955, was quoted by John Paul II, who listed fair play as one of the "many virtues" developed by the "ideal context" of athletics as a "kind of ascesis." Sports ethicists go further in seeing kinship and self-restraint as being necessary to maximize the potential of play.[21] Part of the appeal of the Clericus Cup may be found in the new friendships and sense of kinship that form as a result of the sixteen teams competing against each other.

With soccer being the most popular sport globally, seminarians and priests from all over the world may be sufficiently adept at the game to compete. Few of the teams are comprised of players from only one or two countries—many of the participants hail from South America and Africa. Despite the global nature of the game, sports commentators were still astounded by the late success of the North American Martyrs from the Pontifical North American College, a team mostly comprised of players from the United States at a college under the direct supervision of the U.S. Conference of Catholic Bishops.[22] The North American Martyrs had a name and a history of losing that preceded the tournament by decades. Explaining the Clericus Cup team to the *Wall Street Journal,*

---

[20] Janelle Peters, "Reading the Corinthian Veils through Hijabs and Habits," *1–2 Corinthians* (Minneapolis: Fortress, 2013), 131.

[21] Randolph Feezell, *Sport, Play, and Ethical Reflection* (Urbana: University of Illinois, 2004), 95.

[22] A similar phenomenon might be seen in the world of rugby.

rector Monsignor James Checchio traced the name to the losing record of the Pontifical North American College, which stretched back to his days as a student there.[23] Before the turnaround, the multiple losing seasons of the Martyrs confirmed initial expectations that British and U.S. imperialism would be permanently upended by third-world teams. As trends in worldwide participation in soccer currently stand, American male priests have no distinct advantage over other countries (though American women would, given the dominance of the United States in women's soccer).

The Clericus Cup as a Commentary on Modern Sports

The Clericus Cup tournament was introduced and modified by the Vatican's Secretary of State in response to scandals in Italian and international professional soccer. In 2006, in what became known as the Calciopoli scandal, the Juventus general managers were accused of calling referees and fixing the outcome of matches. According to Italian law professor Gianfranco Garancini in an interview with Vatican Radio, the scandal cast doubt upon the entire Italian justice system.[24]

The implicated teams included Juventus, AC Milan, SS Lazio, and Fiorentina Temporary Federazione Italiana Giuoco Calcio. Guido Rossi, a professor, appointed retired judge Franceso Saverio Borelli to assemble a team to spearhead the investigations of match fixing. They found the teams to be guilty. The initial punishments pushed SS Lazio and Fiorentina down to Serie B while Juventus fell even further to Serie C. Eventually all of the sentences were reduced, but Juventus still fell to Serie B for a brief period. After the expiration date on the accusations before the high court had passed, Juventus attempted to claim €443 million in damages from the Italian FA.

By establishing the Clericus Cup, the Vatican sought to reintroduce a sense of justice and fair play into soccer on the Italian peninsula. To encourage collaboration between the development of sports in secular Italian society and the Vatican, the first Serie A referee Stefano Farina

---

[23] Joshua Robinson, "American Team Reigns in This Devout Soccer League," *Wall Street Journal*, 28 April 2013, www.wsj.com/articles/SB1000 14241278873244937045784308211 80147676.

[24] "Garancini: Con Reati Prescritti non si fa Giustizia," *Radio Vaticana*, 24 March 2015, http://it.radiovaticana.va/news/2015/03/24/calciopoli_ garancini_con_reati_prescritti_non_è_giustizia/1131795.

was on the field at the Clericus Cup in 2009. The date chosen for that 2009 final, May 23, was selected to anticipate the Champions League Final at Rome's Olympic Stadium by four days.[25] By playing in the Cup, priests helped model ethical sports behavior for FIFA and other athletic regulatory agencies, and the Vatican was able to differentiate itself from the Italian nation. Priest players were not simply connecting to youth through sport or demonstrating the possibilities for sport to open dialogue across national and regional lines, they were helping to reshape attitudes. The Clericus Cup was not the Vatican's only intervention in the Italian soccer system. Not only did the Vatican hope to lead by the example of a soccer tournament played by its priests and seminarians, it actually bought a secular team.

In 2007, the Vatican purchased an 80 percent stake in AC Ancona, the top team of Italy's third division. As reported in *The Telegraph*, the Vatican sought to "bring some ethics back into the game, which has been undergoing a grave crisis in terms of sportsmanship," according to Archbishop Edoardo Menichelli of Ancona. The profit model also changed in that ticket prices dropped and profits went to projects in the third world.[26] This move was in keeping with the interest of the Catholic Church in the sports stadium as a medium for communicating cultural values and ethical principles. As Cardinal Bertone noted in his announcement of his Vatican plans, soccer stadiums possess the power to transform the lives of young soccer devotees: "Stadiums are modern temples, frequented by thousands of youths. I once carried out a Stations of the Cross service in the Ferraris stadium."[27]

---

[25] Given the chants by Clericus Cup fans in the stands that the referees could be called Cyclops should they gain an eye, it is unlikely that the Catholic influence in soccer games is too clean for an enjoyable sport. See Joshua Robinson, "American Team Reigns in This Devout Soccer League," *Wall Street Journal*, 28 April 2013, www.wsj.com/articles/SB10001424127887324493704578430821180147676).

[26] Malcolm Moore, "Vatican Buys Team to Clean Up Italian Football," *Telegraph*, 4 October 2007, www.telegraph.co.uk/news/worldnews/1565130/Vatican-buys-team-to-clean-up-Italian-football.html.

[27] Moore, "Vatican Wants to Play Priests in Serie A," 16 December 2006.

Conclusion

More than just an intramural activity, the Clericus Cup allows seminarians studying in Rome to participate in a soccer tournament likened by priests to the World Cup. This intersection of secular and religious realms is not a happy accident as Vatican theology holds that sports develop the human spirit and its ethical understanding, and the Clericus Cup allows seminarians to engage in a public ministry as religious figures. In the liminal space of the Clericus Cup, not only do seminarians learn to see themselves as priests, they envision themselves as the cardinals who come to cheer them on as fans. Seminarians explore their identities as educators, pastors, colleagues, and priests. When the Cup coincides with the conclave, the seminarian players have been compared to the priests selecting the next pope.

The Clericus Cup exists as part of a larger program by the Vatican to promote sports as necessary for the human spirit. Vatican theology construes sports as a human right essential for the development of citizens. To that end, the Vatican also sponsors a cricket team that tours the world to play against teams representing other religious traditions. While the Clericus Cup limits itself to Rome, the Vatican's soccer tournament resembles its cricket tournament in that both combine spiritual authority with sports. Catholic theology already allows for Catholic women religious to be included in the Vatican soccer and cricket tournaments as competitors, but women religious have not yet independently organized such events.

Finally, the Clericus Cup supports Vatican efforts to promote ethics in secular sports. Established in the wake of the Calciopoli scandal in Italian soccer, the Clericus Cup reaffirms the value of soccer play for its own sake. Priests and seminarians affirm the gift of self through their participation in the Clericus Cup and underscore the ability of everyone to act in a spiritual manner. Priests show us how to play for the eternal, but everyone can participate in this divine game.

PART II

BEYOND THE HOLY TRINITY

Pole Dance as a Counter-Cultural, Feminist, Embodied Practice for the Reclamation of Eros

Jennifer Baldwin

> Pole fitness is one of the most physically and emotionally exhilarating sports I have ever done. It not only tests your body but it tests your mind spiritually and emotionally It has helped me to express myself more sexually When I pole, I feel sexy and free when otherwise I would be much more conservative. — Survey response[1]

When most people hear "pole dance," their minds conjure images of women dancing in seven-inch pleaser shoes on a stage, surrounded by men throwing money. They think of strippers—exotic dancers who elicit strong responses from both men and women: Men are either enticed or shamed; women are either threatened or jealous. These are, of course, gross generalizations because in reality there is a far greater variety of responses. One thing that is consistent, however, is the presence of judgment.

The dominant culture loves to presume things about the lives of strippers (daddy issues, uneducated, etc.), project our own sexual shame onto strippers, and summarily denigrate and scapegoat them—in cartoons, sermons, movies, memes, and marches. At the same time, stripping and exotic dance is big business.[2]

So, what does this have to do with pole dance, sports, and religion? Oddly enough, everything. This chapter explores the connections among the sexual ethics that emerge out of Christian theology, the ways in which those religious mandates demonize exotic dancers specifically and female sexual expression generally, and the ways in which the pole dance

---

[1] Pamela Amanda Martino, survey response to unpublished research, Vertical Exploration Foundation, 2013.

[2] For a fuller analysis on the economic and business dimension of exotic dance, see Jessica Bearson, *The Naked Re$ult: How Exotic Dance Became Big Business* (New York, Oxford University Press, 2016).

community negotiates the mainstreaming of its embodied, feminine, sensual practice into a sport that minimizes its connection to sexuality.

The main argument of this chapter is that pole dance as a sport, art, or exotic movement is a counter-cultural, feminist, embodied practice for the reclamation of eros—love and power. Because pole dance outside the exotic dance club is a recent phenomenon, most people only know pole movement as stripper movement.

Pole dance is in the nascent stage of becoming a sport. The first section of this essay offers a necessary introduction to the reader. Pole is also newly conceived as a research subject, so a brief survey of the development of pole dance distinct from the club serves a dual purpose: it offers an orientation to the community for those encountering pole dance for the first time, as well as providing a record of the history of contemporary pole dance in scholarly literature. Finally, this section discusses the variety of movement within pole dance and connects it to the category of alternative sports. Largely male-dominated, alternative sports are exempt from the criticisms that are often leveled at pole dance as an activity and pole dancers as participants. For example, boys demonstrating their skateboarding skills on a daytime news show are not likely to receive the strong cultural backlash that girls receive when demonstrating their pole dance skills.

The second section of this essay traces the slippery slope from women's embracing of their sensual power to "slut or stripper shaming." The punitive nomenclature and shaming of women in an attempt to enforce conformity to established norms of sexual expression is a dynamic that extends beyond the realm of pole dance as a sport and permeates the lives of all pole dancers. As second-wave feminists remind us, the personal is political. With regard to religion and pole dance, I would add that the personal is theological. "Slut or stripper shaming" is a theological problem, it is a sport problem, and, finally, it is a justice problem.

The third section of this essay takes up the theological problems that emerge from the challenges pole athletes and dancers encounter. It considers theological re/formations that more clearly and acutely address the notion of sin. The last section, finally, offers a notion of soteriology that emerges from, and is informed by, the practice of pole sport and dance.

Pole Dance 101

Pole dance as a movement style, fitness option, performance art, and competitive sport, has emerged from the strip club and is finding a place for itself at the edge of mainstream culture. Exclusive to the strip clubs until 1994,[3] pole dance and pole fitness has exploded as an option for fitness, self-discovery, and healing across the globe. Currently, participants of pole dance include people aged 6 and up: men, women, trans persons, lawyers, veterinarians, high-school students, and clergy, as well as mothers, fathers, and grandmothers from more than fifty nations.[4]

Pole dancers come in all shapes, ages, sizes, and movement forms. Some embrace contemporary pole's roots in the strip clubs and adopt the shoes, body waves, self-touch, and sexual-movement vocabulary of exotic dancers. While there are plenty of avenues of analysis on the adaptation of stripper culture into the sanitized spaces of suburban studios, there is also an enticing fascination with the raw accessibility of reclaiming feminine sexuality that draws women (and some men) in as a movement practice of healing. Such positive gestures of acceptance coexist with a shunning of pole dance as taboo and inappropriate. Other individuals approach pole dance as a performance art akin to contemporary dance or artistic circus à la Cirque du Soleil. For these individuals, the dance pole provides a means to explore the vertical space in addition to the horizon-

---

[3] Pole Fitness Studio, Las Vegas, NV; see http://www.polefitnessstudio. com/history-of-pole/ (accessed 8 Dec. 2016).

[4] Offering a glimpse into the growth of pole dance as an activity and subculture, Pole Expo is the largest annual gathering of pole dancers from around the world (see www.poleexpo.com/vendors-sponsorship). While it does not draw participants from every nation that has pole dancers, in 2016 more than fifty nations were represented. In the five years (2011–2016) that Pole Expo has been held, it has grown from 475 to 1800 participants, 550 to 1800 spectators, 12 to 50 countries represented, 50 to 180 workshops with leading performers and instructors, 27 to 80 national and international instructors, and 20 to 64 vendors offering products and services to the pole community, including apparatuses (poles, lyras, silks, etc.), apparel (pole shorts, sports bras, pole specific shirts), grip aids, and body care products. Additionally, touring artist and teacher Marlo Fisken has taught workshops and teacher trainings in 48 different countries according to her touring manager (personal conversation with Meredith Greisman, 30 November 2016). Kristy Craig, manager for Poles on Tour, indicates that her organization has worked with pole studios in 56 different nations (personal correspondence, 1 December 2016).

tal space of the dance floor in personal expression and artistic creation. The third primary form or style of pole dance is as fitness or sport. Athletes who engage pole as sport generally have backgrounds in gymnastics or similar sports and are initially drawn to pole tricks that require significant full-body strength and flexibility.

While the "pole world" is largely supportive and celebratory of differences, one of the ongoing points of debate as the activity continues to grow is the question of the benefits and drawbacks associated with the mainstreaming of pole dance into the larger culture. The year 1994 is generally designated as the beginning of pole dance as a related—though separate—activity to stripping. Prior to this, there were only a handful of studios offering instruction in pole dance in the United States. Contemporary pole dance really took root in Australia in 2004 with the opening of Bobbi's Gold Pole Dance, the founding of Miss Pole Dance Australia (MPDA) in 2005, the first MPDA event in 2006, and sport's first competitive champion, Felix Cane. Pole dance in the United States began emerging more fully in the mid-2000s alongside the founding and growth of YouTube. Many of the individuals and studios who shepherded pole dance's migration from the world of exotic dance into studios, gyms, and homes were introduced to pole dance in strip clubs. In the formative decade of pole dance as an activity performed outside of strip clubs, most of the participants were self-taught at home via growing social media platforms. Pole dance in the late 1990s and early 2000s was primarily sensual/sexual in its movement style. For many women, pole's sensuality and sexuality was, and continues to be, the initial draw.

As the pole dance movement gained exposure, more people began to recognize the full-body strength that was cultivated in pole dance. Pole dance or pole fitness began to emerge in 2003, according to the International Pole Sports Federation (IPSF).[5] The IPSF, created in 2008, is the organization spearheading the development of pole as an alternative sport, with the intention of requesting the International Olympic Committee for pole sport as an Olympic event. From 2011–2016, the IPSF has developed a sport and federation from scratch by creating rules, regulations, scoring systems, policies, health and safety, equipment standards, judges training, thirty national championships, a world cham-

---

[5] See http://www.polesports.org/about-us/history-of-pole-sports/ (accessed 4 December 2016). It is curious that IPSF identifies 2003 as a key year for the beginning of pole as a sport, particularly since most competitions for pole dancers did not begin until 2006 in Australia and 2009 in the United States.

pionship competition, and now a coaching and judging framework. In 2012, the first World Pole Sports Championships took place with 45 athletes, including only five men. "In 2015 more than 2,500 athletes competed in 26 countries to qualify for the world championships, with a growing number of men and children now" participating,[6] IPSF competitions are distinguished from other pole competitions around the world by the rules related to music guidelines, attire, and a highly codified system of moves and points that are patterned after the "Olympic standard sports such as gymnastics, diving, and ice skating."[7] In October 2017, IPSF was awarded the Global Association of International Sports Federation Observer Status.

> The Observer Status allows new, young International Federations to take advantage of the GAISF network to grow and develop, and has been designed as the first step in a clear path towards full GAISF membership. Observers will be accompanied by GAISF in their development towards fulfillment of all criteria required for membership, such as increasing the number of members in various countries and receiving the required recognitions by National Olympic Committees or by national sports authorities.[8]

Just as people revel in the gains of physical strength, flexibility, and cardiovascular fitness, participants of pole dance also regularly speak about pole as art, expression, or healing. Pole dance is also expanding as an artistic form, prompting hundreds of local performances in studios, incorporation of pole performances in burlesque or circus shows, and the cultivation of at least three dance companies[9] in the United States, as well as the incorporation of pole acts into residential Cirque du Soleil

---

[6] "Quick Pole Sports History," http://www.polesports.org/ipsf/ipsf-pole-sports-history/ (accessed 4 Dec. 2016).

[7] See http://www.polesports.org/competitions/pole-sports/ (accessed 4 December 2016). For link to the IPSF code of points, see http://www.polesports.org/ipsf/document-policies/

[8] "Pole Sports Recognition Announcement, http://www.polesports.org/news/04-10-17-gaisf-status/ (accessed 4 December 2016).

[9] Aera is an aerial dance company based in New York City that was founded by several pole dancers. Jagged is a California-based pole dance company that has performed in mainstream televised dance competitions. *Girl Next Door/Seven* is a recurring dance show featuring a core company of pole performers. All three companies were founded in 2009.

shows *Zumanity* and *MJ One*.[10] Pole dance as a movement medium is largely an artistic "blank check." Within the artistic arena, pole performances have incorporated movement vocabulary from a wide range of established dance forms, including tango, ballet, contemporary, tap, and hip hop/bgirl.[11] [12] [13] Artistic pole performers have also incorporated features of theater, including elaborate costuming to evoke classic fantasy,[14] video and lighting innovations,[15] and casts of several performers who can support a primary character in constructing performances that have elements of theater as well as dance.[16] Performances can range from drama, to comedy, to religious critique and reimagining of religious and cultural narratives.[17]

Given the rich variety of movement styles, to what extent does pole movement meet the criteria of "sport?" In her essay focusing on the tension in the BMX community on the mainstreaming and commercialization of BMX, Joy Honea examines Richard Rinehart's criteria of alternative/extreme sports. She writes, "Historically, these sports have existed outside the mainstream world of sport and have promoted values largely antithetical to dominant sport forms, including organization by the participants themselves, less emphasis on competition, and an individual focus. Additionally, these sports often include a lifestyle component, in which authentic participation requires acceptance into the sport subcul-

---

[10]Felix Cane was a featured performer in *Zumanity* and *Michael Jackson the Immortal Tour*. Jenyne Butterfly was a featured performer in *MJ One*.

[11]"Scent of a Woman," choreographed by Svetlana Lutoshkina and performed by Pink Puma, Pole Sport Organization Choreography Cup, 2014, http://www.youtube.com/watch?v=oGRcAH9NBjw.

[12]Elena Gibson, guest performance, UK Professional Pole Championship, 2013, http://www.youtube.com/watch?v=FuHYZ1Sb2zE.

[13]Shaina Cruea, national champion, U.S. National Pole Championship, 2014, http://ww.youtube.com/watch?v=xExR_LSbUZE.

[14] Brandon Grimm, "Wunderland," Showcase, Pole Expo 2016, http://www.youtube.com/watch?v=sLYRzYaEeo4.

[15]Kristy Sellars, "The Abduction," drama champion, Pole Theatre World, 2016, http://www.youtube.com/watch?v=3I6k4nAaqM8.

[16]Crystal Belcher, "A Little Taste of Shug," Miss Pole Dance America, 2015, http://www.youtube.com/watch?v=u_JeGtYPRn4.

[17] Chilli Rox, opening number, Miss Pole Dance Australia, 2016, http://www.youtube.com/watch?v=rzIrOmzQAQA.

ture."[18] According to Rinehart's criteria, pole dance/sport certainly qualifies as an alternative sport. Pole, while often taught in a group fitness/dance class context, is predominantly an individual practice. Progress is measured as personal progression in flexibility, strength, skill acquisition, and flow. The pole community's most consistent values are expression, personal growth, fierce acceptance of all bodies, abilities, ages, and sexualities, and support of the community. The value most antithetical to the dominant sport and cultural forms is the very foundation from which contemporary pole dance emerged as an unapologetic embodiment of feminine sexuality. Pole studios, competitions, events, and supporting industries are almost all owned by women, and all of them emerge from the community itself. Consequently, participation in the activity of pole dance very quickly incorporated into a tight-knit subculture that extends beyond the bounds of an individual's presence at community events.

Pole dance as a movement form has a rich variety of incarnations. For those within the community, the diversity of expression, cultivation of strength, and embodied sensuality, whether or not explicitly sexual, is pole's primary strength. Newcomers to pole are frequently surprised by the strength required, the radical acceptance of the community, the accessibility of the apparatus as a support for whatever movement is desired, and the feelings of accomplishment, power, and pride that facilitate emotional processing and self-awareness. For those outside the community, pole is regularly seen only as an apparatus for exotic dance and stripping for the male gaze. In this outsider understanding, pole is seen a tool for the objectification and exploitation of women. One way this mindset presents is the unilateral equivocation with poles as "stripper poles." This nomenclature is problematic in that it projects onto a fairly neutral object a particular view and valuation that links this object with a societally denigrated profession. The problem is not exotic dancers as a professional community but the reduction of the pole apparatus to a single signifier. Poles are found all over the place—in firehouses, on playgrounds, and on construction rigging. A pole is simply a vertical apparatus, as is clear when one reflects on how rarely people who equate pole dance with objectification prohibit their children from playing on playgrounds or from admiring firefighters. Those who can only see sexual

---

[18]Joy Crissy Honea, "Beyond the Alternative vs. Mainstream Dichotomy: Olympic BMX and the Future of Action Sports," *The Journal of Popular Culture* 46, no. 6 (2013): 1253.

exploitation in the movement of pole dancers betray their own internalized misogyny and deleterious sexual ethics.

Sensual, Sexual, Slutty:
The Slippery Slope to Slut/Stripper Shaming

While pole dance demonstrates a radically inclusive community dynamic in which the only criteria for full inclusion is participation, the stigma of "being a stripper" that is attributed to recreational, competitive, and professional pole dancers generates tension within the community and, for some within the individual, that demands attention to the role of sensual movement as a fundamental component of pole dance. On the community level, this tension reveals itself in controversies over competition rules, drama issuing from the performances in the Sexy Style Showcases, public outrage over children participating in pole classes and movement, debates on the "history of pole dance," and numerous media articles and blogs. In social media such controversies are evident in the #notastripper and #yesastripper hashtags. On the individual level, it shows up in decisions about whether or not to "out" oneself to family, friends, or the larger public. Deciding who in one's life is open-minded enough to hear about pole dance without jumping to conclusions is a recurring question for those who pole, especially if their professional life could be negatively affected by the mainstream interpretation of pole-dance participation.

The issue, of course, is not with the activity of pole dancing itself or even the profession of stripping or exotic dance. Much more significant are the ways that society boxes female sexuality. In much of contemporary Western culture, the embodiment of healthy and active female sexuality—unconstrained by the limitations of heteronormativity—has been taboo, shunned, or shamed, relegated to dark back rooms or hushed whispers. At the same time, the hypersexualization of female bodies has been used to sell everything from shampoo to hamburgers to luxury cars. The societal mandate that "girls" (no matter their age) need to be "good," where goodness conforms to patriarchal structures, has served as a foundation of Western cultural norms, but such practices privilege reason while denigrating the body and sensuality.

Viewed through such dichotomies, binaries such as female/male, body/mind, pure/defiled, environment/human, or sensation/reason emerge. These polarities, with one end deemed of greater value than the other, are untenable when viewing the world, or even the person, holistically. Gender is far more complicated than our current toy aisles would indicate. As we learn more, we see with increasing clarity how interconnected are the body and mind—or, as we might say more accurately, bodymind. When it comes to female embodiment, the binary of the good girl or dirty whore is highly destructive. Reducing life expressions to binary and polarized positions limits full acknowledgement and accessibility of the variety of existence. If female sexual expression through bodily movements—including but not limited to sex acts—is only permitted to occupy the space of body, defilement, sensation, then all female sexual expression that does not function in the service of heterosexual monogamy, is taboo, dirty, shameful. This is clearly untenable.

The reduction of the sensual (pertaining to human senses and bodily epistemology), the sexual ("relating to the instincts, physiological processes, and activities connected with physical attraction or intimate physical contact between individuals"[19]) and the slut (a derogatory term for a woman "with many casual sexual partners"[20]) is both sloppy and destructive. While there is important work being done in deconstructing the vilification of the "slut" as morally suspect, the key point here is the slippery slope leading to the conflation of the sensual, the sexual, and the slut, so that all three are viewed with the contempt leveled against the "slut." Pole dance, in all styles, is sensual. It requires attention to body sensations, kinesthetic awareness, and connection between movement, emotion, and expression. Some pole dance, most obviously (but not exclusively) the sexy/erotic/classique style, evokes the sexual. Artistic and sexy pole dance can, but does not always, choose to embody movement patterns that evoke sexualized activity or desire. Finally, an individual's choice to participate in pole dance as sport, art, or reclamation of sexual energy should not be understood as communicating anything about their personal sexual partnerships, practices, or degree of "slut."

There are few other subcultures (burlesque and polyamory are two), and no other alternative or extreme sports, that contend so overtly with

---

[19] "Sexual," Oxford English Dictionary, https://en.oxforddictionaries.com/definition/sexual (accessed 5 December 2016).

[20] "Slut," Oxford English Dictionary, https://en.oxforddictionaries.com/definition/slut (accessed 5 December 2016). The OED also defines "slut" as a "dated" term for a "woman with low standards of cleanliness," suggesting the transformation of the word "slut" from an indicator of standards of cleanliness to one of sexual availability. It is clear that female sexual availability is considered "dirty," thus invoking taboo and shame. It is also important to remember that men are rarely called "sluts."

this conflation of the sensual, the sexual, and the slut. As a result, pole dance/sport is situated on the front lines of the reclamation of feminine sexuality as good and moral. The crux of the issue for those within the pole community is the degree to which individuals and studios do or do not embrace the sexual or physical sensuality most visibly embodied by women and men who perform in strip clubs. While pole dance, as practiced in many studios, gyms, and homes, has important distinctions from the clubs, the distinctions are less in the realm of movement or footwear than they are in the function and intention of the movement. For instance, even when pole dancers invite sensual gaze from audience members in a performance, video, competition, or class exercise (genuinely or ironically), the gaze itself is the goal or statement rather than a teaser for further interaction as is the function of sexualized movements on the main stage at a club (i.e. lap dances). Moreover, the majority of pole-dance performance, whether for a formal audience, for the informal audience of other classmates, or for one's own appreciation, does not generally invite sexualized behavior. The projection of sexual intent and subsequent objectification onto pole dancers regardless of age or the performer's intent by those outside the pole dance community is received as a denigration of women's sexuality and empowerment.[21] When people, media, and culture outside the pole community equate pole dancers with exotic dancers, thereby reducing the sensual or sexualized gestures of movement by the pole and/or exotic dancer into a means of social control, it ignites either a defensive response to the misidentification that slides into a form of "slut shaming" or "stripper shaming" to undermine feminine eros or calls forth a defense of feminine sexuality and the foremothers of contemporary pole dance, exotic dancers.

While support and advocacy for strippers and contemporary pole's origins in the strip club do not always translate into a participant's personal movement, there is a tension between those in the community who want to honor pole's origin in the club—arguing that the "naughtiness" of pole should not be sanitized and is essential for women's reclamation

---

[21]This dispute recently (2016) emerged in the United Kingdom when a morning talk show showcasing young dancers wearing biking shorts and tank tops became the center of a controversy about whether or not adults were sexualizing these girls. Ironically, it was the outraged audience who functioned as the agent of sexualization, ignoring the "tricks" and movement of the girls, http://www.huffingtonpost.co.uk/2016/02/16/this-morning-girls-pole-dancing_n_9242412.html (accessed 4 December 2016).

of the feminine eros—and those who believe that pole dance should sever any ties to strip clubs in order to gain acceptance into mainstream culture. This tension is never more heated than when a mainstream audience equates pole dance with the objectification and subjugation of women: In September 2016, the London (Ontario) Abused Women's Centre (LAWC) spread a meme equating taking or teaching a pole dance class with "actions taken to normalize men's violence against women."[22] Initial comments to the organization's thread that criticized the image focused on arguments that "pole is not the same as stripping," "pole dance is a sport," etc. As the image spread, more nuanced arguments from pole dancers shifted to the need of an organization like LAWC to embrace all women and refrain from scapegoating entire groups of women—in this case pole dancers and, by proxy, strippers.

Female Eros, Strippers, and Theology: Original Sin or Original Offense?

Despite efforts to wash pole dance and sport of its roots in the strip club, pole dance as a movement form has the sensual, fluid, round movement of women in its kinesthetic DNA. Everything from the rotations of spins to the various points of contact between the pole and the body required to remain aerial were crafted in communion with female bodily form. This argument expands into other research areas outside the scope of this chapter. Pole is inextricably feminine, sensual, and counter-cultural to established exercise patterns and movement. In almost every way, pole dance and sport defy mainstream conventions. Is it any wonder, then,

---

[22]The meme generated several levels of resistance and offense in the pole community, ranging from existential identity concerns to the legality of the meme. The initial offense was the mischaracterization of pole dance as something antithetical to how the activity is experienced in the community. The second concern was that the image used without permission was taken in perhaps the best known and most respected pole studio in the world, Body and Pole in New York. In a sense, this was an unwitting attack on "pole mecca." Thirdly, the image featured one of the most beloved, admired, and sought-after pole dance innovators and instructors, Marlo Fisken. Marlo, as indicated previously, travels globally teaching pole and floor movement and is perhaps the most globally recognized pole dancer. The LAWC's meme ignorantly attacked key pillars of the global pole community and consequently was met with thousands of comments in protest that shut down the LAWC's site, garnering cease-and-desist court orders from both Body and Pole and Marlo.

that pole dance would cultivate a spirituality that embraces feminine eros and critiques the "given" of mainstream religious reflection?[23] As a community, there is little explicit reflection on the role of religion, spirituality, or theology in pole dance, and it is rare that anyone directly claims any kind of religious affiliation since the only criteria for inclusion in participation.[24] Consequently, the only thing you would find in a "pole bible" is a series of "tricks," guidelines for enhanced grip, the honoring of pole stars (internationally recognized performers and instructors), and pole-centric gatherings (studios, conventions, competitions, etc.). Instead of asking, "should Christians be pole dancing?" it is more interesting to consider the religious dimension of pole dance and sport through the implicit spirituality and embodied practice of the sport.[25] In the Tillichian tradition, it is looking more for the dynamics of faith rather than

---

[23] One of the most intriguing manifestations of this counter establishment is the work of LuxATL, the stripper with a PhD. Her performance, literary, and scholastic work all reject dominant forms of religious institutions while also performing "religion." Her primary business branding is "Stripcraft," a clear juxtaposition of "stripping" and "witchcraft." While Lux adamantly claims her identity as an atheist, it is challenging for a Christian, feminist, theological scholar to dismiss the points of resonance between the work of LuxATL and Mary Daly and other goddess religion scholars.

[24] One instance of explicitly claiming religious affiliation occurred in Texas in 2011, when a pole studio caught the attention of national media. The studio was offering a class following church on Sundays that was marketed as pole fitness for Jesus. The class was offered for free if a student brought in a church bulletin and played Christian music in the background. While it is tempting for religious/theological scholars to draw on this as a point of intersection between pole and religion/spirituality, it is a mistake or at least low hanging fruit. See https://www.youtube.com/watch?v=tplfas9OIFI (accessed 5 December 2016.)

[25] See Ray Nothstine, "Should Christians Pole Dance?" *The Christian Post*, September 2015. In this perplexing article, Nothstine pairs and falsely equivocates comments from Mary Bowden, dance ministry director, in which she questions explicitly sexualized choreography and costumes in children's dance that is par for course in many competition circuits with the participation of adults who participate in pole as fitness in full length yoga pants—just in case you were worried about showing some leg. The aim is to join together dance ministries that advocate for the full embodiment of participants in worship and life with the fitness branch of pole that sterilizes the full bodiedness of pole on behalf of mainstream comfort to promote the self-policing of the bodies of Christian women.

for predetermined categories of the content of faith.[26] With this more expansive view, theological themes of ecclesiology,[27] hamartiology, soteriology, and ethics emerge.

When Christian systematic theologians begin the work of constructive theology, one of the first questions considered is "what's the problem?" or, in other words "what's the 'sin'?" While the concept of sin has a long and varying trajectory with a variety of answers to the question of "what fundamentally separates human beings from God/the divine, each other, and one self?" perhaps the most well-known conception of sin is Augustine's doctrine of original sin. The popular understanding of original sin (whether or not Augustinian scholars would agree or even recognize it) is that Eve bit the apple, breaking God's rule; the consequence of biting the apple was that Adam and Eve were cast out of the garden. The sin of Eve (and Adam) was passed down to every person through biology/sex; therefore all people are sinful at birth and have to make restitution to God through faith. In this popularized theology, the combination of women and sexuality is highly threatening and causative of humanity's existential distress. This rendition of the doctrine of original sin, which has made its way into the matrix of popularized western religion and culture, fuels much of the antagonism and violence towards women who embody, without reservation or explanation, feminine eros and erotic energy.

In her 2009 TedX talk "Let's Get Naked,"[28] Sheila Kelley, founder of S Factor, argues that pole dance is a "symbol for the fourth wave of the feminist movement: the personal recollection of the female body and the sexuality within."[29] Kelley proposes that feminine power is wounded ini-

---

[26] Paul Tillich, *Dynamics of Faith* (New York: Harper & Row, 1958).

[27] The systematic theological locus of ecclesiology is extraordinarily rich when taken as lens of analysis and understanding. Unfortunately, the scope of this analysis exceeds the current project. I hope to take up this task in future manuscripts.

[28] Sheila Kelley, "Let's Get Naked," Tedx American Rivera, 2012, http://tedxtalks.ted.com/video/Lets-Get-Naked-Sheila-Kelley-at (accessed 5 December 2016).

[29] As of 2016, the notion of a "fourth wave of feminism" is a burgeoning concept, with its distinguishing features continuing to be contested and clarified. Diana Diamond identifies the fourth wave as "the idea that these [the first three waves of the feminist movement] unfinished agendas will contribute to the fourth wave, in which social action and spiritual-psychological practice con-

tially through an "original offense," in which girls first learn that there are different rules for girls than for boys and that living in a girl's body is not as safe or acceptable as living in a boy's body. The learning that results from this "original offense" is replicated multiple times throughout women's lives, either through implicit socialization or sexualization, explicit "rules" for being a girl/woman, and/or traumatic violence. While many "original offenses" occur under the guise of protecting or educating girls on "proper" social behavior, this pedagogical shaming occurs in a social context that overly sexualizes women. Kelley's "original offense" is a fairly broad term that encompasses experiences of covert assault and a wide range of microaggressions that most, if not all, women experience. While "original offense" is not confined to the categories of sexual assault and violation, it is also helpful to note the prevalence of sexual assault. In addition to oft-cited statistics that one in four girls and one in six boys will experience sexual assault by the age of eighteen,[30] in June 2016, LuxATL, a pole dancer with a large social media following, posted an invitation for people to share their experiences of assault. LuxATL wrote, "if you have ever been the victim of a rape you chose not to report—and feel comfortable revealing that about yourself—please comment here. "Within six days, 931 people commented and over seventy persons private messaged their stories, many of which were previously undisclosed experiences of assaults."[31]

Contemporary Christian theology has an established lineage of feminist and womanist theologians who have highlighted and critiqued patriarchal dimensions of Christian tradition that support and sanctify "original offenses," rending girls and women from their bodies and sexuality. The projection of "original offenses" onto the body-selves of girls and women functions primarily to reinforce heteronormative power dynamics in which the male is king and the female must be submissive to

---

verge." She identifies the fourth wave as a combination of "politics, psychology, and spirituality in an overarching vision of change." The combination of social activism, psychological resiliency, and spirituality (at least broadly conceived) is readily viewable in the social media activity of participants of pole dance. See Diana Diamond, "The Fourth Wave of Feminism: Pyschoanalytic Perspectives," *Studies in Gender and Sexuality* 10 (2009): 213–223.

[30] National Sexual Violence Resource Center, "Statistics about Sexual Violence," https://www.nsvrc.org/statistics.

[31] LuxATL, Facebook comment, www.facebook.com/lux.atl, June 9, 2016 (accessed 5 March 2019).

his needs and wants. Whenever women re-collect their body and sexuality and then demonstrate their agency to determine care and movement of their body and sexuality, patriarchy leaps into action to shame, control, legislate, or victimize. Kelley and LuxATL both draw unwittingly from the well of theologian Mary Daly. In considering the theological trope of the Fall, original sin, and the role of patriarchy and religion in the oppression of women and feminine eros (which is not limited to persons with female biology), Daly writes,

> In a real sense the projection of guilt upon women *is* patriarchy's Fall, the primordial lie. Together with its offspring—the theology of "original sin"—the myth reveals the "Fall" of religion into the role of patriarchy's prostitute.... The message that it unintentionally conveys—the full implications of which we are only now beginning to grasp—is that in patriarchy, with the aid of religion, women have been the primordial scapegoats.[32]

Daly reconceives via reversal the theological trope of the Fall and original sin. For Daly, both instances of the offspring of the Genesis 2-3 narrative function to support systems that implicitly and explicitly endorse the perpetuation of "original offenses."

One of the most effective strategies of oppression is internalized oppression, through which the objects of subjugation police themselves. Religiously, oppression that rends women from their body and sexuality is manifested in centuries of theological discourse that teaches women to be submissive and silent, instructs adherents that the material is to be rejected or cut off in service of the rational/spiritual, and that communion with the divine necessitates either abuse or neglect of the body. In Western cultures, these mandates have been and continue to be woven into the fabric of society and culture. One overt and focused manifestation of theologically derived social controls of women's bodies and sexuality is the activism of the Christian Religious Right in the areas of reproductive health and exotic dance. Judith Lynne Hanna, anthropologist and dance scholar and critic, has become the leading expert on exotic dance as performance art covered as protected speech under the First Amendment. In her text, *Naked Truth: Strip Clubs, Democracy, and a Christian Right*, Hanna documents Christian Right activists and their strategic and calculated actions to close strip clubs, despite many of their arguments proving baseless. Her decades of research and experience as an

---

[32] Mary Daly, *Beyond God the Father* (Boston: Beacon Press, 1973), 47.

expert witness in trials across the nation document the ways in which conservative Christian discourse demonizes the movement of women's bodies and sexuality and generates a culture that heightens the divide between women and their experience of erotic power.

The division of women from their body and power of eros is one of the primary symptoms of the oppression Daly combats. In 1973, Daly wrote:

> [t]his problem, which has been perceived as the dilemma of all oppressed groups, is most tragically the case with women—divided beings *par excellence*...Having been divided against the self, women want to speak, but remain silent. The desire for action is by and large reduced to acting vicariously through men. Instead of living out the dynamics of the authentic self, women generally are submerged in roles believed to be pleasing to males. When a rebel tries to raise up her own identity, that is, to create her own image, she exposes herself to threatened existence in sexist society.[33]

It is hard to read Daly's work today without thinking about contemporary attitudes toward catcalling, dress codes for female students, or the lethal risk of leaving a domestically violent male. Part of Kelley's notion of the "original offenses" is the way all women learn from an early age the everyday diminishments of agency and authority required to "remain safe." Don't wear that. Don't walk to your car late at night. Don't say or do anything to upset him. If you walk alone at night, make sure to keep your keys in hand so they can double as a weapon. In fact, Daly's claim that "original sin" generates the God-endorsed permission for the "original offense" is why exotic dancers are violently demeaned in "Christian" societies. Both categories of women own their embodied eros as Daly's "rebels" without concern for the rules of patriarchy. In the case of exotic performers, their embodiment of erotic power threatens the narrative of the rewards for being a "good girl," thereby unleashing the retaliation of women who play by the rules of patriarchal religion. In the case of the slut, embodiment of erotic power threatens the centrality of the heterosexual male as a relational necessity. The threat of the slut lies in highlighting the disposability of the male as the primary agent and determiner of relationship.

While the vast majority of women and men who participate in pole dance and sport would not *explicitly* make the connection between their

---

[33] Ibid., 48.

attraction and participation in this movement discipline and the theo-cultural underpinnings of the oppression of women and suppression of feminine eros, they do make it clear that their primary interest towards this movement is a reclamation of feeling "sexy" in a supportive and non-judgmental community.

Pole Dance as a Remedy for Original Offense and Means of Restoration: A Soteriology

If we take the idea of "sin" as "original offense" seriously, where the "of-fense" is the relegation of feminine eros and erotic power to the realm of the taboo and shameful and the loss of vital power for full self-actualization that accompanies loss of parts of self, then the "search for what saves us"[34] must include the restoration of exiled parts of the indi-vidual and by extension of the community. This evocative phrase, "the search for what saves us" is part of the subtitle of Rebecca Ann Parker and Rita Nakashima Brock's *Proverbs of Ashes*, a dialogical theological memoir in which Parker and Brock recount their own experiences of "original offenses" and how they found salvation in the presence and compassion of authentic community. The search for what saves us is so-teriology, and what saves us is directly tied as a remedy for what within us needs saving or reclaiming. For many women and some men (espe-cially those who don't neatly fit into heteronormative patterns and roles) in Western culture, the separation and denigration of feminine eros-from the self is debilitating and complicates full self actualization and holistic growth.

What is feminine eros? Is eros the same as the erotic or the sexual? While eros does include the erotic or sexual energy within each person, it is not exclusive to the erotic. Eros signifies life exemplified in wholeness, fulfillment, harmony, and delight. Eros is not perfection but is the an-tithesis of death or Thanatos.[35] Eros is the power of love for fullness of self that vivifies authentic, holistic, complete living. Feminine eros is also those dimensions of personhood that are culturally designated as more

---

[34] Rita Nakashima Brock and Rebecca Ann Parker, *Provers of Ashes: Vio-lence, Redemptive Suffering, and the Search for What Saves Us* (Boston: Beacon Press, 2001).

[35] Phyllis Trible, *God and the Rhetoric of Sexuality* (Philadelphia: Fortress Press, 1978).

innate—however problematic this is—to persons who are gendered "women." These parts of full personhood that most clearly embody feminine eros are those that are most wounded by the sin of original offenses. The dimensions of self that are told to be quiet, be humble, don't take up space, only perform your sexuality for the pleasure of men, be "good," be predictable/knowable/controllable, don't claim too much agency, and never claim space for your own life if it "takes away" from your "real" task of supporting others (kids, partners, employers, etc.). Be one thing. These mandates strangle the life out of eros. They cut persons off from the fullness of life. They are not the desire of divine love and energy.

Fullness of life requires relationships with a multiplicity of human beings. Each of us is many—a wisdom apparent in many of the world's religious traditions. It is seen in the many/oneness of the yin and yang, the multidimensionality of the chakra system, the divine multiplicity of the Trinity, the plurality of Hindu divinity, the popular rhetoric of the head/heart/gut, and the conversational phrase of "part of me wants A, but part of me wants B." Health is authentic wholeness unreduced to unity. Health requires a restoration of all the parts or energies within oneself. It requires careful reconnection to those parts of self that have been shamed, exiled, or wounded...and a community that can witness, support, sustain, and celebrate this bold reclamation of the wounded and diminished parts of oneself.

For many people who first come to pole dance, the lure of the pole is the opportunity to reclaim feminine movement, embodiment, and sexual power. It is the opportunity to safely "be bad, naughty, or dirty" without the public scorn that Daly highlights as the risk of the rebel. Few would question whether participation in pole dance is seen in the larger cultural milieu as counter-cultural or taboo. Pole dance and sport, precisely because of its contemporary roots in exotic dance, is a rebellious act against social norms that promote and sustain practices that diminish feminine eros and movement patterns that celebrate female bodies for their own benefit.[36] Robust, tight-knit celebratory communities are required in order to sustain and protect rebellious and counter-cultural acts designed to promote fullness of being in the face of dominant systems that benefit from belittlement. While many individuals begin pole dance

---

[36] There is certainly space here to also discuss the cultural taboos of breast feeding in public spaces, female nipples, or discussion of menstrual cycles, birth outside a hospital setting, or, to press the point further, any of the issues related to trans identity and gender presentation.

or sport as a means of reclaiming personal "sexiness" or health, the primary reason people continue is the pole community, a sister- (and, increasingly, brother-) hood of the spinning pole. The pole community is both worldwide and profoundly personal and local. Like other alternative or marginalized communities, the pole community demonstrates strong support for those within the community; globally, this is manifest in openness for inclusion and welcome when travelling to another region or nation. Personally or locally, it is seen in presence, compassion, and witness of personal growth.

In her TedX talk, Sheila Kelley claims pole dance as a symbol of the fourth wave of feminism; perhaps she has not claimed enough.[37] What if pole dance and sport are, rather than a symbol, a midwife of the fourth wave? What if those "rebellious, slutty, strippers" who own and find a way to generate a living wage from their sexual power; who crafted a movement form that transcends the bounds of sport, art, dance, and personal growth; who are despised by all the "good" and righteous women and men of conventional faith; who courageously risk life and sanity to beat systems of market, taboo, and patriarchy at their own game—what if those foremothers of contemporary pole dance and sport are the heralds and crafters of a new wave of feminism whose marks are new revolutions in political, psychological, and spiritual life? For women and men who participate in pole to reclaim a part of their being that has been actively harmed or shamed into being less than, the ongoing power of participation in pole is a reclamation of holistic, authentic, life-affirming embodied power, whether that embodied power is found in the strength needed to hold an iron-x, the courage to fonji, the power of expressions of vulnerability, the boldness of cultural critique via comedy, or the raw sensuality of self-touch, high heels, and sensual floor work.

Blogger and community-building pole dancer known as Aerial Amy, writes,

> When I think of the biggest gift pole has given me, I think about this:
> Through pole dance, I learned to DRESS sexy.
> Then I learned to ACT sexy.
> Then I learned to LOOK sexy.
> But then one day I realized that I AM sexy—whatever I dress like, act like, or look like.

---

[37] Kelley, "Let's Get Naked."

105

Do you want to know what power really is? It's knowing you don't have to fill in anyone else's checklist to know your worth.[38]

Is this not "what saves us" from the many "original offenses?"

Pole dance is much more than just a recreational activity. It is a global, thriving community, a growing multidimensional industry, a performance art, a sport with professional athletes, and a counter-cultural movement that celebrates and includes those who are regularly marginalized by dominant Western culture and society. To look for established religious markers in this vast, diverse, and burgeoning community as a means of theological or religious studies misses the many ways in which this community is its own church and creates its own religion—binding together itself and community. From the outside, pole dance is frequently conflated with stripping and exotic dance. While it is tempting for some to correct this external conflation by creating a sharp divide between pole dancers and strippers, this tactic is unconvincing and misses the larger issue—reclamation of feminine eros and healing from the "original offenses." From within the community of pole dancers (some of whom are also or originally were strippers), this movement form offers an embodied practice that allows women and men to reconnect with their physical, emotional, and erotic power. The ability to nourish injured and diminished dimensions of oneself through movement, community, expression, embodied self-awareness, and sensuality is profoundly healing and empowering—perhaps even salvific.

---

[38] Amy Kim, Facebook, www.facebook.com/Aerialamyy, 21 November 2016.

Casting for Meaning
The Mythical, Mystical, and
Metaphysical Significance of Fly Fishing

Joseph L. Price

The first day of trout season in the High Sierras introduces the celebration of "Fishmas" for fly fishing devotees who are lured to be among the first to wade into the waters of the mountains' snowmelt-fed streams and lakes.[1] Near Buckeye Creek and the East Walker River, local motels outfitted with outdoor sinks for cleaning up and cleaning fish are booked months in advance, and some standing reservations at a resort near Crowley Lake are passed down from one generation to another like a family Bible. On the late Friday night in April before trout season opens in Mono County, California, the solid line of headlights coursing up Highway 395 from Los Angeles toward the streams and lakes near Mammoth demarks a pilgrimage of cars, much like the stream of headlights heading toward Ray Kinsella's ballpark in the final scene of *Field of Dreams*.

The fly fishers who make the journey toward the mountains and their waters, like many of the sport's disciples around the world, often refer to their wilderness river encounters in spiritual terms. As Rev. Michael Attas, an accomplished angler and author, has noted, devoted fly fishers will identify "rivers as their church and...nature as sacred."[2] They often offer testimonies that include claims of conversion. For instance, John Gierach, the dean of angler-authors, confesses that once he experienced the thrill of fly fishing, he "eschewed all lesser forms of fishing and

---

[1] Christopher Reynolds, "Trout Season Nears in Mono County, where Angling for Rooms Is Part of the Big Fish Frenzy," *Los Angeles Times*, 16 March 2016, http://www.latimes.com/travel/la-tr-d-spring-trout-20160313-story.html (accessed 4 February 2017).

[2] Eric Eisenkramer and Michael Attas, *Fly-Fishing—The Sacred Art: Casting a Fly as Spiritual Practice* (Woodstock, VT: Skylight Paths Publishing, 2012), 118.

immediately became a born-again dry-fly fisherman."[3] These fly-fishing devotees use a language of awe and wonder to express their experience of achieving personal contentment and fulfillment and of sensing a peace that passes all understanding. This numinous experience of the *totaliter aliter*, as Rudolf Otto determined, identifies an experience of the holy.

The community or "church" of faithful fly fishers has been astutely analyzed by Samuel Snider as an instance of what Robert Orsi calls "lived religion," the practice of world-making and world-maintaining that orients the daily activities and deeply held values of practitioners and advocates.[4] To supplement his analysis, Snider connects the concept of "lived religion" with characteristics of "nature religion" (as set forth by Catherine Albanese, among others) and "material religion" (as identified by Colleen McDannell). Material elements of a religion provide a visual identification of affiliates with a particular community. When a youth or adult wears a yarmulke, for instance, his or her identity as a Jew is unmistakably displayed, and when someone wears earrings or a necklace with a cross, one's Christian identity is affirmed. Similarly, fly fishers also display their identity as a tribe of anglers by the functional and ritual objects that they wear and carry—bamboo rods, overall waders, barbless hooks, and handtied flies or bug puppets.

The kind of rod that a fly fisher uses is a special indication of his or her depth of devotion since, as expert angler David James Duncan has observed, "a rod extends a fly fisher's being as surely as the imagination, empathy, or prayer."[5] Even though a fly fisher develops a personal relationship with a rod, the natural intimacy that one experiences with a bamboo rod expands far beyond the metrics related to its swing weight and elasticity because it is possible for one material to transmit the power of an activity from hand to heart better than another. A bamboo rod in particular carries with it "a sense of something supernatural," elite rod maker Glenn Brackett proclaims, since it conveys the spirit of its crafters whose hands turned and rubbed it thousands of times during the process

---

[3] John Gierach, *All Fishermen Are Liars* (New York: Simon and Schuster, 2014),113.

[4] Samuel Snider, "New Streams of Religion: Fly Fishing as a Lived Religion of Nature," *Journal of the American Academy of Religion* 75, no. 4 (December 2007): 898.

[5] David James Duncan, *Trout Grass.* Documentary film produced by Volcano Motion Pictures, 2007.

of its creation and of the harvesters of the bamboo whose careful cutting of the grass respected its vitality.[6]

In his documentary film *Trout Grass* about the concordant connection between stalks of bamboo and their transformed state as fly rods, Duncan confesses that "on a river without a fly rod I am a tourist; with rod in hand I become something else."[7] The "something else" that he becomes is not simply the complex persona of a fly fisher, but a mystic, a seer, an empathizer. As Duncan suggests, fly fishers can take on a new identity in the way that they use their rod. Fly fishers utilize their bamboo wands to open up new ways of seeing the world, as Matthew Dickerson (an environmental writing professor and occasional fishing guide) has noted—ways "of making contact with a part of the world that would otherwise remain unknown to us."[8] Even though Dickerson is specifically referring the hidden realm of trout, his insight also applies to the fisher's discovery of selfhood that would otherwise remain undisclosed.

Like the attachment that one experiences to a particular rod, one's collection—one's jewel case—of flies also identifies one as a member of the fly-fishing community. The respect and care that a fisher devotes to the preservation and presentation of flies attest to their iconic significance. Writing about these lures, fly-master Tom McGuane celebrates the ongoing usefulness and functional beauty even of some traditional flies, like the Adams and the Cahills. "They remind us of the poetic history of our passion as well as its deficiencies," he observes. "They don't look much like the flies they imitate except in the most basic way, and they encapsulate certain preconceptions about fish which are aesthetic at base, such as the notion that trout really prefer beautiful mayflies to such tiresome things as caddises, stoneflies, midges, and worms."[9]

The fascination with flies extends beyond their image and delicacy to the practice of tying them. Effective pursuit of the craft requires patience and precision, two characteristics of spiritual exercises in meditation. The discipline necessary to work with tiny hooks and minute elements often discourages avid fly fishers from beginning the practice of

---

[6] Brackett makes this comment in Duncan's film *Trout Grass*.

[7] Duncan, *Trout Grass*.

[8] David O'Hara and Matthew Dickerson, *Downstream: Reflections on Brook Trout, Fly Fishing, and the Waters of Appalachia* (Eugene, OR: Cascade Books, 2014), 36.

[9] Thomas McGuane, *The Longest Silence: A Life in Fishing* (New York: Vintage Books, 2001), 67.

tying. Once Michael Attas began fly-tying lessons during recuperation from ankle foot surgery, however, he found the practice of fly tying "to be one of the most profound spiritual disciplines that [he] had ever experienced," and he concluded that the practice can provide a calming effect once one becomes familiar with the delicate movements. Then the deliberate and precise moves invoke an introspective journey akin to meditation.[10] Like Attas, McGuane had been a life-long student of aesthetic and effective flies before somewhat reluctantly joining the cult of fly-tyers. Even though he does not invoke typical terminology associated with meditative practices, he acknowledges that his satisfaction in the process comes from his particular motivation and goal. "I try to tie flies that will make me fish better, to fish more often, to dream of fish when I can't fish," he confesses, "to remind myself to do what I can do to make the world more accommodating to fish and, in short, to take further steps toward becoming a fish myself."[11] While fly-tyers create material objects that become signs of their devotion, the process of their creation can also be a spiritual exercise.

While Snider's essay deals with various material elements that mark membership in the troop of fly fishers, his argument focuses on the evocative, spiritual character of nature that distinguishes anglers' interactions with diverse elements of creation—water, light, aquatic life, insect activity, and more. As Mircea Eliade has averred, because "the cosmos is a divine creation...the world is impregnated with sacredness."[12] In multiple ways nature provides a context for humans to experience a breadth of connections with the sacred—the terrifying threat of the overwhelming power of the divine, as well as intimate harmony with the foundation of reality in the Created Order. A natural disaster such as a hurricane or a lightning strike during a thunderstorm can be experienced as terrifying, as the *mysterium tremendum*, as Wholly Other. By contrast, a simple spring blossom, the sight of a glorious sunset, or an encounter in a forest with a fawn can evoke a sense of harmony with seemingly simple, pure, and majestic elements of nature. In related ways, fly fishers can sense the power of the Other when they wade into the current of a river or stand in canyon stream surrounded by majestic peaks. It is also possible for these anglers to experience a spiritual connection with the entirety of fish habi-

---

[10] Eisenkramer and Attas, *Fly-Fishing*, 104–105.

[11] McGuane, *Longest Silence*, 71.

[12] Mircea Eliade, *The Sacred and the Profane: The Nature of Religion*, trans. by Willard R. Trask (New York: Harcourt, Brace and World, Inc., 1959), 116.

tat since they strive to understand how fish environments work in order to lure, hook, and net the salmon and trout. As Gierach notes, a good fly fisher "might eventually get cagey enough to know when and where the hatches [of midges] would come off and arrive at the river half an hour before the first dimple appeared on the surface."[13]

In his essay on fly fishing as a lived religion, Snider also effectively identifies communal and ritual activities of fly fishers by surveying significant fly-fishing manuals, sampling the range of rhapsodic internet posts written by sports enthusiasts, and interviewing sportsmen who thrill to wade in the river.[14] Taking a different approach to the spiritual character of this sporting experience, I will focus on the mythical, mystical, and metaphysical significance of fly fishing by examining the testimonies in memoir and fiction by two expert anglers: Norman Maclean's *A River Runs through It* and David James Duncan's *The River Why*. Both works express the spiritual dimension of the sport in narrative form, an appropriate genre since, as Cory Willard has noted, "the casting of a fly itself is a sort of narrative and rhetorical act."[15]

Mythical Tradition

The spiritual orientation of both angler-authors is grounded in biblical myths celebrated by the Christian tradition, which have included fishing stories and symbols in a variety of ways. Maclean forthrightly discloses his Calvinist heritage as the son of a Presbyterian minister. In other works, Duncan discloses his upbringing in Seventh Day Adventism. Both authors refer to Jesus and his fondness for fishers by directing attention to the gospel story about Jesus calling his first disciples to abandon their fishing nets in Galilee and to follow him to become "fishers of men." Other gospel narratives about fishing are identified with the miracles of Jesus. On one occasion the gospels record that Jesus took two small fish and five loaves from a boy's lunch, blessed the food, broke the

---

[13] Gierach, 114.

[14] Although Snider's essay discusses various rituals that fly fishers routinely perform, he does not adequately distinguish ritual from habit. According to Ronald L. Grimes, ritual carries with the action a shared meaning that exceeds the function of the action itself. See *Beginnings in Ritual Studies* (Lanham, MD: University Press of America, 1982).

[15] Cory Willard, "On Fly Fishing and Rhetoric: Ethos, Experience, and Fly Fishing's Rhetorical Proofs." *Aethlon* 31, no. 1 (Winter 2014): 70.

small salt-fish (probably the size of sardines) and distributed them to thousands in the crowd.[16] In the Gospel of John, meanwhile, there is a single biblical rendering of a post-resurrection fishing expedition of the backsliding disciples, who had spent all night fishing without catching a thing. Standing on shore at dawn, the risen Christ told the luckless fishermen to cast their net on the opposite side of their boat, a act of trust that yielded a haul of 153 fish. Beyond the gospel accounts of these fish stories, it is also meaningful that the earliest Christians aligned this ichthyology with their messianic theology by utilizing the symbol of a fish as a cipher to identify their affiliation with Christ.

During the pre-textual decades of oral transmission of these stories, it is possible that the inclusion and expansion of specific numbers were introduced to emphasize the miraculous power of Jesus and his messianic identity. At the very least, the phenomenal numbers in these gospel accounts are in keeping with the tendency of tellers of "fish stories" to exaggerate the size and haul of their effort in order to communicate the extraordinary character of their catch or the depth of their disappointment in letting the big one get away. Taking the Johannine tally of 153 fish as a prompt for musing about the penchant of fishermen to expand the size of their success, Gus Orviston, the obsessed, young fly-fisher and narrator in *The River Why*, muses at length about the theological significance of the count. While he knows that anglers adore statistics, he is stunned by the disciples' state of mind that led them to turn their attention away from the newly risen Jesus in order to calculate their catch. Think about their situation, he suggests:

> Mustn't it have happened thus: upon hauling the net to shore, the disciples squatted down by that immense, writhing fish pile and started tossing them into a second pile, painstakingly counting "one, two, three, four, five, six, seven ..." all the way up to an hundred and fifty and three, while the newly risen Lord of Creation, the Sustainer of their beings, he who died for them and for whom they would gladly die, stood waiting, ignored till the heap of fish was quantified. Such is the fisherman's compulsion toward rudimentary mathematics.[17]

---

[16] With some variations, the story of the feeding of the multitude is the only miracle story included in all four gospels.

[17] David James Duncan, *The River Why* (San Francisco: Sierra Club Books, 1983), 15.

The phenomenal numbers in these biblical stories—the itemization of the few items in the boy's lunch box, the estimation of the size of the crowd, the specification of the amount of leftovers, and the precise tally of fish that the disciples snared after the resurrection—are also in keeping with the exaggerated elements that typify "fish stories." For fishers of any kind or method, however, the *reality* of fish, the verification of their existence—whether trapped in a seine net, hooked with a bobber teasing them with live worms or crickets, caught with a spin reel using shiners or power bait, or teased to a strike with a dry fly—is determined by specific numbers associated with them: the size of the haul or the measurement of length and weight, numbers that are also used to determine the largest catch of the day or of one's life. Gus admits that fishers share a compulsion toward "rudimentary mathematics," for the numbers in a fish story not only affirm the reality of the fish, they also lend legitimacy to the account. "A fish story without an exact weight and length is a nonentity," he claims, "whereas the sixteen-incher or the twelve-pounder leaps out of the imagination, splashing the brain with cold spray. The strange implication is that the numbers are more tangible than flesh; fish without vital statistics are fish without being."[18]

The profound meaning of fishing, however, extends far beyond the bloated numbers and fantastic elements that drive and typify fish stories. Their mythic significance begins with water, which, according to one of the biblical accounts of creation, preceded the formation of *terra firma* by separating the dry land *from* the waters. Even though this Genesis story of creation is formative for Jewish and Christian traditions, Eliade recognizes that throughout history and the world the cosmogonies of numerous peoples repeatedly identify the primordial presence and function of water. He avers that "waters invariably retain their function; they disintegrate, abolish forms, 'wash away sins'; they are at once purifying and regenerating. Their destiny is to precede the Creation and to reabsorb it, since they are incapable of transcending their own mode of being, incapable, that is of manifesting themselves in *forms*."[19]

Water in motion—like that in the flow of the Jordan or the troubled waters of the pool at Bethesda—is especially associated with beneficent aspects of life: its generation, purification, or sacralization (as in baptism)—specifically its healing potential. By donning waders and entering the stream, fly fishers thus become part of this cleansing and renewing

---

[18] Ibid.
[19] Eliade, *The Sacred and the Profane*, 131.

power. For some anglers, the rhythm of casting a fly while standing in water becomes a sacramental act by unifying a sense of timelessness with the sacred space of the flowing river, which in myth often serves as a metaphor for the passage of time itself. This connection between the sacred space of the river and the suspension of time—or the sensation of its immediacy—is celebrated by John Gierach who judges that "the best thing about fishing is that it takes place entirely in the present tense, so even if you feel vaguely cheated, you're not brooding about the past, worrying about the future or wondering What am I doing here?" That question, he concludes, is irrelevant for someone experiencing the sacred character of both time and space.[20] The convergence of the sacred character of time is most effectively signified by a river, a body of water that is ever changing and continuous, ever moving, coming and going. To step into the current of a stream is to experience immediately the unifying sense of time and place, to stand momentarily in the immediacy of existence and history.

In this fleeting reprieve from the press of time, it is also possible for a fisher to experience a heightened sense of light, the initial accomplishment in the process of the creation, according to the first account in Genesis. Especially at sunset and dusk, Attas observes, "The shadows move across the water, the colors become more muted, and the air takes on a palpable texture." He concludes that it is then that one becomes aware of the gift of light: how it "shifts, changes, emerges, and softly fades."[21]

Mystical Experience

Because fish stories have a tendency to grow, often becoming tall tales in their retelling, Gierach titled one of his score of fly-fishing books *All Fishermen Are Liars*. This assertion accounts for the pattern of fishing stories to describe challenging conditions and successful outings in mythic terms. Invariably, as Attas notes, since "the biggest fish is the one that got away"—the one whose length is often demonstrated by ever expanding hands—it's possible that this "particular riff is a part of every angler's gene pool."[22] While typical fish stories focus on difficult conditions, the size of the fish that broke the line, or, when applicable, how quickly the

---

[20] Gierach, *All Fishermen Are Liars*, 112.
[21] Eisenkramer and Attas, *Fly Fishing—The Sacred Art*, 54.
[22] Ibid.

limit was reached, the narratives by Maclean and Duncan deal with more profound questions and issues than a precise description and computation of the catch. They explore the mystical and metaphysical significance of the art and act of fly fishing. In part, it has to do with the ephemeral mayflies that in a single day mature, mate, die, and feed trout. Writing about these live lures, Gierach has wondered further, using non-biological, non-philosophical, and non-spiritual terms: "I don't know what fly fishing teaches us," he ponders, "but it's something we need to know."[23] This mystical intuition feeds the reflections on fishing in Maclean and Duncan's works, which personalize and dramatize spiritual lessons that fly fishing teaches: patience, perseverance, hope and beauty, among others.

Identifying his family's unifying rituals and visions, Norman Maclean begins his autobiographic reflections in *A River Runs through It* with the simple observation that in his family "there was no line between religion and fly fishing."[24] As sons of a Calvinist minister in Montana, Norman and Paul Maclean perceived divine order in the precision of the art of fly fishing, and they understood the condensed dogmas of *The Shorter Westminster Catechism* in terms of the sport as a spiritual exercise. Routinely, then, Norman aligned the sporting possibilities of learning the art of fly fishing with the theological possibility of human redemption. Neither is natural, he observed, but through their exercise of discipline both can become aesthetically transformed, even beautiful. It is this dual experience and expression of beauty, in sport and theology that Maclean celebrates throughout his memoir.

During routine Sunday afternoon walks with their father, Norman and Paul listened to him expound upon theological points made in his morning sermon. Repeatedly the boys responded to his instruction in the catechism: "What is the chief end of man?" Faithfully they would answer, "Man's chief end is to glorify God, and to enjoy him forever." The lack of a clear line—whether a metaphorical one of faith or a casting one of filament—between religion and fly fishing prompted the two young Macleans to think of fly fishing as the primary way in which God could be glorified and enjoyed. Weekly, they received as much instruction from their father in the art of fly fishing as they did in the dogmas of the cate-

---

[23] John Gierach, *Sex, Death, and Fly Fishing* (New York: Simon and Schuster, 1990), 20.

[24] Norman Maclean, *A River Runs through It* (Chicago, University of Chicago Press, 1976), 1.

chism. The paradox that they encountered through these lessons was that the divine could be perceived pleasantly though physical senses that are typically sublimated by Calvinists in deference to cognitive, creedal expressions of faith.

In his ruminations about fly fishing, Maclean points out several theological lessons that can also be learned in the sport, lessons related to the doctrines, for instance, of original sin and salvation—or in Calvinist terms, election. Novices to the practice of fly casting, Maclean observes, confirm the Christian dogma of the fallenness of humans: "if you have never picked up a fly rod before," Maclean warns, "you will soon find it factually and theologically true that man by nature is a damn mess. The four-and-a-half-ounce thing in silk wrappings that trembles with the underskin motions of the flesh becomes a stick without brains."[25] The experience of becoming a skilled fly fisher is akin to that of being re-deemed: It is a predestined gift that can be mastered by the elect according to the Calvinist theology of Maclean's father. Some who have been found lacking in the skills necessary for developing artistry with the four-and-a-half-ounce wand have themselves confirmed in their destitute condition, as Paul Maclean notes about Norman's brother-in-law, who had moved to the West Coast and fished with worms, a certain sign of reprobate status. "Practically everybody on the West Coast," Paul remarks, "was born in the Rocky Mountains where they failed as fly fishermen, so they migrated to the West Coast and became lawyers, certified public accountants, presidents of airplane companies, gamblers, or Mormon missionaries."[26] The sure sign of divine election, it seemed to the Macleans, was whether or not one could fish with a fly. In fact, Norman and Paul thought that, since Jesus' disciples were fishermen, "all first-class fishermen on the Sea of Galilee were fly fishermen and that John, the favorite [apostle], was a dry-fly fisherman."[27]

Maclean's elegant story achieved popularity in a faithful, cinematic recasting by the same title, *A River Runs through It*. The lure of both the memoir and the film lies in the image of the river as a route for retreat into the purity of wilderness—the place where time and space converge in the immediacy of the moment—and the ethereal image of a whispering filament that suggests a mystical connection between fly fishing and faith. Through a metaphorical understanding of fly fishing, then, Mac-

---

[25] Ibid., 3.
[26] Ibid., 9–10.
[27] Ibid., 1.

lean locates the mystery of redemption in the imagined innocence of the wilderness, the pristine flow of trout streams and a sense of the lightness of being in the process of luring, hooking, and catching secluded fish.

Metaphysical Significance

While Maclean explores the mystical tug of fly fishing by making metaphorical connections between systems of belief and lore about the sport, David James Duncan uses a different weight and leader to align fly fishing with spiritual impulses, experiences and pursuits. About a decade after the publication of Maclean's book, Duncan completed his first novel, *The River Why*, which celebrates the physical harmony between fly fishing and nature while venturing into metaphysical meditations about existence and destiny. Most of these philosophical and spiritual insights, interwoven throughout the narrative, are voiced by narrator Gus Orviston, whose name combines a theological allusion to Saint Augustine and an angling reference to the Orvis Company, America's premier fly-fishing business. His reflections include descriptions of his piscatorial passion, commentary on the physical harmony between fly fishing and nature, and metaphysical musings about the meaning of existence in its relation to water.

Late in his teens, Gus had realized "that Not-Fishing was the Bad, Fishing was the Good, everything else under sun and moon was the indifferent, and 'too much of the Good' was inconceivable."[28] In response to this insight, he devised a contentment scale to measure how many minutes were spent daily in pleasing pursuits (exclusively identified with fishing), displeasing pursuits (including non-angling conversation), or neutral pursuits (such as consuming food and bathing). With such a measurement system in mind, he then designed a salvific program of "Unending Satisfaction Actualization," for which he envisioned an ideal schedule that could allow for more than fourteen hours a day spent in pursuit of fishing: tying flies, making rods, reading about and discussing techniques, and—of course—wading in the water and casting the line with a bamboo rod. By pursuing the life of a hermit and moving to an isolated shack on the Tamawanis River (subsequently dubbed "the Why" because of the shape of its path from the mountains to the sea) Gus completed a process that Eliade has identified as a kind of initiation into a mystic vocation. That religious process instills in the inductee "a totally

---

[28] Duncan, *River Why*, 56.

different being," prompting her or him to "become *another*."[29] For Gus, his induction into fly fishing as a vocation shifted its importance to a level beyond avocational passion; it now became a way of life.

Prior to the emergence of this consciousness of vocational destiny and identity, Gus had manifested a predestined character to fish. Before Gus's birth, his father, Henning Hale-Orviston (whom Gus subsequently nicknamed H2O) had taken fly fishing so seriously and devoutly that it was recognized by others as his religion. Sometimes called "The Bishop of the Brooks," H2O was best known as the author of the massive *Summa Piscatoria*, obviously an "ichthyological" parody of Thomas Aquinas's magisterial *Summa Theologica*, especially since in Duncan's narrative, H2O's text was often regarded as the angler's Bible. Adding to these parodic references, Duncan underscores the spiritual significance of his own narrative by assigning important biblical, philosophical, and theological names to concocted characters and fictional texts.

At the time of Gus's birth, H2O had also published a fanciful—yes, a fishy account—with the title "Gus the Fish." The story tells of an obstetrician's angling adventure "in hooking and landing 'a chubby eight-pounder' who had 'eluded all anglers for over nine months' despite being tapped in 'a small pool in a river only five feet, five inches long'"[30] In the final paragraph of the satirical story, H2O had disclosed the allegorical nature of his tale, including the fact that the "hooking" referred to the forceps style of delivery required for the landing of Augustine, the name given to his son. Like fish whose entire existence is spent in water, Gus's life is paradoxically shaped by water, which itself has no form. His aquatic identity is signified in his DNA since he was conceived by his mother "Ma" (a name that in Arabic means "water" as pointed out by Titus, his philosopher tutor) and father whose sobriquet was the chemical formula for water.

This parental predilection for fishing was effectively transmitted to Gus. As a precocious preschooler, Gus landed his first steelhead weighing ten pounds. For that catch he had used a worm as bait, a method described by his high-church, dry-fly father as "fishing fundamentalism." At the tender age of six, Gus had landed his first steelhead with a fly; by late adolescence he had become so devoted to fishing that he believed he had been divinely called to the sport. "Because if God is everything the

---

[29] Mircea Eliade, *The Quest: History and Meaning in Religion* (Chicago: University of Chicago Press, 1969), 112.

[30] Duncan, *River Why*, 1.

Bible and the Compleat Angler crack Him up to be," he had written in his journal, "it's Him that's making me want to fish anyhow, and Him who will turn me into a fish or worm or fly or angel or star or saint or sun or frog or taco whenever He decides and what could I do about it? Nothing. Just keep fishing. That's all."[31]

In an expression of intensifying empathy with salmon and trout, then, Gus begins to dissolve his ego as he learns to think like them. "It is simply not enough to know that trout eat insects," Cory Willard suggests in a rhetorical analysis of fly fishing; "the successful fly fisher must come to know what insects, where, when, and the life cycles of these insects as well as the holding and feeding patterns of the trout in particular streams."[32] This attempt to understand the world from the perspective of the trout—this inversion or reversal of the normal role of self in approaching the world—resembles a Buddhist worldview. Adopting such an approach, co-authors and expert fly fishers David O'Hara and Matthew Dickerson observe that the act of fly fishing disrupts their routines and expectations like a Zen koan that upsets the way one sees the world. Embracing this inverted perception, they delight in the fact that "fishing for trout requires us to try to see the world as trout see it, to imagine their riparian cosmos, in which everything is connected, everything flows together and the aim is to find your place in that flow."[33]

Building on this kind of knowledge, Gus is able to recall all data about his catches, in part because he records the information faithfully in a journal that he calls "the God-notebook"—where and how he caught each fish, what kind of cast and what angle he had made in hooking it, what bait or lure he had used for each catch, and what the size and kind of each fish had been. Because of his accurate accounting and keen sense of recall, Gus likens his flawless fishing record to the impeccable memory of God: it is remarkable not because details can be precisely recounted but because it is impossible to forget them.

Through acts of social and self-renunciation Gus fully embraces his calling to be a piscatorial hermit, and he starts to lose touch with his human identity. The more he engages in fishing and focuses on thinking like a fish, the more he fumbles with language when trying to speak to an occasional passerby. During his obsessive descent into the reality of fish life, his typical daily conversation had become restricted to his instruc-

---

[31] Ibid., 44.
[32] Willard, "On Fly Fishing and Rhetoric," 69.
[33] O'Hara and Dickerson, *Downstream*, 5.

tions and admonitions to Rod, the name that he gives to his fishing gear, and to the pet fish that he feeds in the large tank in his cabin. His focus on fishing alone, however, gradually deprives him of so much of his personhood that he starts to suffer insomnia, sleeping less and less and worrying more and more about whether and how he might enjoy complete daily devotion to fishing.

His egression into fishing solitude, however, is abruptly reversed into human interactivity when, in a dense fog, he snags and drags the corpse of a drowned fisherman named Abe. For Gus, clarity about existence is ironically discerned in a fog. In a reversal that resonates with the message of Ingmar Bergman's film *The Seventh Seal*, Death becomes the authoritative teacher about Life. Gus's encounter with the corpse prompts him to reflect on the meaning of *human* life, not exclusively on the habits of Pisces. Shifting his focus to the meaning of human existence, he gains a new appreciation for life itself—for the friendships that it allows, and for the possibility of human communication—when he hears Abe's companion plaintively calling out while searching for him.

Gus's restoration of human relationships significantly progresses when, following his interview with the police about his discovery of the corpse, he hitches a ride back to his cabin with Titus, a philosophizing duffer fisherman with a sense of humor. Riding in a beat-up Plymouth that Titus calls "The Carp," simply because it looks like one, Gus perceives human playfulness each time Titus applies the brakes. A tiny plastic Jesus in the back window of the old, dented car would raise its arm in benediction, while also mimicking the fondness for fishing by the biblical Jesus. For Titus "had glued a flyrod made of three joined toothpicks to His hand, with an ephemeral line of monofilament ending in a No. 20 Royal Coachman. Each time the Carp came to a halt the Good Fisher hauled back, set the hook and somewhere in the world a saved sinner lay gasping on the planks of His boat, a transmundane dry fly still dangling from his spiritual lip."[34]

While this fusion of fishing and spiritual humor intensified Gus's movement to restore his *human* identity, it is his contemplative interaction with Titus that truly revitalizes his personhood. Earlier, from a mountaintop view of the Tamawanis River, Gus had recognized that the cursive course of the river to the ocean carved out the fundamental metaphysical question: WHY? Why is there something rather than nothing?

---

[34] Duncan, *River Why*, 105.

Seeing that question naturally curved by water, spelled in a single word in creation itself, Gus considers its existential and spiritual challenge, turning to Titus for guidance. What can one love? Gus asks. What can one believe?

Noting that fly fishers perceive and pursue trout that remain invisible to ordinary folk and holiday anglers, Titus responds with an assertion and question of his own. "Fishermen should be the easiest of men to convince to commence to search for the soul," he declares. Before Gus can respond, however, Titus asks, "How can you be so sagacious and patient in seeking fish, and so hasty and thick as to write off your soul because you can't see it?"[35]

For Gus, the reclamation of his genuine human identity—his recognition of a human soul—is finally accomplished in two reconciliatory acts with and in his fishing vocation: specifically, his physical quest to find the source of the pristine headwaters of the river Why and his epic, miraculously successful wrestle with a trophy-sized chinook.

Motivated by existential questions and his love of the water, Gus begins his trek toward the top left-wing of the "W" in the Why, hiking farther and farther from his cabin, now more than ten miles, now more than twenty. As difficulties mount with increasing distance from his cabin, he realizes that he is searching for Eden itself, emblematically for the spring that gives birth to the mystifying stream whose existence, whose shape, poses the fundamental metaphysical question: "Why? Why is there something rather than nothing? What is existence and what is its meaning?" Ill-prepared for the fifty-mile pilgrimage to the source, Gus perseveres nonetheless, sleeping in new frost, eating huckleberries, and finally ascending to the ur-spring where he drinks from its pure font, filling a cup that had been left at the site. With the realization that someone had preceded him to the spring, Gus understands that the water's origin does not supply the answer to the river's metaphysical query but only locates its starting point. The existential question about identity is answered, he concludes, not by the river's cause but by its course—the shape of its movement to the sea—even as the life of a fisher (particularly his own water-oriented life that had been conceived by Ma and H20) is not determined by one's birth but by the trajectories of living day to day.

Gus also experiences a fly fisher's contact with incorruption in his romance with a spawning, fifty-pound Chinook salmon snared on a

---

[35] Ibid., 179.

three-pound leader and a No. 4 hook, both far too fragile to land such a catch. The "sacred dance," as Gus calls his temporarily tethered relationship with the fish, begins as he plays with and prays about the Chinook throughout the day and across miles of the river's surge while they maneuver upstream. As the fish dives deeper and dusk begins to engulf them, Gus reasons that the threatening conditions paradoxically increase the risk to his safety, even as they command his will and skills to stay tied to the fish on the line. During this marathon dance toward the possibility of death, he recalls instruction from Titus about a stress point being the place where a line would break. "If the fisherman experiences no stress, and if he transmits this experience through his hands to his pole, to his line, to his hook," Titus had reasoned, "then there will be no stress point, therefore no point at which the strand can break."[36] Gus senses that the application of this Daoist principle about dulling the impact of a force by submissively receiving its contact would enable a fisher to catch the biggest fish by releasing stress at vulnerable moments and places.[37]

Titus's insight guides Gus through this intimate relationship with water and the Chinook. As fictional as this account may be, it follows the lesson from an ancient Chinese fish story in *The Book of Lieh-tzu*, which resembles the tall-tale character of fish stories with exaggerated extremes. According to the story, there was a fisher who assembled gear of a negligible silk filament, a natural hook from a stalk, and simple bait of a split grain of rice. All pieces of the fishing gear were exaggerated to emphasize the miracle of setting the hook and catching the largest fish in the deepest water. Incredibly, the story goes, "the line did not snap, the hook did not straighten out, the rod did not bend, because he let out and drew in the line following the pull and give of the water." When the King asked the fisher how he had managed to catch such a huge fish with such an impossibly inadequate rig, the fisher replied:

> I contemplate nothing but the fish. When I cast my line and sink the hook, my hand does not pull too hard nor give too easily, so that nothing can disturb it. When the fish see the bait on my hook, it is like sinking dust or gathered foam, and they swallow it without suspecting.

---

[36] Ibid., 274.

[37] See Michael L. Raposa, *Meditation and the Martial Arts* (Charlottesville: University of Virginia Press, 2003), 44–45.

This is how I am able to use weak things to control strong ones, light things to bring in heavy ones.[38]

With a similar spiritual orientation and understanding, Gus is able to dance the "hen"—the name of the female Chinook—for the many miles upstream from the pool near his cabin where the fish had been hooked. At one with nature and the fish, while periodically submerging and swimming in the stream, Gus recalls the end of their dance when he looked at the fish and gently lifted her, now relaxed in the cool comfort of his left hand. There, he revels, *"She suffered my touch, and stayed."*[39] With this intimate, caressing embrace of the fish whom he had grown to love during the night of their dance up the Why, Gus is not only restored to community; he is fully transformed.

The evidence of Gus's conversion is revealed in a Damascus road experience during his return to his cabin. Virtually blinded by light, he perceives the depth of being, an experience enabled by his dance with the Chinook and his contact with her. "And then I felt it—a sharp pain in the heart, like a hook being set," he recalls. "I whirled around: sunlight struck me full face."[40] Like the Apostle Paul, who had persecuted Christians before his conversion, Augustine Orviston had routinely sought to apprehend trout, shackling them during the course of their tethered dance and depriving them of freedom (even if only temporarily) in their habitat. Like Paul, Gus recognizes the transcendent origin and transformative power of the blinding light. Somewhat like Paul, who knew that the brilliance was an appearance of the resurrected Christ directed singly to himself, Gus senses that the sunlight that struck him full force had specifically chosen him in a way corresponding to his call to be a fly fisher. He believes that the subtle shaft of light that pierced his heart and head was connected to a transcendent realm, reserved for light alone. Immediately and joyfully, he recalls,

> I sank to my knees on the white road, and I felt the hand, resting like sunlight on my head. And I knew that the line of light led not to a realm but to a Being, and that the light and the hook were his, and that they were made of love alone. My heart was pierced. I began to weep. I

---

[38] Quoted in Kenneth Robinson, *The Way and the Wilderness* (Edinburgh: The Pentland Press Ltd., 1993), 165.

[39] Duncan, *River Why*, 277.

[40] Ibid.

felt the Ancient One drawing me toward him, coaxing me out of this autumn landscape, beckoning me on toward undying joy.[41]

Although Duncan's novel focuses on the perceptions, ideas, and actions of Augustine Orviston, the experience of Gus with the Ancient One—a force older than time—is emblematic of a fly fisher's mystical and metaphysical orientation, practice and discovery.

Ethical Issues

Even though Maclean and Duncan eloquently and vividly describe the fly-fishing experience, and even though they explore the mythical, mystical, and metaphysical meaning that it generates, neither of them raises fundamental ethical questions about the sport as an activity that disrupts nature and puts fish at risk. It is one thing for an angler to fish for sustenance—to provide food for oneself and one's family, or to engage in commerce that indirectly feeds and supports oneself and one's family. It is altogether a different thing to catch fish simply for the sport of it.

The singeing edge of this issue was posed simply and innocently by the ten-year-old son of David O'Hara, an expert angler and environmental philosopher. When O'Hara once returned from a fishing outing without any fish, his young son asked why he was fishing since they didn't need fish for food. That curious inquiry precipitated a series of ethical questions by O'Hara: Is it justifiable to catch fish and cause them even modest pain when there is no intent to eat them? Is it fair to cause fish to struggle for freedom merely to enjoy the thrill of capturing them? Given that a fish's struggle to get free from the hook and line occasionally results in its injury or death without the angler's finally eating it, is it reasonable to engage in a sport that so victimizes its target? To be sure, these profound questions are addressed at times by avid anglers. Most often, though, they tend to avoid pondering such questions, instead rationalizing their fishing by suggesting that the mouth and jaw tissue of fish have few nerves, or that fish pain is unlike human pain, or that whatever pain might be caused will be quickly forgotten, as evidenced by a fish occasionally being caught twice on the same lure on the same evening.[42]

The most sensitive fly fishers operate with a code designed to protect the health of trout and salmon as much as possible. They practice

---

[41] Ibid., 277–278.
[42] O'Hara and Dickerson, *Downstream*, 98–99.

"catch and release" and use barbless hooks. They bring in a fish as quickly as possible to avoid excess stress on it. They avoid touching the fish, hoping that it will spit out the hook once it has been brought in. When they must hold the fish, finally, they first will wet their hands to minimize the removal of the mucous layer that protects the fish's scales. In the unlikely event that the fish must be killed, this code stresses, it should be done quickly.[43]

Aware of these moral challenges and operating with this fishing ethic, O'Hara and Dickerson avidly pursue the sport of fly fishing. They admit that they fish because they are curious and because in the practice of fly fishing they experience a sense of harmony with creation. Although they infrequently utilize religious terminology in the analysis of their motivations and in the descriptions of their experiences, they allude separately to two Christian hymns and spirituals in their explanation about why they fish and what they derive from the experience. They intimate repeatedly that they fish because they are curious, a mind-activity (rather than a mind*set*) that drives them to discoveries under rocks in rivulets, amid the insect life in riparian habitat, and within the flow of pristine waters. Dickerson further connects his dynamic curiosity to a sense of anticipation akin to hope. He is able thereby to derive deep satisfaction simply through the act of "wanding" a fly toward a likely spot where a trout might hide. Even if he is unable to lure the fish to strike, he is able to enjoy every cast as long as there is the prospect—the hope—of catching a fish.

In their reflections on the art and act of fly fishing, O'Hara and Dickerson allude to the Christian spirituals "Peace like a River" and "Balm in Gilead," because their celebration of the calm and contentment that come with healing—with salvation—resonates with the experience that fly fishing provides to anglers. When I mull over the spiritual significance of the sport, I think instead about a different slave song, "Wade in the Water." Not only does the title of the song identify the action of a fly fisher entering a stream, it also carries a deeper meaning of liberation and healing. Although the verses of the song in no way make reference to fly fishing, their celebration of healing and freedom resonate with the physi-

---

[43] Ibid., 99–100. It is also interesting to note that fly fishing devotee Rabbi Eisenkramer indicates that some anglers use a designated tool to kill the fish, "a small wooden mallet [popularly] called a 'priest'" since it is used to administer last rites (Eisenkramer and Attas, *Fly-Fishing—The Sacred Art*, 40–41).

cal and spiritual call for fly fishers to wade in the water. At one level the title of the slave song refers to the biblical story of the pool at Bethesda where invalids and the ill gathered to wait for God to "trouble" the water, thereby imbuing it with the power to restore physical health for the first entrant. The title of the song, a phrase repeated throughout the refrain, also served to remind escaping slaves to walk in creeks and streams to lose the scent that tracking dogs could follow. For them, to "Wade in the Water" immediately meant that their scent would be washed away, and it suggested the promise for their physical liberation and their spiritual nurture. In an analogous way for fly fishers, the retreat into wilderness waters cleanses and calms their minds and spirits, liberates them from the routines of the workaday world and inspires them to reflect on the meaning of their place in nature.

As adequate as the poetic refrain of "Wade in the Water" might be for denoting aspects of fly fishers' spiritual experience, narratives provide a more expansive literary form for probing the depth of anglers' journeys outward and inward, into nature and into self. Furthermore, because fly fishing itself is a kind of narrative act, as Willard notes, the exploration of the spiritual significance of its discipline can more effectively be pursued in accounts about one's devotion to the sport and the meaning derived from it. In this sense, then, the practice of fly fishing is a story told by the act, an ethereal filament wisping toward a calm pool where its plot hovers in hope and wonder. As a novel, *The River Why* is an exemplary tale through which the narrative act of fly fishing can be cast. It explores the metaphysical quest for existential identity through the art of fly fishing. As a memoir, *A River Runs through It* celebrates the metaphorical kinship between religion and fly fishing, a mystical experience that embraces the wonder, purity, and alterity of wilderness. In both of these literary works, fly fishing serves as an analogical structure for the vocation through which one engages with the world, ordering it as a cosmos and experiencing it as a spiritual mystery. In both of these literary works, moreover, the mystical allure of fly fishing provides the fluid framework through which personal relationships are cast, the meaning of life is perceived, and time itself is set free in the wonder of being.

Muscular Affect
The Power Team and the
Heavy Lifting of Evangelical Salvation

Annie Blazer

"Power is…standing at 6 feet 3 inches, weighing nearly 300 pounds, able to bench press more than 600 pounds…but none of those things even matter, because this man has a love for Jesus in his heart! Please, welcome to the stage…the Bear!"[1]

The audience rose to applaud the massively muscled man running down the aisle of New Hope Baptist Church to join his other Power Team members on the stage. The Power Team is an evangelical organization that sends groups of strong men (and a few women) to churches for multi-day "crusades" meant to bolster church membership and deliver messages of evangelical salvation. I observed the four members of the Power Team that visited Raleigh, North Carolina, for five days in February 2007. The group performed nightly at New Hope Baptist Church and spent their days visiting area schools to conduct motivational assemblies. (The team used a secular version of their performance for public schools and was openly religious at private schools.) At the nightly church performances, the men would bend steel rods, tear phone books in half, and break stacks of bricks, all the while praising Jesus and thanking him for the strength to perform these tasks. I attended these events and talked with the performers, managers, and the huge number of New Hope Baptist Church volunteers responsible for ensuring that all events ran smoothly.

---

[1]I have designated my informants by pseudonyms to preserve confidentiality. These pseudonyms are consistent throughout the text. I have identified some people by their generic position rather than a pseudonym when this was more effective for preserving confidentiality. Whenever I quote someone without a citation, this was an interaction that occurred either during fieldwork, interview or informal conversation.

Before the Power Team's arrival, I met with ministry staff at New Hope Baptist Church to discuss my plan to research the Power Team and write about their performances. The church staff enthusiastically invited me to all the Power Team events they had planned that week. I attended four of the five nightly performances in the church sanctuary, one public school assembly at a local middle school, and a motivational speaking event at Eckerd residential facilities—a juvenile justice short-term residential camp for adjudicated males, ages thirteen to seventeen. I had very little access to the members of the Power Team themselves; they traveled separately and did not socialize before or after performances. Their manager spoke to me often and arranged for me to have a half-hour sit-down interview with one member, Jay, while we were at Eckerd. My descriptions of Power Team performances are composites drawn from the multiple performances I saw during their visit to Raleigh.[2]

The Power Team's church performances oscillated between strength and vulnerability; they delivered narratives that painted themselves as vulnerable (to temptation, to sin, to pride) and then symbolized overcoming this vulnerability through physical feats of strength. The Power Team's embodied performances induced an affective sensation of both power and weakness in the audience, a sensation that aligns with evangelical understandings of humans' relationship to the divine. Many evangelicals see the decision to commit to Christianity as brave or strong, yet requiring weakness and vulnerability on the part of the believer in order to eventually access divine strength.

John Jacobs formed the Power Team in 1976 in Dallas, Texas, as the first evangelistic group devoted to feats of strength.[3] Jacobs's divorce

---

[2] The use of composite anthropology and first-person narratives in religious studies scholarship remains controversial. Karen McCarthy Brown's award-winning *Mama Lola: A Vodou Priestess in Brooklyn* (Berkeley: University of California Press, 1991) did much to mainstream this practice, but some critics see this practice as self-indulgent, since it requires the ethnographer to be a consistent part of the text. In my own work, I have found this approach helpful for working toward the feminist goal of transparent positionality. See *Playing for God: Evangelical Women and the Unintended Consequences of Sports Ministry* (New York: NYU Press, 2015).

[3] The Power Team 2.0, http://www.thepowerteam.com/press.html (accessed 12 August 2016).

in May 2000 scandalized his community[4], and about a dozen members of the Power Team left to form their own ministry—Team Impact, a ministry dedicated to feats of strength that strongly resembled the Power Team in their performances and self-presentation.[5] Jacobs retired from the Power Team in May 2003 following several unsavory incidents including a hasty marriage that was later annulled, charges of assault against Team Impact member Jeff Audas that were later dropped, ministry bankruptcy proceedings that resulted in a reorganization of the Power Team's management, and personal bankruptcy proceedings that were later reversed.[6] Covered extensively in *Charisma Magazine* (a print and online Christian publication aimed at Pentecostal and charismatic Christians), reporters often presented Jacobs's saga as a cautionary tale, but continued to support feats of strength as an effective technique for evangelism. Jacobs eventually went on to form another ministry team dedicated to feats of strength, also headquartered in Dallas, the Next Generation Power Force. All three of these teams seem remarkably similar—they perform the same feats of strength and showcase their muscular bodies in red, white, and blue uniforms.[7]

Given the ongoing success of the original Power Team and the existence of these spin-offs, there can be little doubt that the Power Team

---

[4] Andy Butcher, "'Power Team' Founder Jacobs Divorces," *Charisma Magazine*, 31 October 2000, http://www.charismamag.com/site-archives/134-peopleevents/people-events/180-power-team-founder-jacobs-divorces (accessed 12 August 2016).

[5] About—Team Impact, http://team-impact.com/about (accessed 12 August 2016).

[6] Jeremy Reynalds, "Power Team Founder John Jacobs Faces Assault Charges in Dallas," *Charisma Magazine*, June 2001, http://www.charismamag.com/site-archives/134-peopleevents/people-events/395-power-team-founder-john-jacobs-faces-assault-charge-in-dallas (accessed 12 August 2016). See also "Jon [sic] Jacobs Retires from the Power Team," *Charisma Magazine*, 30 June 2003, http://www.charismamag.com/site-archives/154-peopleevents/people-and-events/955-jon-jacobs-retires-from-the-power-team (accessed 12 August 2016).

[7] A recent article from *Vice* traces the history of the Power Team and suggests that Jacobs's Next Generation Power Force is now defunct. See Rick Paulas, "The Power Team Was the Bloody, Evangelical Freakshow That Ruled the 80s," *Vice*, 4 February 2015, http://www.vice.com/read/evangelical-freak-show-the-power-team-were-christian-superstars-of-the-80s-456 (accessed 12 August 2016).

is very good at what they do. The feats they perform are not fake; they are not charlatans exploiting a gullible audience.[8] They are professional strongmen and expert evangelists, well-trained and experienced, and they have been relying on the same performance structure for forty years. They do this because it works; this performance structure achieves their goals of growing their nightly attendance and gaining conversion decisions from their audience.

All the Power Team performances in Raleigh opened with dramatic introductions of the performers. Like Bear's introduction, the announcer would call out some strength statistics, but then negate the importance of these statistics by identifying the performer as a believer in Christianity. This pattern of focusing on strength followed by emphasizing Christianity continued through each two-hour show. Taking the stage after their introductions, the members of the Power Team took positions behind stacks of bricks. The crowd cheered as the men smashed the brick stacks with their forearms, their fists, even their forehead. Members of the Power Team demanded audience participation during feats of strength: they called for standing up, clapping, shouting, foot-stomping. At the same time, the audience could not participate in the actual brick bashing. The Power Team have well-trained bodies that allow them to demolish obstacles that most of us in attendance would never attempt. As much as audience participation mattered, it also signaled our own weakness in comparison to the strong bodies on stage.

Directly following this first round of demolition, the Power Team gestured to the crowd to sit down, quiet down, and listen. Bear took the microphone and stepped into the spotlight as the audience that had recently been on their feet shouting settled into quiet attention. This moment mirrored his opening introduction; Bear was about to tell us that he is more than a strong body. As is common in evangelical practice, Bear recounted the story of his conversion to Christianity. He followed an oft-

---

[8] Churches that host the Power Team are required to buy all the props that the Power Team uses in their performance. When I toured New Hope Baptist Church before the Power Team's visit, I handled the props. To the best of my knowledge, the steel rods, baseball bats, license plates, and other objects were not manipulated.

employed witnessing strategy—describing how life after conversion was fundamentally different (and better) than life before.[9]

Bear began, "I was a messed-up kid with a lot of anger." He told us that he tried to channel that anger into a career as a professional boxer, and although he became very rich, he eventually lost everything. "I moved home to Minnesota and was sleeping on my mom's couch."

The audience at New Hope Baptist Church had likely heard many stories of conversion and could anticipate that this story of dramatic loss would have a redemptive turn. As was clear, Bear was no longer sleeping on his mom's couch; he was on tour with the Power Team. He continued his story:

> One day, this pretty blonde woman asked me to go to church with her. Now, I didn't want to go to church, but she was so fine, I would have followed her anywhere. So, I went to church. I was walking up to the church and I felt something I had never felt before: fear. And I didn't like it. A man walked up to me and hugged me, saying, "I love you, brother." And I didn't like that. I was not used to men hugging me and certainly not saying I love you. That man couldn't have been more than 150 pounds, but he scared me by telling me that he loved me.

In this story, Bear was not powerful; he was weak. He was scared by a hug; he was afraid of church. This was how we the audience could indeed be like the Power Team. Every member of that crowd could potentially be like Bear by experiencing weakness. Perhaps this church that we all sat in together could be like the loving and scary church that Bear described. At least, it was possible to imagine.

Bear continued his story. He did enter that church, and after a conversation with the pastor agreed to give it a chance for one month. But, he told us, he mainly agreed because he was interested in the blonde. He said:

> I came back the next week and sat in the back row and I thought about what I was going to have for lunch, and then—there was like an arrow went straight into my heart [sound effect on the mic—Phoom!], and another [Phoom!], and another [Phoom!], and the arrows just kept coming. [Phoom! Phoom! Phoom!] And that day, I gave my life to Jesus.

---

[9] For an excellent analysis of witnessing in conservative Christianity, see Susan Friend Harding, *The Book of Jerry Falwell: Fundamentalist Language and Politics* (Princeton, NJ: Princeton University Press, 2001).

The audience began to cheer. Bear waited a beat, and with perfect timing, finished his story, "And that blonde, I married her."[10]

In this story, Bear was like us—he was sitting in an audience in a church listening to a preacher. Here we were, sitting and listening to him, hearing the sounds of invisible arrows [Phoom! Phoom! Phoom!] coming from God or the preacher, capable of changing one's life and guaranteeing marriage to a pretty girl. Bear's story invited the audience to become him, to experience the invisible arrows, to be weak.

After Bear finished his story, the celebratory mood of his conversion tale easily turned to more cheering as the strongmen on stage lined up to showcase their muscular abilities once again. The structure of the night's performance continued to follow this pattern—oscillating between dramatic narratives of human weakness and God's strength and impressive feats of human strength that highlighted the comparative weakness of the onlookers, who did not possess the mighty muscles of the Power Team. I argue that this was intentional and incredibly effective for invoking an emotionally charged atmosphere where audience members could imagine overcoming weakness through evangelical salvation. I hope to show that theory of affect can shed light on why this works.

When I teach about affect theory in my classes, I write this definition of affect on the board: "Affect is the stuff that makes you feel things." What I like about this definition is its vagueness. Theorists of affect often define affect negatively: it is not the same as emotion; it is not linguistic. It is the "stuff" that occurs before or outside of these categories and informs emotional reactions and linguistic interpretations. Cultural theorist Brian Massumi defines affect as a two-sided feedback reaction between potentiality and expression.[11] Affect is the stuff that funnels potentiality into language and action.

A concrete example that scholar of philosophy and religion Abby Kluchin uses to illustrate affect is the experience of walking into a room where two people have been fighting or being a passenger in a car with a

---

[10] The heteronormative implications of this kind of storytelling deserve much more attention than this chapter allows. For excellent examples of scholarship on evangelical gender norms, see Sally K. Gallagher, *Evangelical Identity and Gendered Family Life* (New Brunswick, NJ: Rutgers University Press, 2003) and John P. Bartkowski, *Remaking the Godly Marriage: Gender Negotiation in Evangelical Families* (New Brunswick, NJ: Rutgers University Press, 2001).

[11] Brian Massumi, *Parables for the Virtual: Movement, Affect, Sensation* (Durham, NC: Duke University Press, 2002), 35.

nervous driver. In these instances, one's body reacts to the others' experiences, and this informs how one reacts to the situation. Kluchin emphasizes that affect is not purely individual or subjective; it is transmissible.[12] Affect is not the same as emotional reactions; it is the unidentifiable "stuff" that occurs before we perceive our feelings and before we name our emotions.

Affect contributes to our perceptions and emotions by intensifying or dampening potentialities. In *The Affect Theory Reader*, editors Gregory Seigworth and Melissa Greg offer this description of affect: "Cast forward by its open-ended in-between-ness, affect is integral to a body's perpetual *becoming* (always becoming otherwise, however subtly, than what it already is), pulled beyond its seeming surface-boundedness by way of its relation to, indeed its composition through, the forces of encounter."[13] This description emphasizes that affect is visceral—it is an embodied force that fluctuates between restraining and opening different capacities to act and react. Kathleen Stewart, anthropologist of everyday life, calls affect "lines of promise and threat."[14] Affect is an embodied, pre-linguistic, extra-emotional valence that varies in intensity and foreshadows our emotional responses, interpretations and actions.[15]

The Power Team is first and foremost performative. More akin to sports entertainment than to sports competition, the Power Team constructs itself through narratives and bodily demonstrations without the trappings of referees, rules, and final scores. They are athletic bodies unfettered, and the narrative frames they embrace emerge from both sporting and evangelical arenas. Attention to affect can help us see how this intersection shores up evangelical theology through embodied narratives.

---

[12] Abby Kluchin, "Visceral Theory: Affect and Embodiment," course description for *Folksonomy*, 11 December 2013, http://folksonomy.co/?permalink=3582; accessed 15 August 2016).

[13] Gregory J. Seigworth and Melissa Greg, "An Inventory of Shimmers" in *The Affect Theory Reader*, ed. Gregory J. Seigworth and Melissa Greg (Durham, NC: Duke University Press, 2010), 3.

[14] Kathleen Stewart, *Ordinary Affects* (Durham, NC: Duke University Press, 2007), 129.

[15] Donovan Schaefer's recent book, *Religious Affects*, uses affect theory to push readers to see religion as the realm of emotive relations, rather than essentializable to belief or text. *Religious Affects: Animality, Evolution, and Power* (Durham, NC: Duke University Press, 2015).

During their performances, the Power Team deployed affective tools intended to produce a desire for conversion and belonging. They masterfully delivered highly dramatic stories. Each tale narrated personal and material changes in the life of the athlete, highlighting concrete benefits of converting to Christianity. Josh, the leader of this Power Team contingent, offered a story different from Bear's but following a similar format—life before conversion was bad in some way, and commitment to Christianity changed those bad attributes.

Josh's story is also interesting because it included the Power Team itself as a force that changed his life. As the cheers from watching a high-intensity round of brick-bashing, rod-bending, and phonebook tearing diminished and the energetic music faded out, Josh moved into the spotlight, taking the microphone to tell his life story. "I grew up in Detroit," he began.

> Both my parents were alcoholics and addicted to drugs. My mom waited tables, and my dad sold drugs. I remember being seven years old, waiting in the car for my dad to finish a drug deal. And I knew what was going on. Seven years old, and I knew what was going on.

Josh's delivery was well timed. He knew when to pause to maximize the dramatic effect of his tale. "There would be days when my dad would come home drunk and beat my mom," he continued. "I would be hiding under my bunk bed with my little brother, knowing that he would be coming for me next." Josh detailed the fear that he felt, as well as his desire to protect his little brother from his father's violence. This was the part of the story that illustrated the difficulties and pain of a life without Christianity. Most of the audience would be familiar with this format and primed for the next component, the story of conversion.

"When I was nine years old, the kid that lived next door invited me to a Power Team rally." This piece of information was exciting for the audience. Like Bear's story, which subtly integrated the audience by recounting his experience of sitting in church, Josh made the crowd part of his story too, invoking the idea of a nine-year-old Josh among us in the audience. "That was in 1984. I'd never heard of the Power Team, but it sounded cool, and I wanted to go." The mid-1980s would have been a moment of growth for John Jacob's Power Team. The team would have been touring almost constantly at this time, working hard to establish their legitimacy as a ministry. By the late 1980s, they had reached national fame, and videos of their performances appeared on TBN and other Christian television stations.

The structure of Power Team performances has remained remarkably consistent since that time. Perhaps the audience knew that, perhaps not, but it wasn't difficult to imagine a nine-year-old boy's excitement to see the muscular spectacle of the Power Team. Josh told us that he was able to convince his mother to let him go, despite her reservations about church activities. However, she refused to allow his little brother to go with him. Josh paused dramatically before telling us, "I went, and I was saved that night." The audience cheered.

This was another turn in the narrative that many in the audience might have been able to predict. Josh converted, made a decision to change his life, and now the story should contain rewards for that decision. Josh did not disappoint the audience. He told of a desire to attend church regularly, and when his parents refused to take him, he took a bus that the church provided for children who attended church without their parents. "I remember they handed out Tootsie Rolls on the bus. I started rubbing it into my little brother. Like, hey, I'm getting candy, and you're not. He started bugging my mom to let him go too, and eventually she let him. He got saved when he was seven years old."

Again, there was applause. Josh was starting to build now. Many in the audience could anticipate what would happen next as these two children would surely turn to their parents with a desire to convert them. Just as the Power Team's feats of strength over the course of the night became progressively more difficult, Josh's story built to his largest challenge: the conversion of his drug-addicted and abusive parents.

"My mom started to notice some changes in us, and she worried that the church was brainwashing us. She decided to check it out for herself." Josh paused here, perhaps to let us know that another celebratory moment was coming. "And she was saved that day." There was more applause, but Josh did not pause long enough to lose momentum. He continued, "Eventually, we convinced our dad to come too. That day, I saw my father cry, shed tears in church, and commit his life to Jesus Christ." The applause was thunderous.

Josh's story was thin on details, providing just enough information for the audience to envision his family's struggles and their desire to live differently. This lack of detail could invoke a sense of solidarity in the crowd, a way to imagine similarities between Josh's troubled home and the variety of home lives surely present. Josh paused to look at the audience, proud to deliver the icing on the cake: the beneficial life that followed conversion. "My dad is now a pastor to a church of 15,000 in Texas." The applause began again and continued as Josh concluded his tale. "My mom and my brother are also in the ministry full-time. And as for me, well ..." He stretched his arms wide, gesturing to the stage, puffing his chest and emphasizing his muscularity. "I'm a leader in the Power Team!" The story had come full circle. The nine-year-old boy who committed to Christianity at a Power Team rally in 1984 was now standing before us celebrating his life changes and his career as a muscular evangelist.

Josh's tale was thrilling. He inspired visible reactions in the crowd—gasps, cheers, perhaps even tears. Josh's story mirrored the structure of the night's performance—obstacles must be surmounted (or destroyed) to achieve salvation and success. For Josh and for many of the evangelicals present, the decision to commit to Christianity (to "get saved") was the most important decision a person could make. They would see it as a decision that God wanted to reward (with material and social success) and that had eternal consequences (because they believe this decision is the sole factor in human access to heaven after death). Listeners might have had an affective, visceral sense of satisfaction when Josh concluded his story; standing before us as the leader of the Power Team, his body serving as evidence of his own success. After telling the story of his conversion, he then demonstrated the power of his body by stepping behind a tall stack of ice blocks and bringing his forearms down to smash the ice to pieces—a slippage between the power of God to change lives and the power of Josh to change, to destroy, the objects before him.

Josh's narrative offered to include us, the audience, as capable of change, power and fulfillment through Christian conversion. It also held us (literally) at arm's length by concluding the tale with a feat of strength that was beyond our power. This is perhaps most usefully analyzed through the lens of "cruel optimism," an analysis of affect developed by Lauren Berlant. Berlant argues that life in the contemporary age includes affective attachments to unattainable fantasies of "the good life." Our inability to recognize the unattainability of such fantasies makes our optimism cruel. She shows that humans cling to these fantasies to navigate day-to-day life, despite the fact that these fantasies lack concrete strategies for improving material conditions.[16] Watching Josh tell a story of spiritual and material reward cultivated an emotional optimism and sense of celebration. While it might seem that watching him then smash a

---

[16] Lauren Berlant, *Cruel Optimism* (Durham, NC: Duke University Press, 2011).

stack of ice blocks, a feat that separated him from the audience, would shatter the fantasy of rewards for conversion, I observed the opposite. Josh's embodied power shored up his narrative, became evidence for his claim that conversion offers a good life full of familial connection, social success and muscular mastery.

Another consistent element of a Power Team performance is the collection of donations. This money goes toward the operating budget of the Power Team. The "love offering" continued the Power Team performance pattern of oscillating between energetic feats of strength and dramatic story telling. At New Hope Baptist Church, as the volunteer cleanup crew swept up the ice shards, the four strong men lined up at the front of the stage, each preparing a different human feat. Jay stepped forward with an old-fashioned rubber hot water bottle and told the crowd that he would blow into it until it exploded. He began to blow into the water bottle, inflating it and increasing the pressure. The water bottle flew out of his hands, surprising him. "That's not supposed to happen," he exclaimed to the laughter of the crowd. He started again, huffing and puffing into the pink rubber bag. He gestured with his hands for the crowd to cheer him on, but apparently he was dissatisfied with the level of audience energy. He took a break from inflating the bottle to turn to Josh and say, "Hey, remember when we were working that retirement home? Those old ladies were cheering louder than this crowd!" He said it good-humoredly, but the audience got the message, increasing their applause and cheering. The hot water bottle exploded into shreds of pink rubber with a loud pop.

Wasting no time, Josh stepped forward holding two decks of playing cards, and told us that he would tear the decks in half with the strength of his hands. The crowd cheered, as he tore through the cards and tossed them into the air like confetti. Big Tom stepped forward with three iron rods, each one inch in diameter. He held the three of them together over his head to show the audience. The crowd cheered expectantly—bending these heavy rods in half had occurred on previous nights, but never three at the same time. Tom lowered the bars behind his body, bracing them diagonally against his torso to bend them partway. Then, he gripped the end of the bars in front of his muscular, sweaty body, and grunted as he bent the rods in half. He held the bent bars over his head in victory as the crowd cheered wildly, the crowd's energy increasing with each member's performance.

Bear was the final strongman in the lineup, and he declared that he would rip apart eight cans of soda with the strength of his bare hands. As Jay handed him the sodas, he twisted the cans in half, spraying Sprite onto the first few rows of the audience. Jay handed him the cans in quick succession, the audience yelling out the count of how many Bear had destroyed: "Five! Six! Seven!" When he reached the eighth can, he did not twist it apart like the others, but smashed it full against his forehead, yelling, "Yeah! Yeah!" heightening further the pumped up energy of the crowd.

Josh stepped forward, holding a microphone. Riding the energy of the crowd, he began speaking: "Something is wrong with our schools in America today!" The crowd cheered in agreement, but their intensity was dying down. Josh launched into statistics on teen pregnancy and teen suicide, repeating his refrain after each, "Something is wrong with schools in America." The Power Team claims to be one of the top school assemblies in America, and the crowd was likely familiar with the Power Team's mission to speak to school groups.[17] As Josh continued to talk about the problems with American schools, volunteers began to station themselves throughout the sanctuary with white buckets, signaling to those familiar with church services that this was the moment when the Power Team would collect donations.

Josh told us about one reporter who asked him if he really thought he was making a difference with the Power Team's school assembly program. In response to this reporter (and to those in the audience that might be asking themselves the same question), Josh told the story of one assembly at an elementary school where he had called on a seven-year-old girl in the bleachers, asking her, "What's your dream?" She responded that she wanted to be a singer, and Josh told her, "Oh, that's a great dream! Come on down here!" The girl came down to the front of the assembly, and Josh handed her one end of a towel. He held the other end and pulled a little so that she had to pull back to keep hold of it. "I kept telling her: hold onto your dreams, hold on to your dreams! And I could tell that she was getting excited, so I decided to play it up even more. I was telling her, 'You're going to be the best singer. I'm going to buy your CD one day!'"

Josh paused here to signal that he was coming to a climactic and serious moment in his anecdote. "After that assembly, a teacher came up to

---

[17] "Power Team Press Release," http://www.thepowerteam.com/images/uploads/Power_Team_Press_Release.pdf (accessed 12 August 2016).

138

me and said, 'You don't know what you've done for that little girl. Both her parents died in a car accident a month ago, and she really needed that kind of encouragement.'" Josh looked out into the crowd and returned to the reporter's question, saying, "So, yes, I think I am making a difference in our schools." The crowd cheered.

The stories that the Power Team tells may or may not be true. There is no way to find out whether Josh really had that conversation with the reporter or whether there really was a little girl who lost her parents inspired by his assembly performance. However, the veracity of these stories is irrelevant when analyzing affect. Whether or not that story actually happened, audience members could feel like they were part of making stories like that become real by donating to the Power Team. They could feel like they too were making a difference in American schools. The volunteers began circulating with the white buckets, collecting donations. Josh called out that they were $9000 short of their budget for this trip; they needed a "love offering" from this crowd so that they could keep doing their work and keep making a difference. "You know," Josh continued, "a dinner out costs $100; a movie out with the family costs $100—maybe you could sacrifice those things this month to help the Power Team." Donating could become empowering—most members of the audience could not tear soda cans apart with their bare hands, but donating could become a form of participation that connected the audience member to the Power Team. Just like the strongmen needed the support of the audience's cheers to complete their feats of strength, this was another moment when the Power Team needed the audience's help.

When Sharon Mazer published her analysis of a 1991 Power Team performance, she expressed deep discomfort with the economic portion of the event. She described several different pitches for donations that John Jacobs delivered throughout the performance including three framed pages from the "original 1613 King James Bible" available for a donation of $1000 each. According to Mazer's description of the show: "The commodification of salvation is unrelenting."[18] Perhaps Mazer was not the only one to raise these concerns, because by 2008, the Power Team's call for donations had shifted; it only occurred once and no Bible pages were on offer. Josh called out to the crowd, "If you don't have money, then don't give it! We don't want your money if you need your money. If you decide to give with a credit card, don't give more than you

---

[18] Sharon Mazer, "The Power Team: Muscular Christianity and the Spectacle of Conversion," *The Drama Review* 38 no. 4 (Winter 1994): 178.

can pay back in a month. We only want cheerful givers!" There was much shuffling in the crowd as people filled out donation cards, shoved cash into envelopes, wrote checks, and dropped their donations into the passing white buckets. Wanting to give people plenty of time to complete their donations, but also not wanting to lose the momentum of the performance, the Power Team manager took to the stage to raffle off Power Team merchandise (also available for sale in the lobby after the show).

For Mazer, the collection of donations cast a shadow on the Power Team's credibility, but it did not seem disruptive at New Hope Baptist Church. The collection of an offering happened every Sunday in that sanctuary, and the concurrent raffle maintained the feeling of being at a sporting event—a mashing of contexts that made both activities feel appropriate for the situation.

As the raffle winners claimed their prizes, New Hope Baptist Church volunteers assembled the props for the final feat of strength. There were two large rectangular boards with hundreds of nails sticking through to create a bed of nails. There was also a giant log with handles attached to it. Josh returned to the microphone to explain what was about to happen; Jay was going to lie in-between these boards of nails, and Bear was going to lie on the top board and bench press that giant log.

"Now, this is a dangerous thing to do," Josh told the crowd. "If these boards of nails are misplaced, they can go into your body. We had one Power Team member do this with improperly placed boards, and the nails went a quarter inch into his abdomen!" I heard gasps around me, and tension built as Bear and Big Tom helped Jay lie down with his back on the bed of nails. They then positioned the other board of nails on top of him so that he had nails facing both sides of his body. Josh continued, "Bear is going to bench press this 300-pound log, and Bear himself weighs about 300 pounds, so that's 600 pounds of pressure on Jay's body!"

Some volunteers helped Bear get into position, lying face up on top of the wooden board, stacked on top of the nail-sandwiched Jay. Jay's arms tensed as he began to push against the wooden board on top of him. It took three straining volunteers and Big Tom to lift the giant log and position it so that Bear could grip the handles. When they let go, the full 600 pounds of pressure weighed down on Jay's body.

"How many times do you think he can bench press this? Ten? Fifteen? Count with me! One! Two!" The crowd joined Josh's counting as Bear began bench pressing the log. Growing louder and louder, the crowd went wild when Bear reached his final lift, number twenty-five. When Bear came down from the board, he was excited, gesturing with his arms for the crowd to keep cheering. Volunteers carefully removed the board from Jay's body and helped him up. I could see even from halfway back in the sanctuary that there were red marks on his skin from the nail points. Josh held up his hand to quell the cheering, asking Jay if he was okay. When Jay nodded yes and Josh clapped him on the shoulder, the cheering erupted again.

This was the final strength feat that the Power Team executed that evening, but it was not the climax of the performance. All the Power Team's church performances culminated in an altar call. An altar call is a widespread evangelical ritual where a religious leader asks those present to make a public declaration of their commitment to Christianity. Most evangelicals adhere to a narrow understanding of salvation: only those who openly declare their belief in Jesus's divine sacrifice are able to enter heaven after death. All others are doomed to hell.[19]

Josh began the altar call by reminding the audience of these principles. He told the crowd, "This has been God's plan since the beginning of time." Josh told us that God plans for our salvation, that God desires humans to choose salvation and that we can do this by expressing belief in Jesus's resurrection. He also told us that failure to do so would have eternal consequences. "God designed heaven for people who accept Jesus Christ as their savior. Without Jesus, you will go to hell. It's so simple. Why do people choose the devil and hell? I don't know. Why would you want to spend eternity in a place called hell? I want Jesus!" The sanctuary erupted with applause.

The lights in the sanctuary dimmed and the crowd grew expectantly quiet. Josh asked the audience to bow their heads. The woman sitting next to me whispered to her son, "Do you want to go up there?" Clearly, she was aware of the altar call practice of inviting believers forward to the front of the crowd. When her son nodded, she whispered, "I'm so proud

---

[19] For two excellent analyses of evangelical theology regarding salvation and damnation, see Christian Smith, *American Evangelicalism: Embattled and Thriving* (Chicago: Chicago University Press, 1998) and Jason Bivins, *Religion of Fear: The Politics of Horror in Conservative Evangelicalism* (New York: Oxford University Press, 2008).

of you." I saw several whispered conversations occurring throughout the sanctuary. Some families and groups stood to leave, but nearly all of the gathered people followed Josh's instructions and lowered their heads.

"With all heads bowed and nobody looking around," Josh continued, "who wants to be part of this prayer? Who wants to commit their life to Jesus?" He asked for those who wanted to commit to raise their hands, and he led a prayer that most evangelicals would be familiar with as a "sinner's prayer." While this prayer does not have a specific wording, it generally contains several elements central to evangelical theology including an acknowledgement of the sinful state of humanity, a belief in Jesus as the son of God, a belief in the reality of Jesus's crucifixion and resurrection, and a personal commitment to prioritize these beliefs in one's life.[20] There was an embodied component to the prayer; believers were asked to "open their hearts" to accept Jesus within. Throughout the night, the Power Team had given Jesus the credit for their strength. This prayer was an opportunity to also access that strength. The feeling of being so different in ability from these muscular men could be mitigated by the solidarity of saying the same words as Josh, as imagining the same divine being dwelling in their hearts.

It is hard to say how many people in that sanctuary were participating in this ritual for the first time. In general, evangelicals encourage recommitment, and many evangelicals have walked forward at more than one altar call, reaffirming their original commitments. As Josh's prayer ended and the audience lifted their heads, the praying people might have noticed the small groups of people slipping out the sanctuary door—but from where I sat, halfway back on the lower level, most faces remained riveted on Josh, seemingly totally invested in this climactic religious moment of the night. More important than the muscular exploits we had watched all evening, this moment of public submission was the Power Team's central mission.

Josh began a short, highly charged story, emphasizing the seriousness of publicly declaring a commitment to Christianity. He told us that during the Boxer Rebellion in China, Christianity was outlawed and po-

---

[20] Bill Bright, the founder of Campus Crusade for Christ (now called Cru), established the standardized elements to this prayer in his early publications for his organization. See John G. Turner, Bill Bright and Campus Crusade for Christ: The Renewal of Evangelicalism in Postwar America (Chapel Hill: University of North Carolina Press, 2008).

lice forced Christians to abandon their religion. Josh recounted one example, telling us that the police showed up at a Christian school and demanded that the students and teachers spit on a cross or else be killed. He said:

> Eleven people came forward and spit on that cross, but a little twelve-year-old girl, she came forward and refused to spit on the cross. She said, "I will never spit on that cross because that man died for me when no one else would." And they put a gun to her head and shot her.

Josh formed his hand into the shape of a gun and gestured as if to kill an imaginary child in front of him. His expression was serious.

This story of the twelve-year-old girl may or may not be true, but it was compelling because it provided a powerful juxtaposition to the feats of strength we had been watching all night. Josh stood on the stage, dripping with sweat from bending steel rods and tearing phonebooks, and expressed admiration for a young girl who didn't fight back but submitted to her own death. Josh's muscular, vital body starkly opposed the image of a dead twelve-year-old girl, and he described a different idea of strength—strength through submission—than the idea of strength as dominance that the Power Team's bodies demonstrated. With this new version of strength layered over the previous one, Josh became strongman, brave submitter, and revival leader all wrapped into one.

He extended the promises of these identities to the audience. Remember, Josh himself first committed to Christianity at a Power Team rally when he was a child—this was the audience's chance to be like Josh, to be like the twelve-year-old girl, to be both kinds of strong. The anticipation continued to build as Josh told us he would count to three, and then those who wished to commit should come forward. When he reached three, there was a dramatic swell of people toward the stage. Many of them were children, but I also saw whole families, couples, and older men joining the growing pack. Most of the congregation rose to their feet, cheering for those walking by, making gestures of prayer or joining the stream of people heading to the stage. Josh looked down at the crowd, saying, "I just want to hug you right now! But, you probably don't want that though, because I'm all sweaty." He was very sweaty, and this moment of levity amplified a feeling of celebration that was growing among those who had stayed to watch or participate in this ritual. The lights had come up after the count of three and there was a sense of release after the tension of Josh's story of the shooting of a twelve-year-old girl.

As the crowd at the stage continued to grow, I could no longer tell who was actively committing and who was just standing up. Josh said to the gathering crowd, "God loves you. I'm proud of you. Let's honor them," and the whole church applauded. "You out there," Josh addressed those who refrained from approaching the stage,

> You can't rejoice, you need to be here! If Jesus were here, would you still be sitting there or would you be jumping? It is no accident that you are here tonight; God planned for you to be here tonight. Satan wants to make us think this isn't real. But we can rejoice, because it is real.

Josh extended the promise of his saved identity, but accompanied this with a threat; only those who have committed to Christianity can rejoice, and those who fail to commit have fallen prey to Satan's lies and are doomed to hell. The energy of the room affectively reinforced his promise and threat.

A leader from New Hope Baptist Church said a short prayer over the crowd at the foot of the stage, and volunteers led them out of the sanctuary to another room where there would be more praying and they would be asked to fill out commitment cards. Josh called out over the noisy crowd, "Parents, if you have a son or daughter down here, you are more than welcome to go with them. We're not doing any brainwashing; we're not going to give them any creepy Kool-Aid. We just want to send them a letter, keep in touch, reaffirm the commitment they made here tonight." He asked the audience to cheer until every last one of them had left the sanctuary. The crowd cheered exuberantly.

The cheers and applause echoed the previous cheers of the night—those that encouraged the Power Team members to complete their feats of strength. Then too, the Power Team had demanded that the crowd cheer until they had fully finished their feat. This was a different moment, cheering for the physically ordinary figures of children and adults walking out of the sanctuary. Their bodies were so unlike the Power Team, but they experienced the same enthusiastic applause as the strongmen. Overshadowing the Power Team with the sheer force of their numbers, this advancing crowd was now the star of the show. Josh's story had aligned these believers with the vulnerable twelve-year-old girl, but this applause likened them to the strong Power Team.

Evangelical understandings of salvation rely on this combination of vulnerability and strength—the decision to commit to God is brave and strong but requires submission and weakness that will then allow access to divine strength. Jesus is both vulnerable to human death and an example of divine strength and power over death. The Power Team's altar call, and indeed the whole structure of their performance, walked this tightrope of vulnerability and strength, managing to celebrate both and to include the audience in this balancing act. Through cheering, donating, or walking forward for the altar call, the Power Team invited the audience to experience intense vulnerability and strength. The Power Team invoked their own vulnerability to encourage vulnerability in others, even as they displayed and promised strength.

Below the surface of the Power Team's ongoing success is an affective dimension, carefully curated to promise (and threaten) the audience with the intensity of human vulnerability, human power and communal action. It is because the Power Team's affect resonates with and amplifies evangelical ideas of salvation that they have been able to consistently tour, draw crowds and hold altar calls for forty years, and will likely do so for years to come. They hold out a fantasy to the audience through their muscular power and promise access to that power through conversion to evangelical Christianity. The Power Team's masterfully crafted extension of power/vulnerability/strength/weakness affectively appeals to their audience by enveloping them in a larger narrative of divine meaning.

Redeeming Sports Violence
Mixed Martial Arts Ministries as a Remedy for Gender Anxieties in American Evangelicalism

Scott Strednak Singer

Blessed be the Lord my rock, who trains my hands for war,
and my fingers for battle.
—Psalm 144:1, NKJV

When I'm in the cage, I'm full of rage
I'll ground-pound, I'll kick you in the face
Yeah it's all good, 'cause I'm in the right place
The power I get is driven from God,
So don't be mad 'cause it's just my job.
—K-Drama, *Jesus Didn't Tap*

A few minutes after breaking Frankie Edgar's nose with a kick to the face late in the second round, the African-American-Korean mixed martial artist (MMA) Ben Henderson celebrated earning the Ultimate Fighting Championship (UFC) lightweight title by dedicating the victory to his Lord and Savior Jesus Christ, a message that was immediately translated for thousands of witnesses in the Saitama, Japan, arena. There is nothing unusual about Christian athletes giving the glory to God post-contest, nor about Henderson's claim that his faith shapes his personal conduct in his professional world. To see the bloodied and bruised Henderson, however, or his UFC compatriots Randy Couture and Vitor Belfort offer their testimonies after demonstrating their superior talents for inflicting and enduring pain, is disconcerting for many who see a disconnect between the professional obligations of fighters and the ethical dictates of the faith they proclaim on international television.

The issue of sports violence has troubled a number of scholars who are suspicious of the viability of professional sports as an arena for evangelism, or at least one fraught with problems from a theological perspective. This is particularly true of Christian scholars working at secular universities. Researchers Robert Higgs and Michael Braswell conclude that "sports are about the chosen ones, those who are able to make the team—the fit, the able and the talented. All religions at their best are about caring for the unchosen, the rejects, those who don't qualify for any team."[1] Kinesiologist Shirl J. Hoffman claims that "any reasonable person of any theological persuasion"[2] can recognize that a sport such as MMA is too dangerous for participation. Focusing on the ethical quandaries of MMA, UK-based theologians Nick Watson and Brian Brock conclude that "boxing and MMA are immoral and, are thus, not appropriate or helpful for humans (with Christian belief) to participate in, and/or watch; however, within God's economy these activities may engender some moral goods (e.g., positive character development and healthy civil engagement = social harmony)."[3] For such scholars, having a professional career as a pain-inducing, back-fisting, spin-kicking fighter, or being a fan, promoter, or sponsor of such contests, is anathema to Christian faith. Cage fighting and Christianity just don't mix.

Despite the misgivings among such academics, however, MMA is becoming a commonplace site of witnessing in the twenty-first century. Para-church MMA ministries such as Anointed Fighter and the MMA Chaplains Association cater to fierce flocks of men and women, encouraging amateur competitors to integrate their pastime with their faith, at the same time as professional fighters use this public platform to promote the faith of Jesus Christ. At the local level, numerous congregations across the United States have begun to add amateur MMA training to their ministerial programming.[4] While some ministries offer this service

---

[1] Robert Higgs and Michael Braswell, *An Unholy Alliance: The Sacred and Modern Sports* (Macon, GA: Mercer University Press, 2004), 236.

[2] Shirl J. Hoffman, *Good Game: Christianity and the Culture of Sports* (Waco, TX: Baylor University Press), 192.

[3] Nick Watson and Brian Brock, "Christianity, Boxing, and Mixed Martial Arts: Reflections on Morality, Vocation, and Well-Being," *Journal of Religion and Society* 17 (2015): 12–13. See also Joe Carter et al., "Is Cage Fighting Ethical for Christians?" *The Christian Post*, 25 January 2012, http://www.christianitytoday.com/ct/2012/january/cage-fighting.html (accessed 1 July 2016).

[4] A *New York Times* article from 2010 estimated the number of such programs to be around 700. Although this number has been repeated in academic articles and around the blogosphere, this estimate was based solely on conjecture. Hard figures are hard to come by, in part because Christian MMA gyms,

to female congregants, most of the organizational leadership, participants, and spectators of these programs are the men of the congregations. The spread and development of such ministries shows that MMA-related programming, sermons, and viewing parties are becoming increasingly popular ways of attracting men to the Christian faith.

This integration of faith, fists, machismo, commercialism, and entertainment raises numerous questions. Chiefly, if Christianity and MMA are as antithetical as some scholars, senators, liberal Protestant ministers, evangelical authors—such as *The Gospel Coalition's* Joe Carter—and other members of the genteel, intellectual class have suggested, then why do such ministries continue to have massive appeal among so many evangelical Protestants?[5] Conversely, why do other evangelical luminaries—including charismatic pastor Mark Driscoll, Focus on the Family's Ryan Dobson, and the Southern Baptist Theological Seminary's president, Rev. Dr. Albert Mohler—defend the sport's integration into Christian men's outreach programs? What are the qualities of MMA that some U.S. evangelical communities find so attractive, and what outcomes do proponents of Christian MMA ministries hope they will produce?

This essay seeks to answer these questions by contextualizing Christian MMA within a larger historical framework and showcasing the internal logic of the Christian MMA worldview. I contend that these ministries are best understood as a means by which U.S. evangelical communities, typically but not exclusively middle-class and conservative, negotiate masculine Christian identity, and through which they counteract the perceived emasculation of Protestant Christianity. To do so, I look back at sporting violence in western Christian theological history, before turning my attention to the advent of professionalized MMA in the early 1990s and the gender anxieties evident in middle-class Protes-

---

summer camps, participant ministries, church viewing parties, Christian MMA conferences, and the like are often infrequent, are founded quickly and are often dissolved quickly. In that way, they tend to mirror larger association and disassociation trends within evangelical communities. See R.M. Schneiderman, "Flock is Now a Fight Team in Some Ministries," *The New York Times*, 1 February 2010, http://www.nytimes.com/2010/02/02/us/02fight.html (accessed 14 May 2016).

[5] Joe Carter, "Jesus Is Not a Cage Fighter," *The Gospel Coalition*, 30 May, 2014, https://www.thegospelcoalition.org/article/jesus-is-not-a-cagefighter (accessed 1 May 2016).

tantism. From there I examine how Christian MMA seeks to assuage those anxieties by re-masculinizing Jesus and presenting MMA as an arena in which the "truth" of masculine Christian identity can be established.

A History of Violence

Though commercialized mixed martial arts is a modern phenomenon designed for a contemporary audience and utilizing twenty-first century techniques of mass communication and advertising to build a global brand, it also has important historical antecedents that inform today's interpretations of religion, gender, and sporting violence. Early Christians interpreted the relation between religious practice and sporting participation through the Hellenistic athletic culture of the city-states in which their communities first flourished. In the *gymnasia* (all-male schools), boys from well-to-do families trained in wrestling, javelin tossing, and *pankration* (a forerunner to mixed martial arts), alongside lessons in rhetoric, math, and philosophy. Training in the arts of war aided in the internalization of gender-specific roles, such as protectors or conquerors, and helped privileged boys prepare for their social duties within the city-state. From very early on, elite male athletic training was tied to militarism, nationalism, and masculine identity.[6]

Over the next five centuries, as Christianity spread around the Mediterranean, Church fathers struggled to curb their flocks' enthusiasm for gladiatorial spectacle. John Chrysostom, Tertullian, and Augustine each chastised their fellow Christians for attending the games of the colosseums and amphitheaters, which Theodore of Mopseustia suggested "the Devil introduced into the world under the pretext of amusement, and through which he leads the souls of men into perdition."[7] St. Augustine, perhaps the most influential of post-biblical Christian thinkers, lamented that viewing such blood sports altered the dispositions of good men, turning them into men who were "delighted with the wicked contest and

---

[6] See Stephen G. Miller, *Ancient Greek Athletics* (New Haven, CT: Yale University Press, 2004); Stephen G. Miller and Paul Christesen, *Arete: Greek Sports from Ancient Sources* (Berkeley: University of California Press, 2012).

[7] Quoted in Shirl J. Hoffman, "Harvesting Souls in the Stadium: The Rise of Sport Evangelism," in *Sport and Christianity: Historical and Contemporary Perspectives*, ed. Nick J. Watson and Andrew Parker (New York: Routledge Press, 2013), 131–149.

drunk with blood lust."[8] Such warnings and exhortations, however, apparently did little to curb the laity's infatuation. Hoffman notes that while gentile athletic culture contained many elements anathematic to proto-Christian culture (self-aggrandizement, aggression, and so on), it is "naïve to imagine that [initiates'] conversions brought swift and sweeping changes in their view of sports."[9] Such prohibitions continued to be issued by ecclesiastic figures over the next few centuries, indicating how pervasive and entrenched pagan athletic culture was in early Christian societies.

Throughout the Middle Ages, athletic contests that church leaders had once prohibited were occasionally integrated into institutional religious practice, once their financial and evangelistic utility had been demonstrated. In the High and Late Middle Ages, Christian sport discourse largely focused on militaristic sports and the manner in which they could aid or hinder the growth of the faith. In the eleventh century, Bishop Odo of Bayeux encouraged monks under his command to train in the arts of medieval jousting tournaments, finding them well suited to his political agenda and that of his half-brother, William the Conqueror.[10] Even though participation in those tournaments was prohibited at several church councils throughout the twelfth and thirteenth centuries, they were permitted by other clerical leaders on the grounds that they attracted what Bernard of Clairvaux called "mighty men of valor" into the faith, who might themselves spread the domain of the Roman church through putting skills honed in the tournaments and melees to work in the Crusades against Muslims, Jews, and Byzantine Christians.[11] Elsewhere, the Bishop of Tréguier denounced the peasant sport of mob-football as a "dangerous and pernicious" game which engendered "ill-feeling, rancor,

---

[8] Augustine, *The Confessions of St. Augustine*, book 6, chs. vii–viii, trans. and ed. by Albert Cook Outler (Mineola, NY: Dover Publications, 2002), 94.

[9] Hoffman, *Good Game*, 24.

[10] John Marshall Carter, "Sport, War, and the Three Orders of Feudal Society: 700–1300," *Military Affairs* 49, no. 3 (July 1985): 132–139.

[11] These festivals were banned by papal prohibition at the Councils of Clermont (1130), Reims (1131), the Second Lateran (1139), the Synod of Reims (1148) and the Third Lateran (1179), among others. See Richard W. Kauper, *Chivalry and Violence in Medieval Europe* (Cambridge, UK: Oxford University Press, 1999), 80; Bernard of Clairvaux quoted in Christopher Tyerman, *England and the Crusades: 1095–1588* (Chicago: University of Chicago Press, 1988), 167.

and enmities" among the men who played it. However, local priests, whose parishes hosted these games and whose coffers were dependent upon the donations such events generated, continued to support the practice, despite official sanction from their superiors.[12] Financial incentives and local bragging rights seem to have supplanted moral dilemmas among the leaders, participants, and spectators of local congregations, despite official sanction from institutional superiors. Infused with evangelism, militarism, money, competition, and ideals of masculinity, these contests proved to be excellent recruiting grounds for church leaders, who believed such men could aid in the preservation and advancement of the faith.

During the Reformation, the value of physical exertion lay within its recuperative function and its ability to promote docility. Despite Puritan calls to restrain leisure activities, the English King Charles I's Declaration on Sport insisted that English men were not to be denied running, fencing, and wrestling. Recognizing their political utility, the king remarked that "if these times were taken from them, the meaner (read: rougher, less socially respectable) sort that labor[ed] hard all week should have no recreations at all to refresh their spirits."[13] For Charles, as for latter social reformers, the more violent sports provided an acceptable social outlet for aggressiveness that might otherwise manifest in social unrest.

Combat sports also found a home within colonial America, the practice of which often reflected shifting interpretations of manhood grounded in distinctions of social class. In the colonial South, plantation owners, royal governors, and others of the gentry held contests in targeting (archery), wrestling, running, and cudgeling among themselves. The games and their prizes—swords, rifles, boots, saddles and money—continued to valorize those contests whose martial utility, and thus their

---

[12] L. Gougaud, "La Soule en Bretagne et les Jeux Similaires du Cornwall et du Pays de Galles," *Annales de Bretagne* 27, no. 4 (1911), 571–604; Robert W. Henderson, *Bat, Ball, and Bishop: The Origin of Ballgames* (Champaign: University of Illinois Press, 2001).

[13] Charles I, "The King's Majesty's Declaration to His Subjects Concerning Lawful Sports to Be Used," in *Documents Illustrative of English Church History*, ed. Henry Gee and William John Hardy (New York: Macmillan, 1896), 528–532.

masculinity, was self-evident.[14] Such games also provided a space in which landed gentlemen could display their conformity to an elite standard of masculinity that was increasingly (but not completely) distinguished from manual labor, while retaining significant emphasis upon physical prowess.

By the eighteenth century, the landed gentry had developed its own more genteel forms of lower-class contests, replacing gouging (a no-holds barred competition which frequently ended with competitors ripping each-other's eyes out or ears off or biting off a nose) with the more formalized contests of boxing and duels, which were popularly construed as a tests of internal grit, framed as a superior substitute for brute force.[15] These class distinctions between legitimate and illegitimate means of displaying conformity to hegemonic masculinity continued to frame clerical discussions of sports ethics in what became the United States, becoming a recurrent feature of Christian sport discourse.

In the late nineteenth century, reformers in both the United States and Great Britain called for the church to return to a robust manliness, a term synonymous with both physical and moral strength. This muscular Christianity, as it came to be known, was a response to a perceived "crisis of masculinity" among Victorian-era reformers who feared that middle-class managerial work had an emasculating effect upon men in the cities. Games such as rugby and boxing, once prohibited for being too violent, were deemed permissible and legitimate channels through which boyish rambunctiousness could be harnessed into martial skill. Not insignificantly, these games were first promoted at the elite schools like Oxford University and the boarding schools for the male heirs of British lords and the sons of England's emerging managerial class, before they emerged in the urban reform movements like the Young Men's Christian Association.[16] If such boys were to become men, it was thought, they would need to be properly socialized through physical struggle.

Proponents of muscular Christianity considered a properly guided violent disposition innate to true manliness. Advocate Thomas Carlyle

---

[14] See Nancy L. Struna, *People of Prowess: Sport, Leisure, and Labor in Early Anglo-America* (Urbana: University of Illinois Press, 1996), 114–115.

[15] See Elliott J. Gorn, "Gouge and Bite, Pull Hair and Scratch: The Social Significance of Fighting in the Southern Backcountry," *The American Historical Review* 90 (1985): 18–43.

[16] Nick Watson et al., "The Development of Muscular Christianity in Victorian Britain and Beyond," *Journal of Religion and Society* 7 (2005).

believed "[m]an is created to fight; he is perhaps best of all definable as a born soldier; his life 'a battle and a march' under the right General."[17] His fellow enthusiast, novelist Thomas Hughes concurred, adding "[f]rom the cradle to the grave, fighting, rightly understood, is...the real, highest, honest business, of every son of man."[18] The belief that manliness involved fighting for a good cause under the direction of God simultaneously tied the muscular Christian movement to British imperialism and to the Christian faith's historic legacy of authorizing violent recreations when they became politically expedient. For advocates of muscular Christianity, such a position counteracted what theologian Charles Kingsley dubbed "the poison of effeminacy [...] sapping the vitality of the Anglican Church."[19]

Like their English counterparts, U.S. leaders of muscular Christianity championed some violent forms of physical exertion which were taboo but which they viewed as necessary trainings for boys to healthily develop *as* men. Bruce Barton, an influential writer, presumed that healthy, well-socialized boys had an innate taste for and infatuation with violence from a young age:

> Who of us does not remember the fine thrill of appreciation with which he welcomed Samson into his list of heroes—and David? ... When they killed a lion or a giant, or wiped out an army, they had our admiration, every bit of it.[20]

Episcopal Bishop Samuel Fallows publicly advocated boxing as an environment in which boys could express their rough and tumble "inherited proclivities," without which they would not develop the strong bodies and internal dispositions necessary to do moral battle.[21] Pugilism was, in the words of YMCA boys' secretary Edgar Robinson, "positive right-

---

[17] Quoted in David Rosen, "The Volcano and the Cathedral: Muscular Christianity and the Origins of Primal Manliness," in *Muscular Christianity: Embodying the Victorian Age*, ed. Donald Hall (New York: Cambridge University Press, 1994), 25–26.

[18] Quoted in Rosen, "The Volcano and the Cathedral," 26. Note Kingsley's use of the epitaph "Son of Man," a reference to Jesus that Kingsley suggests equally applied to "real" men of violence.

[19] Quoted in David Newsome, *Godliness and Good Learning: Four Studies on a Victorian Ideal* (London: Cassell Publishers, 1961), 207.

[20] Bruce Barton, *A Young Man's Jesus* (Boston: Pilgrim Press, 1914), ix-xi.

[21] Samuel Fallows, "Seconds Dr. Hall's Opinion," *Chicago Record*, 10 April 1899.

eousness physically expressed."[22] Such ideas, found among U.S. social reformers, businessmen, theologians, and child psychologists, remained as part of the undercurrent of American public thought.

Our contemporary discussions about the place of mixed martial arts in Christianity, and of the morality of Christian spectatorship of such a violent sport, are continuations of a longstanding ambivalence. What is interesting is that the arguments for reconciling violent sporting events with Christian praxis have two common threads: that such sports are initially prohibited by elites (both social and ecclesial) for being too violent, and that they are subsequently justified by others under the assumption that the church will benefit from bringing in men who excel in and are attracted to such contests. Similarly, MMA has found a home within U.S. evangelicalism, particularly as the sport was codified (legitimated and professionalized by adding rules and regulations) over the past quarter century, as evangelical intelligentsia reaffirmed the idea that the church was in the midst of a crisis of masculinity.

MMA's Origins and Male-Oriented Entertainment

From its earliest iterations, the founding figures of professionalized MMA have presented their product as a sport of entertainment through which hierarchies of masculine supremacy can be established and maintained. Hollywood films such as *Bloodsport* (1988) and video games such as *Street Fighter* (1987) and the *Mortal Kombat* series highlighted an entertainment industry market that flaunted the superiority of fighting styles, as well as the nationalities or ethnicities that bore their names. Seeing a market opportunity, U.S. businessmen Art Davie and Robert Meyorwitz—along with the Brazilian jiu-jitsu family dynasty of Rickson and Rorion Gracie, Hollywood producer and former NRA board member John Milius (of *Conan the Barbarian* fame) and fighter Ken Shamrock—organized the first Ultimate Fighting Championship in Denver, Colorado, in 1993.[23] Touting its product as the most violent and brutal

---

[22] Quoted in Clifford Putney, *Muscular Christianity: Manhood and Sports in Protestant America, 1880–1920* (Cambridge, MA: Harvard University Press, 2001), 170.

[23] For more on Hollywood and the entertainment industry's role in the creation of professional MMA, see Christopher D. Thrasher, *Fight Sports and American Masculinity: Salvation in Violence from 1607 to the Present* (Jefferson, NC: McFarland and Company, 2015), 208–215.

sport in U.S. entertainment, the UFC would go on to become the largest promotional body in the sport. By pitting muay thai, Chinese kung fu, Brazilian jiu-jitsu, Japanese sumo, French savate, Israeli krav maga and other schools of boxing, wrestling, and kickboxing against one another, the sport's promoters claimed that the Octagon was a "no-holds-barred" crucible in which "There Are No Rules," and through which fighters could defend the honor of their chosen fighting style.[24]

As MMA's popularity mushroomed, calls to regulate—or even eliminate—the sport grew as well. Senators Ben Nighthorse Campbell, Roy Romer, Nolbert Chavez, and John McCain condemned the sport as an organized street fight, reminiscent of similar criticisms leveled against boxing a century earlier.[25] McCain—a boxing aficionado with ties to the gambling industry, then chairman of the Senate Communications Committee—demonized MMA as "human cockfighting," and attempted to prevent cable providers from carrying UFC broadcasts.[26] Athletic commissions across the country began to outlaw MMA events. As had happened with previous combat sports, MMA was condemned for its perceived barbarism by a socially elite group of critics.

UFC organizers, like the great boxing promoters of the previous century, successfully instituted a public relations campaign to redefine the sport. The old slogan, "There Are No Rules" highlighted a lack of re-straint. The new slogan, introduced by UFC president Dana White in 2002, legitimized the UFC by rebranding it as serious sport and chang-ing the tagline to "As Real As It Gets."[27] Trading in narratives of danger

---

[24] For a closer look at the origins of MMA, see Miles Adam Park, "In the Octagon: Mixed Martial Arts Comes to Life," *American History Through American Sport: From Colonial Lacrosse to Extreme Sports*, vol. 3, ed. Danielle Sarver Combs and Bob Batchelor (Santa Barbara, CA: Praeger Press, 2013), 295–314.

[25] *Larry King Live*, "Ultimate Fighting," CNN, 6 December 1995.

[26] Quoted in Martin Marty, "Blood Sport," *The Christian Century*, 27 November 2007, http://www.christiancentury.org/article/2007-11/blood-sport (accessed 21 April 2016).

[27] The UFC changed hands in January 2001 when it was bought by Zuffa, the promotional company started by current UFC chairman Dana White and casino magnates Frank and Lorenzo Fertitta, for a mere $2 million. The government of Abu Dhabi was one investor, claiming a 10 percent stake in the company. In July 2016, Zuffa sold the company for $4 billion, indicating that the global market for the sport had increased two thousand-fold over the past fifteen years. See Darren Rovell and Brett Okamato, "Dana White on $4 billion UFC sale; 'Sport is going to the next level'," 11 July 2016,

for authenticity, UFC leadership repositioned itself as a laboratory in which competitors could prove their claims to be "the best." The UFC's reality TV series, *The Ultimate Fighter*, first broadcast on male-oriented Spike TV cable channel in 2005, provided amateur competitors an opportunity to prove their mettle. It also provided the UFC with a growing fan base across the United States and eventually across the globe, attracting 2.6 million viewers for the series finale.[28] Since then, MMA has become one of the fastest-growing and most profitable branches of the sports industry, hosting events in more than 15 countries, with growing audiences in Europe, South America, and East Asia.[29] In the United States, the sport has attracted more than 31 million fans, 75 percent of whom are men, and nearly a third of whom are men aged 18 to 34.[30] Like martial sports of old, MMA had demonstrable economic utility and attractiveness to young American men.

The rise in popularity of mixed martial arts over the past twenty years has correlated with an increased effort to provide a version of Christianity attractive to men of all ages, and young men in particular. Responding to concerns about the absence of men in the pews and a lack of testosterone in Christian iconography, some evangelical Christian authors and clerical leaders have made the argument that in order to bring men back to church the Christian community had to replace what they perceived as the dominantly feminine mode of the faith with one enticing to men. By the time the UFC was getting off the ground, the Promise Keepers were already filling football stadiums and admonishing men to worship God with all the might they might bring to cheering on their

---

http://espn.go.com/mma/story/_/id/16970360/ufc-sold-unprecedented-4-billion-dana-white-confirms (accessed 14 June 2016).

[28] Thrasher, *Fight Sports*, 227–231.

[29] Julie Scelfo, "Blood, Guts and Money: Don't Look Now, But Mixed Martial Arts Has Gone Mainstream," *Newsweek* 148, no. 13 (2006): 50.

[30] Scarborough Sports Marketing, "Mixed Martial Arts (MMA) Attracts Young Adults with Purchasing Power," *PR Newswire*, 23 November 2009, http://search.proquest.com/docview/450396692?accountid=14270 (accessed 25 February 2016), and Kelsey Philpott, "The UFC Fan Base," *Payout—The Business of MMA*, 29 November 2010, http://mmapayout.com/2010/11/the-ufc-fan-base/ (accessed 25 February 2016). See also Nancy Cheever, "The Uses and Gratifications of Viewing Mixed Martial Arts," *Journal of Sports Media* 4, no. 1 (2009): 25–53.

favorite team.[31] Trying to identify why men were less interested in religion, Christian men's authors critiqued the feminized church for having failed to appeal to men's quintessentially *masculine* characteristics. President of Ransomed Heart ministries John Eldredge contended that men's absence from the pews was because of the church's overly feminized culture, one which emphasized Christ's pacifism, meekness, and gentleness over his manhood and power. This, Eldredge argued in his best-selling *Wild at Heart*, discouraged men's masculine nature, forgetting that "aggression is part of the masculine design,"[32] and that for a boy to "become truly masculine," he needs a "battle to fight; he needs a place for the warrior in him to come alive."[33] Focus on the Family's founder James Dobson's *Bringing Up Boys* blamed "radical feminism" for today's "masculine confusion," and endorsed English philosopher Roger Scruton's contention that feminism had "snuffed out male pride wherever it had grown and ruthlessly uprooted it…downgrad[ing] or reject[ing] such masculine virtues as courage, tenacity, and military prowess in favor of more gentle, more 'socially inclusive' habits."[34] In his 2005 book, *Why Men Hate Going to Church*, Church for Men founder David Murrow posited that men find church "dull and irrelevant" because it doesn't reflect their "masculine heart[s]."[35] The over-civilizing world of middle-class mainstream Protestantism, like secular societies groaning under the weight of feminist critique, they claimed, had edged men out.[36] Frequently, the solution these authors offered was to make Christianity appealing to men again by recreating a masculinized version of the faith.

---

[31] See *Standing on the Promises: The* Promise Keepers *and the Revival of Manhood*, ed. Dane Claussen (Cleveland: Pilgrim Press, 2000).

[32] John Eldredge, *Wild at Heart: Discovering the Secrets of a Man's Soul* (Nashville: Thomas Nelson Publishers, 2001), 10.

[33] John Eldredge, *Wild at Heart*, 140.

[34] James Dobson, *Bringing Up Boys: Shaping the Next Generation of Men* (Carol Stream, IL: Tyndale Publishers, 2005), 213, 169.

[35] David Murrow, *Why Men Hate Going to Church* (Nashville: Thomas Nelson Publishers, 2005), 16.

[36] This concern about over-civilization is a trope that goes back to the early history of muscular Christianity in America. See Gail Bederman, *Manliness and Civilization: A Cultural History of Gender and Race in the United States, 1880–1917* (Chicago: Chicago University Press, 1995); John J. Brent and Peter Kraska, "'Fighting Is the Most Real and Honest Thing': Violence and the Civilization/Barbarism Dialectic," *British Journal of Criminology*, 11 February 2013, https://doi: 10.1093/bjc/azt001.

The Growth of Christian Martial Arts Ministries

Growing out of this desire to create a version of Christianity palatable to the perceived innate aggression of the masculine soul, MMA became an increasingly enticing form of popular culture that could be adapted to evangelistic purposes. U.S. religious historian Darryl Hart has convincingly demonstrated that "as much as people perceive evangelicalism as old-fashioned and conservative, it has actually been one of the most modern and innovative forms of Christianity in using the cultural vernacular to restate the claims of an ancient faith in a modern tongue."[37] Seeing the immense following the sport had among the coveted 18 to 34 male demographic, a group with high levels of disposable income and few family obligations, several evangelical communities anxious to bring men back to the pews eagerly integrated the sport into ministerial programming. The International Network of Christian Martial Artists, founded in 1999, sought to connect MMA instructors, practitioners, and enthusiasts with one another, forming a social network that was nondenominational with regard to theology and fighting style. Older Christian martial arts advocacy groups like the Christian Martial Arts Council began extending services to the MMA community in order to—according to their website's mission statement—"facilitate Christ's admonition to fulfill the Great Commission through the medium of the martial arts." Such ministries, along with international programs like Anointed Fighter, provide the same sort of chaplaincy support and outreach found in every major U.S. sport.

At the local level, some pastors have incorporated MMA instruction into ministerial programming, with the expressed goal of recruiting men who would otherwise not attend church. At Xtreme Ministries in Clarksville, Tennessee, John "The Saint" Renken—a retired pro fighter, Fort Campbell Combatives Team instructor and former lead pastor—succinctly stated his justification for incorporating MMA programming into his church. "Mainstream Christianity," he says, "has feminized men... I think most of our problems in society today are due to a lack of a warrior ethos....At the end of the day it's about reaching people with gospel, regardless of what you do to introduce them into a relationship

---

[37] Darryl G. Hart, *That Old-Time Religion in Modern America: Evangelical Protestantism in the Twentieth Century* (Chicago: I.R. Dee Publishers, 2002), 175.

with Jesus Christ." [38] Images on Renken's website www.fighting-preacher.com and book, *Peaceful in a Violent Sort of Way,* fashion him as a crusader with an American eagle as his totem. He argues that the sport ministry "gives me an avenue to reach those guys I probably would not have if it wasn't for MMA."[39] Just to the east, Rick Hocker, lead pastor of Freedom Fellowship in Virginia Beach, signed off on his son and associate pastor Preston Hocker's creation of a fight ministry, because "tough guys need Jesus too."[40] For men like Renken and Hocker, U.S. Christianity is desperately in need of a testosterone boost. MMA is one such means of attractive those "rough men" or "tough guys," men who the church needs just as much as they need Jesus.

Although several religious leaders initially panned MMA for its unabashedly violent nature, many U.S. evangelical leaders began to make concessions for MMA subculture within their churches. In an apology for these ministries, Albert Mohler, president of the Southern Baptist Theological Seminary, argues "[t]he main issue is not the legitimacy of martial arts, but the fact that these churches are making a self-conscious effort to reach young men and boys with some kind of proof that Christianity is not a feminized and testosterone-free faith that appeals only to women."[41] Megachurch pastor Mark Driscoll, formerly of Mars Hill Church in Seattle, echoed the sentiments of Eldredge and Murrow when he said men are turned off from churches which ignore or otherwise try to dissuade their violent nature: "As a pastor and as a Bible teacher," says Driscoll, "I think that God made men masculine ... Men are made for combat, men are made for conflict, men are made for dominion ... That's just the way men are made."[42] Contemporary American evangelicals incorporating MMA into their churches, or at least tacitly endorsing its presence in other churches, are not too far removed from the arguments of the first generations of Muscular Christians who also suggested that

---

[38] *Fight Church*, directed by Daniel Junge and Bryan Storkel (Northridge, CA: Film Harvest Studios, 2014), DVD.

[39] *Fox and Friends,* "Fight in the Name of the Lord?" 7 April 2010.

[40] Junge and Storkel, *Fight Church.*

[41] Albert Mohler, "News Note: Masculinity in a Can, Fight Club at Church, and the Crisis of Manhood," 5 February 2010, http://www.albert-mohler.com/2010/02/05/newsnote-masculinity-in-a-can-fight-club-at-church-and-the-crisis-of-manhood/ (accessed 24 February 2016).

[42] *Fighting Politics*, directed by Emily Vahey (2009).

men abandoned the church because the sentimental church had first abandoned them.

MMA ministries, supporters have argued, are appropriate antidotes to this problem. MMA is a means of reaching non–church going, rough-and-tumble men who do not identify with "feminized" Christianity. God, the church and society *need* these men, and the end result—their hopeful Christianization—justifies the means. Reading such justifications, one is left with the impression that MMA ministries don't necessarily work *because* God approves of them, but that supporters believe God approves of MMA ministries because they get results among this niche market. Retired fighter Jason Freeman relays the story of how fighting, once merely an acceptable social outlet for his aggressiveness, became a means through which God could use him to attract others to his brand of Protestantism. In true evangelical fashion, Freeman believes God "built up a stage underneath [him] to speak off of and reach others."[43] Charles Pettitt, author of the novel, *The Warrior*, prefaces his book by claiming that "[w]e need spiritually strong young men and women for Christ to stand up in arena like MMA, and proclaim their love of Christ."[44] This also seems to be a common view among the mostly white male crowd of internet commentators on MMA enthusiast websites. Ian Borer and Tyler Schafer's review of unsolicited threads asking whether or not MMA and Christianity were compatible revealed that most commentators (unsurprisingly) believed they were, often invoking the idea that MMA has a "unique position to serve as a *recruitment tool* which could help *restore* traditional masculinity."[45] God's church, it seems, is in desperate need of real "warrior" men.

---

[43] Quoted in Annika Young, "Fighting Your Family's Demons," *The 700 Club* clips, Christian Broadcast Network, http://www1.cbn.com/700club/fighting-your-familys-demons (accessed 5 June 2016). See also Dannon Svab, *Knocking Out the Devil: The Jay Freeman Story* (self-published e-book).

[44] Charles J. Pettitt, *The Warrior: Can Mixed Martial Arts and Christianity Coexist?* (Bloomington, IN: WestBow Press, 2014), xv.

[45] Ian Borer and Tyler S. Schafer, "Culture War Confessionals: Conflicting Accounts of Christianity, Violence, and Mixed Martial Arts," *Journal of Media and Religion* 10 (2011), 165–184 (emphasis in original).

Christian Warriors in Post-9/11 America

What precipitated this strong call for a return to a violent masculinity within the church? On the one hand, calls for a restoration of gender balance in the pews, a portrayal of the ambiguously "feminine" as the root causes of social evil and the belief that sports could be used to attract men who would otherwise go unchurched have defined the muscular Christian movement. The emergence of MMA ministries at this particular time, however, is also tied to a uniquely twenty-first century U.S. crisis of masculinity, built upon a decade and half of post-9/11 national vulnerability and bellicose foreign policy. This section examines the politics of warrior Christianity through the lens of the war on terror.

When two planes hit the towers of New York's World Trade Center on the morning on September 11, 2001, while another plane crashed into the Pentagon and a fourth went down in a field in western Pennsylvania, many U.S. men spent the following weeks trying to assess the likelihood of a draft, considered enlistment, and otherwise tried to make sense of the new world. What was made clear—through presidential speeches, op-eds, editorials, Sunday sermons, and pamphlets at the army recruiter's station—was that the nation had been attacked, and that this required a righteously violent reply from the American people. In his speech before a joint session of Congress on 20 September, President George W. Bush spoke about a national response defined by "courage," "endurance," "the giving of blood," and "the saying of prayers."[46] The president continued by asserting that the nation's new defense would best be served by a military offensive. Like Jesus warning the disciples about the Day of the Lord in Matthew 24, Bush alerted the armed services to "be ready," for "the hour is coming when America will act."[47] Rhetorically, the president had positioned the U.S. Armed Services as the advanced forces in God's army at Judgment Day, assuring the nation that God "is not neutral in this conflict."[48] With God on our side, who could be against us?

President Bush's speech, along with its theo-political overtones, also invoked common clichés of sporting culture and militaristic patriotism. The necessity for courage in the face of adversity, endurance in spite of

---

[46] George W. Bush, "Address to the Joint Session of Congress Following 9/11 Attacks," 20 September 2001.

[47] Ibid.

[48] Ibid.

pain, and the willing self-sacrifice of national blood for the sake of a greater cause could easily have been lifted from a coach's pre-game speech to a beleaguered team. The communal experience of victimization resulted in a dramatic increase in calls to restore a hyper-violent masculinity.

Gender historians have pointed out that the emergence of contemporary American sporting culture can largely be defined by a desire to create "a homosocial cultural sphere which provided men with psychological separation from the perceived 'feminization' of society"[49] in the late nineteenth century. More recently, French sociologist Pierre Bourdieu attempted to explain why societies would invest themselves in inculcating violent dispositions among young men, largely as an extension of a patriarchal project that included both the subordination of women at home and "inferior" masculine subjects abroad. He posited that western societies tended to define manliness through violence—especially violence as righteous revenge. "Manliness," Bourdieu argued, is largely defined as "the capacity to fight and to exercise violence (especially in acts of revenge)," and "is first and foremost a *duty*,"[50] of "real" men. This, he contends, is the arena in which virility is established. Because this masculine virility can never be eternally established, it is also "the source of an immense vulnerability,"[51] a fear of eventually becoming feminized. It is this fear of feminization that Bourdieu identifies as the genesis for societies investing in "all the masculine games of violence, such as sports in modern societies, and most especially those which most tend to produce the visible signs of masculinity, and to manifest and also test what are called manly virtues, such as combat sports."[52] The national experience of the 9/11 attacks provided just such an experience of vulnerability, one that demanded a reinvestment in the games of violence that produced visible signs of masculinity.

---

[49] Michael A. Messner, "When Bodies Are Weapons: Masculinity and Violence in Sport," *International Review for the Sociology of Sport* 25 (1990): 204. See also Michael A. Messner, "Sport and Male Domination: The Female Athlete as Contested Ideological Terrain," *Sociology of Sport Journal* 5 (1988): 197–211.

[50] Pierre Bourdieu, *Masculine Domination*, translated by Richard Nice (Stanford: Stanford University Press, 2001), 50.

[51] Ibid.

[52] Ibid, 51.

Undoubtedly, MMA has enjoyed unprecedented commercial success in since the 9/11 attacks. Zuffa, the promotional company started by current UFC chairman Dana White and casino magnates Frank and Lorenzo Fertitta, purchased the UFC in January 2001 for $2 million. In the eight-year history of the UFC prior to 9/11, the largest promotional body in the sport had hosted a mere thirty-six events, or four-and-a-half events per year. However, from 28 September 2001 to the present, the UFC has hosted an additional 320 events at a rate of twenty-one events per year, nearly five times as many as they did in the 1990s.[53] In July 2016, White and the Fertitta's sold the UFC for $4 billion, indicating that the worldwide market for its product had risen two thousand fold since 2001.[54] It is impossible to ignore the fact that MMA achieved this massive success amid the war on terror and what it reveals about the financial value of combat sports in an era of warfare. September 11 did not cause the rise of the UFC, but there is substantial evidence to suggest that images of men's bodies in pain, inflicting damage upon one another particularly resonated with a majority of white, male, heterosexual, millennial, American audience in the post-9/11 world in a way it didn't before.

In the years since 9/11, God's pressing need for Christian warriors has grown within U.S. evangelical culture, reflecting a society responding to its own vulnerability and its post-colonial wars abroad. In *He Fights for You: 40 Promises for Everyday Battles*, the prolific men's devotional author Max Lucado charges his readers to "March like a Promised Land conqueror,"[55] assured in the knowledge of God's complete victory over the devil and his grip on the reader's life. The men's ministry *Core 300* calls for men to "get out of the stands and into the arena," because the "violent men of God" must take the Kingdom "by force, through faith."[56] Even

---

[53] *Ultimate Fighting Championship* website, https://www.ufc.com (accessed 1 June 2016).

[54] Darren Rovell and Brett Okamato, "Dana White on $4 billion UFC sale, 'Sport Is Going to the Next Level," 11 July 2016, http://espn.go.com/mma/story/_/id/16970360/ufc-sold-unprecedented-4-billion-dana-white-confirms (accessed 20 July 2016).

[55] Max Lucado and Andrea Lucado, *He Fights for You: Forty Promises for Everyday Battles* (Nashville: Thomas Nelson, 2015), 14.

[56] *Core 300* website, http://www.core300.org/core-300-beliefs/ (accessed 21 July 2016). The name is a reference to a gory 2006 action film featuring a mostly

the Promise Keepers—whose diminishing role in evangelical men's ministries in the 1990s coincided with MMA's rise to popularity—has gotten in on the action, hosting an *Awakening the Warrior* and *Battle Lines* series of men's conferences in 2013 and 2015, respectively.[57] This strong desire for a bellicose Christian masculinity isn't confined to evangelicals either; Catholic writer Leon Podles has also contended that "sacred violence is the ultimate meaning of masculinity," and that "masculinity is, at heart, a willingness to sacrifice oneself even unto bloody death for the other."[58] A writer for the evangelical periodical *Christianity Today* went so far as to say that men "can't grow in godliness unless we are fighting," by which he meant fighting to "lead, love and protect,"[59] that which men hold dear. Real men need to become warriors to achieve true masculinity; they need a battle to fight. Warriors never surrender; they never tap out in a fight (unless of course, they are submitting to Jesus).[60]

While this has echoes of earlier muscular Christians, it also reflects the bellicose foreign policy of the past fifteen years. As the Bush administration sold the Iraq War to the American public under the guise of protecting U.S. interests from outside aggressors, the same evangelical leaders who espoused the virtues of warrior masculinity vigorously supported the decision of the president and his advisors. Lucado, invoking

---

naked and supremely buff collection of white soldiers who fight to the last man to defend their homeland from an overwhelming, brown-skinned Persian army.

[57] Eleanor Osborne, "Spirit Warriors: Promise Keepers Hope to Reach the Hearts and Minds of Men and Boys at Daytona Beach Conference," *Daytona Beach News*, 19 October 2013 (see also https://promisekeepers.org/event-details).

[58] Quoted in Timothy Nonn, "Renewal as Retreat: The Battle for Men's Souls," in *The Politics of Manhood: Profeminist Men Respond to the Mythopetic Men's Movement*, ed. Michael S. Kimmel (Philadelphia: Temple University Press, 1995), 178.

[59] Ed Stetzer, "Act Like Men: What It Means to Fight Like a Man," *Christianity Today*, 6 August 2014, http://www.christianitytoday.com/ edstetzer/2014/august/act-like-men-what-it-means-to-fight.html (accessed 6 June 2016).

[60] In his autobiography, *Tapped Out by Jesus*, former professional fighter and current Team Impact Ministries strongman Ron Waterman explains that no matter how many fights he participated in, he couldn't achieve true victory until, paradoxically, he "tapped out" (submitted) his life to Christ. Ron Waterman, *Tapped Out by Jesus: From the Cage to the Cross* (Alachua, FL: Bridge-Logos Publishers, 2011).

iustum bellum ("just war"), defended the invasion of Iraq because "innocent people need to be protected."[61] He continued by saying the president "has a moral obligation to protect innocent people here and abroad, but especially here."[62] Of course in this case the protectionist military strategy took the form of a large-scale invasion of a country thousands of miles from U.S. shores. Jerry Falwell published an article simply entitled, "God Is Pro-War," in which he outlined his belief that "our God-authored freedoms must be defended," and that "President Bush declared war in Iraq to defend innocent people."[63] On his daily radio show, Dobson argued that "America comes as a liberator, not as a conqueror," and that the American people have a "moral obligation"[64] to fight. What is most interesting is that Dobson and Falwell have been among the most ardent supports of the muscular Christian movement, often using the same language to call upon men to fight for the establishment of a proper, God-oriented (and androcentric) society.

They are not alone, either. *Fight Church*, Daniel Junge and Brian Storkel's documentary about Christian MMA ministries, captures a wide variety of individuals who support MMA and MMA ministries using very similar language to the hawkish group above, claiming that participation in MMA gives men a "warrior ethos" and "the strength to stand up to evil, wickedness, and unrighteousness," that is out there, "trying to seek and destroy us."[65] "This is a battlefield," says pastor Joe Burress. "We need to charge them, not wait for them to come to us."[66] Although he may be speaking of the devil, he uses the rhetoric of the war on terror used to justify the 2003 invasion of Iraq. In the era of the war on terror, MMA ministries are a crucible through which men can be trained in the habits and dispositions necessary for the survival of the church and the nation in this moment of crisis.

---

[61] *Larry King Live*, "Panel of Christians Speaks Out on War with Iraq, CNN, 11 March 2003. Transcript available at http://transcripts.cnn.com/TRANSCRIPTS/0303/11/lkl.00.html.

[62] Ibid.

[63] Jerry Falwell, "God Is Pro-War," *World News Daily*, 1 January 2004, http://www.wnd.com/2004/01/23022/ (accessed 1 March 2016).

[64] U.S. Newswire, "Dobson Supports War Efforts in Iraq; Pro-Family Leader Calls for Support, Prayer for Troops on National Daily Broadcast," 21 March 2003, 1.

[65] Junge and Storkel, *Fight Church*.

[66] Ibid.

Amid this cultural nexus of hawkish patriotism, foreign aggression, and a perceived lack of testosterone in the pews, MMA ministries emerged as a vehicle through which churches could train men to carry out the righteous, protective violence of God. As with many of the sports ministries discussed earlier, MMA ministries present a version of God that highlights the characteristics that the sport is supposed to inculcate in its participants. As we will see, the Jesus of MMA is as tough as they come, exercising his righteously violent prerogative to establish the Kingdom of God on earth.

MMA Jesus

Such ministries have a shared hope of counteracting a perceived stereotype of Christianity among non-churchgoing men: that it is a domesticated faith revolving around an effete Jesus. Apologists for these ministries tend to remasculinize Jesus himself through violent imagery in order to present a form of Christianity they find more palatable to their senses. Mark Driscoll has suggested that the problem some Christians see with their brethren participating in MMA stems from their false, effeminate image of Christ that is common in many U.S. churches. "Their picture of Jesus is basically a guy in a dress with fabulous long hair, drinking decaf and in touch with his feelings, who would never hurt anyone." Driscoll's preferred iconography is of Jesus the carpenter, whose "cloth is dipped in blood" (Rev. 19:11-18), a man who "took a beating" on his first trip to earth but who will return "to hand them out to unrepentant sinners."[67] This manlier version Driscoll dubs "Ultimate Fighting Jesus."[68] Paul Burress, a former MMA fighter and pastor at Victory Church in Rochester, New York, echoes this when he says that Jesus' original followers were "roughnecks," defining meekness as "controlled strength" and scoffing at the idea that "if you're a Christian, you have to be a sissy."[69] These

---

[67] Mark Driscoll, "A Christian Evaluation of Mixed Martial Arts," 9 November 2011, http://pastormark.tv/2011/11/09/a-christian-evaluation-of-mixed-martial-arts (accessed 12 February 2016).

[68] Quoted in Brandon O'Brien, "A Jesus for Real Men: What the New Masculinity Movement Gets Right and Wrong," *Christianity Today* 52, no. 4 (2008), 48.

[69] Quoted in Brownie Marie, "Pastor's 'Fight Ministry' Incorporates Mixed Martial Arts; Sees It as a Counter to 'Feminized' Church," *Christianity Today*, 12 September 2014, http://www.christiantoday.com/article/pastors.fight. minis-

images of Jesus are not too far removed from older muscular Christian presumptions about what kind of Christ is most attractive. Warren Conant's 1915 claim that "hard-fisted men…are not likely to be impressed or attracted by a feminine Christ," is a perennial theme seen in Jerry Falwell's declaration that "Christ wasn't effeminate…Christ was a he-man!"[70] Driscoll and Burress simply present a twenty-first century version of this idea.

These comments highlight a common presumption in Christian MMA subculture: The masculine qualities of Christianity—construed as virile, powerful, aggressive, competitive and physically endowed—must be stressed (and perhaps exaggerated) if non-churchgoing men will find it worthy of their time, energy, and material resources. If Jesus is to be emulated, he must be a Jesus who already conforms to and approves of the MMA lifestyle. The website for Pastor Nathan Kirby's Rock City MMA assures such men that even when they feel the "ground-n-pound at work or at school," Jesus is their "ultimate Cornerman," as they go through "the cage of life." Dave Hatfield, an organizer for MMA at Victory Christian Fellowship in State College, Pennsylvania claims aggressiveness is next to godliness:

> The Bible talks about the Lord being a victorious warrior and says we're created in his image. I believe God has given each one of us a divine desire to conquer and overcome…We use our MMA outreaches to tap into guys' natural desire[s] to conquer and compete and point them to their creator and the fact He has plans for them to become not only beloved sons, but also warriors for Him.[71]

Such language suggests that the nineteenth-century hymn "Onward Christian Soldiers" hasn't lost its place in twenty-first century Protestantism.

This hypermasculine image of Jesus also has commercial value for astute Christian MMA entrepreneurs. The popular Jesus Didn't Tap

---

try.incorporates.mixed.martial.arts.sees.it.as.a.counter.to.feminised.church/4059 1.htm (accessed 10 March 2016).

[70] Warren Conant, *The Virility of Christ: A New View*, 2nd ed. (Whitefish, MT: Kessinger Publishing, 2009 [1915]), 92–93. See also Falwell quoted in Michael Kimmel, *Misframing Men: The Politics of Contemporary Masculinities* (New Brunswick, NJ: Rutgers University Press, 2010), 23.

[71] Quoted in Lee Warren, "Is MMA Compatible with Christianity?" *The Christian Post*, 23 April 2011, http://www.christianpost.com/news/is-mma-compatible-with-christianity-49947/ (accessed 6 June 2016).

clothing line, the brainchild of martial arts enthusiast and former Power Ranger Jason David Frank, offers tee-shirts, headgear, and other paraphernalia reinforcing the masculine asceticism of Christ who, according to the company's website, "didn't quit after going through unimaginable suffering and pain when he was crucified on the cross." With street and training clothes for both men and women, the company's slogan promotes the notion that real Christians emulating their Lord do not succumb to the demands of the flesh, they tough it out and fight through. Two tee-shirts in particular feature Jesus' martial skills, presenting him as the exemplary fighter who bests the devil through submission. "Get a Hold of Your Life" shows Jesus putting Satan into a chokehold, while "Break Your Bad Habits" has Satan trapped in Jesus' arm bar. Another shirt, "Jesus Didn't Tap—Neither Does This Country," weds nationalism within macho Christianity, using the Crusader's Cross to position Christian MMA as a training program for the theo-political struggle between Islam and an imagined Christian America. These material artifacts of MMA evangelism denote the wearer's membership in the body of faith and promoting their hyper-masculine version of Jesus. As Justine Greve summarizes, the MMA Jesus is "self-sufficient and strong-minded." This is important because "when manliness is connected to fitness and to godliness, Jesus' image imparts theological and ideological truths."[72] Jesus doesn't tap because submission is a sign of weakness. If Jesus is "the Ultimate Fighter" and the object of Christian emulation, then *real* Christian men—American men—must always be dominant, never submissive, and by extension never effeminate or queer. Such images also highlight the connections between masculinity, patriotism, and U.S. foreign policy within Christian MMA subculture.

Teaching Evangelical Masculinity in MMA

Aside from attracting new members and rebranding Jesus, MMA has also been construed as a means of teaching an idealized version of masculinity to male participants. What is at stake for many of these pastors is the future of the faith. Beset by the anxious notion that the church is losing the battle for men's souls, several Christian MMA participants, spectators, and supporters turned to the sport as an antidote for many of

---

· [72] Justine Greve, "Jesus Didn't Tap: Masculinity, Theology, and Ideology in Christian Mixed Martial Arts," *Religion and American Culture* 24, no. 2 (2014), 167, https://doi: 10.1525/rac.2014.24.2.141.

problems of the modern church. Most of all, Christian MMA supporters hope that the sport provides the necessary physical and moral training to engender desirable masculine qualities in young men and boys, who in turn will become the future leaders of both church and society: as pastors, lay ministers, businessmen, coworkers, patriarchal domestic figures, headstrong husbands, and dependable brothers.

One hope, repeating aspirations found throughout muscular Christian literature, is that MMA will provide the necessary structure for moral living by teaching the values of discipline, hard work, and self-determination. Some ministries invite female congregants to participate in training (though few do so, and mixed-gender competitions are infrequent) on the grounds that they can benefit from the spiritual exercises of physical training and sporting asceticism. This is particularly the case with younger members. Professional fighter and Pentecostal preacher Jason Barrett says, "young people need discipline in their lives, and mixed martial arts gives them exactly that."[73] Giving and receiving hits, kicks, eye-gouges, body-slams, cauliflower ear, chokeholds, arm-bars, groin shots, cracked ribs, broken noses, and broken bones, in addition to other injuries common in sports training, are thus integrated into a disciplinary practice designed for preparing young people for the hardships of the adult world.

Thinking primarily of the males in these congregations, other defenders hope that MMA participation will enable boys and young men to take over family responsibilities. "The man should be the overall leader of the household," according to Ryan Dobson, son of James Dobson and vice president of his father's "Family Talk" radio show. The reason so many men fail to take on this duty, according to Ryan Dobson, is that the church has "raised a generation of little boys."[74] His hope is that masculinizing efforts like Christian MMA will reverse this trend. Virginia Beach pastor Preston Hocker said that he moved from the pulpit into the cage when he considered his then-inability to protect his family: "I was newly married, and had a real beautiful wife—and heaven forbid anybody want to take her life or take her away from me. I wanted to know that I

---

[73] Quoted in Marty, "Blood Sport," 47.

[74] Quoted in Bill Forman, "Dobson 2.0: As the Doctor Leaves Focus, His Son Talks about a Second Coming," *Colorado Springs Independent*, 25 February 2010, http://www.csindy.com/coloradosprings/dobson-20/Content?oid=1633735 (accessed 6 June 2016).

had the ability to at the very least defend her life."[75] For him, honing his skills in inflicting pain would enable him to fulfill his Christian duty as the protector of his family—something that has increasingly occupied the minds of American men in the post-9/11 world.[76] Albert Mohler hopes that these ministries prepare men for:

> the most important fight to which a Christian man is called...the fight to grow up into godly manhood, to be true to wife and provide for his children, to make a real contribution in the home, in the church, and in the society...This means a fight for truth, for the Gospels, and for the virtues of the Christian life.[77]

The image of the masculine gospel of Jesus on the offensive reveals something of the sense of embattlement that is pervasive in U.S. evangelicalism broadly and the gender coding of both familial and social salvation within MMA apologetic discourse. Whatever the problems of society, fighting preacher John Renken knows that "If we would raise our boys to be men, these kinds of problems go away."[78] For some U.S. evangelicals, MMA is a silver bullet for many of the nation's gender troubles.

The Octagon as Instrument of Truth

The Octagon serves as a proving ground in which realities are contested and (temporarily) established, both in terms of establishing truths about the self and about the world. The desire for authenticity among MMA participants and spectators suggests that the post-modern world has failed to provide a sufficient space for grounding reality. Certainly, the UFC has presented its product as "As Real As It Gets." Even from its beginnings amid the birth of reality TV in the early 1990s, the UFC distinguished itself as a form of authentic entertainment different from the scripted shows that comprised the majority of programming. For MMA enthusiasts, the sport is an opportunity to create reality.

---

[75] Quoted in Bob Woodruff and Ben Newman, "In Jesus' Name, Throw Punches: 'Fight Church' Christian Ministries Believe in Fight Clubs," *ABC News*, 3 October 2014, http://abcnews.go.com/US/jesus-throw-punches-fight-church-christian-ministries-fight/story?id=25953786 (accessed 6 Jun. 2016).

[76] Susan Faludi, *The Terror Dream: Fear and Fantasy in Post 9/11 America* (New York: Metropolitan Books, 2007).

[77] Mohler, "Masculinity in a Can."

[78] Quoted in Junge and Storkel, *Fight Church*.

For MMA participants, personal identities are formed, challenged, and improved in the Octagon. As John Brent and Peter Kraska's interviews with MMA participants suggest, "fighters seek excitement, power and control and even a type of self-actualization."[79] The purpose it serves for many of them is that it gives them a sense of control over their own lives, which are often structured and dictated by the rules and tasks set upon them by others (bosses, family obligations, and so on). "Fighting gets me to let go," said one fighter, implying that the cathartic release from these stressors is the ultimate reward.[80] The documentary film *Fightville* highlights this quest for an authentic life among the conditions of rural poverty in the southern United States.[81] MMA competition also reinforces the great American myth of radical self-invention through a great dramaturgical production with clear winners and losers, establishing a fighter's place in the social pecking order while also providing some with the opportunity for upward social mobility. In this sense, MMA is an avenue for transcending the mundane, providing a sense of salvation from the various devils that beset participants.

The Octagon, moreover, is also a space in which realities about the world are contested. As Corey Abramson and Darren Modzelewski contend, fighting is a space in which "the deeply held ideals that make up [fighters'] moral world[s] can be realized rather than thwarted."[82] Like other "sacred spaces," the Octagon is a physical space demarcated for certain purposes and in which certain otherwise illicit behaviors are temporarily permissible. What are criminal acts outside of the cage are allowable within the confines of chain-link fences. In ritual and in sport, spaces are set aside where rules do not apply and where the norms of the world are momentarily upended. As Victor Turner and Clifford Geertz suggest, however, "rituals of status reversal" have a tendency to reinforce the

---

[79] Brent and Kraska, "Fighting Is the Most Real and Honest Thing," 3.

[80] Ibid., 9.

[81] *Fightville*, directed by Petra Epperlein and Michael Tucker (New York: Showtime Networks, 2011), DVD.

[82] Corey Abramson and Darren Modzelewski, "Caged Morality: Moral Worlds, Subculture, and Stratification Among Middle-Class Cage Fighters," *Qualitative Sociology* 34 (2010), http://cmabramson.com/uploads/1caged-morality-cma-dm.pdf; https://doi: 10.1007/s11133-010-9175-8.

social order.[83] For men who believe that the institutions of modern society have an over-civilizing or emasculating effect, MMA provides a powerful corrective to such constraining forces.

Participating in cage fighting is a rebuttal against the social impera-
tives towards docility, repudiating liberal Protestant visions of a society
that transcends violence. In fact, this is one of MMA's greatest pleasures.
At the same time, cage fighting reminds the audience of the sheer
Hobbesian horror of a world in which physical strength is the primary
arbiter. Christian MMA ministries reinforce the idea that the survival of
the faith—and of American society in general—is dependent upon the
judicious use of righteous violence. This is made all the more obvious in
light of Preston Hocker's claim that his MMA work is for the protection
of loved ones, John Renken's self-image as all-American Christian crusader and involvement with Fort Campbell's Combatives team, and the
numerous articles of Jesus Didn't Tap merchandise that frame MMA as
a training regimen for Christian patriotism.

Conclusion

One the great strengths of religious studies is that it is a field in which
students can learn *why* certain beliefs—which may seem wholly irrational
to outsiders—make perfectly logical sense for insiders. Certain premises,
once accepted, lead to other beliefs, compromising a total system with its
own internal structures and ways of understanding the world. Although a
great number of academics, priests, rabbis, pundits, politicians, and casual observers have denounced mixed martial arts as antisocial, and have
lambasted MMA ministries as a perversion of Christian faith, few such
critiques have come from those already successfully integrated into the
muscular Christian world of twenty-first century U.S. evangelical sporting culture. As Randall Stephens and Karl Giberson have detailed, evangelical communities have their own centers of knowledge production
which may run afoul of secular society.[84] Even though elite academics of
evangelical Christian persuasion like Higgs and Hoffman question the
wisdom of adapting combative U.S. sporting culture for evangelistic pur-

---

[83] Victor Turner, *The Ritual Process: Structure and Anti-Structure* (Chicago:
Aldine Publishing, 1966); Clifford Geertz, *The Interpretation of Cultures* (New
York: Basic Books, 1973).

[84] Randall Stephen and Karl Giberson, *The Anointed: Evangelical Truth in a
Secular Age* (Cambridge, MA: Harvard University Press, 2011).

poses, other, more popular, truth speakers from the U.S. evangelical community—such as Lucado, Mohler, Driscoll, Falwell, Dobson, or Eldredge—have defended the Christian warrior culture of post-9/11 U.S. Protestantism. What outsiders fail to grasp is that displays of the violent capabilities of the Christian warrior (both meted out and received) perform a valuable psychosocial function for a particular subset of American males at this particular moment in time.

In the wake of 9/11, in response to a chorus of theologians and other men's ministers calling for a return to "dangerous masculinity" defined through fighting, and in response to the perceived deleterious forces of docile sentimentality, feminism, and foreign aggressors, MMA ministries offer a (largely) homosocial space in Christian men can be physically and psychologically molded into a model of hegemonic masculinity invested with soteriological significance. For those on the inside, such parachurch ministries provide Christian men opportunities to reclaim their own manhood, along with that of the church and the nation.

Although many Christian MMA critics rightly focus on the disconnect between Jesus's nonviolent lifestyle and that of a cage-fighter, few acknowledge the distinct overlap between the Octagon and the Jesus's crucifixion. Such criticisms often reflect a presumption that "what is religious is inherently good, and therefore cannot be violent," or the mirror presumption, "violence is inherently bad, and therefore it cannot be religious." One of Kent Brintnall's key arguments in *Ecce Homo*, echoing earlier feminist theologians like Mary Daly and Rebecca Parker, was that "Christians have fled from the abyss opened by nails and spear for the saner, safer religious imaginary of salvation."[85] By espousing theological discourses that "focus[ed] exclusively on love, forgiveness, or reconciliation," many Christians failed "to grapple with the messy details of the event."[86] Brintnall demanded that attention be paid to the "content of the crucifixion," which is "the brutalization, humiliation, and degradation of a male body."[87] Christian soteriology, like MMA, is grounded in broken bodies. Evangelicalism's focus upon a personal relationship with that broken body, and its iconographic and hymnological emphasis upon that body's blood and the torture it endured, make perfect sense within an

---

[85] Kent Brintnall, *Ecce Homo: The Male-Body-In-Pain as Redemptive Figure* (Chicago: University of Chicago Press, 2011), 22.

[86] Ibid, 131.

[87] Ibid.

MMA framework. Both are meaning-making systems that invest broken male bodies with mystical significance. For those on the inside, the sport is legitimated not in spite of its violent nature, but because of it.

Sybil "Syd" Koff
Track and Field Star in American Jewish Life

Linda J. Borish

From the settlement houses of the late nineteenth century where immigrant Jewish females first learned about sports and physical culture in American life, to the Olympic stadiums of the twentieth century where superb Jewish sportswomen competed and excelled, Jewish women have a made a significant contribution to American sport history, religious history, and popular culture. The study of Jewish women in American sports, however, remains scarcely explored in American sports history, women's and gender history, American Jewish history, and Jewish Studies. One outstanding female athlete, Sybil "Syd" Koff, earned accolades from the American and Jewish presses in the 1920s and 1930s for her track and field triumphs. The *Jewish Telegraphic Agency* (JTA) reported on 11 April 1934 that "Syd" Koff entered in the women's national Amateur Athletic Union (AAU) indoor track and field championships and would compete against the great 1932 Los Angeles Olympic champion Mildred "Babe" Didrikson. "We have heard a good deal about Syd, as she is known. She first came into prominence two years ago, when she won the Jewish sprint championship title at Tel Aviv, Palestine. She was one the two women members of the U.S. Maccabi team that placed second in international competition." The JTA reporter continued that in this AAU championship meet, "Syd has filed her entry for the fifty-meter hurdle race. In the event she will meet among others Evelyn Hall, national champion and the word's best amateur hurdler." The journalist emphasized for male readers of this sports story the importance of this national athletic meet for women: "For the male track enthusiasts who may be reading this column, the women's hurdle events are to them what the Casey 600, the Wanamaker mile, and the Penn relays are to you!"[1]

---

[1] "Women in Sports. Syd Koff Entered," *Jewish Telegraphic Agency*, 11 April 1934.

Nonetheless, representations about Jewish women's lack of physical capability and participation in sports persist in historical views and in some popular accounts about women in Jewish sports. Journalist Bertha A. Loeb described in 1914 in *The Sentinel*, the American Jewish newspaper in Chicago, the stereotype of the Ashkenazi Jewish woman as a lower-class, weak, and weary immigrant without bodily verve. She articulated the prevailing stereotype about Jews of both sexes in relation to sports and physical health in the early twentieth century: "The undersized, anemic 'Jewish weakling' will soon be a recollection of bygone days." Some Jewish institutions were building gymnasiums "for the youth of both sexes."[2] Indeed, historians of Jewish Studies, American Studies, and women and sport will find documented in diverse historical sources evidence of Jewish women's physical well-being and their various achievements in sports. Many historians have thought that Jewish women, because of their domestic roles and religiosity, particularly for the most observant Jewish females, did not participate in sport. I have investigated the historical experiences of several Jewish women and asked if this lack of sporting participation has been borne out by historical sources.

The study of American Jewish men in sports has yielded evidence over time of sporting experiences and assimilation into American sporting and popular culture. Several scholars have written about Jewish men in American sports, noting that Jews have historically been perceived as "people of the book" (the Torah) rather "than men and women of the bat." Such scholars have explored how Jewish men played baseball and basketball, as well as competed in boxing and other sports. Jewish men vied for victory in American sports to demonstrate their masculinity—belying the historical stereotype of weak and sickly Jewish men; men of brains, not brawn. These Jewish men became "Tough Jews," as historian Steven Riess termed it, in sports such as boxing.[3] Indeed, historical works

---

[2] B.A. Loeb, "The Temple of the Body. How the Hebrew Institute Is Laboring to Make Jews Physically Fit," *The Sentinel*, 1 May 1914, Jacob M. Loeb Collection, Chicago Hebrew Institute (hereafter cited as CHI), American Jewish Archives, Cincinnati, OH. On Jewish women's roles in the early twentieth century, see C. Baum et al., *The Jewish Woman in America* (New York: Plume Books, 1977), and Pamela S. Nadell, ed., *American Jewish Women's History* (New York: New York University Press, 2003).

[3] Steven A. Riess, ed., *Sports and the American Jew* (Syracuse, NY: Syracuse University Press, 1998): 1–2; on "Tough Jews" see Chapter 2 about American Jewish men and boxing, 60–104; Linda J. Borish, " 'Athletic Activities of Various

about Jewish life and sports typically focus on sportsmen. Alan Klein argues "that in the U.S., Jews used sport as a vehicle for assimilation and in certain sports put up impressive numbers. The first half of the twentieth century had Jewish men performing at an elite level in boxing and basketball."[4] Jews in baseball, for example, also showed their manly athletic prowess, challenging images of scrawny Jewish men.[5] In reality, Jewish women as well as men, strove to participate in a range of sports as a way of gaining access to American culture and defying stereotypes about Jewish women as weak, sickly, and uninterested in sports.

Historians, however have neglected to research how and why Jewish women participated in sports and competed in athletics. Historians of women and American Jewish life and religion have explored Jewish women in literature, politics, theater and music, media and television, for example, yet have overlooked the role of Jewish women in sports. A study of American sport history and culture reveals that Jewish women have played a substantial role in influencing sports and have, at times, expanded traditional gender, ethnic, and religious roles in the field of sports. As Edna R. Seligman reported in 1917 in the *American Hebrew*, although "[t]he field of athletics is one of the last that the Jewish woman has entered," in "the last year or two they have come to the front in this field too."[6] American Jewish sportswomen have in fact, played an important role in the sporting landscape in America from the late nineteenth century to the present. American Jewish women played on teams for the Young Women's Hebrew Associations and settlement houses such as the Irene Kaufmann Settlement or the Chicago Hebrew Insti-

---

Kinds': Physical Health and Sport Programs for Jewish American Women," *Journal of Sport History* 26 (Summer 1999): 240–270; Peter Levine, *Ellis Island to Ebbets Field: Sport and the American Jewish Experience* (New York: Oxford University Press, 1992); Steven A. Riess, "Jews and American Sports," *The Routledge History of American Sport*, eds. Linda J. Borish et al. (New York: Routledge, 2017), 172–186.

[4] Alan M. Klein, "Anti-Semitism and Anti-Somatism: Seeking the Elusive Sporting Jew." *Sport in Society: Cultures, Commerce, Media, Politics* 10, no. 6 (Oct. 2007): 1120–1121. See also Jeffrey S. Gurock, *Judaism's Encounter with American Sports* (Bloomington, IN: Indiana University Press, 2005), which focuses mainly on men in the twentieth century.

[5] *Ellis Island to Ebbets Field;*. See also Steven A. Riess, "Jews and American Sports," *The Routledge History of American Sport*, ed. Linda J. Borish et al.

[6] Edna R. Seligman, "Versatility of Jewish Women," *American Hebrew*, 102 (14 September 1917), 526.

tute, and later for Jewish Community Centers. In sports such as swimming, basketball, and tennis, American Jewish sportswomen have shattered stereotypes about the unathletic and uninterested Jewish woman who displays sparse participation in sporting activities.[7] Sybil "Syd" Koff's story of exceling in track and field adds importance to the historical understanding of Jewish women in American sports.

Known to those around her as "Syd," Sybil Koff Cooper (1913–1998) achieved success in track and field during her athletic career, which started in New York City and continued across the United States. She was also successful in international competitions during the interwar period of the twentieth century. Koff maintained her Jewish identity as a champion in the Maccabiah Games—known as the "Jewish Olympics"—earning an astonishing seven gold medals during the 1932 and 1935

[7] For information on the various YM and YWHAs and sporting programs for Jewish women at settlement houses see Linda J. Borish, "'An Interest in Physical Well-Being Among the Feminine Membership': Sporting Activities for Women at Young Men's and Young Women's Hebrew Associations," *American Jewish History* 87 (March 1999): 61–93; Borish, "Women, Sports, and American Jewish Identity in the Late Nineteenth and Early Twentieth Centuries," in *With God on their Side: Sport in the Service of Religion*, Tara Magdalinksi and Timothy J.L. Chandler, eds. (London: Routledge Press, 2002), 71–98; Borish, "Place, Identity, Physical Culture and Sport for Women in Jewish Americanization Organizations" in *STADION: Internationale Zeitschrift für Geschichte des Sports/Internationa/ Journal of the History of Sport/Revue International d' Histoire du Sport*, 35 (2009): 87–108; Borish, "Jewish Sportswomen," in *Jews and American Popular Culture* 3, Sports, Leisure, and Lifestyle, ed. Paul Buhle (Westport, CT: Praeger, 2006): 71–101. On American Jewish women excelling in certain sports and involved in sporting contests against Jewish and non-Jewish competitors, see Borish, "Jewish Women in the American Gym: Basketball, Ethnicity, and Gender in the Early Twentieth Century," in *Jews in the Gym: Judaism, Sports, and Athletics*, ed. Leonard Greenspoon 3, Studies in Jewish Civilization (West Lafayette, IN: Purdue University Press, 2012): 213–237; Borish, "'The Cradle of American Champions, Women Champions…Swim Champions': Charlotte Epstein, Gender and Jewish Identity, and the Physical Emancipation of Women in Aquatic Sports," *The International Journal of the History of Sport* 21, no. 2 (March 2004): 197–235; Borish, "American Jewish Women on the Court: Seeking an Identity in Tennis in the Early Decades of the Twentieth Century," in *Beyond Stereotypes: American Jews and Sports, the University of Southern California Casden Institute for the Study of the Jewish Role in America Life*, Annual Review 12, eds. Bruce Zuckerman, Ari F. Sclar (guest editor) and Lisa Ansell (West Lafayette, IN: Purdue University Press, 2014), 43–72.

Games. Koff just missed making the 1932 Olympic team for track and field in Los Angeles, and she boycotted the 1936 Olympics in Berlin, held under the Nazi government. However, Koff continued her athletic prowess in women's track and field, serving as a national 80-yard hurdle champion in 1940 at the National Championships/Olympic trials, beating U.S. record holder Marie Cottrell. This meet qualified Koff for the 1940 Helsinki Olympic Games, although the games were cancelled due to World War II.[8] Koff missed two Olympic Games, the pinnacle of track and field competition, which perhaps accounts for some of her lack of recognition in U.S. sports history. The current investigation of Koff also reveals how gender, ethnicity, and religiosity shaped her sporting experiences in the early decades of the twentieth century. As a young Jewish woman, she asserted her religious affiliation and challenged the gendered perception of Jewish women as lacking athletic ability. Koff's impressive athletic career shows how she maintained her American and Jewish identities and competed as an American Jewish woman in high-level competitions.

Sybil "Syd" Koff's Early Years and Interest in Athletics

Born Celia Tabachnikoff in 1913, Syd Koff, the youngest of five children of Russian immigrants, had her name changed as she entered sporting competition; her father, Sam, used the shortened family name. Koff earned acclaim at the first Maccabi Games, the "Jewish Olympics," at age nineteen with her impressive athletic performance, earning three gold medals. She showed interest in sports at an even earlier age, though her parents held no interest. Koff grew up in New York City and, as with many young women of immigrant backgrounds, her family did not encourage her enthusiasm for sports. However, Koff was a fierce competitor and wanted to participate in track and field. During his time in a nursing home, Koff's father decided to write his autobiography, providing insight into the life of Koff and her family. Unfortunately, the entire autobiography is not provided in the archive of Koff's son, Steve Cooper, but the pages written by Koff's father, Sam Tabachnikoff, do provide information regarding Koff's early athletic career, her trips around the

---

[8] Borish, "Jewish Sportswomen, 94; "Sybil Cooper, Track Star, 85," *Forward* (29 May 1998): 10; Steve Cooper, "The Story of Sybille—True and Complete," *Sybille Gallery Newsletter* (Premiere Issue Summer 1998): 1–2; Steve Cooper Archives, New York, NY. (hereafter Steve Cooper Archives).

world, and her later marriage to Felix Cooper. In this autobiography, Koff's father recalled her interest in track and field:

> [O]ur baby daughter, who had grown up to be a leggy youngster, was a tomboy, her greatest delight was athletics. She was a member of the German-American Club, and she was in her glory there. She was on the running team, and often came home with medals that she had won in the races. Her specialty was the hurdle race, her long legs stood her in good stead here. About this time, Palestine held an athletic meet for Jewish youth of the entire world. The American Macabees club was sending a team, six boys and six girls. Three days before the boat was scheduled to sail, the German-American Club had a meet on Long Island, and the American Macabees team were there as observers. Syd won a silver cup for her running. The manager of the visiting team was interested, and when he heard that she was Jewish, he approached her, introduced himself, and told her that she would have a place on their team for the Palestinian trip.[9]

In biographical information in the family archives, it can be ascertained that a track observer discovered Koff jumping at Coney Island, New York, and invited her to join the Millrose Athletic Club; she won gold in her first race on 22 January 1930. By 1931, prior to the Maccabiah Games, Koff had earned twenty-two medals; she later qualified as one of the twelve members of the first U.S. Maccabiah team.[10]

Like some immigrant parents, Koff's father was reluctant to have his daughter participate in athletics, wondering what benefits it might yield for her.[11] When Koff came home after being recognized for her athletic skill by the Maccabiah team, "[s]he was overwhelmed with joy, and came rushing home to tell us the good news." Koffs' parents, however, unfamiliar with the culture of sports for young women, initially held an unenthusiastic perspective on athletics for their daughter. As Koff's father explained, "[w]e had scoffed at her preoccupation with athletics. [R]unning was all right for a boy, but where did a girl get off, thinking only about racing?" Her father expected a girl to grow up and follow gender conventions for young women of the time: "she should learn to earn her own money and prepare for marriage." Koff's parents did not show sympathy toward her athletic interest, and friction emerged in the house. Koff's father recalled that when she, "rushed in, all enthused over

---

[9] Sam Tabachnikoff, "An Autobiography," Steve Cooper Archives.

[10] Syd Koff, "Biographical Information," 1. Steve Cooper Archives.

[11] Tabachnikoff, "An Autobiography."

the chance to go to Palestine, we did not know what to tell her. To send a girl alone half way around the world, without us. But Syd would not take no for an answer. She made me go to the American Macabee office on Fifth Avenue to get more information."[12]

Her father also expressed some doubts about Koff competing in international sporting events. Sam recollected the experience of helping Koff get ready to sail overseas to Palestine because he worried about his daughter traveling such a long distance. One of the men involved with the trip informed him that there would twenty-eight nations participating; the boat for Palestine with the U.S. team, he added, planned to sail in two days. Koff's father complained, "[w]hat form of insanity was this, I asked them, People going all the way to Palestine just to run and jump." One of the men asked Syd's father how long he had been in the United States, informing him "'that you do not know what athletic contests are, and how much they mean to everyone.'" Sam answered that he had lived in the United States for more than twenty years but that he never heard of such athletic activities. One of the men patiently explained that

> these contests were international, and did much to increase the good will among the nations. This one had been undertaken to show that Jewish youth [were] the equal of all youth in the world in their athletic prowess, and since it was a Jewish show, the Jewish boys and girls from twenty-eight countries participating, the logical place to hold it was Palestine.[13]

Sam continued his thoughts on the prospect of his daughter joining in such sporting activities:

> I was in a daze—running and jumping should be so important that people were [willing] to spend money to sponsor such exhibition, it still seemed crazy to me. When the men told me that I would have to decide at once, I thought, how can I send a young girl so far away, alone, and she has never been out of New York.[14]

Koff's father recollected, "[b]ut the men pressed me for an answer, and very reluctantly, I said yes. They explained that a nurse and a doctor would accompany the team, that [Koff] would be well taken care of, that chaperones were also in the company, and that I had nothing to worry

---

[12] Sam Tabachnikoff, "An Autobiography," Steve Cooper Archives.

[13] Tabachnikoff, "An Autobiography."

[14] Ibid.

about." Sam countered, "Not worry, I thought. Were any of them a father sending a young daughter away from her family over the seven seas? But I had agreed."[15]

Indeed, Syd Koff would embark on her international sporting career by participating in the Maccabiah Games. The send-off would involve U.S. and Jewish officials wishing the team well in its athletic endeavors, and once again Sam remembered the event and shared his views:

> The men in the office thank me for giving my permission for Syd to go with them, they felt that she would be an important addition to their team, after all to be the winning team would be quite a feather in their cap. Then they told me to read tomorrow morning's paper, and I left. The next morning I read in the paper that the entire team, with Syd, were to be at City Hall at noon. When we reached downtown, we found a platform had been erected in front of the City Hall, and that there was a crowd of several thousand people waiting there. The mayor came out and greeted every member of the team, and when he greeted Syd, he made a little speech, telling her how proud we must be of her victory on Long Island the day before, and that if she repeated this performance in Palestine, the whole world would hear of her excellence as an athlete. We didn't know what to think, whether to be proud of her, or to think that the whole affair was whacky. Since everyone was making such a fuss, maybe we were wrong, and we should give her the benefit of the doubt.[16]

Given the popular interest in sport and the persuasion of the Maccabiah leaders informing Koff's father of the importance and pride in this Jewish sports competition, Sam offered a changed viewpoint on Koff participating in the Maccabiah Games. As part of a national recognition of this first U.S. Maccabiah team of twelve athletes, the grand sendoff on 11 March 1932 included New York City Mayor Jimmy Walker and other dignitaries. The desire for Americans to win in international competition included this Jewish competition. In fact, the sendoff group included heralded 1924 Olympic swimmer and first woman to swim the English Channel in 1926, Gertrude Ederle. Ederle, teammate of renowned swimming leader and Jewish sportswomen Charlotte Epstein (founder of the Women's Swimming Association fostering Olympic champions) certainly supported these American Jewish athletes. With Epstein's guidance, Ederle swam at the New York Young Women's Hebrew Associa-

---

[15] Ibid.
[16] Ibid.

tion where national championships were contested, and Epstein served as chaperone-manager of the U.S. Women's swimming team for three Olympic Games, as well as for the 1935 Maccabiah Games.[17]

Syd Koff, the Maccabiah Games, and Jewish Identity

At nineteen years old Koff began the journey on the ship sailing to Palestine to compete in the first ever Maccabiah Games in March 1932. These games comprised athletes from fourteen countries. The U.S. women's team consisted of the outstanding track athlete Syd Koff as well as swimmer Eva Bein, the only two U.S. women to compete in these games. On 11 March 1932, The *Brooklyn Daily Eagle* reported, "Jewish Stars to Sail Tonight for Palestine. Six Brooklyn Athletes on Team Presenting U.S. at Tel Aviv," indicating that the New York media covered the event. The article specifically recognized Koff, stating, "Miss Syd Koff, prominent girl sprinter, who won the dash events at the AAU [Amateur Athletic Union] development meet and at the Knights of Columbus Games. She has a mark of 8.8 for the seventy-five yard dash, has traveled over sixteen feet in the broad jump, and has reared five feet in the high jump."[18] The *New York Times* also commented on 29 March 1932 that "25,000 Jam Stadium as First Event of its Kind Gets Underway Way in Tel Aviv; Miss Koff Is a Victor; New York Girl Wins Semi-Final of 100 Meter Race." Another *New York Times* article highlighted Koff's achievements in the track and field finals, writing that "Miss Sybil Koff of New York won the women's 100-meter dash, the women's triathlon and the high jump."[19] Koff recalled, "I was the whole women's'

---

[17] Linda J. Borish, "'The Cradle of American Champions, Women Champions...Swim Champions': Charlotte Epstein, Gender and Jewish Identity, and the Physical Emancipation of Women in Aquatic Sports"; for information on the 1920s and 1930s U.S. Women Olympic Swimmers and Gertrude Ederle's 1926 English Channel swim see Gerald R. Gems et al., *Sports in American History: From Colonization to Globalization*, 2nd ed. (Champaign, IL: Human Kinetics, 2017).

[18] "Jewish Starts to Sail for Palestine: Six Brooklyn Athletes on Team Representing U.S. At Tel Aviv," *Brooklyn Daily Eagle*, 11 March 1932, 14, Steve Cooper Archives.

[19] Joseph M. Levy, "Jewish Olympics Open in Palestine: 25,000 Jam Stadium as First Event of Its Kind Gets Underway in Tel Aviv," *New York Times*, 29 March 1932, 14, Steve Cooper Archives; "Miss Koff Scores in Jewish Games:

track team, literally," and she won more medals—three golds—than anyone else on the U.S. team.[20] Koff showed how, as a Jewish woman representing both her Jewish faith and the U.S. nation, sports were a significant part of her life. Her victories propelled her to popular acclaim in
sports—an area in which few in the media anticipated a Jewish woman to
excel.

To honor the achievement of Koff and her U.S. teammates, the
Maccabiah team members were to be recognized in an event showing
their pride in being Jewish. Koff received a letter on 20 May 1932 from
Dr. Solomon Flink, chairman of the U.S. Maccabee Association. The
letter reveals the importance of the Maccabiah team's athletic success and
how the team ought to display its ethnic pride at the event. The letter
stated the protocol for receiving medals they won in Palestine:

> Dear Friend. As you know the U.S. Maccabee team will be presented
> to the Mayor of York City on Sunday afternoon at the Polo [Grounds]
> where they will receive the medals in Palestine. It is imperative that
> every member of the team be there with their Maccabee uniform for
> the parade and presentation to the Mayor.[21]

The success of the first Maccabiah Games led to the organization of
the second Maccabiah Games in 1935. In the time between the two
competitions, Koff continued her athletic endeavors. She again led the
track and field team for the United States, and was joined by Jewish track
star Lillian Copeland, the 1932 Los Angeles Olympics discus champion.
Both Koff and Copeland competed against the great Mildred "Babe"
Didrikson. At the second Maccabiah Games, thirty countries competed.
Lou Cohen of the *Brooklyn Daily Eagle* crowned Koff as "Bensonhurt's
One-Girl Track Team," expressing Jewish pride in her achievements on
the track. Cohen also wrote about Koff's appearance, writing that she
bucked traditional male conventions of female athletes lacking feminine
attributes: "For the Koff girl from Bensonhurst, although tall and ex-
ceedingly well built, is pleasant-looking and indeed quite attractive. She
lacks the hard-features commonly associated with the female athlete."

New York Girl Captures Three Final Events as Maccabiah in Palestine Ends;
25,000 Watch Contests," *New York Times*, 1 April 1932, 14, Steve Cooper Archives.

[20] "Miss Koff Scores in Jewish Games," *New York Times*, 1 April 1932, 1.

[21] Letter to Sybil Koff from Dr. Solomon Flink, 20 May 1932, Steve
Cooper Archives.

Cohen described Koff's competitiveness and passion to regain her title in the second Maccabiah Games, explaining: "[t]here is nothing from which she derives so much enjoyment as track and to prove how entertaining her career has been thus far, she has won her way to possession of fifty-six medals, two trophies and various certificates, necklaces, and wristwatches."[22]

In 1935, Koff once again shined in the international spotlight of the Maccabiah Games in Tel Aviv, along with an expanded roster of female teammates. Tens of thousands crowded into the Tel Aviv Stadium for the opening ceremony. The festivities featured the hoisting of the Maccabi flag, and expressions of Jewish identity manifested in the "Blue and White clad Maccabi" and the singing of "Hatikvah," the song that would become Israel's national anthem: "Every building, every shop and every home proudly displayed the Zionist colors".[23] In his opening address, translated from Hebrew into English, Lord Melchett, official British leader of Palestine, proclaimed, "[w]e represent here today a movement of 200,000 young men and women imbued with high ideals and with the knowledge that the physical development of Jewry, the inculcation in the heart of Jewry of the love of athletics, is a necessary element in the up-building of our nation and of our land." To the Jews who came from the Diaspora, Maccabiah officials stated that they must return to their countries after the Maccabiah Games, despite the plea by Melchett that, "I wish to remind all Maccabis of the solemn promise which I have given upon their behalf, to leave this country before the period by the authorities expires." Many competitors, however, took advantage of their being in the Palestine and decided to stay, "defying British government's strict limitations on *aliyah* [seeking permanent residence], the *Palestine Post* reported.[24] Koff also stayed in Palestine for a time after her competitions ended.

---

[22] Lou E. Cohen, "Syd Koff—She Suddenly Became an Athlete and Rose to Champion," *Brooklyn Daily Eagle*, 22 Aug. 1934, 16, Steve Cooper Archives.

[23] Quoted from "Second Maccabiah Flag Hoisted," *The Palestine Post*, Tel Aviv, 2 April 1935, and "Gay Pageantry Marks Opening of Maccabiah," *The Palestine Post*, Jerusalem, 3 April 1935, p. 1. In New York Public Library (hereafter NYPL), Dorot Jewish Division.

[24] Rivka Rabinowitz, ed., "History of the Maccabiah Games," *Sixteenth Maccabiah: One People, One Dream*, Israel, July 2001. Archival Material from the Pierre Gildesgame Maccabi Sports Museum and Maccabi World Union, Ramat-Gan, Israel; "After the Maccabiah," *The Palestine Post*, Jerusalem, 9 April

Koff excelled at the Games, winning three first places in the 50-meter dash, 200-meter dash, and 400-meter hurdle; she took second in the broad jump. Koff won a total of seven gold medals between these first two Maccabiads.[25] The *American Hebrew* remarked in 1935 that "Miss Koff, the Maccabiad star, was the leading Jewish girl athlete of the year winning the 200 Meter Metropolitan AAU title."[26] Joined by teammate Lillian Copeland, their elite athletic feats earned them victories. According to the *American Hebrew*, "Outstanding was Lillian Copeland of Los Angeles, 1932 Olympic champion, who scored first in the javelin throw, shotput and discus at Tel Aviv."[27]

In the 1935 Maccabiad, Copeland and Koff led the American team to win "the Manischewitz Trophy," named for a major manufacturer of kosher food and wine products. Manischewitz's sponsorship of the trophy not only exemplified U.S. supremacy in track and field events, but also linked these athletes to the Jewish community.[28] In the 4x100 relay race, Copeland and Koff were joined by their teammates—who happened to be swimmers—to win a bronze medal: "It was quite a relay team...Janice Lifson led off, Lillian Copeland...ran the second leg. Swimmer Doris Kelman ran third leg. And then me."[29] On competing in the Maccabi Games, Koff recollected, "I felt very strongly that it was an innovative thing...I wanted to do something really spectacular to make a dent in it for American Jews participating. I saw it as a marvelous opportunity for me to do something."[30]

In 1936, journalist Lou Cohen again wrote about Koff in terms of gender, noting that "Sybil Koff is one of those pleasant creatures who

---

1935, 5, NYPL, Dorot Jewish Division. For additional information on athletes wanting to stay in Palestine see Rabinowitz "History of the Maccabiah Games."

[25] "Jewish Sportsmen on Parade," *American Hebrew* 136 (7 June 1935): 94; "Jewish Who's Who–1935, Sports," *American Hebrew*, 193.

[26] "Jewish Who's Who–1935, Sports," 192.

[27] Ibid., 192–3.

[28] Linda J. Borish, "Women, Sports, and American Jewish Identity in the Late Nineteenth and Early Twentieth Centuries," in *With God on their Side: Sport in the Service of Religion*, Tara Magdalinksi and Timothy J.L. Chandler, eds. (London: Routledge, 2002), 71–98. See also "Miss Koff Scores in Jewish Games," *New York Times*, 1 April 1932; "Jewish Sportsmen on Parade," 94; "Jewish Who's Who–1935, Sports," 192–193.

[29] Article in Syd Koff Album, Steve Cooper Archives.

[30] "Reflections of Past Maccabiet," Steve Cooper Archives.

would rather conquer the world all by herself than stay home and do the dishes. Four years ago she competed in Palestine at the Maccabi Games and tallied forty-four points to single-handedly win the team prize." He continued, "Last year she returned to the Holy Land and came back with three first places."[31]

In a piece titled, "Two-Woman Team," the *Palestine Post* articulated the outstanding athleticism of Koff and Copeland. The newspaper commentated that "Miss Sybil Koff continued to show her fast-stepping heels to a smart field of women sprinters in winning the 200-meter dash in 27.6 seconds, cracking the old Palestine (Maccabiah) record. Syd is as versatile in the track events as Lilian Copeland is in the field events."[32] The American Jewish press, too, noted Koff's sporting victories. In a column in Philadelphia's *Jewish Exponent*, "Womankind: Jewish Women in Sports, Baroness Levi, Miss Copeland and Miss Koff Lead in Various Fields," editor Emma Brylawski extolled the sporting prowess of Koff in the international sporting arena:

> Syd in one of her races was coasting around the turn planning to put on steam in the last steps of the home stretch. The girl is a front runner...However, the fact that she was in the lead not withstanding, the crowd of 50,000 spectators were wildly exhorting her to put on even more steam and smash the world's record. She answered to their cries valiantly and put on a burst of speed that had not been seen since the Tel Aviv Stadium was built. Hers was the fastest time a human being had covered 200 meters in Palestine since the history of the world.[33]

Koff and the American Jewish women who excelled in sports expressed pride and patriotism at home and in their affiliation with Jewish life.

Koff's Boycott of the 1936 Berlin Nazi Olympics

As Jews and Americans, athletes such as Koff and Copeland continued with their sporting careers, in the knowledge that the Berlin Olympics

---

[31] Lou E. Cohen, article in *The Brooklyn Daily Eagle*, 6 April 1936, 19, Steve Cooper Archives.

[32] "Two-Woman Team," *Palestine Post*, 5 April 1935, 17. In Steve Cooper Archives.

[33] Emma Brylawski, "Womankind: Jewish Women in Sports, Baroness Levi, Miss Copeland and Miss Koff Lead in Various Fields," *Jewish Exponent*, 13 May 1935, 5.

would be held the following year, in 1936. Both were aware of the threat of Nazism in Europe, and during her stay in Palestine following the Maccabiah Games, Koff corresponded with family members and shared her view of the growing crisis in Germany, which would lead her to boycott the 1936 Olympics. In the letter written on Wednesday, 29 May 1935, Koff wrote:

> Before I go further let me tell you of a lovely holiday spent here in Haifa. It is called the Log-Bomar Day. A day on which they always burn large pieces of wood and make real bonfires. All the young Maccabim gathered around the fire and sing songs. And nearly everywhere you go you may find fires of this sort. The real beauty of them was the fact that they had all burned effigies of Hitler. They made stuffed heads and bodies and I swear they looked just like the old Geezer. As he burned away the higher the singing went, and everyone sighed because they knew that it was only in effigy that he was burning....Nevertheless it is a happy holiday and they all acted the part.[34]]

Koff and Copeland also corresponded about the impending Olympics. In a letter from Copeland to Koff, written 11 December 1935, Copeland remarked, "You know...how very, very much interested I will be to hear from you at length about Palestine during your extended sojourn. One can conclude that you were afforded ample opportunity to form an opinion about the Promised Land." Copeland shared that she corresponded with other "Maccabi's," including swimmers Janice Lifson and Doris Kelman, and male team members, and focused on the rise of Hitler and Nazism. Her letter to Koff continued, "It appears that nothing short of a war involving Deutschland will prevent the Olympics from going there. What is the attitude of regarding the Amer. Jewish athletes?" Copeland offered Koff her analysis of Jewish athletes competing in the Nazi Olympics:

> The "jolly fishes" governing the A.O.T. for 1936, had they not been blinded to and by poor reasoning, would have taken the bull by the horns and voted against Amer. [p]articipation...Of course, the Jews had a difficult row...to hoe: theirs was a true dilemma of logic; for one had to ask what support they had ever given to sports to have the privilege of using the Games as a boomerang. One need only know their interest in the Maccabis. It is all too bad: but there are two sides to this

---

[34] Letter from Sybil Syd Koff, Palestine, to family, 29 May 1935, Steve Cooper Archives.

controversy and, unfortunately, the Jews have the weight of conviction on their side, without meriting the weight.[35]

Copeland noted she would miss seeing Koff at the track and field ("nationals indoors or out,") but their correspondence continued, as did decisions by these American Jewish sportswomen to not compete in the 1936 Nazi Olympics. Copeland, who considered her gold medal her triumph in the 1932 Olympics, joined with other Jewish women athletes to boycott Hitler at the Berlin Olympics in 1936, and thus did not defend her Olympic title.[36]

Copeland, recalling her connection with Koff as a teammate at the 1935 Maccabiad, wanted to know Koff's decision about paticipating in the 1936 Olympics. On 7 April 1936, Copeland wrote, "Its [sic] track season, Olympic Games year, etc. A year ago today we stood in that windswept sun-burned, humanity-laden sport in Tel-Aviv participating in the closing ceremony of the Maccabiah." Copeland declared that, "armed conflict before August 1st would indeed upset the picture and my feeling is much will be acceded to short of obliterating German's [sic] staging of the Games." She also noted that "arch-sadist Hitler will not be stilled" and that "as a member of the Women's Track & Field Committee of the Amer. Olympic Committee I owe the utmost duty as such member as a member of former American Teams." Copeland urged Koff good success in her final tryouts for the 1936 U.S Olympic team on 4 July and expressed that the "big shot on the scene"—Helen Stephens—with her prowess, would "help one to forget Babe Didrikson." Commenting on her own event of the discus throw, Copeland asserted her patriotism; with a lack of "capable standard bearers" she stated she should "hate to see no American flag raised after that event in August." She then

---

[35] Letter from Lillian Copeland, Los Angeles, to Sybil Koff, Brooklyn, 11 December1935, underline in original letter, Steve Cooper Archives.

[36] Letter from Lillian Copeland, Los Angeles, to Sybil Koff, Brooklyn, 11 December 1935, Steve Cooper Archives. Linda J. Borish, "Lillian Copeland," in *The Encyclopedia of Ethnicity and Sports in the United States*, ed. George B. Kirsch et al. (Westport CT: Greenwood Press, 200), 110; "Lillian Copeland, 59, Dies; Won Olympic Medal in 1932," *The New York Times*, 8 July 1964, 35; "Miss Copeland Sets Mark in Shot-Put," *The New York Times*, 13 Aug. 1928, 12:4. For information on Copeland's views on the Olympic Games, see Paul Soifer, "Lillian Copeland Speaks Out on the Olympics: Los Angles, 1932, Berlin 1936, *Western States Jewish History* 38 (Fall 2005): 3–16.

asked Koff, to send her a "copy of the paper containing the article on Jewish athletes."[37]

Koff needed to decide her own position on participating on the U.S. Women's Track and Field Team after qualifying in the broad and high jumps for the 1936 Berlin Olympics. Koff identified strongly with the struggles of Jews in Palestine (then under British government) and with Jews in peril in Germany. She worked in Palestine helping to build communities desiring an independent Jewish state. Koff joined the boycott against the Nazi Olympics and gave up her chance for Olympic triumphs. As Koff recollected, "we knew was going on, I had just come back from Palestine. There was no question of going to the Olympics, none at all...there was no interest, no desire to compete over there. There was no hesitation, no regret, nothing at all."[38]

Koff maintained her elite athletic competitive status in the late 1930s with national titles and triumphs against other Olympians. She followed the lead, communicated in 1935 by the Maccabi World Union in the *American Hebrew*, that stated, "Maccabee World Union Urges All Jewish Athletes Boycott Olympics." In December 1935, the *American Hebrew* also registered its opposition to the U.S. sending athletes to the Berlin Olympics. Other members of the Maccabi team also decided against participating: "[Those] who have also resigned from the Olympic Executive Committee and all other Olympic connections are Miss Charlotte Epstein, coach of the American Women's Swimming Association, one of the leading figures in women's sports."[39] Koff joined in the boycott as an elite athlete in the prime of her career. Not competing in the 1936 Nazi Olympic Games showed her stance as a Jew and a woman in gender, ethnic, and religious contexts in her political protest.

---

[37] Letter from Lillian Copeland, Los Angeles, to Sybil Koff, Brooklyn, 7 April 1936, Steve Cooper Archives.

[38] "Sybil Koff Biography," Steve Cooper Archives. Letters and materials from Syd Koff indicate her time in Palestine and her interest in helping in the country.

[39] "Maccabee World Union Urges All Jewish Athletes Boycott Olympics; Sport Group Notes Progress," *American Hebrew* 137 (27 September 1935): 328; "The Olympic Muddle," *American Hebrew* 138 (13 December 1935): 151; Linda J. Borish, "Epstein, Charlotte," 382; see also J. T. Mahoney, "America Should Refuse Participation in Olympics: The Case for Withdrawal of the United States from the Olympics in Germany Is Eloquently Stated by A.A.U. Head," *American Hebrew* 137 (30 August 1935): 259, 261.

Enroute to the Maccabiah Games.
Syd resting after a workout on board the S.S. Patria
crossing the Mediterranean, March 24, 1932, age 19.
Courtesy of Steve Cooper Archives of Syd Koff, New York City

Lillian Copeland and Syd Koff at the 1935 Maccabiah Games.
"Lillian C. and myself going to the stadium to start the day of competition."
Courtesy of Steve Cooper Archives of Syd Koff, New York City

Syd High Jumps.
"Sybil Koff Cooper, metropolitan women's high jump champion, is shown
in midair as she clears the bar in scissor twist high jump at the German A.C.
gymnasium in New York," April 25 1940.

Courtesy Steve Cooper Archives of Syd Koff, New York City.

Syd with her medals and trophies, Flatbush, Brooklyn, 1948.
Courtesy Steve Cooper Archives of Syd Koff, New York City

Koff continued to train for track and field events. In 1940 she won the woman's 80-yard hurdles at the National Championships/Olympic Trials for the upcoming Olympic Games, beating U.S. record holder Marie Cottrel. She qualified for the 1940 Olympic Games in Helsinki, but the Games were cancelled due to World War II.[40] The *Jewish Advocate* published an article citing Koff as an example of a stellar Jewish athlete in its piece about Jews from pre-state Palestine participating in the 1940 Japanese Olympiad, which had been considered as an Olympic site prior to Helsinki being selected. Participating as an all-Jewish contingent, the Jews could participate as their own team for their desired homeland. "Sybil Koff, outstanding star of the first Jewish Olympics and the girl who beat Jesse Owens' four first places by four years, declared, 'There is no doubt in my mind but that women athletes of Palestine can be developed into world champions in the track and field and water events.'"[41] Koff wrote passionately in the *Jewish Examiner* on the need for a Maccabi organization in America, especially for women athletes. In 1939 she declared "[i]t is almost imperative to have a Maccabi" as Jews needed to "compete for decidedly non-Jewish clubs, i.e. Swedish-American, German-American, Park Central, Millrose A.A., etc." About women in sports, Koff wrote: "[t]here are five champions in the Metropolitan Area who must compete against one another...They are Jewish, and should they be representatives of Jewry wearing the 'Star of David,' then that would be enlightening and give some strength in the hearts that are mourning the Fate of the Jews."[42]

Jewish sportswomen displayed courage and integrity in their roles in public as accomplished sportswomen in the 1930s. At a time when relatively few women competed in world-class competitions, Syd Koff, her fellow American Jewish sportswomen, and Maccabi athletes Lillian Copeland and Jason Lifson, demonstrated their commitment to upholding their Jewish identities.[43]

---

[40] "Sybil Cooper, Track Star, 85," *Forward* (29 May 1998): 10; Steve Cooper, "The Story of Sybille—True and Complete," *Sybille Gallery Newsletter* (Premiere Issue Summer 1998): 1–2, Steve Cooper Archives.

[41] "Our Sports World," by Loyal Rooters, *The Jewish Advocate*, 29 August 1938, 19.

[42] Sybil Syd Koff, "An Appeal for a Maccabi," *The Jewish Examiner*, 14 July 1939, Steve Cooper Archives.

[43] For information on these other American Jewish women athletes and the Nazi Olympic boycott, see Linda J. Borish, "American Jewish Sportswomen:

Koff maintained her enthusiasm for sports in her Jewish life. She displayed and upheld her Jewishness while highlighting her athletic talents in numerous ways. According to her father's reminiscences after her return from overseas (likely after 1935), Koff challenged anti-Semitism surrounding her successful sporting feats competing as a Jew after they were called into question:

> Upon her return, she came across an article in the sporting pages of the newspaper, that the American Olympic Committee had investigated the alleged championship of the Jewish Girl from Brooklyn wasn't kosher, that graft had been paid to proclaim her the champion. This was an attempted whitewash, as the committee's hands weren't too clean in the affair of the Western Meet, four years previous, it had been rushed three months in advance, and we felt that the reason had been that they did not want to acclaim a Jewish girl as the champion. How upon reading this article, Syd became very angry, and called the manager of the team, and told him to refute this slander. He did not want to start anything, and said, it was over four years since the races, better let sleeping dogs lie. But she was not satisfied, and insisted that in all fairness, the Olympic committee must let her compete with their team, to prove that she had won her laurels fairly. So a racing meeting was arranged in Atlantic City, Syd against the Olympic racing team, and before a large crowd, Syd won. She was very happy, she had proved that her title had been won fairly, and even though there was not any title at stake here, she felt that she had been exonerated. She was asked to say a few words to the public, so she told them she was very happy that she had won, as this proved that she was a champion in fact, if not in name, and that was all she wanted. She held up her left hand, and pointing to her wedding band, announced that now she was thru with racing, she was very happily married, and would now start raising a family.[44]

Koff, indeed, married Felix Cooper in 1938 and started a family.

Conclusion

Sybil "Syd" Koff earned a remarkable career of achievement in track and field from the 1920s through the 1940. Although she never earned an

---

The 1935 Maccabi Games and the 1936 Berlin Olympics," lecture series presented by the Schusterman Center for Jewish Studies in conjunction with the H.J. Luther Stark Center for Physical Culture and Sports and the Texas Program in Sport and Media, University of Texas-Austin, 24 January 2016.

[44] Tabachnikoff, "An Autobiography," Steve Cooper Archives.

Olympic medal due to the political turmoil of the 1936 Nazi Olympics and the cancellation of the 1940 Helsinki games, she garnered media attention from the American and Jewish press and earned noteworthy championships on the track. Koff upheld her convictions as a Jewish woman, supporting sport in pre-state Palestine in the 1930s, and by displaying ethnic and gender pride as a champion track-and-field athlete. Koff also expressed her identity as a Jewish woman as she boycotted the Nazi Olympics in 1936. As one observer of Jews in sports stated, in looking back at the 1936 Olympics and recognizing Koff's seven gold medals in the Maccabiah Games, "[h]ow many Olympic medals she might have won in the Games for which she qualified is conjecture."[45] The next Maccabiah Games would take place fifteen years after the 1935 games in which Koff shined, due to World War II. Years later, in 1968, Koff resumed her athletic career at age fifty-five in the Masters Track Meet. She continued to add to her medals and accolades. During her impressive career, Koff won 110 medals and trophies.[46] The impact of Sybil "Syd" Koff adds to our historical understanding of American sport and religious history and the understanding of Jewish women in American sports.

Acknowledgment

I am especially grateful to Steve Cooper for sharing the Steve Cooper Archives with the holdings of archival materials about Sybil Syd Koff. It has been a pleasure to work with Steve Cooper and to learn about the remarkable life of Sybil Syd Koff.

---

[45] Steve Lipman, "The Olympics and the Holocaust: Their Participation in the Games Did Not Spare them from Shoah Horrors," *The Jewish Week*, 12 August 2004, 40, Steve Cooper Archives.

[46] Koff, Biographical Information, 1, Steve Cooper Archives.

PART III

EMERGING THEORETICAL INSIGHTS

"I Pray that I Can Be Contagious"
Exploring the Faith of Christian Elite Athletes
Using a Socio-Theological Approach

Tom Gibbons and Stuart Braye

I believe God made me for a purpose, but he also made me fast!
And when I run I feel his pleasure.[1]

Eric Liddell epitomized muscular Christianity.[2] He was a Scottish track athlete, rugby union international, and missionary and is most famous for refusing to run in the men's 100-meter heats at the 1924 Paris Olympics because they were being held on a Sunday. This was depicted in the 1981 film *Chariots of Fire*, which elevated Liddell to even greater fame compared to when he was alive.[3] The decision not to run is, perhaps, one of the best-known examples of an elite Christian athlete publicly putting his faith before the requirements of his sport, but Liddell is not the only example.[4] C.T. Studd and the "Cambridge Seven" in the 1880s is another well-known example from sporting history.[5]

---

[1] Eric Liddell's character in *Chariots of Fire*, directed by Hugh Hudson, UK: 20th Century Fox, 1981.

[2] For more on the historical development of the concept/ideology of "muscular Christianity" see Nick J. Watson et al., "The Development of Muscular Christianity in Victorian Britain and Beyond," *Journal of Religion and Society* 7 (2005): 1–25.

[3] For more on Eric Liddell see John W. Keddie, *Running the Race: Eric Liddell, Olympic Champion and Missionary* (Darlington, Evangelical Press, 2007); Sally Magnusson. *The Flying Scotsman: Biography of Eric Liddell* (London: Quartet, 1981); William J. Weatherby et al., *Chariots of Fire* (London: HarperCollins, 1983); Ellis Cashmore, "Chariots of Fire: Bigotry, Manhood and Moral Certitude in an Age Of Individualism," *Sport in Society* 11 (2008): 159–173.

[4] See also Dennis Brailsford, "The Lord's Day Observance Society and Sunday Sport 1834–1914," *Sport in History* 16 (1996): 140–155.

[5] Norman P. Grubb, *C.T. Studd, Cricketer and Pioneer*, 3rd ed. (Cambridge: Lutterworth Press, 1982); John Pollock, *The Cambridge Seven: The True Story of Ordinary Men Used in No Ordinary Way* (London: Christian Focus, 2006).

Fast-forward a hundred years. In the second decade of the twenty-first century, elite Christian athletes are still expressing their faith through sports in a variety of ways, explicitly and implicitly. For example, after scoring the winning goal securing England's 2-1 victory over Wales in the group stages of the European Soccer Championships (Euro 2016) at the Stade Bollaert-Delelis in Lens, France, on 16 June 2016, Daniel Sturridge said to a BBC reporter in a post-match pitch-side interview, "Great feeling, unbelievable. I'm grateful for the opportunity from the gaffer, grateful to God for allowing me to score."[6] Similarly, after a recent World Heavyweight boxing title fight, *Christianity Today* reported that in a post-fight interview British boxer Tyson Fury gave thanks to Jesus after his victory over Wladimir Klitschko.[7] These are just two examples where elite British, Christian athletes have openly expressed their faith to a global audience. It is not just in post-event interviews that this occurs—other common expressions of faith in elite sport include athletes crossing their chest before they run onto the field, pitch, or court; unveiling statements written across t-shirts worn underneath their team jerseys with sayings such things as "I belong to Jesus"; and bending down on one or both knees to pray before, after, or even during sporting contests.[8] While such expressions of faith are not uncommon in elite sport, questions about the authenticity of the athletes' faith are rarely asked by sports reporters, commentators, or pundits involved in the media production of live sports events.

---

[6] Thomas Bristow, "Watch Winning Goal Scorer Daniel Sturridge's Post-Match Reaction to "Unbelievable" England Win." *Mirror*, 16 June 2016, http://www.mirror.co.uk/sport/football/news/watch-winning-goalscorer-daniel-sturridges-8210241 (accessed 7 July 2016).

[7] Nate Flannagan, "Tyson Fury Testifies 'It Was Only by the Power of Jesus I Won This Fight,' After Claiming World Heavyweight Titles from Wladimir Klitschko," *Christianity Today*, 29 November 2015, http://www.christiantoday.com/article/tyson.fury.testifies.only.by.power.of.jesus.won.this.fight.world.heavyweight.title.wladimir.klitschko/71947.htm (accessed 12 July 2016).

[8] Recent essays on the uses of prayer in sport include Shirl J. Hoffman, "Prayer Out of Bounds" in *Theology, Ethics and Transcendence in Sports*, ed. Jim Parry, et al. (London: Routledge, 2011); Joseph L. Price, "Playing and Praying, Sport and Spirit: The Forms and Functions of Prayer in Sports," *International Journal of Religion and Sport* 1 (2009): 55–80; and Pete Ward, *Gods Behaving Badly: Media, Religion and Celebrity Culture* (Waco, TX: Baylor University Press, 2011).

It is difficult to know the extent of these brief expressions, their full meaning, and why such talented, high-profile athletes make a deliberate point of expressing their beliefs publicly. Surprisingly, few researchers have endeavored to ask elite athletes themselves about their faith. Every other area of the lives of famous sportspeople is under the media's microscope; thus, it seems only right and proper to explore this particular element as well. Sociologist Christopher Stevenson was one of the first to conduct an empirical study using interviews with Christian athletes in Canada, examining "the ways in which certain athletes who were also professing Christians juxtaposed the two role-identities...of Christian and athlete."[9] Few more recent studies exist, however. Toward the end of their systematic review of the multi-disciplinary literature on the topic of sport and Christianity, Nick Watson and Andrew Parker note that:

> [T]he difficulty of course, is discerning the "motivation of the heart" ("a person's inner nature") of a sportsperson who crosses him/herself while running onto the field of play, points to the sky when scoring, and/or gives thanks to God on bended-knee (e.g., Tim Tebow). And thus, theologians need to exercise caution when "judging" (Romans 2:1-3) the external ritualistic behavior of sports celebrities.[10]

The motivations underlying displays of faith by elite sportspeople should not be based on assumptions. We aim to explore this area through a socio-theological lens by critical analysis of narratives collected from a small sample of elite British athletes who defined themselves as "born-again" Christians.[11] At present, narratives from athletes are lacking in academic literature, and there is little focus on the spiritual nature of being "born again" specifically. We seek to develop a thematic framework that can be applied and tested by future researchers in order to gauge the "authenticity" of the faith of supposedly Christian athletes. We aim for future researchers to be able to use this framework as a starting point to examine whether athletes fall into the biblical definition of "born again," to understand how and why athletes express their faith in Jesus Christ, and to demystify current popular views of Christians in sport as often

---

[9] Christopher L. Stevenson, "The Christian-Athlete: An Interactionist-Developmental Analysis." *Sociology of Sport Journal* 8 (1991): 362–379.

[10] Nick J. Watson and Andrew Parker, *Sport and the Christian Religion: A Systematic Review of Literature* (Newcastle-upon-Tyne, Cambridge Scholars Publishing, 2014), 102.

[11] John 3:3, NIV.

presented in the media. Thus, the primary goal of the current chapter is to provide some evidence to address this gap in the literature of religion and sports.

Our secondary goal is to build upon previous purely theoretical work by Tom Gibbons, which aimed to identify Christian approaches to sociology that are yet to be drawn upon by sociologists of sport.[12] In their essay published in the *Sociology of Sport Journal* (one of the leading journals in this sub-discipline), Shilling and Mellor argued that the topic of "religion" has been "marginalized" in sociological analyses of sport over the last two decades.[13] Part of their argument was that "analyzing sport purely as a secular phenomenon, and marginalizing its religious significance, is potentially antagonistic to a broader attempt to grasp its societal importance."[14] They also state that research "studies focused purely on the secular dimensions of sport can be unhelpfully narrow."[15] The current chapter is based upon the kind of "socio-theological" approach pioneered by Robin Gill,[16] through utilizing biblical themes and sociological concepts together to analyze narratives provided by elite Christian sports people.

In what follows, we begin by outlining the socio-theological approach we aim to employ and its relevance to exploring the authenticity of the faith of elite Christian athletes. Here we primarily refer to the work of Gill while also critically analyzing the applicability of *habitus*—now a widely used concept primarily associated with the distinct sociological approach of the late-twentieth-century French social theorist Pierre Bourdieu. We then go on to explain the methodology for the

---

[12] Tom Gibbons, "Challenging the Secular Bias in the Sociology of Sport: Scratching the Surface of Christian Approaches to Sociology," in *Global Perspectives on Sports and Christianity*, ed. Afe Adogame et al. (London: Routledge, 2017); see also Andrew Parker and Nick J. Watson, "Spiritualized and Religious Bodies" in *Routledge Handbook of Physical Cultural Studies*, ed. David L. Andrews et al. (London: Routledge, 2017).

[13] Chris Shilling and Philip A. Mellor, "Re-Conceptualizing Sport as a Sacred Phenomenon," *Sociology of Sport Journal* 31 (2014): 350.

[14] Ibid., 351.

[15] Ibid., 352.

[16] Robin Gill, *Society Shaped by Theology: Sociological Theology*, vol. 3 (Surrey: Ashgate, 2013); Robin Gill, *Theology in a Social Context: Sociological Theology*, vol. 1 (Surrey: Ashgate, 2012); and Robin Gill, *Theology Shaped by Society: Sociological Theology*, vol. 2 (Surrey: Ashgate, 2012).

study before discussing the findings themselves. We end with a conclusion and call for further research to build upon this exploratory study.

Using a Socio-theological Approach to Explore the Faith of Elite Christian Athletes

John Brewer makes an interesting distinction between what he terms "religious sociology," where "sociology is put to serve faith," and the "secular sociology of religion," where "religion is studied scientifically."[17] "Religious" sociology, which (to be clear) is purely Christian in nature, contributed significantly to the development of early sociology in Britain, France, and the United States, although its development within these countries differs somewhat. There have been attempts since the late nineteenth century to consider the interface between Christianity and sociology seriously from the perspective of the Christian faith.[18] This form of sociology, however, lies underdeveloped and has been obscured from the history of the development of the discipline of sociology.[19]

The late 1970s saw new "sociological work by Biblical scholars" emerging in Britain.[20] Robin Gill, an Anglican clergyman and Emeritus Professor in Applied Theology at the University of Kent (UK), has been one of the key advocates of socio-theological approaches and recently produced three volumes on what he terms "Sociological Theology."[21] Gill revisits the dialogue between theologians and sociologists, inviting both to explore the intersections, conflicts, and consensuses between the two disciplines.[22]

Gill's approach to the collocation of theology and sociology is enlightening in the sense that he shows how these two distinct and seemingly opposing disciplines can actually complement one another. This

---

[17] John D. Brewer, "Sociology and Theology Reconsidered: Religious Sociology and the Sociology of Religion in Britain," *History of the Human Sciences*, 20 (2007): 7.

[18] These are discussed in more detail in Gibbons, "Challenging the Secular Bias in the Sociology of Sport."

[19] Brewer, "Sociology and theology reconsidered," 8; Gill, *Theology in a Social Context*, 25.

[20] Brewer, "Sociology and theology reconsidered," 21.

[21] Gill, *Society Shaped by Theology*; Gill, *Theology in a Social Context*; Gill, *Theology Shaped by Society*.

[22] Gill, *Theology in a Social Context*, 11.

kind of socio-theological approach has so far not been applied to a sporting context; the current study sought to begin to address this through exploring the use of biblical themes alongside the sociological concept of habitus in the interpretation of the narratives of elite Christian athletes.

Gill compares and contrasts the works of many past theologians and sociologists of religion (the latter both religious and secular) in order to identify areas of common ground while also suggesting ways of overcoming seemingly irreconcilable polemics. He argues that there have been "pitfalls involved in socio-theological forms of cooperation" in the past, and he seeks to address many of these.[23] One of the main issues discussed by Gill was the tendency of some theologians who attempted to use sociology to make sociological assumptions without using the work of sociologists or evidence gathered from sociological research and suggested they were "in danger of jumping straight from the 'is' to the 'ought'. In the process sociological descriptions and theological prescriptions had become thoroughly confused."[24] Gill goes on to criticize such theologians for being "amateur sociologists" who ignored the work of professional sociologists and assumed their views to represent the rest of society.[25] This issue is one that we seek to avoid in the current chapter through letting the narratives of elite Christian athletes speak for themselves while at the same time exploring how these might align with existing biblical themes and the sociological concept of habitus.

The term *habitus* refers to a specific set of acquired dispositions of thought, behaviors, and actions that are embedded in individuals through long-term socialization into particular cultures. Although habitus is a term thought to have originated in the work of Aristotle, Bourdieu is most commonly associated with its modern usage in sociology and latterly in the sociology of sport.[26] Yet it is important to clarify that the term was actually used in a sociological context prior to this by Norbert Elias

---

[23] Gill, *Theology in a Social Context*, 61.

[24] Gill, *Theology in a Social Context*, 66.

[25] Gill, *Theology in a Social Context*, 67.

[26] Pierre Bourdieu, *Outline of a Theory of Practice,* originally published in French 1972, trans. Richard Nice (Cambridge: Cambridge University Press, 1977). See also John Scott and Gordon Marshall, *A Dictionary of Sociology* 3rd rev. ed. (Oxford: Oxford University Press, 2009), 299; Alan Tomlinson, "Pierre Bourdieu and the sociological study of sport: habitus, capital and field," in *Sport and Modern Social Theorists,* ed. Richard Giulianotti (London, Palgrave-Macmillan, 2004), 161–172.

in *The Civilizing Process*.[27] Elias contends that human beings have developed multi-layered, shared identities, and he refers to these as the "social habitus," which exists within the personality structure of every human being. According to Stephen Mennell:

> Habitus is a useful word in referring to the modes of conduct, taste, and feeling which predominate among members of particular groups. It can refer to shared traits of which the people who share them may be largely unconscious; for the meaning of the technical term "habitus" is, as Norbert Elias used to remark, captured exactly in the everyday English expression *second nature*—an expression defined by the *Oxford English Dictionary* as "an acquired tendency that has become instinctive."[28]

The concept of habitus has been applied in a number of different sporting contexts, though not alongside biblical themes.

Methodology

Design and Rationale

One of the initial aims of the current study was to use narratives from athletes who have competed at an international level.[29] The reason for choosing international athletes was that it was felt that sport had to play a significant part in their lives to the point where it encroaches on every other aspect of their lives, including their faith. In addition, their profile in sport had to be such that they were influencing other people, including spectators, commentators, coaches, and fellow athletes, although this varies depending on their sport and reputation. Three of the athletes interviewed had sport as their source of income, either through professional status or other sources of funding from governing bodies and sponsors. This study is not about athletes having a spiritual aspect to their personality, nor is it about spirituality as a notion within sport, nor is "spirit" seen as an experience to be attained through sport. This research is about speaking to athletes who defined themselves as being

---

[27] Norbert Elias, *The Civilizing Process*, rev. ed. (Oxford: Basil Blackwell, 1939/2000).

[28] Stephen Mennell, "The Formation of We-Images: A Process Theory," In *Social Theory and the Politics of Identity*, ed. Craig Calhoun (Oxford: Blackwell, 1994), 177.

[29] The sport, age or gender of athletes was not our primary consideration but should be explored further by future studies.

"born again" or "born of the Spirit,"[30] and examining how they describe their faith.

The reason for using a narrative method is to gain data that can be examined to provide meaning around the subject of the born-again athlete. We also wanted the athletes to determine the direction of their responses rather than the researchers leading them. The aim was to be able to state with some precision what these athletes really believe—what do athletes mean when they make statements about their faith?

Participants

Narratives from four elite British athletes (three male and one female) who defined themselves as "born-again" Christians were collected in 2009. Each of the four athletes participated internationally in different sports, including: boxing, rugby league, rowing, and squash. All gave consent for their names to be used in the research. While the narratives were gathered slightly differently (see below), the similarity is that respondents were able to talk at length with limited intervention, which is true to the narrative method.[31] All respondents were aware that information related to their faith was the key area under examination. The athletes were not all from the same church denomination.

Our first participant was Ben Falaga (aged 22 at interview),[32] a boxer from the northeast English town of Middlesbrough who fought in the 70-74 kg weight category. Ben was formerly Tyne and Wear Champion and was also an England international. Ben's boxer nickname was "Born Again Ben," a phrase he had emblazoned across the waistband of his shorts whenever he competed. Our second participant was Jamie Jones-Buchanan (aged 27 at interview),[33] a rugby league player (second row) from Leeds, West Yorkshire. Jamie has played for Leeds Rhinos since 1999. He has represented England on fourteen occasions and also Great

---

[30] John 3:3, NIV.

[31] Jane Elliot, *Using Narrative in Social Research: Qualitative and Quantitative Approaches* (London: Sage, 2005).

[32] Ben was interviewed by Stuart Braye and Kevin Dixon in March 2009.

[33] Jamie was interviewed by Paul Hinton at a church outreach event in Leeds in April 2009. He granted permission for us to use this interview for research purposes.

Britain in 2007. He has been defined as a "devout Christian" by the media.[34]

Our third participant was Debbie Flood (aged 28 at interview),[35] a rower from Harrogate in Yorkshire. Debbie has been a full-time rower since 1998 and was the first British woman to win the prestigious Henley Regatta. She has also won two silver medals in the quadruple sculls at the Athens 2004 and Beijing 2008 Olympic Games, as well as a gold medal at the 2006 world championships. Like Jamie, Debbie has been described in the media as a "devout Christian" and works as a member of the "Performance Team" for the organization "Christians in Sport," where she supports other elite Christian athletes.[36]

Our final participant was Philip Nightingale (aged 27 at interview),[37] a pro–squash player from Surrey in southeast England. Philip became a member of the Professional Squash Association (PSA) in 2003 and is a world-ranked player. He has won two PSA titles and also coaches squash to a high level. Philip is currently an Anglican ordinand at the University of Oxford. On his "player bio" on the PSA website, he lists one of his interests as being "Christian Faith."[38]

Analysis

The transcripts containing the narratives were analyzed using a coding approach termed "qualitative discourse analysis." Practically, the qualitative discourse analysis used was similar to that suggested by Mike Miles and Michael Huberman.[39] "Codes," also referred to as "tags or la-

---

[34] Yorkshire Evening Post, "Leeds Rhinos: Simple life for Jamie Jones Buchanan: Interview," http://www.yorkshireeveningpost.co.uk/news/leeds-rhinos-simple-life-for-jamie-jones-buchanan-interview-1-2250462 (accessed 1 July 2016).

[35] Much like Jamie, Debbie was interviewed by Paul Hinton at a church outreach event in Leeds in May 2009. She granted permission for us to use this interview for research purposes.

[36] Paul Kelso, "Flood aims to turn tide for Britain on a sea of faith," *The Guardian*, 6 August 2008, https://www.theguardian.com/sport/2008/aug/06/olympics2008.olympicsrowing (accessed 1 July 2016).

[37] Philip was interviewed by Stuart Braye in July 2009.

[38] PSA, "Players," https://psaworldtour.com/players/view/785/info (accessed 2 July 2016).

[39] Michael B. Miles and A. Michael Huberman, *Qualitative Data Analysis: An Expanded Sourcebook* (Thousand Oaks, CA: Sage, 1994), 56.

bels for assigning units of meaning," were developed using a "semi-inductive" coding technique.[40] Analysis of the data began by manually developing a list of initial codes based upon an interpretation of the meanings the authors extracted from the narratives under analysis. Analysis involved extracts from narratives being assigned an initial theme before being grouped into codes with similar extracts. This initial coding process resulted in a long list of provisional codes, and so it was essential to reread the narratives a number of times in order to reduce the number of codes into fewer but more comprehensive qualitative categories that were distinct enough from one another to be classed as separate codes, but still related to the overall research objectives.[41]

The analysis discovered the prevalence of the following three themes under a collective biblical understanding and framework of "the Kingdom of God" that was at the core of the narratives provided by each athlete: "Set Apart," "Familiarity with God," and "Evangelism." These biblical themes appeared to be embedded within the narratives of these athletes. In what follows, dominant codes are indicated by bold subheadings. Key extracts are used to demonstrate recurrent themes in the narratives.

Discussion of Findings

Set Apart

In his first letter to the Corinthians, the Apostle Paul writes: "We have not received the spirit of the world but the Spirit who is from God, that we may understand what God has freely given us."[42] Each of the athletes' narratives referred to a specific point in their lives when they were "born again" and first became a Christian.[43] For instance, Philip said the following:

> I gave my life to Christ, then I began my Christian walk, as it is now really I suppose.

---

[40] Miles and Huberman, *Qualitative Data Analysis*, 56.

[41] Chris Gratton and Ian Jones, *Research Methods for Sports Studies*, 2nd ed. (London: Routledge, 2010), 240.

[42] 1 Cor. 2:12, NIV.

[43] John 3:3, NIV; see Grudem, Wayne. *Systematic Theology: An Introduction to Biblical Doctrine* (Leicester: Inter-Varsity Press, 1994), 670.

This "new birth" experience of the elite Christian athletes in our sample meant that they regarded themselves as behaving and thinking differently to other non-Christians around them. Jamie said:

> The majority of people I mix with every day are not Christians. …The lads were a bit shy to start with, thinking that to become a Christian you've got to become like Ned Flanders. They don't realize that that is not what Christianity is about.[44]

In a similar way, Debbie referred to being regarded by other non-Christians that she interacted with on a daily basis as "different" due to her faith:

> I am a Christian and it comes up in conversation all the time, whether it's questions with good intentions or not, it's good conversation. People are really interested and it sort of explains a lot of how I am and why I am.

Finally, Ben made reference to himself as distinct in comparison to other non-Christian boxers in terms of how he viewed role models:

> I can't think of a role model, the only person who I really think is Jesus. But ask loads of other boxers and they'll say "Ricky Hatton's my favourite boxer." But I don't really have a favourite boxer.

Distinction is a key aspect of habitus for Bourdieu.[45] How one regards oneself "in relation to" others is key to determining social classes. For Bourdieu, social classes are not real groups mobilized for social struggles. A social class refers to a group of social agents who share similar experiences, interests and value systems, and who define themselves in relation to other groups of people. Bourdieu's social classes can also be characterized by any kind of socially constructed trait, like gender or disability for example.[46] What seems to be clear for Philip, Jamie, Debbie, and Ben here is that their new-birth experiences included a separation in their minds between themselves as Christians and the non-Christians they spend time with in their everyday lives. This similarity suggests the-

---

[44] Ned Flanders is a Christian character from the hit TV cartoon series *The Simpsons*.

[45] Michael Grenfell, *Pierre Bourdieu: Key Concepts*. Stocksfield: Acumen, 2008.

[46] Suzanne Laberge and Joanne Kay, "Pierre Bourdieu's Sociocultural Theory and Sport Practice," in *Theory, Sport and Society*, ed. Joseph Maguire and Kevin Young (Amsterdam: JAI Press, 2002), 241.

se athletes share the same "Christian social habitus." They share a specific set of acquired dispositions of thought, behavior, and actions that are embedded through them becoming Christians.

In the following extracts, one can see how Ben, Debbie, and Philip each look to God rather than any aspect of their socialization into the world to determine their success in their respective sports, thus reinforcing Jesus' words to his disciples in John's gospel: "you do not belong to the world, but I have chosen you out of the world."[47]

Ben: Whatever happens it's not in my hands, it's in God's hands.

Debbie: God does have my life in his hands and that makes a difference to me.

Philip: I think what's there is that I have a quiet trust in God in my squash so I don't go nuts and I don't lose it if I haven't won or been defeated in tournaments. I am able to have a perspective and have a peace about things.

The problem with attempting to apply the sociological concept of habitus to the Christian experience of being "born again" (and thus "set apart") is that this is a spiritual, often instantaneous, experience provided by God alone. This means that in essence it is not something that can ever be acquired from long-term socialization into a particular culture. While habitus has been applied to understanding "religion" as a "lifestyle" that one is simply socialized into, such as sport or music,[48] being born again means to be "born of God."[49] This is a key distinction to make and one that has been missed by many sociologists of religion when discussing what they generically term "religious habitus" when discussing conversion to any "religion."[50] Philip Mellor and Chris Shilling,

---

[47] John 15:19.

[48] See for example Stephen Grusendorf, "Bourdieu's Field, Capital, and Habitus in Religion," *Journal for the Sociological Integration of Religion and Society* 6 (2016): 1–13.

[49] John 1:13; 1 John 3:9; 1 John 4:7; 1 John 5:1; 1 John 5:4; 1 John 5:18, NIV.

[50] See for example Yafa Shanneik, "Conversion and Religious Habitus: The Experiences of Irish Women Converts to Islam in the Pre-Celtic Tiger Era," *Journal of Muslim Minority Affairs* 31 (2011): 503–517. For Bourdieu, "religion" is simply a "field"— a microcosm of society with its own rules, regularities and forms of authority. See Terry Rey, *Bourdieu on Religion: Imposing Faith and Legitimacy* (New York: Routledge, 2007).

when focusing part of their argument on the Christian Pentecostal movement, recognize the limitations of Bourdieu's habitus for explaining the "born-again subject" and seek to reconceptualize the concept of "religious habitus" in relation to this.[51] Yet their analysis is limited by their lack of engagement with systematic theology, specifically the "doctrine of the application of redemption." Within this Christian doctrine "regeneration" is the element used to explain what it means to be born again. Unlike "conversion," "sanctification," and "perseverance," "in the work of regeneration we play no active role at all. It is instead totally a work of God."[52]

Mellor and Shilling suggest that humans are somehow "active" in terms of "preparing" themselves for receiving the Holy Spirit, but this vocabulary is in fact not biblical. For example, at the beginning of John's gospel the apostle writes: "Yet to all who did receive him, to those who believed in his name, he gave the right to become children of God—children born not of natural descent, nor of human decision or a husband's will, but born of God."[53] Perhaps the clearest evidence for the biblical basis underlying the regeneration doctrine comes later in John's gospel in the story of Jesus teaching a Pharisee named Nicodemus.[54] Here Jesus is quoted as stating that being spiritually born again (or "born from above") is different from physical birth, when Jesus says to Nicodemus: "Flesh gives birth to flesh, but the Spirit gives birth to spirit."[55] This doctrine is also reinforced by the teaching of the apostles found later in the New Testament.[56]

Familiarity with God

The limitations of the applicability of the concept of habitus to these narratives were also apparent when the athletes talked about God in personal, relational terms. The athletes were again pointing to God rather than to any significant others involved in their socialization, either

---

[51] Philip A. Mellor and Chris Shilling, "Re-conceptualizing the Religious Habitus: Reflexivity and Embodied Subjectivity in Global Modernity," *Culture and Religion* 15 (2014): 275–297.

[52] See Grudem, *Systematic Theology*, 699.

[53] John 1:12-13, NIV.

[54] John 3:3-8, NIV.

[55] John 3:6, NIV.

[56] See, for example, Jas. 1:18; 1 Pt. 1:3, NIV.

inside or outside sport. For instance, when explaining her own personal relationship with God, Debbie said:

> It's actually about choosing to ask Jesus to come into my life and if I choose to do so then that's a relationship with Jesus.

Jesus is quoted in John's gospel as saying: "I know my sheep and my sheep know me—just as the Father knows me and I know the Father".[57] Jamie talked about submitting everything in his life to God and trusting in Him:

> I want God to be my leader and my shepherd and my guide.

Jamie later added:

> You sort of realize that Jesus is your savior, he died for us to have faith in him.

Ben and Philip both stressed the importance of their own personal relationships with God in terms of how he had affected their lives. Ben says clearly:

> God has turned my life around....God is definitely the most important thing in my life....Like it says in the Bible. "If God is for me who can be against me?"[58]

Philip talked about how God had never left him when he had gone through difficult times and was struggling to continue to have faith:

> God sort of held onto me even though I'd become very barren in my faith....We have to remember that God is God, he's very powerful and he holds onto people and he held onto me.

Thus, while a shared "Christian habitus" appears to be identifiable through their narratives, it is important to reiterate that this "born again nature" is understood by these athletes as coming from God rather than human beings.

All of the athletes referred to prayer a number of times throughout their interviews. The New Testament teaches that prayer is the way Christians develop and sustain an ongoing relationship with God. Unlike regeneration, which is a work of God alone, praying is something Christians are actively involved in.[59] For example, in Paul's letter to the church

---

[57] John 10:14-15, NIV.

[58] Rom. 8:31, NIV.

[59] Grudem, *Systematic Theology*, 376–396.

in Ephesus the apostle writes: "And pray in the Spirit on all occasions with all kinds of prayers and requests."[60] In the past it has been assumed that athletes pray to win,[61] but that was not the case for any of the athletes in our sample. All four athletes talked about how they pray immediately prior to competing and what they pray for specifically. Philip provided the most detailed insight into his prayer life:

> I pray daily about my squash. I don't generally pray, "Please Lord make we win." What I usually pray, I have a kind of a set prayer I almost say it every time. I even say it before training, I say, "Lord, please grant that this session might be really worthwhile, help glorify yourself through me in it in Godliness and excellence and be pleased to prosper me in what I'm doing in my squash and may this session count towards that," or "may this match count towards that." So what I'm in effect saying is, "God I can't do this without you; please grant me your blessing. Thank you for this and please prosper me in it." So whether that means I win that day or lose I'm just asking that He will be pleased to prosper me in it, which I think is warranted Biblically; you can pray that and trust that he would be pleased to do that.

Like Philip, Debbie was also clear about not praying to win:

> I would always pray before a race and pray that I could always do my best because that is all we can do. So I would never pray to win, definitely not.

At the point of the interview with Ben, he was considering hanging up his boxing gloves and retiring from the sport even though he was only 22:

> I'm praying that God would tell me whether I should give up this job and spend more time with Him.

It was clear that one of the reasons for this was that Ben was struggling with the violence inherent in the sport:[62]

---

[60] Eph. 6:18, NIV.

[61] See Hoffman, "Prayer out of Bounds"; Price, "Playing and Praying, Sport and Spirit"; Ward, *Gods Behaving Badly*.

[62] The acceptability of Christians participating in violent sports has been considered in various studies, see, for instance, Tracy Trothen, "Holy Acceptable Violence? Violence in Hockey and Christian Atonement Theories," *Journal of Religion and Popular Culture* 21 (2009): 3.

I always pray for the other person before boxing, that he, none of us, gets hurt and that God's will be done.

Whereas Jamie's focus for prayer prior to competing was more focused on evangelizing those around him:

I pray that I am contagious with it [Christianity].

These extracts show the importance of prayer to these athletes and provide insights into why they pray prior to competing. According to Wayne Grudem, God wants Christians to pray because prayer expresses trust in God and is a means through which "trust in him can increase."[63] The fact that all these athletes pray in their everyday lives is evidence that they have a real relationship with God through being spiritually born again.

Evangelism

The final common theme across all four narratives was the desire of the athletes to tell other people about their faith and to use their sporting prowess as a platform to do so. This is consistent with the last recorded words of Jesus to his disciples in Matthew's gospel: "[G]o and make disciples of all nations, baptizing them in the name of the Father and of the Son and of the Holy Spirit, and teaching them to obey everything I have commanded you."[64] For instance, Jamie commented:

To be honest with you, sport is a great medium for being able to spread the word, Jesus' word, and spread the Gospel.

He goes on to say how he wants to evangelize in every area of his life using sport as his primary vehicle:

I pray that I can be contagious in passing the Gospel onto everybody, the fact that I'm with these kids coaching them, at University, you know...when I'm in the paper when we're winning or on TV that I can shine out.

This resonates with the famous muscular Christians of the nineteenth and early twentieth centuries such as C.T. Studd and Eric Liddell. As was accurately depicted in the film *Chariots of Fire*, Liddell used to regularly preach before or after the events in which he competed as an athlete. Following his decision not to race in the 100-meter heats at the

---

[63] Grudem, *Systematic Theology*, 376.
[64] Matt. 28:19-20, NIV.

Paris Olympiad he preached in the Scots church in Paris instead.[65] Jamie and Debbie's narratives were recorded at outreach events, which are a regular part of their extremely busy lives. Both athletes were keen to stress the importance of such events for promoting evangelism. As Debbie noted:

> I've driven four hours to be here because it is important—it's important to everyone's lives.

Ben (an ex-drug addict himself) visits prisons on a regular basis with the intention of sharing his faith:

> When I get up in front of these inmates and tell them my testimony, I mean, they should all be laughing at me...but they listen 'cos it's true and when people hear the truth they can't deny the truth can they?...I'd like to help young people who've been in the situation that I've been in...and just tell them that if you truly believe in God and Jesus and if you follow him...he'll bless you.

Finally, Philip explained how he actively seeks opportunities for evangelistic conversations with the athletes he trains with on a regular basis:

> I've had loads of conversations with guys over the years and a few guys have become Christians, brilliantly!...There have been good opportunities to have conversations. I think these guys will be thinking about these things quietly within their own hearts and minds and mulling it over, I hope.

The fact that all of these athletes were willingly involved in evangelism provides further evidence to suggest that they are "born again" Christians. This evangelistic work is regarded as "the primary ministry that the church has toward the world," regardless of denomination."[66]

Conclusion

Nick Watson and Andrew Parker previously suggested that accurately discerning the motivations underlying expressions of faith by sports celebrities has been difficult, as it is based largely on assumptions regarding

---

[65] BBC. "A Sporting Nation—Eric Liddell," http://www.bbc.co.uk/scotland/sportscotland/asportingnation/article/0019/print.shtml (accessed 18 June 2016).

[66] Grudem, *Systematic Theology*, 868.

the authenticity of the athletes' faith.[67] The primary aim of the exploratory study presented in this chapter was to begin to address this problem through critical analysis of narratives collected from a small sample of elite British athletes who defined themselves as "born-again" Christians.[68] An attempt was made to utilize biblical themes and sociological concepts together in this analysis of elite Christian athletes using the kind of "socio-theological" approach pioneered by Robin Gill, an approach that previously has had not been applied to a sporting context.

Despite being involved in different sports in different areas of England and being from different church denominations, all four elite Christian athletes in our exploratory study appeared to share a born-again "Christian habitus." However, we recognized that the term habitus is limited in the context of fully explaining the born-again nature of Christian experience. While habitus usually depends on long-term socialization, it is important to bear in mind the reality that being spiritually born again can be instantaneous and is understood to be totally a work of God rather than human beings. Under our biblical framework of the "Kingdom of God" three recurrent themes were present in the athletes' narratives. These were: "set apart," "familiarity with God," and "evangelism." While these are admittedly not the only aspects of Christian faith, they are some of the most important signifiers of authentic Christian faith (regardless of denomination).

More empirical studies using a socio-theological approach are required to build upon this exploratory study to add to current knowledge regarding the authenticity of the faith of elite athletes who either verbally identify as Christians or appear so through their behavior. We hope that this three-point "Kingdom of God" thematic framework can be applied and tested by future researchers in order to gauge the "authenticity" of the faith of athletes who define themselves as Christians. More interviews with athletes are required and further theological and sociological explanations are needed to bring greater meaning to these findings.

---

[67] Watson and Parker, *Sport and the Christian Religion*, 102
[68] John 3:3, NIV.

The Scandalizing of Religion, Fanaticism, and Modern Sport

Roberto Sirvent and Duncan Reyburn

Introduction

The following essay offers a response to the observation that the terms "religion" and "fanaticism" are commonly used in a pejorative sense in relation to sport, both in popular writing and in more critical academic discourse. "Religion" is often used as code for "violent," and "fanaticism" is often used as code for "religion." Far from being an innocent rhetorical move, this usage poses several problems. In particular, when the connection between "religion" and "fanaticism" is taken for granted, especially in relation to "modern sport," certain groups are more easily marginalized and othered; their voices are then dismissed as aberrations and thus unfairly subordinated to the dominant ideology. In the process, critical sport studies scholars may be blinded to the very nature of sport, religion, and fanaticism, as well as to the nature of a devotion that is complicit in problematic aspects of state politics. Because of the uncritical use of common terms such as "religion" and "fanaticism," other fanaticisms—connected with secular projects and institutions such as the nation-state, for instance—are rendered indiscernible.[1]

---

[1] Almost endless examples of the scandalizing of "religion" in sport scholarship can be found, though we will name only a few examples here. To begin with, there is Eric Bain-Selbo's use of religion as something akin to sport, but which seems particularly guilty of perpetuating crimes against humanity; in *Game Day and God: Football, Faith, and Politics in the American South* (Macon, GA: Mercer University Press 2009), 67. Then, there is Joan M. Chandler's distinction between sport and religion, which sees sport and religion as utterly separate phenomena. For Chandler, "religion" is an "other"—it is far removed from the ordinary experience and preoccupations of the sports fan, in "Sport is Not a Religion," in Shirl J. Hoffman, ed., *Sport and Religion* (Champaign, IL: Human Kinetics Publication), 59. Charles Prebish at least notices that not all religions are the same, and thus suggests that so-called "secular" and "civil reli-

We thus propose here that sport scholars should more carefully examine how these terms function, both in regard to the larger political context within which sport operates and in regard to sport itself. To develop a more discerning hermeneutic, we root the following critique in recent developments in hermeneutics within the interdisciplinary field of mimetic theory. Furthermore, we apply and expand on Jeremiah Alberg's deployment of René Girard's[2] notion of "scandal," which is at the center of the language of political violence. Scandal suggests a hermeneutic enclosure that enforces very particular coordinates for interpretive understanding. A critical engagement with how scandal operates in terms such as "religion" and "fanaticism," and even in the invention of "modern sport," proves a helpful strategy for uncovering what is occluded by a scandalizing hermeneutic. Following an explanation of the nature of scandal and how it functions in the context of sports, we offer a brief explanation of how "religion," "fanaticism" and "modern sport" have become scandals on their own, and thereafter present what Alberg terms a "hermeneutics of forgiveness," which resists the logic of scandal and scandalizing.

Scandal

"[S]candal" and "the scandalous," in Alberg's usage, "refers to those events, scenes, and representations to which we are attracted at the same moment that we are repelled. The scandalous is that which excites without satisfying, seduces without delivering, and promises without ful-

---

gions" exist. But even this usage ensures that "religion" is a pejorative term—once again, politics, it seems, is all fine and dandy, unless it becomes "religious"; in *Religion and Sport: The Meeting of Sacred and Profane* (Westport, CT: Greenwood Press, 1993), 13–18, 59.

[2] While the basic parameters of mimetic theory are very productive in sport and religion discourses, we do not wholeheartedly embrace Girard's conception of "religion." Although an argument can be made that Girard makes use of "religion" in a way that subverts the expectations set up by more everyday understandings of the word by using the term to delineate a pattern of human behaviors—mimetic contagion, sacrificial crisis, scapegoating, ritual, *et cetera*—that can be seen in both "secular" and "religious" domains, it is equally true that Girard still treats "religion" as an ahistorical or atemporal mode of being and acting. Since our argument focuses, among other things, on descandalzing "religion," it is also, in fact, an implicit critique of Girard's use of "religion."

filling."[3] Alberg's mention of "representations" is of particular interest for this essay, which focuses on specific words as representations. Scandal suggests an object that is appalling or repulsive and thus worthy of rejection—at the same time that it is also desirable and thus worthy of attention and investigation.[4] In fact, "a scandal is able to attract us precisely to the degree that it repels us and vice versa."[5] The meaning of attraction here implies something that makes us want to look, makes us want to explore and inquire, because in so doing it legitimates our networks of understanding and our in-group hermeneutical biases. This attraction, however, is offset by a concurrent desire to look no further, which results in us finding ourselves disappointed by our looking, or finding that looking itself does not allow full access to the object of our attention. This is to say that, if only unconsciously,[6] we are aware that the scandal, as legitimating framework for interpretive understanding, is nevertheless not a legitimate source of meaning and social cohesion.

Thus, as all of this suggests, a scandal is a representation that grants a certain access to meaning and therefore allows a specific delimitation of the hermeneutic experience. Paradoxically, it is precisely in this access that access is blocked.[7] We may be fascinated by scandals while nevertheless being unable to really see what is going on in them or behind them. This double experience is found in celebrity scandals, for instance, when tabloids grant the world access to the private lives of the rich and famous while simultaneously, perhaps unconsciously, confirming to their readers the fact that they will never really know the whole story. Access is granted at the same time that access is blocked.

---

[3] Jeremiah Alberg, *Beneath the Veil of Strange Verses* (Michigan University, 2014), xiv.

[4] Ibid., xv.

[5] Ibid., 3.

[6] The idea that we may be unconsciously aware of what occurs in scandal is rooted in Girard's suggestion that scandal revolves around a misunderstanding or misrecognition. See, for example, René Girard, *The Scapegoat*, translated by Yvonne Freccero (Baltimore: Johns Hopkins University, 1986), 83. However, especially as we find in Girard's later work, in the light of the Christian demystification of "religion," the violence of scandal is more difficult, if not impossible, to sustain. See René Girard, *Battling to the End: Conversations with Benôit Chantre*, trans. Mary Baker (East Lansing: Michigan State University, 2010), 49, 198.

[7] Ibid., xvi.

To begin to understand the hermeneutic experience of scandal, we need to notice the conflicting desire at the center of this experience—the desire to both look and look away—which is not "conflicted 'in itself,' as it were. The conflict is always between persons."[8] While it is easy to remember the presence of the subject to the scandalous object—the scandalous event, scene or representation—the presence of a mediator is often comfortably forgotten. For a scandal to exist, there must be a mediator who somehow communicates both ideas, both "Look!" and "Look away!" This happens because desire, which is how human beings navigate the world, is always mediated or borrowed.[9] Scandalous mediation occurs when a mediator is situated or perceived as a rival.

The nature of this rival-mediator's rivalry is multifaceted and ambiguous. On the one hand, rivalry exists between the rival-mediator and the one looking at the scandalous object. In this, the rival-mediator is someone or some entity that designates something as being "desirable" (that is, worthy of attention), while simultaneously preventing full access to it (that is, worthy of only a particular kind and degree of attention).[10] To make matters more complicated, on the other hand, the rival-mediator seems to embody and promote a kind of rivalry with the scandalous object itself. Thus, the object is attractive (desired), but also threatening (feared). In this, the one who sees the object of scandal also sees themselves as being somehow above or better than those who have been scandalized by the rival-mediator. Of course, in this hermeneutic process, no one caught in the stream of scandalizing desire is non-scandalized. A scandalizing hermeneutic taints everyone involved in the hermeneutic process.

One example of how this might happen is found in John Oliver's 2014 rant on FIFA and the World Cup on HBO's *Last Week Tonight*. Here, FIFA, including those who sustain and support all that it stands for, is the apparent source of scandal. However, our argument here is that the object of scandal is not the source of the scandal, but the result of a scandalizing hermeneutic. It is the way that something is mediated that creates the scandal. In particular, it is the hermeneutic procedure and coordinates provided by the rival-mediator that determine what is perceived as scandalous.

---

[8] Ibid., 3.

[9] René Girard, *Deceit, Desire and the Novel: Self and Other in Literary Structure*, trans. Yvonne Freccero. (Baltimore: Johns Hopkins, 1965), 63.

[10] Ibid., 4.

In the above-named segment, Oliver refers to soccer as a "religion" and calls FIFA its "church."[11] "Just think about it," Oliver continues, creating an analogy between FIFA and the Roman Catholic church, "[FIFA's] leader is infallible. It compels South American countries to spend money they don't have building opulent cathedrals. *And it may ultimately be responsible for the deaths of shocking numbers people in the Middle East.* But, for millions of people around the world like me, it is also the guardian of the only thing that gives their lives any meaning." In the course of his argument, Oliver highlights that the "religiosity" attached to soccer is also linked with violence. For instance, he mentions that death threats have been connected with FIFA, thus implying that when people take something like soccer too seriously, they must be religious. Moreover, it is as if people will threaten others with death only when "religion" is at work, not when something supposedly "secular" and "mundane"—like oil, money, power, and property—is in the equation. Oliver's rendering of soccer as scandalous is therefore directly connected with the scandalizing of religion. A certain kind of access to the scandal is granted, but only in a limited way.

A similar link between religion and violence in relation to sport is made by Joseph Price in connection with a story about death threats received by American football coach Bill Curry when he moved to the American South. Many fans were not happy with the decision that an outsider from Georgia Tech should coach their team. However, the death threats were explained by Curry's wife as being the result of the fact that "football is a *religion* over [t]here."[12] Price appears to agree with this assessment when he notes that "[w]hile Southerners' football passion often starts with their allegiance to local high school teams, it is in their nearly blind devotion to collegiate teams that their *religious* fervor is manifest most clearly."[13]

The rhetoric we find in the above anecdote, and in Price's argument, is very telling. It connects the idea of religiosity to blind devotion—something that apparently moves past reasonable fidelity—and ultimately suggests that this posture can be taken as a matter-of-fact ex-

---

[11] John Oliver, FIFA and the World Cup, 2014, https://www.youtube.com/watch?v=DlJEt2KU33I.

[12] Joseph Price, "Forward," in Eric Bain-Selbo, *Game Day and God: Football, Faith, and Politics in the American South* (Macon: Mercer University, 2009), xi, emphasis added.

[13] Cited by Joseph Price, "Forward," xi, emphasis added.

planation for the violence of certain fans. Price's rhetoric especially reminds us of what has become something of a truism in recent history (albeit a false one): religion and violence are inseparable. Consider, for example, Mark Juergensmeyer, who argues that religion is particularly adept at aggravating the violent tendencies of others. This leads him to suggest that the violence of secularity is part and parcel of its own religious impulse.[14] Secularity goes wrong, it is implied, when it becomes religious. The implication of this rhetoric is that if we were rid of the "religious impulse" we would find that we struggle far less to get along.

Here, we clearly see how scandal is mediated. In the above examples, people are invited to look—to be drawn into the scandal of what happens when sport becomes "religious"—but are simultaneously blocked from the fuller implications of what is going on. As noted above, "religion" becomes code for "violent;" the fanatical "religious impulse" seems to be framed as a corruption of something inherently good, namely sport or, in the case of FIFA, the organization of sport. For any scandal to function, the "public" needs to have invested an "office holder" (usually also mediated by the rival-mediator)—FIFA, for instance—"with the power to bring certain symbolic realities into existence."[15] Scandal arises in part when this office holder "contravenes what the office symbolizes."[16] In this case, it is "religion" that is named as the root of this contravention. As Alberg notes, whenever scandal arises, the subject sees himself or herself as rival of the original office holder (the object of scandal), unconsciously adopting the posture of one who possesses the moral high ground and who "could do it better" than the original office holder.[17] In the FIFA scandals named by Oliver, for instance, the scandalized viewer might easily assume that she or he is a more ethical—better—person, than those who run FIFA.

When this happens, a sense of regularity and calm is experienced by the scandalized subject, which is to say that three things happen: First, the origin of this desire—that is, the rival-mediator—to perceive the scandalous object in a particular way is forgotten. Second, the scandalized subject senses unconsciously that his or her self is being constituted through adopting this borrowed desire (to look/look away). Third, final-

---

[14] Mark Juergensmeyer, *The New Cold War? Religious Nationalism Confronts the Secular State* (Berkley: University of Califonia Press, 1993), 15.

[15] Alberg, *Beneath the Veil of Strange Verses*, 5.

[16] Ibid., 6.

[17] Ibid.

ly, the terms used to define the scandal itself acquire a sense of normalcy; this means that the rival-mediator's perspective on the scandal is taken as authoritative and correct—"soccer" really can be a "religion" and "religion" really is a description of a primitive impulse inside people that destabilizes an otherwise peaceful thing.[18]

It is thus possible to establish precisely how rivalry is at the heart of all scandal. Such rivalry, however, ought not to be simplistically understood as a rivalry between, for instance, John Oliver, FIFA, and the audience watching *Last Week Tonight*. Rather, the scandal goes deeper. The original rival-mediator is not John Oliver but the state or states whose politics FIFA has contravened. What scandalizing implies here is that one is forced to pick a side: FIFA or the state. The center of this conflict, at least as Oliver's rhetoric suggests, is in something called "religion."

This naturally raises the question of what the rivalry is at the center of our relationship with words such as "religion" and "fanaticism." Answering this question would provide at least some clue as to why there is an appeal to seeing such terms as scandalous and scandalizing. We turn thus to a very brief historical account of how the meanings of these words have developed, beginning with "religion" before moving on to discuss "fanaticism." Following this, it becomes possible to see how the invention of "religion" and "fanaticism" is mirrored in the invention of the "secular order," as well as the invention of "modern sport."

The Scandalizing of "Religion" and "Fanaticism"

Today, especially outside of critical discourse, "religion" is commonly held to refer to an "essentially private or spiritual realm that somehow transcends the mundane world of language and history."[19] In this view, religion—referring to an internal or contemplative experience—has a "timeless and ahistorical" quality separate from history and politics.[20] This understanding relies on a "naïve realism" that renders religion as ontologically "objective."[21] This popular usage of "religion" is naturally

---

[18] See Jean-Michel Oughourlian, *The Mimetic Brain* (East Lansing: Michigan State University, 2016), 39–48.

[19] Brent Nongbri, *Before Religion: A History of a Modern Concept* (New Haven: Yale, 2013), 18.

[20] Ibid., 19.

[21] Adopting this naïve realism, Karen Armstrong remarks, for instance, that "[t]he external history of a religious tradition often seems divorced from the

taken as antithetical to the "secular." The "religious impulse," then, is apparently ancient and primordial—an evolutionary development, perhaps, that humankind was always somehow destined to outgrow. It has stayed with us, however, despite all kinds of material and philosophical developments. It is also commonplace to find the word "religion" used in the singular, despite the fact that this usage causes much confusion. It supports the common view that a simple, singular thing called "religion" is the plainest explanation for "violence." It presumes different manifestations of a solitary and largely irrational concern for what is ultimate.[22] This is a clear example, however, of a "fallacy of misplaced concreteness," also known as "reification," whereby an abstract concept has been treated "as though it were a concrete entity having agency in its own right."[23]

William Cavanaugh has discussed how this understanding of religion was constructed. His argument supports how "religion" has been scandalized. Following a "constructivist" approach, Cavanaugh examines history to see how the "religious" and the "secular" are "invented" categories: they exist as constructions. The really interesting question is always why some things are labeled religious and others are not, because this reveals that particular "types of power are being exercised in the use of these categories."[24] In terms of the present argument, it helps to highlight how the precise nature of the rivalries at play in scandal can be more accurately delineated. To state the obvious, "religion" is not a transhistorical, transcultural term.[25] In his pivotal study *The Meaning and End of Religion*, Wilfred Cantwell Smith notes that the "religious aspect" of humanity ought to be seen as "historical, evolving, in process."[26] This does not mean that there is no such thing as religion or that the category

---

raison d'être of faith. The spiritual quest is an interior journey; it is a psychic rather than political drama." See Karen Armstrong, *Islam: A Short History* (London: Phoenix, 2000), ix. Kevin Schilbrack's critical engagement with this issue is particularly worthy of attention; in Kevin Schilbrack, "Religions: Are There Any?" *Journal of the American Academy of Religion* 78, no. 4 (2010).

[22] Brent Nongbri, *Before Religion: A History of a Modern Concept* (New Haven: Yale University Press, 2013), 20.

[23] Charlene P.E. Burns, *More Moral than God: Taking Responsibility for Religious Violence* (New York: Rowman & Littlefield, 2008).

[24] Ibid., 111.

[25] Ibid., 105.

[26] Wilfred Cantwell Smith, *The Meaning and End of Religion* (New York: Mentor, 1962), 8.

of "religion" should be abandoned, although some scholars have attempted to do this. It merely asks, in keeping with the aim of this essay, for a
more nuanced engagement with how the term "religion" arose in history,
and how it still functions as an ideological category.

As it turns out, the very notion of "religion"—as something separate
from other areas of life, like culture and politics—is translatable into very
few languages.[27] In pre-modern cultures and non-Western cultures not
influenced by the modern West, the idea of "religion" as we commonly
understand it today simply cannot be found.[28] Such peoples would have
found the distinction between "religion" and "secularity" absurd. For instance, "[t]he ancient Romans," Cavanaugh explains, "employed the term
religio" to cover "all kinds of civic duties and relations of respect that we
would consider 'secular'."[29] St. Augustine's use of the word *religio* extends
this understanding, in denoting a bond in human relationships with each
other and the socio-political sphere. Religion, in Augustine's mind, is
therefore not just something confined to the worship of God.[30] Even the
earliest uses of "religion" in the English language, which drew from the
Latin, meant something quite different to what we understand.[31] The
"Latin word *religio*" and the "English word 'religion' (or 'religioun')" preceded definitions of religion that regarded it as an "internal, private experience."[32] In the work of Thomas Aquinas, for example, "religion" has to
do with one's entire way of life as worship for God, not just to something
someone does behind closed doors.[33]

It is only in modernity that the nature of religion, as something that
pervades one's entire life, changes. In modernity, "religion" starts to be
used to refer to an "essentially interior, private impulse"—something
"distinct" from so-called "secular" activities like politics and economics.[34]
In its modern sense, "religion" is thus heavily dependent on the development of the idea of the "secular." Today, in fact, it is almost impossible
to think of religion apart from a religious-secular divide. Again, this di-

---

[27] Ibid., 22.

[28] William T. Cavanaugh, "The Invention of the Fanaticism," *Modern Theology* 27, no. 2 (2011): 227.

[29] Ibid., 227.

[30] Ibid.

[31] Nongbri, *Before* Religion, 21.

[32] Ibid.

[33] Cavanaugh, "The Invention of the Religious-Secular Distinction," 112.

[34] Cavanaugh, "The Invention of Fanaticism," 228.

vide was a modern, Western invention, rather than something drawn from an apparently implicit and timeless division between "religious" life and "non-religious" life.

Even the meaning of the "secular" and the historical-rhetorical process of "secularization"—itself a process of scandalization—must be understood as historically affected. In contemporary discourse, when people write or speak of a resurgence of religion or even a post-secular order, they obscure the political function of the imaginary dichotomy and scandalous rivalry between the so-called "religious" and "secular" orders, which are aimed to establish the state's authority over and against the authority of "religion."[35] In the process, the secular-religious divide becomes a matter of allegiance. Thus, Cavanaugh's answer to why "religion"—in its modern sense—was invented is that it was "part of the ideological apparatus necessary for the reduction of ecclesiastical power in the modern state."[36]

This ideological apparatus resulted in the elevation of Enlightenment rationality over seemingly irrational aspects of human nature, as well as confirming a patriarchal bias of the so-called rational masculine over the hysterical feminine.[37] Accordingly, the secular was set up as the rival-mediator—the structure according to which "religion" and all "irrational" others were first set up as rivals and then sidelined or excluded; that is, scandalized. The scandalous object ("religion" and its associated "others") is thus commonly perceived in a particular way today, while the connection to rivalry that the establishment of this particular definition of religion requires is forgotten and the "secular" order, now firmly established against this "other," is assumed, albeit unconsciously, as the legitimate mediator of all desire.

As this indication of the creation of Enlightenment reason's other suggests, parallel to the development of the modern idea of "religion" is the invention of the religious "fanatic." The terms "religion" and "fanatic" are often synonymous. Like the term "religion," "fanaticism" "often ap-

[35] Cavanaugh, "The Invention of the Religious-Secular Distinction," 113–115.

[36] Cavanaugh, "The Invention of Fanaticism," 228.

37 Roxanne L. Euben, *Enemy in the Mirror: Islamic Fundamentalism and the Limits of Modern Rationalism* (Princeton, NJ: Princeton University Press, 1999), 34.

pears as an invariable that transcends historical events."[38] The significance of the ideas of the "fanatic" and "fanaticism" in political discourse only became apparent through the ideological contests that arose during the Reformation[39]—in the crucible that paralleled and echoed the rise of modernity and so-called "secularity." Without recounting the details, it suffices here to point out that, like "religion," "fanaticism" began as a fairly widely applicable term—a word used to denote enthusiasm in various domains, not just the domain of "religion." This changed, however. As Cavanaugh notes, "fanaticism" goes from being an "accusation against heretics to an accusation against intolerance," to being an "indictment of false prophecy and belief" and then, finally, "an indictment of an irrational and violent passion."[40] Increasingly, as time wore on, and in keeping with the growing marginalization of "religion" by the secular order, "fanaticism" and "religion" became interlinked and even synonymous "problems" posed to the social order maintained by state laws. It is here that the problem of scandal emerges again. As Alberto Toscano notes, "Fanaticism, as we cannot help but notice with painful frequency, is often projected onto an enemy with which, by definition, we cannot negotiate."[41]

The Invention of "Modern Sport"

We can see that the modern usage of the words "religion" and "fanaticism" directly reflects the invention of the so-called secular-religious di-

---

[38] Alberto Toscana, *Fanaticism: A brief history of the concept*, 2006, http://www.eurozine.com/articles/2006-12-07-toscano-en.html.

[39] Martin Luther's use of *Schwärmer*—the German equivalent of the Latin *fanaticus*—in the sixteenth century seems to mark the introduction of the term to modernity. It is not coincidental that *Schwärmer* is a word etymologically linked to the English word *swarm*: it evokes ideas of a mob gone wild and failing to co-operate with the proper order of things. In particular, Luther used the term *Schwärmer* to describe Thomas Müntzer, who had provoked a violent peasant revolt against German lords. At the end of Luther's pen, *Schwärmer* was an insult to these political rebels, but is noteworthy that it was not just used to refer to a violence-producing emotional intensity. Around the same time, Luther's ally Philip Melanchthon referred to Anabaptist opponents as *fanaticus homo*, even though the Anabaptists were pacifists who refused to engage in any sort of violent action. See Cavanaugh, "The Invention of Fanaticism," 229.

[40] Ibid.

[41] Ibid.

vide, the point of which was to create or reinforce a rivalry between the church and the state, as well as the subordination of church to state, and thereby rhetorically enforce the idea that, ultimately, one's allegiance should be primarily to the state. This scandalous rivalry between the "secular" and the "religious" filters into a range of other domains of human action. In particular, we find a politics by another name in the invention of "modern sport."

In his book *Race, Sports and Politics*, Ben Carrington traces the colonial origins of what he calls the "myth of modern sport." While Carrington's discussion on "Sport, Colonialism, and the Primitives" is worth exploring in full, we focus here only on the parallels between the construction of "modern sport" with the constructions of "religion" and "fanaticism." Carrington notes that the supplanting and displacing of non-Western or traditional games and sporting forms were likely motivated by a couple key factors, modernity being one of them and capitalism being the other.[42] He cites Allen Guttmann's famous typology of modern sport found in the book *From Ritual to Record: The Nature of Modern Sports*.[43] According to Carrington, Guttmann's account suggests "that 'primitive' societies are marked by simple forms of spontaneous play, whereas advanced societies develop more complex forms of rule-bound play."[44] This "structuralist account is then used to provide a set of seven core characteristics that are claimed to define and distinguish 'modern sport' from that which came before: these characteristics are secularism, equality of opportunity, specialization of roles, rationalization, bureaucratic organization, quantification and the quest for records."[45]

---

[42] Ben Carrington, *Race, Sport and Politics: The Sporting Black Diaspora* (London: Sage, 2010), 36–40.

[43] See Allen Guttmann, *From Ritual to Record: The Nature of Modern Sports* (New York: Columbia University Press).

[44] Carrington, *Race, Sport and Politics: The Sporting Black Diaspora*, 38–39.

[45] Guttmann, cited in Carrington, *Race, Sport and Politics: The Sporting Black Diaspora*, 39. Carrington's complaints against this structural account are echoed and supported by Lucien Scubla in *Giving Life, Giving Death* (East Lansing: Michigan State University, 2016). Scubla explores how what is often perceived to be a neutral framework (especially in Claude Levi-Strauss's anthropology) according to which human societies may be understood in fact perpetuates the subordination of one group of people to another.

Carrington observes that Guttmann's typology's central implication is that primitive people are "incapable of producing sport" as it is typically constituted in Western contexts.[46] "This argument," he continues, "is based on the notion that 'primitive cultures' are ontologically incapable of producing sports due to their assumed inability to make adequate distinctions between the profane and the sacred within the social structures of their societies, hence their lack of 'secularism' renders them incompletely modern."[47] Here we notice how a scandalizing hermeneutic is at play in Guttmann's work. His typology invents a clear rivalry between the so-called "primitive" and the "secular," and in the process names the latter as the superior configuration.

Carrington suggests that the "problematic binaries" that underpin Guttmann's "operate to distinguish the modern from the traditional, the west and the rest, Europe and its Others, and ultimately the rational civilized moderns contrasted against the irrational violent primitives who, we are told, can barely even speak the language of sport." Binaries such as these can only thrive when the "preconditional assumptions and tropes of alterity that infuse the approach itself" remain unchallenged and unquestioned.[48] As to the effects that these binaries have, Carrington writes the following:

> Defining modern sport is not just a question of chronology. Sport signifies something deeper about the very meaning of western modernity and its constitution. Modernity is cleansed of violence and violence itself is read as a characteristic of the primitive. So a sport such as American football, with its ritualistic, linguistic, symbolic, and actual forms of bodily violence that would otherwise render it "primitive," is instead reframed as an example of a civilizing practice that helps to dissipate latent forms of evolutionary violence that still reside within the modern subject, allowing for a relatively harmless cathartic release of aggression.[49]

It is worth noting how similar the effects are to the creation of the binaries discussed so far regarding the invention of the religious-secular binary and the fanatical-rational binary. Just as the "religious" becomes the scandal according to which the "secular" retains its authority, so the "primitive...becomes the Other through and against which the modern

---

[46] Carrington, *Race, Sport and Politics: The Sporting Black Diaspora*, 39.
[47] Ibid.
[48] Ibid.
[49] Ibid., 40.

sporting self is defined. Primitive games can never be sports and the closer an activity is to that which the primitives play, the less it becomes sport."[50] The so-called "primitive mind" is rendered as being "incapable of complex thought;" it is thought of as gravitating towards the simplistic, remaining "underdeveloped, lacking the complex, multi-dimensional elements of calculation, quantification, secularism, specialization of roles and so on, that are claimed to define western, and hence modern, sport."[51] "Modern sport" therefore becomes subject to the politics of the state. This begins to confirm why it remains problematic to call sport "religion" or "fanatical" when it ceases to conform to strict, so-called "rational" aspects of social conduct. In doing so, the so-called irredeemably "primitive" Other of "modern sport" is confirmed. This is particularly pertinent given that:

> "rationality" was used during the eighteenth and nineteenth centuries to construct the very concept of the white, western, masculine self and became one of the key justifications…for why certain subjects, more often women, Native peoples and blacks, should be restricted from the public sphere and hence from citizenship due to their supposed inherent *irrationality*.[52]

The political use of these inventions and binaries attempt to show that one group (the "modern" West) is civilized and rational, compared to the backwards Others who do not have the ability to engage in any deep calculation or reasoning, and are backwards in their mere "games."

This othering through the "myth of modern sport" also operates in a context different to that of the African diaspora, which serves as Carrington's chief focus. In the book *Latinos in U.S. Sport: A History of Isolation, Cultural Identity, and Acceptance*, we find numerous examples of how certain cultures and people are seen as irrational, divisive, more prone to anger, less in control of their emotions and undisciplined. For instance, during the late nineteenth and early twentieth centuries, in an effort to teach "inferior" Spanish-speaking people how to become "real Americans," many academic and political elites used athletic training to help assimilate them better into the culture. Apart from teaching children specific values related to teamwork and competition, this involved in-

---

[50] Ibid.
[51] Ibid., 41.
[52] Ibid., 41–42.

structing the "often 'dirty' Mexicans on all manner of proper hygiene."[53] The civilized were therefore associated with cleanliness and the uncivilized were called dirty. And it was "modern sport"—as a tool of the state—that was used to help clean them up.

As the authors note, "[b]aseball and eventually other games...would be part of the effort to modernize the peoples of Latin America and teach them how to think strategically and scientifically as well as to improve the Spanish speakers' less-developed physiques."[54] The perceived physical, intellectual, and moral inferiority of Spanish speakers in the United States has meant that "the weak and not very bright progeny of conquistadores and native people could never measure up to the standards set by the conquerors and employers."[55] All of this points to the power plays involved in constructing terms—such as "religion" and "fanaticism" or even the way that "modern sport" is frequently understood. There is a process of scandalizing, whereby an "other" is created (communicated) and then excluded (excommunicated).[56] We must therefore

---

[53] Jorge Iber et al., *Latinos in U.S. Sport: A History of Isolation, Cultural Identity, and Acceptance* (Champaign, IL: Human Kinetics, 2011), 67–68.

[54] Ibid., 70; see also Gerald R. Gems, *The Athletic Crusade: Sports and American Cultural Imperialism*).

[55] Iber et al., *Latinos in U.S. Sport: A History of Isolation, Cultural Identity, and Acceptance*, 71. Other examples show how the construction of "modern sport" serves to solidify the idea of an Other who is inherently irrational, aggressive, or violent. In an article written in a 1922 issue of the *American Physical Education Review*, Elmer D. Mitchell argues that "the emotions, being more on the surface, make the Latin more lighthearted ... and, at the same time, more quickly aroused to temper and more fickle in his ardor." Mitchell goes on to argue that "Latins" are inferior athletes because of their "indolent disposition." They also, according to the author, have less self-control than the Italians or the French and are "cruel," as evidenced "by the bull fights in Mexico and Spain." Furthermore, Mitchell suggests that such people are more emotionally sensitive, unreasonable, and therefore more likely to rebel against the instruction of a coach. In this, Mitchell sets up the same kind of negative stereotyping often associated with a "religious" person. See Elmer D. Mitchell, "Racial Traits in Athletics," *American Physical Education Review* 27, no. 4 (April 1922): 147–152, 197–206; "Racial Traits in Athletics," *American Physical Education Review* 27, no. 5 (April 1922): 197–206.

[56] For more on how the notion of "excommunication" is at work in hermeneutics, see Alexander R. Galloway, Eugene Thacker, and Mackenzie Wark,

question not only who is in charge of creating and establishing these such terms but also the political stakes involved in understanding "sport" in a particular way.

In particular, we would suggest that this scandalizing hermeneutic—this setting up of a hermeneutic enclosure according to which things "ought" to be interpreted—functions primarily to occlude the very processes by which meanings have been set up. Put differently, scandal is created but, in the process, the role of rivalry in the mediation of scandal is hidden from view. As the examples mentioned above show, we see that such a scandalizing hermeneutic presumes, among other things, a language of domination, power, control, rationality and progress. This language is used to overcome or overpower all that is supposedly antithetical to itself, including weakness, irrationality, impulsiveness and backwardness. As suggested above, scandal is at the center of political violence. In particular, it is language itself that is the scandalizing force employed to legitimate a particular kind of political violence.

The Invention of "Religious" Violence

It is not a stretch to say that the setting up of the distinction between the public (politics and the secular order) and the private ("religion" and "religious faith" as being "fanatical"), as well as the creation of a distinction between "modern sport" and "primitive games" and all that has become associated with this, has allowed for the legitimation of one kind of violence and the outlawing of another. As a great deal of political theory after Hobbes intimates, the state's function is largely to mitigate violence—that most central of human problems.[57] Indeed, the "containment and re-channeling of violence" can be argued to be the "fundamental meaning and purpose of politics."[58] This containment and re-channeling of violence takes place through a "unanimous transfer to a single sovereign of our right to defend ourselves," which "creates the institution that

---

Excommunication: Three Inquiries in Media and Mediation (Chicago: University of Chicago, 2014).

[57] Michael Kirwan, *Girard and Theology* (London: Bloomsbury, 2009), 96.
[58] Ibid.

violently puts an end to violent disorder. By renouncing our right to violence (and vengeance), we give the state the monopoly over violence."[59]

In this way, violence—something easily regarded as a universal
evil—is transformed and rendered "legitimate," but only when it is carried out within very specific conditions mediated by the sovereign state.
Because of this process, the state's coercive violence "no longer seems to
be real violence."[60] Indeed, the state's violence—what might be termed
"secular violence"—becomes moral and rational, just as so-called "religious violence" and "fanaticism" are rendered immoral and irrational.
There is, therefore, as this distinction suggests, "good" violence—that is,
violence committed by the state—and "bad" violence—that is, violence
committed by "fanatical religion." But the "good" violence is not really
thought of, generally speaking, as violence.[61] To support this distinction,
a corollary exists in the realm of sport, where we find rational, stable
Western, "modern sport" pitted against irrational, unstable, non-Western
"primitive games," as Carrington discusses.[62] Moreover, as our examples
show, it is frequently accepted that the contamination of the "religious
impulse" that disrupts the otherwise rational core of "modern sport."

We see most clearly that it is not the journalist or academic who uses the scandalization of religion and its associated fanaticism in his or her
argument that is the rival-mediator, but the modern nation-state as a
mythical construct. Even in our language, by using simple words like "religion" and "fanaticism" and "modern sport," that the "unanimous transfer to a single sovereign of our right to defend ourselves"[63] is evident.

The coupling of the state and modern sport with rationality and
morality, and religion and primitive games with irrationality and immo-

---

[59] Paul Dumouchel, *The Barren Sacrifice: An Essay on Political Violence*,
trans. Mary Baker (East Lansing: Michigan State University, 2015), unpaginat-
ed ebook.

[60] Ibid.

[61] An excellent discussion of so-called "good" violence and the way that we
fail to notice it is found in Robert M. Cover, "Violence and the Word" (1986),
Faculty Scholarship Series, Paper 2708. Pp. 1601–1629, http://digitalcommons.
law.yale.edu/fss_papers/2708; see also, Walter Benjamin, *Reflections: Essays,
Aphorisms, Autobiographical Writings* (New York: Schocken, 1978), 277–300.

[62] Carrington, *Race, Sport and Politics: The Sporting Black Diaspora*.

[63] Paul Dumouchel, *The Barren Sacrifice: An Essay on Political Violence*,
translated by Mary Baker (East Lansing: Michigan State University, 2015), un-
paginated ebook.

rality, is inseparable from the rise of the modern secular-sacred distinction. Though it is not our focus, this also sets up a patriarchal dichotomy between so-called "masculine virtues" and so-called "feminine vices"—something that certainly has a part to play in the politics of sport today. As with the uses of the terms "religion" and "fanaticism," this has become so widely accepted that few would question it. As modern political theory has it, rationality is the basis of the state's monopoly on legitimate violence. In reality, society's members subscribe to this so-called legitimate violence on the basis of an apparently rational decision to denounce their own violence. Cavanaugh sarcastically quips, with reference to the wars in Iraq and Afghanistan, that because "secular violence is rational and peace-loving...[a]t times we must regrettably bomb [irrational others] into the higher rationality."[64] Since the "religious" Other cannot be reasoned with, it is therefore the reasonable state that must occasionally take such drastic measures.[65]

Sam Harris epitomizes this so-called "rationality," which sees no reason to reason with the "religiously inclined"—force is often, in his estimation, the only recourse against those who are so obviously out of line with what he deems to be reasonable Western standards.[66] As purblind thinking like this should make evident, though, the assumption of the pure rationality of the state is deeply mythical and therefore conceals what is really going on. Paul Dumouchel notes that the Girardian reading of the relationship between the state and rationality inverts the common understanding: "the monopoly of legitimate violence is what provides reason with its claim to be violence's Other, thus making itself

---

[64] Cavanaugh, "The Invention of the Fanaticism," 235.

[65] Some may cite examples in the writings of various theologians throughout history that argue for positive uses of violence, as in the "just war" theories of Christian theologians like St. Augustine and St. Thomas Aquinas. As such examples would make clear, the relationship between "religion" and the state is often complicated. However, it would be a mistake to take theological justifications for war as proof of a clear link between religion and violence. For instance, in the earliest stages of the development of Christianity, violence of all kinds was deemed illegitimate; and participating in any kind of war was seen as fundamentally ant-Christian. See George Kalantzis, *Early Christian Attitudes on War and Military Service* (Eugene: Cascade, 2012).

[66] Sam Harris, *The End of Faith: Religion, Terror, and the Future of Reason* (New York: W. W. Norton, 2004), 52-53.

'Reason.'"[67] It is not reason that creates the state's monopoly on violence but the state's monopoly on violence that determines the bounds and conditions of reason and, by implication, hermeneutics too. Even "religion" and the "religious impulse" in modern sport may be deemed sane and sensible when they subordinate themselves to the mandates and mythos of the state. Religion is quite fine, in other words, when it accepts and supports state violence. Modern sport is fine, as long as it, too, confirms the state's monopoly on legitimate violence.

As all of this intimates, "religion" is particularly easily used today in a scandalizing hermeneutic, because of the way that it has been set up to function as a scandal through a series of historical processes. Of course, this takes into account the fact that certain "religions" are no doubt easier to scandalize than others, depending on the religion-in-question's willingness to subordinate itself to state interests. The central impetus behind this scandalizing is found in the fact that "religion" carries an implicit challenge to the state's monopoly on violence. If violence were to be done in the name of "religion"—whether by its consent or by an accidental or circumstantial association—this would challenge the state's supposed moral authority in matters of force, coercion and retribution.

Against such simplistic understandings of specific religions, the challenge posed by various religions to secular violence is not only in extremist endorsements of violence. In fact, the challenge to secular violence may be even more potent when religions operate according to the logic of love and mercy. If a religious order challenges the state's violent, legal impositions (as in the case of the many early Christians who challenged the violent impositions Rome)[68]—by indicating toward justice or equality rather than power as a measure of law keeping, for instance—then such religions would be an even more problematic and subversive presence from the perspective of state politics. In such instances, a commitment to justice would also undermine the state's monopoly on violence.

At both its worst and its best, then, in actions considered morally deviant or morally righteous, religion, however well or poorly defined, proposes a different set of coordinates and conditions for allegiance. In the process, "it" claims an alternate moral authority—a subversive exception that is higher and more significant than the state. Insofar as the state

---

[67] Dumouchel, *The Barren Sacrifice: An Essay on Political Violence.*

[68] See George Kalantzis, *Early Christian Attitudes on War and Military Service* (Eugene: Cascade, 2012).

is concerned, measures should be taken to keep "it" out of play—to scandalize it and perhaps even scapegoat it. In the first place, this involves encouraging or enforcing religious repression, an example of which can be found in the relegation of the "religious impulse" to the realm of private belief. In the second place, if repression does not work, outright persecution—through discrimination or physical violence—becomes necessary. At the heart of scandal is the victim, and this victim, as the above assessment has shown, is likely to be any "other" that suits the bolstering of state politics and the social order that it commands.

Escaping Scandal: A Hermeneutics of Forgiveness

As should be clear by now, a scandalizing hermeneutic distorts perceptions. By granting access only in a very limited way, scandal causes us to lose access to the very thing that we are observing. This naturally gives rise to a question: "how, then, does one escape the world of scandal?"[69] Another way to ask this question is this: how does one overcome the paradox of scandal—the fact that one is compelled to both look and to look away? To begin to answer this question, it is necessary to take a step back. We have already noted the way that the words "religion" and "fanaticism" have lost their original meanings. It seems that this is an inherent quality of the nature of language, namely the fact that it is capable of losing its meaning, which includes bending and shifting to suit various historical-rhetorical aims. Signifiers ossify around signifiers, blocking access to them.[70] This, Alberg suggests, is one of the most compelling reasons for why we find scandals interesting: they promise "to make things more interesting, more alive, more real, even if there is an ultimate letdown."[71] The fundamental blockage of meaning, and the misunderstanding that accompanies it, creates a perpetual sense of intrigue. The "Other"—"religion" or "fanaticism," or the "primitive" Other to "modern sport" for instance—remains a mystery, never met or understood on its own terms, but always mediated through (implied or overt) rivalry and conflict. There is a loss of meaning that scandalizing sustains, because by sustaining this loss of meaning, the power of the rival-mediator goes unchallenged.

---

[69] Alberg, *Beneath the Veil of Strange Verses*, 71.
[70] Ibid., 13.
[71] Ibid.

Alberg goes further to suggest that "[t]he loss of meaning and the concomitant loss of reality suggest that the origin of language was itself something of a scandal, something that both opened up reality and occluded it. The ultimate reason why words lose their meaning and reality its density is that from the beginning, even before articulate language, the first signifier was really a corpse."[72] Girard explains that this happened because of the significance, in ancient cultures, of the effects of the unanimous scapegoating of victims, which constituted a prevailing sense of what was before and what came after.[73] Girard therefore suggests, "The signifier is the victim. The signified constitutes all actual and potential meaning the community confers on the victim, and through its intermediacy, onto all things."[74]

To clarify, Alberg writes, "The first signifier is scandalous and underneath that scandal is all of the rivalry that led to the victim's climactic demise."[75] Moreover, "[t]he victim is *the* symbolic office. The victim represents not himself but all of the problems, all of the evil, that the community transfers to him. He also represents all of the blessings that flow from the peace that results from his killing. The victim as signifier holds out the possibility of peace, but only by means of violence."[76] This can be seen in much of what we have already noted: for example, it is in scandalizing "religion"—in a sense, creating a victim of those who align themselves with the core of any religious pattern—that the status quo of "modern sport," state politics and the othering that such things ensure is upheld.

It is precisely when such things are kept in mind that a way out of scandal emerges. In a sense, we have attempted to enact something of an answer to the question of how one escapes scandal in the very construction of this essay. It begins, as does every Girardian hermeneutic, with the recognition of the "innocence of…victims."[77] This recognition is not an absolute pronouncement. It does not mean, for instance, that "religions" are completely innocent of ever being entangled in violence or that "religion" and "fanaticism" are never intertwined. What it means, in this

---

[72] Ibid., 14.

[73] René Girard, *Things Hidden Since the Foundation of the World* (London: Athlone Press, 1987), 100–102.

[74] Ibid., 102.

[75] Alberg, *Beneath the Veil of Strange Verses*, 15.

[76] Ibid., 16.

[77] Girard, *I See Satan Fall Like Lightning*, 73.

case, is that the reasons provided for scandalizing religion are seldom, if ever, legitimate. The victim or scandal has been created to serve a purpose—sustaining a very particular status quo and its associated "universals"—not because of something it has done, but because of something that is needed for particular power structures to thrive. Put in linguistic terms, the "[d]estruction of the bearer of meaning (the signifier) in order to release its meaning (the signified) is grounded in [an] ancient, sacrificial view of meaning: the destruction of the victim brings blessings from the gods."[78] When we see, though, that the victim is innocent, we are then more capable of recognizing how victimization is perpetuated to support more problematic political concerns.

In addition to becoming aware of the innocence of the victim—in this argument, the innocence of "religion" or "fanaticism"—one is able to then identify more accurately what has been rendered scandalous.[79] This opens a way for what Alberg calls a "hermeneutics of forgiveness." Interpretation, he notes, "is the art of transforming scandals into paradoxes."[80] This involves allowing new possibilities of meaning to emerge without binding a text to any kind of strict "necessity."[81] "It does this," Alberg suggests, "by restoring that which has been rejected, thus both completing and undoing the text."[82] This, again, is something we have attempted to do. Cavanaugh's constructivist approach to understanding religion helps in such an endeavor. By insisting that words do in fact undergo transformations under the influence of political regimes, Cavanaugh has noted that what we may have thought gains—particular definitions of particular words—are in fact also losses.

Together with becoming aware of the innocence of victims and identifying what has been rendered scandalous, forgiveness becomes essential. Alberg suggests that this is not done "by forgiving the scandal but by receiving forgiveness from the 'scoundrel' for what we have done to him.[83]" The brilliance of Alberg's hermeneutic here is that it again insists that our hermeneutics are never something arrived at apart from particular mediations, and that such mediations are never simply about texts, but are about people affected, harmed, disenfranchised. The only way to

---

[78] Alberg, *Beneath the Veil of Strange Verses*, 16.

[79] Ibid., 46.

[80] Ibid.

[81] Ibid.

[82] Ibid.

[83] Ibid., 51.

get beyond scandal, to get beyond simplistic binaries that set up excluded, scandalized others, is to step beyond the text, apologize to those who
have been scandalized by our words, and ask for their pardon.

As our argument has begun to show, a great many problems emerge
when terms are used as part of systemic "exclusionary practices."[84] While
our argument has implications for how we understand politics in general,
the application to modern sport is of vital importance. In fact, as Carrington notes, while some may want to argue that "exclusionary practices" in "modern sport" are anomalous, the truth is more sinister: "sports
were born out of and from classed, gendered and racial inequalities."[85]
This claim is similar to the one made by people who hold to the myth of
religious violence.[86] These people claim that there is something inherently violent about religion. When religion is peaceful, it is an exception to
or aberration of its true nature. When secular people, institutions or
practices turn violent, however, they are considered either aberrations,
exceptions, or simply necessary to preserving rational secular order.
Those who believe in the myth of modern sport believe something similar: that they have found the inherently rational, calculated, peaceful civil
way of engaging in athletic competition.

Here, in contrast, Carrington draws on cultural studies literature to
show that the violence in modern sport is not an anomaly or aberration
of modern sport, but is actually constitutive of it. This fits with all that
we have been saying: scandal persists; and, ultimately, what is needed is
for sport scholars and sport journalists to take care not to perpetuate
what is obviously a problematic and hurtful status quo. Perhaps what is
needed is not more explaining, defining, delineating or dichotomizing,
but a sincere utterance of an apology, and a request to those who have
been othered to help us to learn to speak again. This supports what
Hans-Georg Gadamer has argued is of central importance in all truthful
hermeneutics: the vital project of refusing to see any text as neutral, since
this would only foreground and support our own "fore-meanings and
prejudices."[87] Rather, we need to begin to recognize that the text itself is

---

[84] Carrington, *Race, Sport and Politics: The Sporting Black Diaspora*, 65.

[85] Ibid.

[86] See Cavanaugh, *The Myth of Religious Violence*.

[87] Hans-Georg Gadamer, *Truth and Method*, trans. by Joel Weinsheimer
and Donald G. Marshal (London: Continuum, 2004), 271.

an other, which requires us not just to question it, but also ourselves and, by implication, the validity of our allegiances.[88]

[88] Ibid.

Turning Those Others' Cheeks
Racial Martyrdom and the Re-Integration
of Major League Baseball

Carmen Nanko-Fernández

In colloquial Mexican *béisbol* Spanish, an unearned run is "una carrera manchada por el pecado," literally a run stained by sin.[1] This expression captures the relationship between professional baseball and institutional racism, the sin enabled by white privileged acquiescence to social and legal conventions of white supremacy, and rectified, I contend, by employing an exploitative strategy of constructed racial martyrdom. Evident in the memorialization of Jackie Robinson, such strategic martyrdom impacts black and brown bodies by expecting sacrifice, domesticating anger, sanctioning violence, and sanitizing narratives to favor racial reconciliation. Memories of Robinson are deployed in ways that the institutional sinner, professional baseball, scores a run for racial justice by resolving its own intentional sin of racism with the blood of a martyr.

I propose that a framework for this racial martyrdom can be found in Branch Rickey's reading of the Dorothy Canfield Fisher English translation of *Storia di Cristo* (*Life of Christ*, 1923) by the Italian pragmatist and Catholic convert Giovanni Papini. This influential text in Rickey's strategy, while mentioned or alluded to in print and film, has rarely been examined critically. At the heart of this strategy is Rickey's interpretation of the gospel imperative to "turn the other cheek" in a manner that places the burden of dismantling racism on its victims, giving rise to a

---

[1] German Quintero, "Modismos," *El Diario*, 1 February 2013, https://eldiariony.com/2013/02/01/modismos/ (all hyperlinks in the footnotes were accessed on 16 August 2017). Thanks to Alyssa Nanko, an undergraduate at the Savannah College of Art and Design, for her research assistance in checking all links. Please note direct quotations retain the style and punctuation of the original sources cited.

perverted soteriology that fetishizes the violent suffering of the oppressed in order to remedy segregation.[2]

The Intentional Martyrdom of Jackie Robinson

According to the preferred narrative, the desegregation of the sport was orchestrated by baseball executive Branch Rickey, at the time general manager and president of the Brooklyn Dodgers. Jackie Robinson was signed in October 1945 and played his first year in the minor leagues in 1946 in Montreal, Canada, followed by his first major league game with the Brooklyn Dodgers on 15 April 1947. The full integration of Major League Baseball (MLB) was accomplished in a gradual process spanning twelve years from 1947 to 1959.[3]

In 1945, after an allegedly expensive and extensive search, Rickey chose Robinson of the Negro Leagues' Kansas City Monarchs to breach baseball's long-held color line. According to Rickey, this was an international search: "I spent $25,000 in all the Caribbean countries—in Puerto Rico, Cuba—employed two scouts, one for an entire year in Mexico, to find that the greatest negro players were in our own country."[4] The point for Rickey was that an exhaustive search was necessary to find the perfect candidate for his great social experiment: "I had to get a man who could carry the burden on the field. I needed a man to carry the badge of mar-

---

[2] This chapter contains some material also found in chapter 2, "Martyr," in ¿El Santo? Baseball and the Canonization of Roberto Clemente (Atlanta, GA: Mercer University Press, forthcoming).

[3] Technically speaking, baseball was re-integrated with the signing of Jackie Robinson to the National League. Black players such as Moses Fleetwood Walker played professional baseball in the major and minor leagues on predominantly white teams until 1887. Bill Veeck, owner of the Cleveland Indians, signed Larry Dolby directly from the Newark Eagles of the Negro Leagues in July 1947, re-integrating the American League. The term re-integrated will be used in this text.

[4] Branch Rickey, "Speech by Branch Rickey for the 'One Hundred Percent Wrong Club' banquet," Atlanta, 20 January 1956. Broadcast on WERD 860 AM radio. Text available at By Popular Demand: Jackie Robinson and Other Baseball Highlights, 1860s–1960s, Library of Congress, http://www.loc.gov/ collections/jackie-robinson-baseball/articles-and-essays/baseball-the-color-line-and-jackie-robinson/one-hundred-percent-wrong-club-speech/.

tyrdom on the field and off it."[5] That same year, African-American sports writer Doc Young pondered what characteristics would be needed of a black man who dared to play a sport that elevated "rowdies, drunkards, temper tantrum throwers, wastrels, and called them heroes because they could hit or catch a ball."[6] Young's assessment proved prescient:

> the Negro player had actually to be a better man, and at least as skilled an athlete, as the Caucasian, merely to be considered!...the Negro had to be college-bred, one of history's greatest all-around athletes, as honest as Jesus, as clean as laundered white-on-white, as pure as Ivory, as emotionless as Sphinx, as cool as the Sky Blue Waters...merely to get the chance ...[7]

Robinson himself referred to his own martyrdom: "I learned that as long as I appeared to ignore insult and injury, I was a martyred hero to a lot of people who seemed to have sympathy for the underdog."[8] The price for re-integrating baseball was a period of three years of no retaliation for verbal abuse or physical violence from anyone, on the field or off. Its parameters were imposed at the first encounter between Rickey and Robinson at the Dodgers' corporate office in Brooklyn. Any number of sources has reported this first encounter, with some variation, and it has been enshrined in the 2012 movie *42* and in the 1950 film *The Jackie Robinson Story*, which featured Robinson playing himself.[9]

---

[5] "Laws Delay Race Equality Jackie Robinson's Boss Says," *The Milwaukee Sentinel*, 27 February 1950, 2.

[6] Attributed to Doc Young, 1945 in Hamilton J. Bims, "Black America Says 'Goodbye Jackie'," *Ebony* (December 1972):194. Young includes his words from 1945 in A.S. Doc Young, "Jackie Robinson Remembered," *Ebony* (August 1992): 38, 40. This article is an excerpt from A.S. Young, *Negro Firsts in Sports* (Chicago: Johnson Publishing, 1963). The excerpt was reprised in *Ebony* on significant Robinson anniversaries, May 1987, August 1992, and February 1997.

[7] Attributed to Young, in Bims, "Black America Says 'Goodbye Jackie'," 194.

[8] Jackie Robinson and Alfred Duckett, *I Never Had It Made* Kindle edition (New York: HarperCollins, 2013) 78.

[9] See. for example, Lee Lowenfish, *Branch Rickey: Baseball's Ferocious Gentleman* (Lincoln: University of Nebraska Press, 2009) 373–377; Arnold Rampersad, *Jackie Robinson: A Biography* (New York: Knopf, 1997) 125–128; Jackie Robinson, *I Never*, 30–34; Carl T. Rowan with Jackie Robinson, *Wait Til Next Year: The Life Story of Jackie Robinson* (New York: Random House, 1960) 113–

A dramatization of the meeting appears in the script of the 1950 movie, which was heavily influenced by Rickey. In one scene Rickey prepares Robinson for the vitriol to come.

> RICKEY: I want a ball player with guts enough not to fight back. You've got to do this job with base hits and stolen bases and fielding ground balls, Jackie. Nothing else. Now, I'm playing against you in the World Series and I'm hot-headed. I want to win that game, so I go into you spikes first, and you jab the ball in my ribs. The umpire says "Out." I flare—all I see is your face—that black face right on top of me. So I haul off and I punch you right in the cheek. What do you do?
>
> JACKIE: Mr. Rickey, I've got two cheeks.[10]

One of the lobby cards for the film captured the moment graphically, with the white actor portraying Rickey standing over Robinson with a fist in his face.[11] In the staged photo, Rickey's physical action is exaggerated, yet communicates the violence Robinson was expected to take. Robinson's posture displays his response. He sits dignified and stoic with hands folded in his lap, as if prepared to receive the blow.

In his first autobiography, Robinson recalled that event in a significantly understated manner, in comparison to the film and subsequent retellings.

> Then Mr. Rickey told me I would have to stand a lot of gaff without losing my temper or making a scene. He even acted out several situations I'd be likely to face, and then asked how I would meet each one of them, I wasn't too happy over the prospect he foresaw, but I knew too,

---

119; Jules Tygiel, *Baseball's Great Experiment: Jackie Robinson and His Legacy* (New York: Oxford University Press, 1997) 65–67.

[10] *"The Jackie Robinson Story,* Script Excerpt and Additional Lobby Card Images," http://www.loc.gov/collections/jackie-robinson-baseball/articles-and-essays/baseball-the-color-line-and-jackie-robinson/the-jackie-robinson-story/. See also Alfred E. Green, director, *The Jackie Robinson Story* (1950), available in the public domain at Internet Archive, https://archive.org/details/ Jackie_Robinson_Story_The.

[11] "Lobby card promoting *The Jackie Robinson Story,* showing Minor Watson (as Dodgers president Branch Rickey) and Jackie Robinson (as himself)," print, 1950, Library of Congress, http://loc.gov/pictures/resource/ppmsc. 00045/.

that I was pretty sure to run into some name-calling, some insults, some Jim Crow.[12]

In Robinson's initial version he pushes back:

I told him I felt pretty sure I would stay out of rhubarbs on the field and trouble of any sort away from it, but that I couldn't become an obsequious, cringing fellow. Among other things, I couldn't play hard, aggressive ball if I were that sort of man. Mr. Rickey seemed satisfied because he changed the subject.[13]

Papini's Life of Christ

The instruction "to turn the other cheek" can be traced to a 1923 English translation of Papini's *Storia di Cristo* (*Life of Christ*).[14] A Catholic layman writing for a popular audience, Papini synthesized the gospels and recast them with vivid, graphic detail, especially in portraying the suffering of Jesus (along the lines of Mel Gibson's *Passion of the Christ*).[15] In the destructive aftermath of World War I, Papini's goal was to move emotions and "transform human beings"[16] in an era with "a thirst so burning for a supernatural salvation."[17]

The book was unusually popular with mainline Protestants, in part because of certain liberties taken by the translator and her use of the King James Bible.[18] One Methodist reviewer noted that Papini's "conversion

---

[12] Jackie Robinson, *My Own Story*, Wendell Smith, ed. (New York: Greenberg, 1948) 22–23.

[13] Ibid.

[14] Giovanni Papini, *Storia di Cristo* (Firenze: Vallecchi Editore, 1923), digitized by University of Toronto, https://archive.org/stream/storiadicristo00papi#page/n7/mode/2up. Giovanni Papini, *Life of Christ*, trans. Dorothy Canfield Fisher (New York: Harcourt, Brace and Company, 1923), digitized by University of Connecticut Libraries, https://archive.org/details/lifeofchrist00papi.

[15] Stephen Prothero, "The Way We Live Now: The Personal Jesus," *New York Times Magazine*, 29 February 2004, http://www.nytimes.com/2004/02/29/magazine/the-way-we-live-now-2-29-04-essay-the-personal-jesus.html.

[16] Papini, *Life*, 10.

[17] Papini, "Prayer," *America*, 324.

[18] These omissions were pointed out in a letter to the editor of the Catholic magazine *America*, which included a translated note from Papini to the letter writer. See Paul Renaudo De Ville. M.D., "Papini's 'Life of Christ," *America* (4 August 1923): 372–373. In a positive review of the book and the translation by Canfield Fisher, a Catholic book reviewer noted the use of the King James Bible

to Romanism has doubtless been both a gladness and an embarrassment to the Holy Church—as he has enough of the individualistic mind of Protestantism to interpret the Gospels in his own way. His book is rather dogmatic—a dogmatism all his own and not ecclesiastical."[19] This nonfiction bestseller was one of Rickey's favorites.[20] Rickey, who misidentified the philosopher as a priest, on occasion referred to "the Papini doctrine," which was neatly summed up by sportswriter Doc Young as "the ecclesiastical dictum of model behavior: *You can't fight back.*"[21]

The "Papini Doctrine"

The section of the *Life of Christ* that Rickey shared with Robinson was titled "Nonresistance," Papini's reflection on the Sermon on the Mount in the Gospel according to Matthew. Rickey begins with Matthew 5:38–41, the injunction to turn the other cheek.[22] The various retellings in baseball literature abridge the section. In Rickey's own publication of his memory, his condensation seems to indicate that the entire section was under consideration in his initial interrogation of Robinson. An open question is whether Rickey read the pages aloud, or if Robinson read them at his behest, or if they studied them together. The accounts vary on this point.[23]

---

corrected by the Revised Version and cautions Catholic readers that "these versions are not always to be trusted, and should be read with constant reference to our own version." In W.P. review of *Life of Christ* by Giovanni Papini, *America* (12 May 1923): 91.

[19] Book Notices, review of *Life of Christ* by Giovanni Papini, *The Methodist Review*, vol. 106 (1923): 481, https://archive.org/stream/methodistreview1923 jmnewy#page/976/mode/2up/search/481.

[20] Lowenfish, *Ferocious Gentleman*, 375. The book is mentioned in a number of biographical accounts of Rickey and of Robinson, in popular articles about their meeting, as well as in social histories of baseball's integration and in commentaries from religious perspectives. The focus tends to be limited narrowly, however, to the turn-the-other-cheek command.

[21] A.S. (Doc) Young, "The Black Athlete in the Golden Age of Sports (Part 1)," *Ebony* (November 1968): 160.

[22] Papini, *Life*, 104–108.

[23] In Rowan with Jackie Robinson, 118–119, Rickey begins to read aloud then hands the book over to Robinson to read silently. In Red Barber, *1947: When All Hell Broke Loose in Baseball* (New York: DeCapo Press, 1982, 1984) 59–61, Rickey reads the passage aloud in a voice that was "low, strong, intense"

Papini discussed three responses to violence: "revenge, flight, turning the other cheek."[24] He found revenge unacceptable because it did not break the cycle of violence and could exacerbate the damage. Even though retribution may provide relief for the aggrieved or might be accomplished with a desire for good, the chain of violence stretches *ad infinitum*. Flight serves only to bolster the enemy's resolve. With a logic that seems to blame the victim, Papini opined: "Fear of retaliation can on rare occasions hold back the violent hand, but the man who takes flight invites pursuit....His weakness becomes the accomplice of the ferocity of others."[25] For Papini, the only response that also breaks the cycle is to turn the other cheek. In doing so, the second blow is never received because the adversary, expecting retaliation or flight, is confused and humiliated into abstaining from violent action. This self-offering displays courage, particularly moral courage that is respected, even begrudgingly, by the oppressor. In making oneself available for the next blow, the aggrieved demonstrates his superiority by refusing to be coerced into participating in evil.[26] Papini admitted that adherence to this command is difficult, even repugnant, and not without consequence. It requires "a mastery possessed by few, of the blood, of the nerves, and of all the instincts of the baser part of our being."[27] He proposed that it is the only solution to violence, and even if it "has never been obeyed or too rarely obeyed, there is no proof that it cannot be followed, still less that it ought to be rejected."[28]

---

and then asks Robinson if he can turn his cheek for three years. Barber draws on Rickey's book with Robert Riger, *The American Diamond: A Documentary of the Game of Baseball* (New York: Simon and Schuster, 1965). Robinson reads the passage to himself and then looks up to Rickey in Fred Glennon "Baseball's Surprising Moral Example: Branch Rickey, Jackie Robinson, and the Racial Integration of America," in *The Faith of Fifty Million: Baseball, Religion, and American Culture*, ed. Christopher Hodge Evans and William R. Herzog (Louisville, KY: Westminster John Knox Press, 2002) 155. Glennon cites the book by Arthur Mann, Rickey's special assistant and chronicler, *Branch Rickey: American in Action* (Boston: Houghton-Mifflin, 1957). In Rickey-dependent accounts, Robinson's response is depicted in submissive tones; in the Robinson version there is no mention of whispered or quiet responses by the ballplayer.

[24] Papini, *Life*, 105.
[25] Ibid.
[26] Ibid., 106.
[27] Ibid., 106–107.
[28] Ibid., 107.

The "Experiment"

Throughout *Life of Christ* the word "experiment" appears, suggesting a curious translation of Italian terms more typically understood as "experience."[29] This usage is most frequent in a section where Papini discusses love of enemy. In the Italian, he uses a rhetorical formula "abbiamo sperimentato,"[30] in other words "we have tried" or "we have experienced." Canfield Fisher translates the expression as "we have tried the experiment."[31] She underscored the significance of the terminology by imposing a subheading, "The Last Experiment," not present in the Italian, as her organizing principle for Papini's thoughts on Jesus and the love of enemy, which, like turning the other cheek, remains an arduous approach, "contrary to our instincts" which few have tried.[32]

Rickey repeatedly referred to his efforts to integrate baseball as an experiment[33] which hinged on the willingness of the pioneering black player to turn the other cheek. In *The American Diamond* he wrote, "For three years (that was the agreement) this boy was to turn the other cheek. He did, day after day, until he had no other to turn. They were both beat off."[34] Through the re-integration of baseball was Rickey engineering that arduous response to evil that seemed most contrary to human instincts yet had been manifest through the sufferings of Jesus?

---

[29] Thanks to Jean-Pierre Ruiz and Gilberto Cavazos-González for their assistance in translating sections of Papini's *Storia* from the Italian. They both suggest as well that experience and not experiment is a more accurate translation of "esperienza" and "abbiamo sperimentato" in the context of *Storia*.

[30] Papini, *Storia*, 140.

[31] Ibid., 124.

[32] Ibid., 125. In *Storia*, 141, Papini writes "Gesù ci propone la sua esperienza, l'ultima. L'esperienza dell'Amore. Quella che nessuno ha fatto, o pochi hanno tentata e per pochi momenti della loro vita. La più ardua, la più contraria al nostro istinto ma la soia che possa mantenere quel che promette." A more accurate translation would be, "Jesus proposes his own experience, the ultimate experience. The experience of Love."

[33] See for example Rickey's 1955 address to African-American sports enthusiasts in Atlanta "One Hundred Percent Wrong Club." Biographer Murray Polner reported Rickey's gleeful comment to one of his daughters, "We are going to indulge in what most people would call a social experiment." See Murray Polner, *Branch Rickey: A Biography* (New York: Atheneum, 1982) 169.

[34] Branch Rickey with Robert Riger, *The American Diamond: A Documentary of the Game of Baseball* (New York: Simon and Schuster, 1965) 46.

The term "experiment" appears as well in Robinson's recollections of his frustration with the condition of nonresistance. Robinson thought, "To hell with Mr. Rickey's 'noble experiment.'...To hell with the image of patient black freak I was supposed to create."[35] In an interview Rickey biographer Lee Lowenfish expresses uncertainty regarding the source of Rickey's use of the term. "By the way no one seems to know where that term came from. If anyone knows, do inform me."[36] I propose Rickey's use of experiment can be traced to the English translation of *Life of Christ*.

Rickey was determined to transform baseball, and he devised what he called the "Papini doctrine" to accomplish it. He insisted that Robinson was convinced as well that it was necessary and acceptable.[37] He constructed a plan to desegregate in a manner that was the least threatening as possible for whites, yet imposed sacrifice of self on both the black player and the African-American community. He outlined six challenges: the support of baseball ownership, the right man on and off the field, acceptance by the press, an appropriate reception by African Americans, [and] the attitude of teammates.[38] With the exception of the first criteri-

---

[35] Robinson, *I Never*, 58.

[36] Danny Peary, "Lee Lowenfish on His Epic Branch Rickey Biography" *Danny Peary* (blog), 15 February 2012, http://dannypeary.blogspot.com/2012/02/lee-lowenfish-on-his-epic-branch-rickey.html.

[37] See Rickey, *American Diamond*, 46; repeated in Young, "The Black Athlete (Part1)," 160.

[38] The six criteria vary slightly in order and in content. In a 1950 address to the National Association of School Administrators, Rickey identified "six problems" he faced: "I had to get the full support of the ownership in baseball. I had to get a man who could carry the burden on the field. I needed a man who could carry the badge of martyrdom on the field and off it. The press had to accept him. The reaction of the Negro race itself might solidify antagonism of people of other colors. And, I had to consider the attitudes of the man's teammates." Cited in "Laws Delay Race." In a 1955 article, Rickey outlined the criteria in an interview: "Number one the man we finally chose had to be right off the field. Number two, he had to be right on the field. If he turned out to be a lemon, our efforts would fail for that reason alone. Number three, the reaction of his own race had to be right. Number four, the reaction of press and public had to be right. Number five, we had to have a place to put him. Number six, the reaction of his fellow players had to be right." In "Mr. Rickey and the Game," *Sports Illustrated* (7 March 1955),(http://www.si.com/vault/1955/03/07/601015/mr-rickey-and-the-game\.

on, success pivoted on Robinson's cooperation with the "Papini doctrine." In terms of the right man, Ricky expected an athlete with superior skills, intelligence, character, patience, forbearance, and who "could take it."[39] Rickey confided that Robinson was not ideal for the task: "Not that God made him for it. But Robinson understood the problem and that made him safe for the experiment."[40] According to Rickey, "'Punch for punch' was by inheritance, by experience, and by desire Jackie's quick and natural reaction to insult or attack."[41] Rickey thought Robinson demonstrated "the necessary intelligence and strength of personality, but he had more and deeper racial resentment than we hoped for or expected."[42]

This element of resistance made Robinson an attractive candidate for proving the transformative power of turning the other cheek. Proof for the experiment's effectiveness was found in the level of difficulty and the higher motivation for the self-sacrifice. Intimations of Papini hide beneath the surface:

> this example of a strong, sane man who looks like other men, and yet who acts almost like a God, like a being above other beings, above the motives which move other men—this example if repeated more than once…if it is accompanied by proofs of physical courage when physical courage is necessary to enjoy and not to harm—this example has an ef-

---

In a 1956 speech to African Americans, Rickey identifies "Number one was ownership, number two is the man on the field, number three the man off the field. And number four was my public relations, transportation, housing, accommodations here, embarrassments,—feasibility…And the fifth one was the negro race itself,—over-adulation, mass attendance, dinners, of one kind or another of such a public nature that it would have a tendency to create a solidification of the antagonisms and misunderstandings,—over-doing it…And sixth was the acceptance by his colleagues." Rickey, "One Hundred Percent Wrong Club."

In Jackie Robinson, *Baseball Has Done It*, ed. Charles Dexter (Philadelphia and New York: J.B. Lippincott, 1964) 214–215, Rickey presents another iteration of the list of "problems": first, "find a player who could represent the finest qualities of the Negro people" and be a fine athlete; second, "reconcile him and the hundreds of thousands of others, all white, with whom he would associate or before whom he would play;" third, "the Negro people;" fourth, "the hotel situation" especially during travels in the South or during spring training.

[39] Rickey, "One Hundred Percent Wrong Club."

[40] "Branch Rickey Discusses the Negro in Baseball Today," *Ebony* (May 1957): 41.

[41] Rickey, *American Diamond*, 46.

[42] Ibid.

fectiveness which we can imagine, soaked though we are in the ideas of
revenge and reprisals.[43]

Propitiatory Sacrifice

Rickey acknowledged that the type of sacrifice expected of Robinson, "to
self-impose control of every decent reflex was almost too much to ask
from any man."[44] As interpreted by Rickey, the "Papini doctrine" meant
in this case "some Booker T. Washington compromises with surface inequalities for the sake of expediency. It would require constant and silent
reaction to abuse—oral and physical. There could be but one direction of
dedication—the doctrine of turning the other cheek."[45] Robinson's interpretation of the ideal player for "Rickey's noble experiment" reflected
Rickey's expectations yet contained a resistant reframing from an African-American perspective.

> This player…had to be a contradiction in human terms; he still had to
> have spirit. He could not be an "Uncle Tom." His ability to turn the
> other cheek had to be predicated on his determination to gain ac-
> ceptance. Once having proven his ability as a player, teammate, and
> man, he had to be able to cast off humbleness and stand up as a full-
> fledged participant whose triumph did not carry the poison of bitter-
> ness.[46]

Rickey expected sacrifice and self-discipline from the African-
American community as well, and he sought to ensure that through the
meetings he arranged with black leaders and educators. In no uncertain
terms he considered the biggest threat to Robinson's success "the one
enemy most likely to ruin that success—is the Negro people themselves!"[47] His February 1947 address to a group of eminent professionals
from the black community gathered at a New York YMCA was, by his
own admission, cruel. It was harsh in tenor and undeniably racist in its
stereotypical assumptions.

---

[43] Papini, *Life*, 107.

[44] Rickey, *American Diamond*, 46; Young, "The Black Athlete (Part1)," 160.

[45] Ibid.

[46] Robinson, *I Never*, 27–28.

[47] Arthur Mann, "The Truth About the Jackie Robinson Case," *Saturday Evening Post* (20 May 1950): 150.

And yet, on the day that Robinson enters the big league—if he does—
every one of you will go out and form parades and welcoming commit-
tees. You'll hold Jackie Robinson Days and Jackie Robinson Nights.
You'll get drunk. You'll fight. You'll be arrested. You'll wine and dine
the player until he is fat and futile. You'll symbolize his importance into
a national comedy, and an ultimate tragedy—yea, tragedy![48]

Rickey exercised extraordinary white privilege, making threats that
exceeded his reach. He reminded the assembled that the initiative was
his alone:

If any individual group or segment of Negro society uses the advancement of Jackie Robinson in baseball as a symbol of a social "ism" or
schism, as a triumph of race over race, I will curse the day I ever signed
him to a contract, and I will personally see that baseball is never so
abused and misrepresented again![49]

A soteriological dimension was unmistakable in his words of ad-
monishment. While Rickey acknowledged the suffering and blood shed
for racial progress, he insisted that "this step in baseball is being taken for
you by a single person whose wounds you cannot see or share. You haven't fought a single lick for a victory, if there is one."[50] What remains
unclear is whether the wounded single person is Robinson or Rickey.

Rickey preyed on class divides, indicating in other venues that the
threat was not so much from middle class black professionals but from
"those of less understanding, those of a lower grade of education frank-
ly."[51] It was to the popular masses that the "don't spoil Robinson's chances" and "leave your liquor outside the ball park" campaign was aimed,
with a message allegedly "preached from the pulpits to all religious denominations...spoken from the rostrum of every lodge and
club...repeated by the bartenders in virtually every café or saloon frequented by Negroes."[52]

The 1960 version of this meeting as told by Robinson with Carl
Rowan contains similar content, yet is decidedly different in tone than
the retelling by Mann a decade earlier. Here Rickey, described as a
"round man with the wrinkled face and the bushy eyebrows," comes off

---

[48] Mann, 152.
[49] Ibid.
[50] Ibid.
[51] Rickey, "One Hundred Percent Wrong Club."
[52] Mann, 152.

as a benevolent supplicant seeking cooperation from leadership in the black community about a difficult matter. This description mitigates Rickey's bluntness in Mann's account and clearly establishes Robinson's sacrifice.

> I know that I am saying it as cruelly as it can be said…but I must make you appreciate the weight of responsibility that rests upon the shoulders of leading Negro citizens of this community. I don't need to tell people like you how racial progress is made, for every gain that you have made in this country was won by sacrifice, sorrow, and sometimes bloodshed. This step we would like to take in organized baseball is certain to benefit greatly every Negro in this nation, and this step is being made for you by a single individual, by a young man who has already had to undergo racial barbs and humiliations that are sickening to any human being with a heart; by one young man whose wounds you cannot see or share.[53]

Rickey begged these leaders "to do what you can to see that no Negro adds to the burdens of Jackie Robinson," by avoiding inappropriate fan behavior or any obstructions that would jeopardize this potential milestone in race relations.[54] He also placed on their shoulders responsibility for white fragility: "remember that white ballplayers are human beings too. That old green-eyed monster, jealousy, also moves among them, and it is only natural that they will resent the heaping of praise and awards upon a Negro who has not been in the major leagues long enough to prove himself."[55]

In his reminiscences more than a decade later, in 1972, Robinson acknowledged the need for African-American fans "sitting in the stands to keep from overreacting when they sensed a racial slur or unjust decision."[56] He saw black support in more nuanced terms as a complicated matter, attracting baseball enthusiasts as well as those with dreams long repressed needing "a victorious black man as a symbol."[57] He perceived that a sign of hope could just as easily present an occasion for danger if an apparent injustice incited a racial incident giving bigots cause to fur-

---

[53] Rowan with Jackie Robinson, 169. The retelling of Rickey's words are remarkably similar to Mann's account. The tone, however, is significantly different.

[54] Rowan with Robinson, 169–170.

[55] Ibid.

[56] Robinson, *I Never*, preface, 219.

[57] Ibid.

ther impede the fragile progress being made for African Americans in the sport. This tacit acceptance of Rickey's premise that blacks had to control their adulation, celebration, and indignation made turning the other cheek a communal obligation as well as an individual one.

Nonresistance as a tactic to appeal to white sensibilities of the press, fans, and players ended for Robinson with the 1949 season. He had honored his agreement with Rickey to avoid retaliation when faced with abuse. Robinson recalled in his memoir Rickey's explanation for releasing him from the obligation. Rickey was cited as saying:

> I knew also that whereas the wisest policy for Robinson overall for those first two years was to turn the other cheek, not to fight back, there were many in baseball and out of it who, because they did not accept Papini's philosophy, would not understand Robinson's employing it. They could be made to respect only the fierce competition, the fighting back, the things that are the signs of courage to men who know courage only in its physical sense. So I told Robinson that he was on his own.[58]

For Rickey, however, the "Papini philosophy" was a long-term strategy for the assimilation of black and brown players. In a 1957 interview, a couple of years after he had desegregated the Pittsburgh Pirates, Rickey proposed that black players needed to "continue to turn the other cheek as Jackie did."[59] Rickey opined, "Negro players [*must*] remain patient and forbearing because the problem has not been solved, and I think the colored player should want to help solve it by not upsetting the bucket of milk. He should maintain good conduct at all times, both on and off the field."[60] His rationale for the ongoing practice of his "'turn the other cheek' policy" was that "there are a few white players whose aversion toward playing with or against Negroes has not been completely erased."[61]

Released from his promise, a "liberated" Robinson "was eager to cast off his shackles, and Rickey set him free, opening up a chain of events that was to create a new public image of Jackie Robinson, 'social fire-

---

[58] Rowan with Jackie Robinson, 199. See also Robinson, *I Never*, 78. Note that in this 1972 version the reference to Papini's philosophy is gone and replaced by "there were many in baseball who would not understand his lack of action."

[59] "Branch Rickey Discusses," 41.

[60] Ibid.

[61] Ibid.

brand,' 'hothead,' and 'troublemaker.'"[62] This face of Robinson was not appreciated by any number of sportswriters, who preferred the cheek-turner.[63] It also set him on a course of conflict with a gradualist approach to racial justice in the sport he had re-integrated. Robinson cited the crosstown New York Yankees management as an example with their lack of black players on the team or in their farm system. He commented, "It seems to me the Yankee front office has used racial prejudice in its dealings with Negro ball players....I may be wrong but the Yankees will have to prove it to me."[64] Years later Robinson confided that his candor in part was fueled as well by information from several writers who "had told me of conversations with people in the Yankee organization who confided that they would rather not add Negroes to their squad because it was certain to mean that Yankee Stadium would be 'deluged' by Negroes and Puerto Ricans, who would chase away all their good, longstanding customers from Westchester."[65] Twenty years later Robinson was still chiding the sport for its lack of commitment to racial inclusion at all levels. In an interview months before his death in October 1972, coincidentally the same year as the twenty-fifth anniversary of his historic rookie year, Robinson expressed dismay at the prevailing attitudes that kept blacks from leadership positions on and off the field: "It's hard to look at a sport which black athletes have virtually saved and when a managerial job opens they give it to a guy who's failed in other areas because he's white."[66]

Almost four decades later, Rachel Robinson, Jackie's spouse, interpreted the decision to cease the practice of no retaliation in a manner that portrayed Rickey and Robinson as collaborators and partners. From her perspective, the Dodger executive was not an emancipator, and her husband was in control of his own destiny. Reflecting on his agency, she cited the social capital he had amassed in those years, positive relationships with some teammates, support from Brooklyn fans, and cultivation

---

[62] Rowan with Jackie Robinson, 236.

[63] Robinson, *I Never*, 92–93.

[64] "Robinson Charges Yankee Race Bias," *New York Times*, 1 December 1952, 44. See also Rowan with Jackie Robinson, 244–45.

[65] Rowan with Jackie Robinson, 244.

[66] Ron Rapoport, "The Last Word," *Los Angeles Times*, 19 October 1997, articles.latimes.com/1997/oct/19/magazine/tm-44274.

of allies.[67] In those first two years with the Dodgers, she surmised "[Robinson] had shown he could measure up to major league standards. He felt any constraining of himself would also affect his play. His style had to be spontaneous, loose. One thing they had worried about was that his actions might catalyze some kind of demonstration on the part of black fans. They talked about possible riots. None of that took place."[68]

Martyrology: Baseball Remembers Jackie Robinson

In the years following his retirement in 1956, Jackie Robinson was mostly ignored by the baseball establishment, and his calls for integration at the levels of management and the front office went largely unheeded. In his last autobiography, completed a few months before his death, Robinson wrote with dismay and disillusionment: "The sickness of baseball...is that it exploits and uses up young, gifted black and brown talent on the playing field, then throws them away and forgets about them after they have given the best years and the best energies of their lives."[69] Even after his untimely death at age fifty-three, his achievements remained underappreciated within the sport he had re-integrated.

The appropriation of Robinson's memory by MLB, especially after the fiftieth anniversary and the institution of annual public ceremonies in 2004, preserved as an iconic moment, the re-integration by Robinson with a focus on his rookie year. One historian described this memorializing analogically as "the Passover story is to Jews: it must be told to every generation so that we never forget."[70]

In 1997, on the occasion of the fiftieth anniversary, commissioner Bud Selig made the unprecedented decision to retire Robinson's number 42 across all teams in both leagues.[71] In a move prompted by then-National League President Len Coleman, at the time the highest ranking African-American executive in the sport, number 42 was officially

---

[67] Cited in Stan Hochman, "A Man of Action: Robinson's Aggressive, Daring Style Quickly Became the Stuff of Legend," *Philadelphia Inquirer*, 16 April 1987.

[68] Hochman, "A Man of Action."

[69] Robinson, *I Never*, 261.

[70] Attributed to historian Steve Riess in Tygiel, *Baseball's Great* Experiment, 345.

[71] For descriptions of the event, see Rick Weinberg, "93: Baseball Retires Jackie Robinson's No. 42," ESPN, http://espn.go.com/espn/espn25/ story?page=moments/93.

retired in a ceremony at Shea Stadium in New York before a packed house at a game between the Los Angeles Dodgers and the New York Mets. With dramatic flair, the game was briefly interrupted in the fifth inning and a ceremony was held at second base in honor of Robinson's field position throughout the majority of his career. The dignitaries assembled included Selig, Robinson's widow Rachel, his daughter Sharon, his grandson Jesse Simms (a student athlete at his grandfather's alma mater UCLA), and Branch Rickey's grandson and namesake. The presence of the president of the United States, Bill Clinton, also signaled the universal import MLB sought to impart in its remembering of Robinson and his role in the historic "first" crossing of the color line. Clinton's words affirmed the groundbreaking significance of the moment, not only for baseball but for the nation. He expressed gratitude toward "Jackie Robinson and to Branch Rickey and to members of the Dodger team who made him one of their own and proved that America is a bigger, stronger, richer country when we all work together and give everybody a chance."[72] Clinton's conclusion propelled Robinson's legacy beyond past struggles and contemporary advances, "as we sit side by side at baseball games, we must make sure that we walk out of these stadiums together. We must stand for something more magnificent even than a grand slam home run. We ought to have a grand slam society, a good society where all of us have a chance to work together for a better tomorrow for our children."[73]

Seven years later, the sport instituted what one MLB.com reporter called "Major League Baseball's first national holiday."[74] Once again at New York's Shea Stadium, Selig celebrated the inaugural observance of Jackie Robinson Day, 15 April 2004, marking Robinson's 1947 debut

---

[72] "Jackie Robinson Speech by President Bill Clinton (15 April 1997)," *Baseball Almanac*, http://www.baseball-almanac.com/players/p_robij4.shtml.

[73] "Jackie Robinson Speech by President Bill Clinton."

[74] Tom Singer, "Baseball Honors Jackie's Legacy," MLB, 15 April 2004, http://mlb.mlb.com/content/printer_friendly/nym/y2004/m04/d15/c718078.jsp. Note Roberto Clemente Day inaugurated by MLB in 2002 was the first commemorative day. See "Annual Roberto Clemente Day Established," *La Prensa San Diego*, 20 September 2002, http://laprensa-sandiego.org/archieve/september 20-02/roberto.htm.

with the Brooklyn Dodgers.[75] Selig sought to ensure that Robinson's actions would not be forgotten, including by the players whom he felt needed to know not only "who Jackie Robinson is, but what Jackie Robinson did for them."[76] For Selig, Robinson's breaking of the color line was "the most powerful moment in baseball history. It transcended baseball. It took this extraordinary man—going through what we never will understand—to set a path for change in baseball, sports, society."[77]

For the sixtieth anniversary in 2007, there was "widespread use of a 'sacred' No. 42 jersey number by on-field personnel" across MLB teams.[78] The tribute arose from the grassroots initiative of Cincinnati Reds outfielder Ken Griffey Jr., who petitioned Robinson's widow Rachel and commissioner Selig to temporarily "unretire" 42 so that he might wear that number in that day's game as an expression of honor and gratitude to Robinson and his family. In response to a reporter's question a few years later, Griffey explained his motivation:

> if he didn't play, you never know how long it's going to take for another African-American to play, and would my dad have played, and would I have the love for the game if my dad didn't play. So he was the start of it all for not just African-Americans but everybody else to play. It was my way of respecting him for what he did, for him wearing that uniform allowed me to wear my uniform, and you have to give thanks in a certain way, and it was my way of saying thank you to him for allowing that to happen.[79]

The practice evolved to the point that from 2009 on, at the insistence of the commissioner's office, all on-field personnel wear number 42 annually on Jackie Robinson Day.

The commemorations of Robinson's re-integrative act also included a revision to his original plaque in the National Baseball Hall of Fame in

---

[75] The MLB webpage dedicated to the annual commemoration is available at "Jackie Robinson Day," http://web.mlbcommunity.org/index.jsp?content=programs&program=jackie_robinson_foundation.

[76] Singer, "Baseball Honors."

[77] Ibid.

[78] Mark Newman, "'Sacred' No. 42 on Display in Baseball," MLB, 16 April 2007, http://m.mlb.com/news/article/1901218.

[79] Transcript of remarks by Ken Griffey Jr. on the occasion of his receiving the Commissioner's Historic Achievement Award in 2011, available in "MLB World Series: Rangers v. Cardinals," ASAP Sports, 23 October 2011, http://www.asapsports.com/show_interview.php?id=75458.

Cooperstown, New York. Much to his surprise, Robinson was elected in 1962, his first year of eligibility, by the Baseball Writers of America (BBWA), the professional guild that included any number of detractors throughout his ten-year career. He received 77.5 percent of the votes (124/160), barely clearing the seventy-five percent threshold necessary for induction.[80]

Robinson acknowledged that such recognition eclipsed the personal because it symbolized the full acceptance of blacks in the sport. At the same time, Robinson expected that such recognition needed to be founded on the standards established for election: "Voting shall be based upon the player's record, playing ability, integrity, sportsmanship, character and contributions to the team(s) on which the player played."[81] Robinson wrote: "I did not want to win election simply because I was the first black man to be considered. Equally, I did not feel that I deserved rejection simply because I had directed what was called 'my fiery temper' against violations of my personal dignity and the civil rights of my people."[82] The text on his original plaque reflected only his athletic accomplishments.[83] In 2008, the Hall of Fame unveiled and dedicated a revised plaque in order to commemorate his re-integration of the sport as well as his performance. The amended text briefly acknowledged the struggle that formed the context for his Hall worthy achievements:

> A player of extraordinary ability renowned for his electrifying style of play. Over 10 seasons hit .311, scored more than 100 runs six times,

---

[80] "Remembering Jackie," National Baseball Hall of Fame and Museum, http://baseballhall.org/discover/remembering-jackie.

[81] "BBWA Election Rules," *National Baseball Hall of Fame and Museum*, No.5 (Voting) https://baseballhall.org/hall-of-famers/bbwaa-rules-for-election. See also Robinson, *I Never*, 140–41.

[82] Robinson, *I Never*, 141.

[83] "Brooklyn N.L. 1947 to 1956. Leading N.L. batter in 1949. Holds fielding mark for second baseman playing in 150 or more games with .992. Led N.L. in stolen bases in 1947 and 1949. Most valuable player in 1949. Lifetime batting average .311. Joint record holder for most double plays by second baseman, 137 in 1951. Led second baseman in double plays 1949-50-51-52." Plague text and Robinson Hall of Fame Induction Speech (23 July 1962) appear in "News & Notes from the National Baseball Hall of Fame and Museum, Special Edition: Jackie Robinson Day 2011," *Around the Horn* 18, no. 5 (15 April 2011): 2–3. Both plaque texts available at "Remembering Jackie," http://baseballhall.org/discover/remembering-jackie.

named to six All-Star teams and led Brooklyn to six pennants and its only World Series title in 1955. The 1947 Rookie of the Year, and the 1949 N.L. MVP when he hit a league-best .342 with 37 steals. Led second basemen in double plays four times and stole home 19 times. Displayed tremendous courage and poise in 1947, when he integrated the modern major leagues in the face of intense adversity.[84]

Hall of Fame board chair Jane Forbes Clark explained the unusual move: "Today, his impact is not fully defined without mention of his extreme courage in crossing baseball's color line. We are proud of the changes we have made."[85] This revision arose at the suggestion of board vice chair Joe Morgan, a former player and Hall of Famer.[86] The adjusted citation remained essentially the same in terms of identifying Robinson's career achievements; however the addition of the last line situated him as a "civil rights pioneer."[87] The wording on the plaque with its understated acknowledgement of adversity also contributed to the impression that after the integrative year the struggles lessened for Robinson and for all subsequent players of color.

These memorials, in part initiated at the urging of African Americans in the sport, are now established annual rituals. This institutional remembering of Robinson, Gerald Early suggests, represents an "uneasy elegiac symbol of race relations, satisfying everyone's psychic needs: blacks, with a redemptive black hero who did not sell out and in whose personal tragedy was a corporate triumph over racism; whites, with a black hero who showed assimilation to be a triumphant act."[88]

Salvation through the Blood of *the* Martyr

The institutional narrative of MLB as perpetuated in the American imagination is frozen in time at 1947—the rookie year of Jackie Robinson—which it observes annually in self-congratulatory commemorations.

---

[84] "News & Notes Special Edition," 3.

[85] Ibid.

[86] Jack O'Connell, "Robinson's HOF Plaque Rededicated," 25 June 2008, http://m.mlb.com/news/article/3000773/. For a list of the Hall of Fame board members at the time see "Board of Directors," National Baseball Hall of Fame and Museum, http://baseballhall.org/museum/board-of-directors.

[87] O'Connell, "Robinson's HOF Plaque."

[88] Gerald Early, "Performance and Reality Race, Sports and the Modern World," *The Nation* 10, no. 17 August 1998, http://www.ferris.edu/HTMLS/othersrv/isar/archives2/early/homepage.htm.

Commenting on the fiftieth anniversary observance in 1997, columnist Robert Lipsyte noted, "There was more about Robinson the rookie who turned the other cheek than about the fiery veteran who talked back."[89] By privileging "a 'safe' version of Robinson," MLB celebrates its gradualist approach and erases multiple counter-narratives.[90] It glosses over the exorbitant prices paid by black and brown bodies othered for a sin that did not have to be, let alone atoned for by a strategy of brutal cheek-turning imposed on its victims. Ignored are decades of civil rights and grassroots activism by African Americans and others who preceded the re-integration of the sport. Omitted are the efforts of black journalists, U.S.A. communists and socialists, and racially ambiguous players who had been challenging and testing the color line for decades.[91] Forgotten, too, is the price paid by the black community who endured segregated stadiums and facilities, denial of opportunities, unnecessary exclusion, and ultimately the destruction of their own economic enterprise and legacy—the Negro Leagues. The manner in which Robinson is remembered by MLB focuses justifiably on his personal courage; yet in the process of remembering, the institution has subtly rehabilitated its own image. The Robinson memorials function ostensibly as an institutional mea culpa. In the retelling of the story, however, baseball becomes a pioneer in the greater Civil Rights story. So much so that institutional baseball's version of the civil rights movement, which already is narrowly construed and focused on Martin Luther King Jr., now begins in 1947 with Robinson as the pre-eminent martyr, Branch Rickey as the catalyst, and baseball as

---

[89] Robert Lipsyte, "1997 In Review: Three Anniversaries, and Three Heroes," *New York Times*, 28 December 1997, http://www.nytimes.com/1997/12/28/sports/1997-in-review-three-anniversaries-and-three-heroes.html.

[90] Lisa Doris Alexander, *When Baseball Isn't White, Straight and Male*, Kindle Edition (Jefferson, NC: McFarland and Co., 2013), loc. 2297.

[91] See Adrian Burgos Jr., *Playing America's Game: Baseball, Latinos, and the Color Line*, Kindle edition, (Berkeley, CA: University of California Press, 2007) for a critical exploration of the place of Latinos on all sides of baseball's color line. See Chris Lamb, *Conspiracy of Silence: Sportswriters and the Long Campaign to Desegregate Baseball* (Lincoln: University of Nebraska Press, 2012) for a chronicle and analysis of the role of sportswriters and journalists in the campaign for the desegregation of baseball.

the exemplar of the successful mixing of races without legislative interference.[92]

Legal scholar Phoebe Weaver Williams situates Rickey's strategy as an example of a "model citizen/deference paradigm."[93] In these cases the aggrieved party, typically minoritized athletes, were expected to exercise extraordinary emotional control, suppress retaliatory response, and channel anger into a performance advantage.[94] Passivity, the only acceptable response under the circumstances, was reframed positively in ways that "may have included redemptive and conciliatory nonviolent resistance" in the face of "racial harassment."[95] Weaver Williams, however, distinguishes between nonresistance as coerced passivity and as protest freely undertaken. For the athlete placed in this untenable position, "they often experienced an internal violence which accompanied their inability to protest. Their only means of reconciling inaction to blatant racial abuse was the belief that they carried on their shoulders the future prospects of an entire race for participation in interracial competition. They carried these loads alone, and the prices they paid were substantial."[96] Robinson, too, struggled with this conundrum: "Could I turn the other cheek? I

---

[92] Rickey was opposed to advancing integration via legislation. He believed such laws would breed antagonism and compared it to the response to the Eighteenth Amendment to the U.S. Constitution, which he believed set back the cause for temperance. See, for example, "Laws Delay Race Equality Jackie Robinson's Boss Says," 2. Some scholars propose that his signing of Robinson was an attempt to circumvent investigation under New York State's Ives-Quinn Anti-Discrimination Bill, (March 1945), which prohibited employment discrimination on the basis of race, religion, color, and national origin by any for-profit employer with more than six employees. New York's three baseball teams (Yankees, Giants, and Dodgers) were under scrutiny by the public, politicians, and civil rights activists as businesses that needed to come into compliance. Therefore, with or without the signing of Robinson, New York baseball would have been compelled to desegregate. See J. Gordon Hylton, "American Civil Rights Laws and the Legacy of Jackie Robinson," *Marquette Sports Law Review* (Spring1998): 396–399, http://scholarship.law.marquette.edu/sportslaw/vol8/iss2/9.

[93] Phoebe Weaver Williams, "Performing in a Racially Hostile Environment," *Marquette Sports Law Review* (Spring 1996): 304–308, http://scholarship.law.marquette.edu/sportslaw/vol6/iss2/6.

[94] Weaver Williams, 304.

[95] Ibid., 305.

[96] Ibid., 308.

didn't know how I would do it. Yet I knew that I must…For black youth, for my mother, for Rae, for myself. I had already begun to feel I had to do it for Branch Rickey."[97]

This paradigm of deferential model citizen, especially in light of the theological underpinnings of Rickey's strategy, has soteriological implications. Salvation, predicated on an endurance of abuse, fetishizes suffering and places the burden for atonement on the victim, who proves personal dignity by absorbing brutality without retaliation of any sort. In this case the savior of the sport, and of a nation failing to abide by its principles, is the one who is *made to be* the suffering servant. The redemptive value is enjoyed by others: the perpetrators who gradually and begrudgingly change their ways, because they have been morally influenced in the presence of extraordinary and superior restraint; the indifferent who come to recognize the dignity of the one they deemed inferior. In other words, through Robinson's sacrificial self-deprecatory posture racist white Americans are saved from themselves and their own racism, in order to come to an appreciation of desegregation. He suffered for *their* sins against him and those like him.

This schema determines that for African Americans, salvation is inclusion—but on terms set by dominant powers in a manner whose weight can only be borne by one carefully selected representative. In effect, the individualization of emancipatory suffering obviates the sacrifices of others and conceals the reality that the salvific act had less impact than implied by those who have shaped public memory. There is a sense that once the sacrifice is made, it is efficacious for all; all other suffering, therefore, is measured against it and can never be considered on par with the original individual act without diminishing the significance of "the first." In this reconfiguration, there can only be one martyr for the integration of baseball, iconic in his blackness, for if there are more, the experiment failed. In memory, the savior is reduced to a single action, the complexity of his humanity is overlooked, his resistance conveniently forgotten, and his life is proof-texted to fit a dominant, revisionist narrative of racial reconciliation. Turning the other cheek becomes an expectation of subsequent black and brown players, and martyrdom is a way of domesticating dangerous memories 'and complicated inconvenient prophets such as Jackie Robinson.

---

[97] Robinson, *I Never*, 34.

The engagement of a strategy rooted in a particular interpretation of "turn the other cheek" establishes an overtly Christian concept as a means to achieve a just end. Rarely questioned is the justice of the means, the power dynamics embedded in the interpretation, the privileged dominance of the interpreter, and the long-term negative consequences by those victimized in the process. An overly optimistic assessment of Rickey's embrace of nonresistance[98] betrays a failure to attend critically to theological subtexts in the deployment of a gospel imperative mediated through a particular translation of Papini's *Life of Christ*. A preference for a narrow focus on the three years that Robinson cooperated with the arrangement continue to feed what Gerald Early calls "the myth of St. Jackie, who lived selflessly and died prematurely for our racial sins."[99] Ultimately public memory is traditioned in ways that reinforce for those who are othered the reality that racial justice in baseball remains "una carrera manchada por el pecado."

---

[98] See, for example, Glennon, "Baseball's Surprising Moral Example, 145–166.

[99] Gerald L. Early, "Jackie Robinson as Man and Hero," *St. Louis Post-Dispatch*, 16 April 2013, http://www.stltoday.com/news/opinion/columns/jackie-robinson-as-man-and-hero/article_33ede76b-392a-5e0f-9ede-b3b48a5a01db.html.

Sport and the "Search for the Sacred"[1]

Tracy J. Trothen

Is sport a religion? If so, is it a civil religion, folk religion, popular religion, or secular religion? Scholars studying the relationship between sport and religion have made use of Ninian Smart's definition and criteria for a civil religion,[2] or Rudolph Otto's and Friedrich Schleiermacher's,[3] or Émile Durkheim. Certainly there are aspects that can be drawn from the writings of these well-regarded scholars. For example, Durkheim's notion of "collective effervescence" is very applicable to sports fans' experiences of flow. Unlike approaches that focus primarily on the relationship of sports to religion, I explore how sports might satisfy psychologist Kenneth I. Pargament's research-driven understanding of spirituality as "the search for the sacred."[4] In this chapter, using Pargament's understanding of spirituality, I suggest that one reason why sport draws so many followers and participants is because it *can* be a place where the sacred is discovered through the multifaceted presence of hope.

I propose that the concept of hope overlaps with the concept of spirituality. Pastoral theologian Pamela R. McCarroll carried out an in-depth study of hope, investigating fifty-two articles and thirty books

---

[1] Thanks go to the Springer International Publishing for granting permission to publish this chapter, which is an earlier iteration of my chapter in *Spirituality, Sport, and Doping: More than Just a Game (SpringerBriefs Sport and Religion Series)*.

[2] For example, see the very thorough and well thought-out arguments of Joseph L. Price, *Rounding the Bases: Baseball and Religion in America* (Macon, GA: Mercer University Press, 2006) 111–75 and Rebecca T. Alpert, *Religion and Sports: An Introduction and Case Studies* (New York: Columbia University Press, 2015).

[3] See, for example, Eric Bain-Selbo, *Game Day and God: Football, Faith, and Politics in the American South* (Macon, GA: Mercer University Press, 2009).

[4] Kenneth I. Pargament, "Searching for the Sacred: Toward a Non-Reductionist Theory of Spirituality," in *APA Handbooks in Psychology, Religion, and Spirituality: Vol. 1, Context, Theory, and Research*, ed. K. I. Pargament et al, (Washington, DC: American Psychological Association, 2013) 258.

published between 1976 and 2011 that addressed the topic of hope. These sources came from several disciplines, including theology, philosophy, psychology, and health care.[5] She found that there was no consensus regarding the meaning of hope. Hope has been understood as an internal dispositional quality and also as transcendent. Hope can be about the pursuit of varied goals and outcomes—some specific and concrete and others more open-ended. McCarroll describes hope as being about relationship with self, others (community), creation and the transcendent. Interestingly, these domains of hope mirror many understandings of the domains of spirituality, which is also a very difficult concept to define.[6] Based on careful analysis of these many understandings of hope, McCarroll proposes the following broad definition of hope: "Hope is the experience of the opening of horizons of meaning and participation in relationship to time, other human and nonhuman beings, and/or the transcendent."[7] In this chapter, I am interested in hope as defined by McCarroll as it intersects with spirituality as defined by Pargament.

Sport can inspire hope in at least five different ways, which will be discussed later in this chapter:[8] winning, anticipation, and losing; star athletes and "my team;" perfect moments; embodied connections and possibilities of just communities; and flow states. I suggest that these sources or "locations" of hope in sport each hold the potential to meet Pargament's understanding of spirituality as a search for the sacred. In other words, I discuss how the sacred may be discovered in each of these locations of hope.

I write as a Canadian and often use sports examples from the Canadian context. Since the majority of scholarship on sport, religion, and spirituality is written by scholars in the United States and the United Kingdom, examples from sports in these countries are more common. Examples from countries such as Canada that appear less often in this

---

[5] Pamela R. McCarroll, *The End of Hope—The Beginning: Narratives of Hope in the Face of Death and Trauma* (Minneapolis: Fortress Press, 2014), 19.

[6] For example, see John Fisher, "The Four Domains Model: Connecting Spirituality, Health and Well-Being," *Religions* 2 (2011) 17–28, who proposes four domains of spirituality: the personal domain, the communal domain, the environmental domain (connecting with nature) and the transcendental domain ("relating to some-thing or some-One beyond the human level").

[7] McCarroll, *The End of Hope*, 48.

[8] Tracy J. Trothen, *Winning the Race? Religion, Hope, and Reshaping the Sport Enhancement Debate* (Macon, GA: Mercer University Press, 2015).

discipline can generate a more global sense of sport as it relates to religion and spirituality.

The Back-Drop
Why a Consideration of Sport as
Sacred Is Worthwhile

Some see claims of sport's spirituality or religiosity as idolatrous[9] or inaccurate,[10] while others see these claims as very fitting.[11] Divergent understandings of the relationship between the secular and the religious have been one of the factors behind these varied contentions. If the secular and the religious are understood as mutually exclusive, and if spirituality traditionally has been restricted to institutional mainstream religion, then sport and other phenomenon cannot be spiritual. If theologians such as Jürgen Moltmann, Mayra Rivera, and several others are correct, however, the line between the sacred and the profane, and the religious and the secular, is not impermeable, fixed, or even necessarily existent.

Should the spirituality experienced by pop culture fans be dismissed as fake, derivative, self-absorbed, or pathological? Religious studies scholar Jennifer Porter vigorously critiques value-based distinctions between spirituality that is experienced within established institutional religions and spirituality that is experienced within pop culture. Mainstream religions have been considered authentic, while the religious dimension of fandom has often has been considered fake or derivative. After establishing that many scholars have pathologized the implicitly religious dimension of fan experience, Porter makes a convincing case for the authenticity and validity of "pop-culture inspired spiritualities[12] fan communities, she proposes,

---

[9] See, for example, Robert J. Higgs and Michael Braswell, *An Unholy Alliance: The Sacred and Modern Sports* (Macon, GA: Mercer University Press, 2004).

[10] See, for example, Joan M. Chandler, "Sport Is Not a Religion," in *Sport and Religion*, ed. Shirl J. Hoffman (Champaign, IL: Human Kinetics Books, 1992) 57.

[11] See, for example, Price, *Rounding the Bases*; Trothen, *Winning the Race*; and Robert Ellis, *The Games People Play: Theology, Religion, and Sport* (Eugene, Oregon: Wipf & Stock, 2014).

[12] Jennifer Porter, "Implicit Religion in Popular Culture: The Religious Dimensions of Fan Communities," *Implicit Religion* 12, no. 3 (2009): 272.

are, or at least can be, a place that embodies a person's and/or a community's expression of the essence of all meaning: what it means to be human, to be in community, to be in space and time, to be moral or immoral, to be finite or eternal, to simply be. As a result, pop culture fandoms are implicitly religious. Implicit religion underpins ardent pop culture fandom, just as it underpins ardent explicit religion.[13]

The question of meaning need not be explicitly pursued for a spirituality to be authentic, but can be lived or experienced implicitly. The implicit qualities of spirituality inspired by pop culture, religions or both, resist hard-and-fast definitions, just as they open up a multiplicity of ways of experiencing the sacred.

Part of the problem involved in pinning down what some experience as the complex, powerful, and awe-inspiring qualities of sport is the difficulty of defining spirituality and religion. Instead of starting with *definitions* of religion and spirituality, it may be more prudent to start instead with *understandings* of religion and spirituality, since the term "understanding" implies a more provisional conception that is responsive to shifting contexts and new insights. I am persuaded that empirical studies combined with theoretical research may offer constructive and insightful approaches to contemporary spirituality, so long as scientism is avoided.[14]

I have suggested elsewhere that "sport is a secular religion because sport functions as a communal belief system and it is characterized by the spiritual quality of hope."[15] I have been drawn to an understanding of sport as a secular religion in part because this concept implicitly rejects a binary split between the secular and the religious. Likewise, I find it compelling because good arguments have been made for the religious-like function and form, and sometimes content, of sport.

---

[13] Ibid., 275.

[14] Scientism assumes arguments or particular findings and their interpretations as objective fact, camouflaging the influence of investigators' values, assumptions, and perspectives. See, for example, an excellent article by Jim Parry, "Must Scientists Think Philosophically about Science?" in *Philosophy and the Sciences of Exercise, Health and Sport: Critical Perspectives on Research Methods*, ed. Mike McNamee (New York: Routledge, 2005), 22. Scientific, evidence-based methods are built on the assumption that *every claim* is provisional. Every finding and interpretation may be proven false or limited, otherwise there would be no need for further inquiry.

[15] Trothen, *Winning the Race*, 80.

Notwithstanding the value of arguments, including my own, that sport can be similar to an institutional religion, I am becoming more persuaded that sport may be better understood in terms of spirituality rather than as a religion. No matter how strenuously and persuasively counter-arguments are made, the concept of religion tends to be reduced to anthropomorphic theism in much of the Euro-American world. Critiques by Christopher Hitchens, Richard Dawkins and others who reject religion, particularly Christianity and Islam, as irrational (not arational, which is a far more apt claim) and inherently destructive, rely on assumptions that all religious followers ascribe human qualities to an all-powerful, enthroned God who chooses whether or not to respond to prayer requests. Further complicating perceptions of the relationship of sport to religion are faith claims that the Christian God is a jealous God who, anthropomorphically, will not abide any claims of religiosity outside of an explicit Christian structure. One benefit to the exploration of sport as a type of religion is the potential for debating these claims and assumptions in the spirit of the radical reformer. Perhaps, however, we can better address such value-laden assumptions by beginning the discussion differently.[16]

This brings me to the next challenge: how should we understand "spirituality?" One literature review yielded ninety-two different definitions of spirituality.[17] Many of these definitions are based on individual

---

[16] Historian Brent Nongbri in *Before Religion: A History of a Modern Concept* (New Haven and London: Yale University Press, 2013) provides a constructive critique of religion as a constructed category. Nongbri points out that the concept of religion is projected onto many ancient cultures, noting that religion has not been a universal concept. Looking back over the past 2,000 years, Nongbri concludes that the contemporary assumption of religion as being about "inner disposition and concern for salvation" (24) does not apply to antiquity. His analysis supports the notion that through much of antiquity there was no distinction between the religious and the secular. Indeed, it was not until modernity (the sixteenth and seventeenth centuries) that the category of religion as separate from the secular emerged. In sum, Nongbri argues that the category of religion has been assumed to be natural and universal, when it is, in reality, neither.

[17] A.M. Unruh et al., "Spirituality Unplugged: A Review of Commonalities and Contentions and a Resolution," *Canadian Journal of Occupational Therapy* 69, no. 1 (2002): 5–19, referred to in Larry Vandecreek, "Defining and Advocating for Spiritual Care in the Hospital," *Journal of Pastoral Care and Counseling* 64, no. 2 (2010): 2.

subjective experiences, in the absence of systemic attempts to outline a broader narrative. This individualistic approach makes definitions of spirituality susceptible to charges of uncritical reliance on individual inner experiences. Contemporary shaping of the meaning of spirituality has been heavily influenced by the emergence of New Age movements in the 1960s and the postmodern rejection of master narratives.[18] Spirituality, as influenced by New Age movements, often has been variously constructed according to subjective inner experiences alone. The more recent SBNR (spiritual but not religious) tendency (I stop short of calling it a movement as this status is not clear) sometimes includes a social justice component, extending well beyond the self and embracing a value system.

A number of scholars using social-scientific, evidence-based research methods have been studying spirituality. One of the most established and well-regarded scholars engaged in such research on spirituality is Kenneth I. Pargament, an emeritus professor of psychology from Bowling Green State University, who has published more than two hundred papers on the relationship between religion, spirituality, and psychology. Based on a combination of theoretical research and empirical studies using scales with high degrees of reliability and validity, Pargament has constructed a definition of spirituality that reflects common themes distilled from research carried out by himself and colleagues over the years. He describes spirituality as a "'search for the sacred'…and a natural and normal part of life."[19] Supporting his contention that spirituality is part of being human, Pargament cites studies from neuroscience that suggest humans may be "hard-wired" for spirituality.[20] In other words, according to Pargament, a yearning for the sacred is a basic part of being human: "Our yearning for the sacred is what makes us human, healthy, and whole."

---

[18] See, for example, Simon Robinson's analysis of this historical backdrop. Simon Robinson, "The Spiritual Journey," in *Sport and Spirituality: An Introduction,* eds. J. Parry et al. (London: Routledge, 2007), 38–58.

[19] Kenneth I. Pargament, "Searching for the Sacred," 258.

[20] Kenneth I. Pargament (2013), "Spirituality as an Irreducible Human Motivation and Process" in *The International Journal for the Psychology of Religion* 23 (2013): 273.

Spirituality as a Search for the Sacred

Pargament's definition of spirituality as a "search for the sacred" is multifaceted. Consider first the term "sacred," which Pargament defines as referring "not only to ideas of higher powers, God, and transcendent reality, but also to other significant objects that take on spiritual character and meaning by virtue of their association with the divine."[21] "Sacred" can be understood in both theistic and nontheistic terms. Pargament's research suggests that anyone "can perceive spiritual qualities in various aspects of life."[22] These aspects of life are far-ranging and can include sport. He quotes the Brazilian Roman Catholic priest Jose Benedito Filho as saying that "[w]e have so much misery and suffering here. But soccer is our gift from God. Our healing grace so that we Brazilians can go on."[23] The sacred can be discovered in many aspects of life, ranging from nature, institutional religions, relationships, work, and music to sport. One can discover the sacred in more than one facet of life. A commitment to an organized traditional religion, for example, does not preclude experiencing the sacred in sport or other aspects of life such as familial relationships or music. Not everyone, likewise, discovers the sacred in organized religions. One may or may not, moreover, explicitly use the term "sacred" when discussing an aspect of life that satisfies the meaning of sacred.

One may object that this understanding leaves us again with the problem that the concept of spirituality is defined too loosely and too individualistically; I could claim that jam on toast is sacred, simply because I enjoy it. How do we know when we have discovered something that is sacred to us, and not just enjoyable or otherwise pleasure-inducing?

The meaning of "search" adds a thicker dimension to the concept of spirituality. As Pargament explains, his research shows that spirituality as the *search* for the sacred is dynamic and changing throughout one's life and is characterized by three activities that are in constant motion: discovery of the sacred, conservation of the sacred, and transformation of

---

[21] Ibid., 271.

[22] Pargament, "Searching for the Sacred," 260.

[23] Pargament, "Baylor ISR: Implications of Spirituality for Health and Well-Being" 17 April 2013, YouTube (www.youtube.com/watch?v=8qezB_uW4KM). Pargament references the quote as part of an article published in the *Washington Post*: Anthony Faiola, "A Divine Carnival of Glory," 1 July 2002.

the sacred.[24] Spirituality, in Pargament's work, is a search even if this search is not consciously intentional and it is relational. One thus might find or be found during the lifetime process of the search for the sacred; a conscious awareness of finding or being found is part of the discovery. In this chapter I am most interested in the first activity of the search for the sacred: the possibility of the discovery of the sacred in sport. When people *discover* the sacred, there are at least four implications for their lives. Whether or not such implications occur goes to whether or not the sacred is indeed discovered in sport for someone. In this way, Pargament provides us with a model of spirituality that challenges a purely individualistic assessment of what constitutes spirituality as "the discovery of the sacred." If these four implications are not experienced, then what has been discovered is not something that is sacred to the person. (Since the writing of this chapter, Pargament has reframed his findings and has identified six implications.[25])

These four implications for people's lives are as follows. First, partly because the sacred has "attributes of transcendence, boundlessness and ultimacy,"[26] people invest their resources, including time and money, in sacred things. Second, "perceptions of the sacred appear to act like an emotional generator," stimulating feelings of awe, elevation, love, hope, and gratitude. Third, "people derive more support, strength and satisfaction from those parts of their lives that they hold sacred." Fourth, finally, the sacred objects are prioritized and become "organizing forces" in their lives.[27]

I consider how these implications of the discovery of the sacred may be present in the lives of athletes and sports fans. Although I focus on the discovery of the sacred, I suggest some questions regarding sport and the additional two activities that characterize the search for the sacred: conservation and transformation. In sum, I theorize that Pargament's research can help us to appreciate more fully the significance and meaning of sport in the lives of many followers.

---

[24] Pargament, "Spirituality as an Irreducible Human Motivation and Process," 274.

[25] Kenneth I. Pargament and others, "Some contributions of a psychological approach to the study of the sacred," *Religion* 47, no. 4 (2017): 718.

[26] Pargament, *Spiritually Integrated Psychotherapy: Understanding and Addressing the Sacred* (New York: Guilford, 2007), 39.

[27] Pargament, "Searching for the Sacred," 261–262.

The Game Is On!—Why Are Sports Such a Big Deal?

The gold-medal game of the men's 2010 Olympic hockey game was the most watched event (of any kind, not only sport) in Canadian history, with 16.6 million Canadians, almost half of the country's population, watching the entire game, and 26.5 million—about 80 percent of Canada's population at the time—watching at least part of the game.[28] The question of why sport is so important to so many people has been investigated mainly through psychological, sociological, and historical lenses. The reasons why people are motivated to follow sport as spectators or fans are multiple, but most research points to the excitement of competition, stress relief, connecting with others (for example, social issues of belonging and identity), aesthetics, and escapism.[29] Theologian Robert Ellis, in his 2012 empirical study of 468 sports spectators and athletes, had similar findings regarding motives behind both spectating and playing sports: fitness and health (primarily for athletes), stress relief, social motives, enjoyment of competition, and simple enjoyment.[30] What has been ignored in many of these studies, with a very notable exception being Ellis's, is the possibility that these surface motives may have more comprehensive motives underlying them. Ellis suggests that a spiritual underpinning as a driving force may provide a more comprehensive understanding of why so many people are drawn to sports. Although competition, stress relief, social connection, enjoyment, and fitness are persuasive and important motivators, they may not explain fully the pervasive, powerful attraction of sport.

There are few social-scientific research studies that investigate the question of the possible relevance of spirituality or religion to the question of what motivates people to follow sport. The two most notable of such studies, however, suggest that there is indeed a spiritual motivation for many followers. Ellis considers the possibility of underlying religious

---

[28] The most-watched hockey game in thirty years in an Olympic final, https://www.nhl.com/news/olympic-final-most-watched-hockey-game.../c-519476.

[29] See Markovits and Albertson for a very helpful summary of relevant research studies: Andrei S. Markovits and Emily K. Albertson, *Sportista: Female Fandom in the United States* (Philadelphia: Temple University Press, 2012), 159–160.

[30] Included in enjoyment was the appreciation of the aesthetic dimension of sport. Ellis, *The Games People Play*, 251.

motivations, positing that the quest for transcendence, including self-transcendence, characterizes sport and distinguishes it from play.[31] Religious studies scholar Eric Bain-Selbo surveyed 220 fans at college football games in the southern United States and, based on his subjects' usage of words that allude to religious and even mystical concepts to describe the game-day experience, found that such games provided opportunities for fans to have what he calls "religious experiences."[32] Ellis's and Bain-Selbo's contention that sport often has a religious dimension for its followers may be strengthened through the application of Pargament's empirically driven understanding of the discovery of the sacred.

Pargament makes the case that people are drawn to religion primarily because of their search for the sacred. While other motivations, including the need to belong to a united community,[33] make meaning,[34] achieve a sense of control (and serve in part as Karl Marx's "opiate of the people"), and enhance self-esteem,[35] may *partly* explain the motivation for following a religion, the motivations of many followers cannot be reduced to these factors alone. Instead, "spirituality is an important, irreducible motivation and process in and of itself."[36] Religion attracts people for all of these reasons and is also attractive because religions offer a spiritual dimension. All of these factors are important and are entwined, adding depth to spiritual concepts such as hope. Pargament's point is that the quest for spiritual meaning and fulfilment cannot and should not be explained only in terms that do not also include spirituality for its own sake.

---

[31] Ellis, "The Meaning of Sport: An Empirical Study into the Significance Attached to Sporting Participation and Spectating in the UK and US," *Practical Theology* 5, no. 2 (2012): 170, 174; and Ellis, *The Games People Play*, 228–274.

[32] Eric Bain-Selbo, "Ecstasy, Joy, and Sorrow: The Religious Experience of Southern College Football," *Journal of Religion and Popular Culture* 20 (Fall 2008): 1–12.

[33] Émile Durkheim, *The Elementary Forms of the Religious Life* (New York: Free Press, 1965 [1912]).

[34] Clifford Geertz, "Religion as a Cultural System," in *Anthropological Approaches to the Study of Religion*, ed. M. Banton (London: Tavistock, 1966), 1–46.

[35] B. Spilka et al., "A General Attribution Theory for the Psychology of Religion," *Journal for the Scientific Study of Religion* 24 (1985): 1–20.

[36] Pargament, "Spirituality as an Irreducible Human Motivation and Process," 271.

Pargament explains that there has been a tendency within psychological research to diminish or deny spirituality as a motivation in and of itself. Instead, motivations for subscribing to a religion tend to be explained away in "psychological, social, or physiological" terms.[37] What if attempts to understand sports' fans and athletes' motivations have been affected by the same myopic vision?

Several scholars make reference to hope in sport.[38] Like Ellis, professor of sociology Michael Grimshaw makes the point that hope characterizes experiences of reaching toward transcendence in sport. Discussions of the relationship between religion and sport, and of sport's spiritual dimension, almost always address hope and the human quest for meaning as part of that hope. In short, hope is a thread through the elements that draw many people to sport. Based on a review of most scholarly literature regarding the intersection of religion and sport, I have proposed locations of hope in sport for fans and athletes.[39] I will consider five of these locations of hope in turn, making a case for spirituality as a motivating force for many sports followers and athletes. To make this case I ask whether Pargament's four implications of the discovery of the sacred may be experienced by sports fans and athletes.

---

[37] Part of the reason for this overlooking of spirituality as irreducible, Pargament offers, is that psychologists as a group in the United States are much less theistic than the general population of the country (ibid., 271).

[38] For example, see Simon Robinson, "The Spiritual Journey," 38–58; Jeffrey Scholes, "Professional Baseball and Fan Disillusionment: A Religious Ritual Analysis," *Journal of Religion and Popular Culture*, 7 (Summer 2014): 1–14; Joseph L. Price, *Rounding the Bases*, 117, 125; Christopher H. Evans and William R. Herzog, II, eds., *The Faith of Fifty Million: Baseball, Religion, and American Culture* (Louisville, KY: Westminster John Knox Press, 2002) 7, 48; and Michael Grimshaw, "I Can't Believe My Eyes: The Religious Ascetics of Sport as Postmodern Salvific Moments", *Implicit Religion* 3, no. 2 (2002): 87–99.

[39] Elsewhere I have considered the spiritual quality of hope and posit that there are four locations of hope in sport and that these locations of hope attract both fans and athletes. I now suggest that one of the locations of hope that I have identified is better understood as two locations (see *Winning the Race*, 115–132).

It's About Hope[40]

1. Winning, Losing, and Anticipation

We hope to win. We wait with bated breath for record-breaking performances and personal bests. Even when the odds are stacked against us, we hope our team will win. In 1992, immediately following the Toronto Blue Jays' first World Series win, it is estimated that half a million fans flooded Yonge Street from Lake Ontario all the way north to Highway 401. In 2015, when the Blue Jays won the American League East pennant for the first time since this earlier win, fans rejoiced. As one fan tweeted, "22 years. 3,559 games. You're damn right it's time to celebrate!"

Part of the fans' jubilation is the identification that many experience with their teams. Winning can bring a special sort of hope–validating our loyalties and even validating ourselves. This psychological dynamic of identification with a team or individual athlete is called "basking in reflected glory" (BIRG), and is even more pronounced if the win occurs following a challenge to the individual fan's self-esteem.[41] Another part of winning can be the sense of boundlessness, and ultimacy, that characterize the sacred; a big win can make it seem as if anything is possible and that one is on top of the world. Pargament's observation that "perceptions of the sacred appear to act like an emotional generator," stimulating feelings of awe, elevation, love, hope and gratitude, fits well with the emotions that are generated at sports events particularly at championship-level competitions in the wake of a win or outstanding performance.

Winning is important and stokes hope and jubilation. Winning, however, is not required for hope. Fans persist in hoping for a win even in the face of years of losses. I continue, in defiance of much reason, to hope that the Toronto Maple Leafs will win the Stanley Cup, even though they have not won it since 1967. And Chicago Cubs fans kept rooting for their team despite not winning the World Series from 1908 until 2016, when they finally broke the infamous curse of the Billy Goat!

---

[40] An earlier version of this section on locations of hope was published in Trothen, *Winning the Race*, 115–132 (adapted with permission from Mercer University Press).

[41] Robert B. Cialdiniet et al., "Basking in Reflected Glory: Three Football (Field) Studies" *Journal of Personality and Social Psychology* 34 (1976): 366–375.

Losing can be crushing. Philosopher and theologian Michael Novak goes so far as to say that losing in sport can feel like a "death." While there has been critique of this description as going too far,[42] others have supported Novak's contention, arguing that sport is much more than just a game for followers.[43] If sport were just a game, fans should be able to disengage from an unsatisfying or disappointing sports event. Studies show, however, that fans do not see themselves as simply passive observers: "supporters believe they can influence what happens" in a competition.[44] Real people, real dreams, and real struggle are involved; authentic meaning and happiness are not restricted to dramatic existential moments but seem to be generated through more temporary and simple "meaningful activities" such as sport for many people.[45]

Fans of teams that have lost numerous championships may find it even more meaningful when they eventually do win; the years of persistence and humbling status often seem to inculcate a sense of loyalty and community through commiseration and shared stories. This commiseration and shared narratives can open horizons of meaning that McCarroll proposes form the basis of hope. A long struggle can make victory that much sweeter. In the meantime, hope exists in the very persistence of dedicated fans who participate in their teams' struggles, forming part of the wider narrative of persistence. For example, in 2014 tennis player Eugenie Bouchard made it to the Wimbledon finals, becoming the first Canadian to do so. She lost and Canadian fans lamented. Almost immediately, though, the Canadian media began to broadcast interviews focused on optimism and hope for her (our) future successes.

Anticipation of the next season, game, or moment is an important component of hope. Winning is very important and it is not all that matters: athletes and fans in Ellis's study also reported a "good quality game as important, a strong performance from one's team, a good effort."[46] As Pargament asserts, "people derive more support, strength, and satisfac-

---

[42] See, for example, Randolph Feezell, *Sport, Philosophy, and Good Lives* (Lincoln: University of Nebraska Press, 2013), 70.

[43] See, for example, Ellis, "The Meaning of Sport," 183.

[44] Ellis, *The Games People Play*, 259. Ellis proposes that sports spectators are more than spectators and have vicarious relationships with the players, noting that spectators expressed a strong sense of identification with the team (256).

[45] Feezel, *Sport, Philosophy, and Good Lives*, 193.

[46] Ellis, *The Games People Play*, 256.

tion from those parts of their lives that they hold sacred." A loss will not usually compromise the sacredness of sport; the sport usually will remain a prioritized and organizing force with game-time being sacrosanct.

2. Star Athletes and "My Team"

Identification, including BIRG, with a team and their fan group makes one part of a community; one belongs. Research studies and anecdotal evidence show that people can find the "support, strength, and satisfaction" that Pargament outlines as one of the implications of discovering the sacred, by being part of a sports community.[47]

Fans buy shirts with their favorite team's logo or player's number. Posters of individual athletes and teams adorn walls. Time and money are spent on attending games and competitions, as per Pargament's first implication of the discovery of the sacred: "people invest their resources, including time and money, in these sacred things."

Star athletes are regarded by some fans as more than role models; they may become regarded as moral exemplars, even though there is no reason to expect exemplary or even good moral behavior from someone known for their athletic skill alone. Sport does not necessarily instill good character or virtue; athletes are not better people simply because they perform their sport well or even superbly. There are few who perform what may be altruistic acts in the midst of fierce competition such as Canadian speed skater Gilmore Junio in the 2014 winter Olympics. Junio gave up his spot to Denny Morrison in the 1000-meter race, given that Morrison had failed to qualify for the team, despite his impressive record in this particular competition. By giving up his spot, Junio in all probability improved the chances of the Canadian team winning. Morrison achieved a silver medal in the event. Whether or not athletes act as moral role models or even exemplars, fans admire their star athletes, seeing them as symbols of hope and promise because of their exceptional athletic accomplishments.

Belonging to a sport community helps one to shape one's identity, participate in meaningful activities with others and to have inspiring performers or even perceived role models. Not only do these fan activities fit

---

[47] See, for example, Joseph L. Price, "Here I Cheer: Conversion Narratives of Baseball Fans," *Criterion* 42, no. 2 (Spring 2003): 16; Lynn Ellis McCutcheon et al., *Celebrity Worshippers: Inside the Minds of Stargazers* (Baltimore: PublishAmerica, 2004), 82; Ellis, "The Meaning of Sport,"179.

with some of Pargament's implications of the sacred, they also speak of hope: the opening of horizons of meaning and participation through relationship with others.

3. Perfect Moments

Perfect athletic moments are liminal: they stand at the threshold of this world and beyond. The "imperfect performer" bridges the gap between the seemingly possible and impossible. Dick Fosbury's remarkable jump, Nadia Comăneci's perfect ten in the 1976 Olympic gymnastics, Paul Henderson's stunning goal in 1972 Canada-Russia series, and the list goes on. These inspiring moments of athletic perfection generate feelings of awe, akin to Pargament's second implication of discovering the sacred.

Is the quest for perfect moments too egocentric to generate an authentic sense of transcendence? Joseph L. Price, professor of religion, notes that "[e]ven when the pursuit of a perfect performance in sport becomes corrupted or distorted—when it moves toward selfish goals rather than the joy and disclosive possibilities of play itself—it still manifests a fundamental human desire for fulfillment."[48] This desire for fulfillment is part of the search for the sacred: the human desire for something more—for transcendence, ultimacy, and boundlessness. Even when motives are more self-centered than outwardly oriented, the search for the sacred may well provide the underlying propulsion.

The biblical Greek understanding of perfection has more to do with wholeness, being complete,[49] or, I would suggest, becoming more fully human. Instead of perceiving strivings for perfection as attempts to supersede appropriate human limits, or even to become god-like, the quest for perfection is perhaps better understood as the quest to be more fully human, embracing the part of ourselves that is hard-wired for spirituality, including the desire for feelings of awe, elevation, love, hope and gratitude that follow the discovery of that which is sacred to us.

---

[48] Joseph L. Price, "An American Apotheosis: Sport as Popular Religion" in *Religion and Popular Culture in America*, eds. Bruce David Forbes and Jeffrey H. Mahan (Berkeley: University of California Press, 2000), 211.

[49] Eric Bain-Selbo and D. Gregory Sapp, *Understanding Sport as a Religious Phenomenon: An Introduction* (New York: Bloomsbury Academic, 2016), 8. See chapter 3 of this title for an in-depth exploration of the perspectives of several religions on perfection, and the relationship between sport, religion, and perfection.

What it means to be more fully human is not clear. Athletes can go overboard in the pursuit of so-called perfection in sport; this best of impulses can become manifested destructively. Excessive self-violence, for example, is a risk. An overwhelming desire to be the best can lead to dangerous weight loss or high risk-taking in already extreme sports such as snow-boarding.

The quest for perfection and the best possible athletic performance is an organizing principle for many sport fans and athletes. A focus on watching one's team or improving one's performance and hoping for the ultimate sports moment is a priority that most are unwilling to give up unless faced with an overwhelming reason. Fittingly, Pargament's fourth implication is that the sacred is prioritized as and becomes an organizing force in one's life.[50]

When perfect moments are achieved or witnessed, they generate awe and can offer hope that the almost unimaginable, the never before achieved, is indeed possible. In this way, fans and athletes experience "more support, strength, and satisfaction" from sport than from parts of their lives that are not sacred to them. Perfect moments are about hope in that they can open up horizons of meaning. The witnessing of moments in which human limitations are transcended suggest the possibility that we can be or do, or participate in, more than we had thought. This opening up of possibilities is part of hope.

4. Unity and Diversity

At its best, sport does not allow one to forget or devalue one's body, emotions, intellect, or spirit. At its worst, sport can promote unnecessary violence, and athletes can become regarded as machines. Mainstream western culture tends to be either body-denying or body-obsessed. The ethic of winning at all costs encourages an instrumental approach that reduces the athlete to a body that has utility in its potential to win. The value of the athlete is reduced to their capacity to compartmentalize, utilize, and optimize measurable abilities that can produce a win. On the other hand, a sports ethic that centers on becoming the best that one can be holds the potential for the promotion of embodied integrity fostering intrapersonal integration and growth.

Sport has the potential to celebrate and unite a confluence of people from diverse racial, ethnic and socio-economic backgrounds. Top-notch

---

[50] See, for example, Ellis, "The Meaning of Sport," 179.

athletes with physical disabilities challenge assumptions about the meaning and perceived limitations of disability. Hayley Wickenheiser and other women's Olympic hockey players challenged gender stereotypes.[51] An example of a sports event that helped to unify a very divided country is the 1995 Rugby World Cup, which was hosted in South Africa soon after the end of apartheid. Through Nelson Mandela's inspired leadership, the country came together, black and white, to support and celebrate their rugby team in winning the 1995 World Cup.

Sport can be both liberating and oppressive, with athletes, teams, and sports leaders overcoming or reinforcing barriers on the basis of sex, gender, disability, race, ethnicity, age, and sexual orientation. Theologian Jürgen Moltmann sees the promise of Olympia in the expression of protest against barriers, divisiveness and oppression: "Olympia will be 'a symbol of hope' if its character as protest, as alternative, and as the prelude to freedom is stressed, in its contrast to burdened everyday life in the economic, political and social world. This is a primal human longing."[52] When sport is the locus of inclusion, it is a source of "support, strength,…satisfaction" and justice, stimulating feelings of awe, elevation, love, hope, and gratitude.

Sport can be a unifying force, increasing intrapersonal and interpersonal connection, connection with nature, and connection with the transcendent.[53] These connections can provide hope when hope is understood as the "opening of horizons of meaning and participation."[54] The development of these relationships contributes to an awareness of the interdependence of all life and of the possibilities endemic to this interdependence.

5. Flow

A "flow" state, as coined by Mihaly Csikszentmihalyi, is characterized by total absorption in the experience, the sense that all life is con-

---

[51] Some studies suggest that diversity can be promoted effectively in recreational sport, combating societal prejudices. See, for example, William Bridel and Genevieve Rail, "Sport, Sexuality, and the Production of (Resistant) Bodies: De-/Re-Constructing the Meanings of Gay Male Marathon Corporeality," *Sociology of Sport Journal* 24 (2007): 127–144.

[52] Jürgen Moltmann, "Olympia between Politics and Religion," in *Sport*, eds. Gregory Baum and John Coleman (Edinburgh: T&T Clark, 1989), 107.

[53] Pargament, *Spiritually Integrated Psychotherapy*, 112–113.

[54] McCarroll, *The End of Hope*, 48.

nected, a strong sense of self, and the loss of individual ego. As an athlete in flow, one is aware of working very hard but also of not working at all—some describe it as being on automatic pilot. Exceptionally strong athletic performances can be driven by a flow experience. Although particular conditions for flow have been identified, flow experiences cannot be induced.[55]

Most studies focus on flow states in relation to the athlete, but the sports fan seems to experience a similar state.[56] Fans' euphoria has been variously called a wave, effervescence, a type of flow, "anonymous enthusiasm,"[57] or "shining moments." As philosophers Hubert Dreyfus and Sean Dorrance Kelly explain, "there are moments in sport—either in the playing of them or in the witnessing of them—during which something so overpowering happens that it wells up before you as a palpable presence and carries you along as on a powerful wave. At that moment there is no question of ironic distance from the event. That is the moment when the sacred shines."[58] Similar to athletes in flow, fans' shining moments hold transformative potential, are extraordinary, temporary, and can seem to be propelled by an external force. In Pargament's research, whatever is held sacred "act[s] like an emotional generator, stimulating feelings of awe, elevation, love, hope, and gratitude." These emotional responses are associated with flow.

Complicating the dynamics of flow among fans is the reality that crowds at sporting events can be violent. Some have theorized that the violence of sports fans has roots in "personal and political identities involving economic and ethnic issues,"[59] but other research refutes this.[60]

---

[55] Susan Jackson and Mihaly Csikszentmihalyi, *Flow in Sports: The Keys to Optimal Experiences and Performance* (Champaign, IL: Human Kinetics, 1999).

[56] Bain-Selbo ("Ecstasy, Joy, and Sorrow," 9) argues that "the experience of the religious adherent and the experience of the Southern college football fan are essentially the same flow experiences; they are simply labeled differently."

[57] Wolfgang Vondey, "Christian Enthusiasm: Can the Olympic Flame Kindle the Fire of Christianity?," *Word & World* 23, no. 3 (Summer 2003): 319.

[58] Hubert Dreyfus and Sean Dorrance Kelly, *All Things Shining: Reading the Western Classics to Find Meaning in a Secular Age* (New York: Free Press, 2011), 194.

[59] Kevin O'Gorman in *Saving Sport—Sport, Society and Spirituality* (Dublin: The Columbia Press, 2010, 133) addresses fan violence and sums up the explanation for this provided by Franklin Foer, *How Football Explains the World* (London: Arrow Books, 2004): 13.

Studies have found likewise that although crowds can engage in passive "automatic thinking," they can also function proactively.[61] So, why choose violence? Perhaps the difference lies in whether or not sport is a source of the sacred or only a source of adrenaline for followers. More likely, given humanity's history of violence in institutional religion and in sport, the discovery of the sacred does not necessarily preclude bad behavior.

Flow can generate hope through the experiential awareness of the powerful connections between all life, the transcendent, and the extraordinary. Intentional and communal reflection on the meanings of such awe-inspiring moments, however, is necessary if these experiences are to be expressed in consonant actions.

Conservation and Transformation in Sacred Sport

To demonstrate that sport has spiritual meaning for some people, in this chapter I focus most on the discovery of the sacred, since it must first be shown that it is possible to experience the sacred in sport if one is to successfully argue that sport has a spiritual dimension, as understood by Pargament. Two additional activities characterize spirituality in this model: conservation of the sacred and transformation of the sacred.[62] Space allows only for a very brief consideration of these remaining two activities.

The conservation of the sacred is a strong motivating force. People want to hold onto whatever is sacred to them. There are many spiritual pathways to help conserve or deepen one's relationship with the sacred. For people who subscribe to institutional religions, these pathways may include attending worship services, participating in ritual practices, engaging with meditation or prayer, and gathering with others in the faith community. For people who find the sacred in sport, spiritual pathways

---

[60] For example, see Daniel L. Wann, "Preliminary Validation of the Sport Fan Motivation Scale," *Journal of Sport and Social Issues 19* (1995): 377–396. Wann studied the motivations of 272 sports fans and found no "relationship between level of economic motivation and self-proclaimed fandom."

[61] Martyn Percy and Rogan Taylor, "Something for the Weekend, Sir? Leisure, Ecstasy and Identity in Football and Contemporary Religion," *Leisure Studies,* 16 (1997): 38.

[62] Pargament, "Spirituality as an Irreducible Human Motivation and Process," 274.

may include attending sporting events and engaging in rituals such as singing the national anthem before a NHL game, making pilgrimages to sacred sites such as the Hockey Hall of Fame in Toronto, wearing emblematic clothing such as four-time gold medalist Hayley Wickenheiser's hockey number, 22, and gathering with fan communities.

These pathways can fail when one is confronted by what Pargament calls a disorienting issue. For those who experience spirituality in sport, spiritual disorientation could be generated by a disruption to hope: a momentous loss, a career-ending injury, the inability to break records continually, or the revelation that an admired athlete has used banned substances in an effort to break more records or simply to win.

Coping methods that conserve the sacred include trying one's usual pathways again, "spiritual meaning-making, seeking spiritual support and connection, and spiritual purification."[63] Meaning-making[64] usually involves the reframing or redefining of a stressor. For instance, one may have believed that worthy sports icons never cheat by using performance-enhancing drugs (PEDs). Lance Armstrong was an icon for many cycling fans. By beating cancer *and* by being a star athlete, Armstrong was the "ultimate symbol of hope, inspiration, and the limitless potential of the human will and spirit to the American audiences."[65] Similarly, Ben Johnson was an icon for many Canadians. Johnson is Jamaican-born, former Canadian sprinter who won gold and set a new record for the 100-meter race at the 1988 Olympics, which was later rescinded after tests showed he had used banned substances. To cope with the news that Armstrong or Johnson used PEDs, one may need to reframe the use of PEDs: Armstrong used PEDs, but he did it because everyone else did and there was no other good option if he wanted to continue to compete. Similarly, Johnson used PEDs, but he has redeemed himself by confessing and do-

---

[63] Pargament, *Spiritually Integrated Psychotherapy*, 99.

[64] Pastoral theologians have written about embedded and deliberative theologies. See, for example, H.W. Stone and J.O. Duke, *How to Think Theologically* (Minneapolis, MN: Fortress Press, 1996); Carrie Doehring, *The Practice of Pastoral Care: A Postmodern Approach* 2nd ed. (Louisville, KY: Westminster/John Knox Press, 2015). When a faith conviction is not deliberately examined and reevaluated in relation to lived experiences, including those of suffering, loss, and systemic injustice, the faith claim may cease to make sense and not hold up in times of extreme stress.

[65] Kyle Kusz, *Revolt of the White Athlete: Race, Media and the Emergence of Extreme Athletes in America* (New York: Peter Lang Publishing, 2007) 139.

ing educational and mentoring work with youth around sports and drugs.[66] Seeking support could involve something as simple as talking about the scandal with other fans. Spiritual purification involves a ritual in which the disorienting incident or impulse is cleansed. Purification seems most helpful for people who have committed a wrong that offends their understanding of the sacred. The athlete who uses a banned enhancement, for example, may need to confess and do penance for their wrong-doing, as did Johnson.

When these spiritual coping methods do not work, a spiritual struggle ensues, through which one's beliefs are either changed or discarded.[67] Spiritual struggles are "typically marked by isolation from God, self, and/or others and involve topics and/or questioning that are not perceived as socially acceptable."[68] The general expectation is that upset over a big loss or the news that an athlete has cheated is passing. For those fans who become depressed or otherwise stuck, dangerous social norms can suggest that there is something defective about such individuals. It may be that their sense of spiritual meaning has been very damaged and they are struggling to make sense of something that has been sacred to them. There are, however, few safe places for people to be taken seriously and to get help in processing these struggles. Sport is supposedly "just a game." We have failed to understand that sport can be spiritual.

Pargament sees spiritual coping methods as distinctive from other coping mechanisms, in that "spiritual coping methods are tailored to provide solutions to problems of human finitude and insufficiency."[69] Indeed, part of the very reason people discover the sacred in sport is the escape from temporality and the experience of transcending perceived human limits. Sport can put us in touch with something greater than ourselves, a sense of awe, inspiration, and the belief that the impossible may be possible. Paradoxically, with the emphasis on becoming better

---

[66] See, for example, Stephen Brunt, "Ben Johnson: An Attempt at Redemption," 27 September 2013, http://www.sportsnet.ca/more/ben-johnson-an-attempt-at-redemption-brunt/ (accessed 8 October 2016).

[67] Pargament, "Spirituality as an Irreducible Human Motivation and Process," 277.

[68] C.A. Faigin et al., "Spiritual Struggles as a Possible Risk Factor for Addictive Behaviors: An Initial Empirical Investigation," *The International Journal for the Psychology of Religion*, 24 (2014): 211. These conditions seem to be risk factors for the development of addictions.

[69] Pargament, "Searching for the Sacred," 264.

and superseding limits, we come in touch with the reality that we are limited. Transformation must involve the reconfiguring of the meanings of being human, its limits and transcendence toward "more-ness."

Sport as Spiritual

Spirituality is comprised of activities such as discovery of the sacred, conservation of the sacred, and transformation of the sacred.[70] Each has been explored in this chapter as they may apply to sport. We have considered the four implications that the discovery of the sacred has for people's lives and discussed the alignment of these implications with hope in sport. First, people invest their resources in sport. Second, experiences of sport often "act like an emotional generator," stimulating feelings of awe, elevation, love, hope, and gratitude. Third, "people derive more support, strength, and satisfaction" from time they spend on sport. Finally, sport is an "organizing force" in the lives of many fans and athletes.[71]

Pargament's work on the meaning of spirituality can help us to see why people draw on spiritual concepts, some of which are associated also with modern religions, to describe their sport experiences.[72] If people discover the sacred in sport, it explains why sport is so meaningful and absorbing for these people. The discovery of the sacred in sport also explains the intensity of emotional responses to losses, wins, scandals, trades, and other incidents. Significant efforts are made to conserve and, if necessary, transform what one believes about sport, and particular teams and athletes, in the face of disorienting issues.

As I proposed at the beginning of this chapter, sport can be spiritual. To frame this argument, I suggested that spirituality (as defined by Pargament) overlaps with hope (as defined by McCarroll) in sport. I considered five locations of hope in sport. I explored expressions of Pargament's four implications of the sacred in these locations of hope and showed that sport can involve "the opening of horizons of meaning and participation" through relationships with time, others, creation and the transcendent, showing that sport can be spiritual.[73]

---

[70] Pargament, "Spirituality as an Irreducible Human Motivation and Process," 274.

[71] Pargament, "Searching for the Sacred," 261–262.

[72] See Bain-Selbo, *Game Day and God*, and Robert Ellis, *The Games People Play*.

[73] McCarroll, *The End of Hope*, 48.

This contention points to further questions. What is it that is satisfied by sport? For what do we yearn? What does it mean to be human? How do we engage with our limitations and our quest for transcendence? If I am correct and spirituality is part of sport, then it behooves us to be more intentional about how we address this spiritual dimension communally[74] and to take the spirituality of sport seriously.

---

[74] If people discover the sacred in sport, this has implications for therapeutic care. Instead of ignoring sports talk, spiritual care providers need to listen more attentively, assuming that sport may well be one significant location of hope and the sacred.

OVERTIME

Christianity and Ice Hockey in Canada
The Role of Violence

Nick DeLuca

Throughout many forms of Christianity, there are a range of ideas and messages about peace that stand out as key themes of the religion. As such, many denominations of Christianity have taken to these ideas of peace. In a world that is almost constantly violent, it is intriguing to look at how this religion intersects with the culture of violence. This essay seeks to analyze how Christianity and ice hockey coexist, since the peaceful themes of Christianity seem counterintuitive to the violence often seen in ice hockey.

The idea of analyzing Christianity and ice hockey derives from looking at a study done by researchers Robert Dunn and Christopher Stevenson concerning an evangelical church hockey league in Canada.[1] Dunn and Stevenson argued that competitiveness and the "elements of the sport ethic," not violence, were to blame for any difficulties in the application of Christian values to the game.[2] They also found that players struggling to understand their own application of the "Christian role-identity" had an "uncertainty or lack of knowledge about what was expected of a "Christian" in this hockey setting, supplementing these difficulties.[3] Surprisingly, the study proved that the only aspects of ice hockey that could prevent Christian athletes from applying their religious values to the sport were either the athletes' own struggles with their Christian identity or the competitive, dominant nature of the sport. In this study, however, the researchers noted that the league prohibited body contact of any kind, owing to how violence conflicts with the churches' own evangelical beliefs.[4] This essay aims to discuss how the violence prohibited by the league studied by Dunn and Stevenson, and the violence on display

---

[1] Robert Dunn and Christopher Stevenson, "The Paradox of the Church Hockey League," *International Review for the Sociology of Sport* 33, no. 2 (1998): 131.

[2] Ibid., 139–140.

[3] Ibid., 135.

[4] Ibid., 134.

in professional ice hockey, is more Christian than it might seem. Despite Dunn and Stevenson's assumption that hockey and Christianity are paradoxical in nature,[5] Christianity and religion remains a key part of many hockey players' lives. Professional players such as Mike Fisher,[6] Dan Ellis,[7] and Adam McQuaid[8] are all outspoken about their faith and are prime examples of religion's existence in the sport of hockey. While the sport of hockey is inherently violent, Christianity is still evident throughout the sport, despite the assumptions of people such as Dunn and Stevenson.

Christianity and ice hockey can coexist because the violence in hockey, as well as the justifications of that violence, are not unlike the violence and its rationale seen in the Bible. To demonstrate this, we will first discuss the role of violence in hockey before illustrating the connections it has with violence in the Bible. We will discuss the arguments surrounding violence in hockey and the nuances such violence has in the game before suggesting how these nuances connect to discussions about the role of violence in the Bible. We will look to the sport's birthplace of Canada—a country that has adapted the sport into its own identity—and examine how Canada has maintained Christianity as its majority faith while still being heavily influenced by hockey. These arguments will illuminate the similarities between violence in hockey and Christianity, and these similarities, along with Canadians' perceptions of hockey, will demonstrate how Christian theology and hockey can be compatible.

Violence has been part of the sport of ice hockey since its inception. The most commonly tolerated form of violence in hockey is body checking, which involves a player aggressively hitting an opponent in the hopes of freeing the puck from their possession.[9] This technique of winning the

---

[5] Ibid., 132–133.

[6] Kim Washburn, *Defender of the Faith: The Mike Fisher Story* (Grand Rapids, MI: Zondervan, 2011).

[7] Daniel Schopf, "Religion in Hockey Part One: NHL Players," *The Hockey Writers* (21 May 2017), https://thehockeywriters.com/religion-in-hockey-part-one-nhl-players/.

[8] Amalie Benjamin, "Religion Rarely on Display across the NHL," *Boston Globe*, 5 April 2015, https://www.bostonglobe.com/sports/2015/04/05/religion-not-often-display-nhl/TgROsmqu1gFE4IIhB1thOO/story.html.

[9] "Standard of Play and Rule Emphasis—Body Checking," *USA* Hockey, http://www.usahockeyrulebook.com/page/show/1015119-standard-of-play-and-rule-emphasis-body-checking (accessed 1 August 2017).

puck has been a part of hockey for its entire history, with the early years of the game described as "rugby on skates" due to the frequent hitting.[10] In its most natural form, body checking is a violent act and is classified as violence in the Merriam-Webster's dictionary, which describe it as "the use of physical force so as to injure, abuse, damage, or destroy."[11] This tactic is, essentially, abusing the opposing player to regain control of the puck—qualifying it as an act of violence.

But how are we to define violence? The World Health Organization (WHO) proposes ideas about hockey violence that conflict with the Merriam-Webster definition, arguing that violence is "the intentional use of physical force or power, threatened or actual, against oneself, another person, or against a group or community, that either results in or has a high likelihood of resulting in injury, death, psychological harm, maldevelopment or deprivation."[12] According to WHO, any incidental contact during play, although dangerous, is not classified as violence, since it is not intentional. Even intentional body contact could fall outside of this definition because the true intention could be winning possession of the puck and not harming the other player. Subtle changes and interpretations about the nature of violence can change the perception of certain acts. The heart of the debates that surround both violence in ice hockey and violence in the Bible involve discrepancies regarding the genuine definition of violence, and the intent of the person committing the violent act. Understanding the different interpretations of violence will help demonstrate how people can support violence in certain cases.

Debates about violence in hockey commonly revolve around fighting in the National Hockey League (NHL). Fighting officially became a part of the NHL rulebook in 1922 under rule fifty-six[13] and has survived through sustained criticism. The International Ice Hockey Federation (IIHF), which dictates the regulations of many leagues world-

---

[10] Ross Bernstein, *The Code: The Unwritten Rules of Fighting and Retaliation in the NHL* (Chicago: Triumph Books, 2006), 4.

[11] "Violence," *Merriam-Webster*, https://www.merriam-webster.com/ dictionary/violence (accessed 24 June 2017).

[12] Etienne G. Krug, and Linda L. Dahlberg, "Violence—A Global Health Problem," in *World Report on Violence and Health*, ed. Etienne G. Krug, Linda L. Dahlberg, James A. Mercy, Anthony B. Zwi, and Rafael Lozano (Geneva: WHO, 2002), *eBook Collection (EBSCOhost)*, EBSCO*host*, 5.

[13] Bernstein, *The Code*, 4.

wide, including the Winter Olympics, has prohibited fighting.[14] Despite the criticism and actions taken against fighting, philosopher Abe Zakhem argues that fighting under the correct circumstances can be virtuous; for this to be the case, the main intention should not be harm, but justice.[15] While hockey violence concerns many people, and many advocate against it, the difficulty in accurately defining and establishing a boundary for sanctioned versus unsanctioned violence makes it tough to legislate rules that the NHL can actually implement. A hockey principle, known as "the code," poses a similar challenge. "The code" is a set of unwritten rules of fighting in hockey that exists to keep players safer when fighting. It lays out ground rules for enforcers of when,[16] why,[17] how,[18] and with whom[19] it is acceptable to fight. This code applies to all players, but was created for and is commonly used by players who take on the role of an enforcer on the team. Enforcers are hockey players who are essentially participating on the team as intimidation to the other team. They fight, aim for big hits, and act as protection for a team's star players.

Zakhem suggests four criteria that a fight must meet to be virtuous—echoing some of the code's values. First, the fight must provide education in the virtues of fighting fair. Second, the fight must be reasonably safe. Third, the fight must be good for the community involved. Fourth, the fight must be sensitive to tradition, in order to keep fulfilling the first three requirements.[20] "The code" is a key factor that helps satisfy these criteria for fighting in hockey. These unwritten rules, along with some minor rules outlining basic fighting etiquette legislated in the NHL rulebook,[21] teach players the virtue of fighting[22] and keep players safe, satisfying the first two criteria outlined by Zakhem. Specifically, this code keeps players safe by invoking a natural policing; in the case of an illegal play not seen by an official, the player responsible will likely be

---

[14] *IIHF Official Rule Book 2014–2018* (Zurich: IIHF, 2015), 84.

[15] Abe Zakhem, "The Virtues of a Good Fight: Assessing the Ethics of Fighting in the National Hockey League," *Sports, Ethics and Philosophy* 9, no. 1 (2015): 32–33.

[16] Bernstein, *The Code*, 65–71.

[17] Ibid., 34–55.

[18] Ibid., 73–75

[19] Ibid., 60–61.

[20] Zakhem, "The Virtues of a Good Fight," 37–38.

[21] *National Hockey League Official Rules 2015–2016*, 70–75.

[22] Bernstein, *The Code*, 71–72; ibid., 75–77.

met with a fight from a player from the opposing team. This concept of natural policing helps satisfy Zakhem's third requirement of being beneficial to the sport by discouraging more brutal and unnecessary violence. Thus, ice hockey uses these justifications to rationalize the violence and make it appear almost virtuous.

There are, however, many instances of violence in hockey that are not virtuous. For example, the Todd Bertuzzi incident is infamous for demonstrating the unnecessary and unacceptable aggression that still appears in hockey. During this incident, Vancouver Canucks enforcer Todd Bertuzzi was enacting revenge on Steve Moore for a previous violent play that Moore had made in prior game between the two teams.[23] Bertuzzi punched Moore in the back of the head while he was not looking, knocking him to the ice with a concussion and multiple fractures.[24] Most of the hockey world condemned the play, which ended up in court, with Bertuzzi pleading guilty to simple assault.[25] These actions are not tolerated within the sport of hockey, and this incident is a good example of what might happen more frequently without "the code." Players overwhelmingly argue that keeping sanctioned fighting in the sport will prevent similar, negative incidents from becoming commonplace. Without such legislated fighting, players could make illegal and dangerous plays, frequently outside of the referee's view. Players such as veteran Jarome Iginla[26] and enforcer Brandon Prust[27] have publicly supported the efficacy of natural policing and have even gone on to say that the NHL needs controlled fighting in the league to prevent more substantial violence, especially using the stick to injure someone. Thus, many view "the code" in hockey as beneficial to the sport.

Despite much public outcry, such debates about justifiable violence make it difficult to remove fighting from the sport. Concerns exist about

---

[23] John H. Kerr, "Examining the Bertuzzi-Moore NHL Ice Hockey Incident: Crossing the Line Between Sanctioned and Unsanctioned Violence in Sport," *Aggression and Violent Behavior* 11, no. 4 (2006): 315.

[24] Ibid.

[25] Ibid., 317.

[26] "Jarome Iginla Makes Case for Fighting," *ESPN*, http://www.espn.com/boston/nhl/story/_/id/9981354/jarome-iginla-fighting-makes-hockey-safer (last modified 15 November 2013).

[27] Brandon Prust, "Why We Fight," *The Players' Tribune*, https://www.theplayerstribune.com/why-we-fight/ (last modified 3 February 2015).

the role of players as enforcers,[28] the virtues of fighting,[29] and of criminal and legal issues.[30] Questions exist regarding why enforcers fight, as people wonder about the true reason for the aggression. Researchers Richard Burdekin and Matthew Morton suggest that, since fighting allowed them to reach the professional level of play, enforcers might be fighting to keep their jobs, as opposed to truly fighting for the positive values that Zakhem sees.[31] Enforcers exist to respond to prohibited actions of the other team and to protect their team's more skilled players. Given the possibility that enforcers may be risking their salary, the research of Burdekin and Morton suggests enforcers might be fighting for their jobs rather than the good of the sport.[32] With regard to legal issues, the intention of the players' violence is debatable, as described in a detailed analysis of the Todd Bertuzzi incident.[33] As a response to the outcry against fighting, the NHL has claimed that they do not condone fighting, as demonstrated by their policy of penalizing players for five minutes,[34] but this is depends on how you define "condone"—some international hockey leagues offer ejections and suspensions as sanction against fighting. Although fighting has been declining in recent years,[35] its popularity is still high. A 2013 study on attendance in the American Hockey League (AHL) found that "fans were shown to be significantly impacted by fighting during hockey games as fights per game of the home team had a large positive and significant effect."[36] Given the popularity of hockey violence, skeptics are as concerned as ever. These concerns, while valid, do not comprise a strong enough counterargument to

---

[28] Richard C. K. Burdekin and Matthew Grindon Morton, "Blood Money: Violence for Hire in the National Hockey League," *International Journal of Sport Finance* 10, no. 4 (2015): 328–356.

[29] Zakhem, "The Virtues of a Good Fight," 32–46.

[30] Kerr, "Examining the Bertuzzi-Moore Incident," 313–322.

[31] Burdekin and Morton, "Blood Money," 329.

[32] Ibid.

[33] Kerr, "Examining the Bertuzzi-Moore Incident," 317–318.

[34] Corey Masisak, "Bettman Discusses Fighting, CTE in Remarks at BOG," *NHL*, https://www.nhl.com/news/bettman-discusses-fighting-cte-in-remarks-at-bog/c-605081 (last modified 6 December 2011).

[35] "Hockey Fight Statistics—NHL," *Hockey Fights*, http://www.hockey-fights.com/stats/ (accessed 23 July 2017).

[36] Rodney Paul et al., "American Hockey League Attendance: A Study of Fan Preferences for Fighting, Team Performance, and Promotions," *International Journal of Sport Finance* 8, no. 1 (2013): 33.

Zakhem's discussions of "morally good" violence. The NHL, meanwhile, has refused to change its stance on fighting.

Zakhem's ideas are also echoed in ethicist and theologian Tracy Trothen's insights on Christian atonement theories and hockey violence. She states that "religions and other ways of being religious are marked by violence and other distortions, yet this usually neither stops people from participating in religious organizations, nor from passionately defending the ones to which they subscribe."[37] Trothen expands on this as she focuses on the violence of Christ on the cross. She analyzes the cross because, as she discusses, such violence is often overlooked by Christians, since the symbol of Jesus on the cross is one of the defining moments in the Bible.[38] Many ignore the inherent violence of crucifixion because of the importance of the image of Christ on the cross. Many people, however, still passionately defend the cross as a symbol of love. Trothen addresses this by saying that the violence of Jesus on the cross "in no way negates the love and the promise of life in the cross"[39] and that "anger and even wrath can be parts of love particularly in terms of caring enough to be angry at injustice."[40] Both concepts translate well to hockey, as many of the positive aspects taught and practiced in the sport are not negated by the violence, aggression, and wrath in hockey. As Trothen states, hockey "can offer intense physical awareness, including both pleasure and pain, grounded in communal co-operation; it can promote self-knowledge in terms of how to lose, how to work as a team, and how to stand together with others who come with a diversity of social classes and worldviews."[41] These values are not only taught despite the violence in hockey, but some of them (such as physical awareness, pleasure, and pain) actually rely on the violence to be taught. Additionally, the suggestion that anger can be valuable when reacting to injustice is a main factor

---

[37] Tracy Trothen, "Holy Acceptable Violence? Violence in Hockey and Christian Atonement Theories," *Journal of Religion and Popular Culture* 21, no. 1 (Fall 2009): 3, http://go.galegroup.com.libproxy.temple.edu/ps/i.do?p=AONE &sw=w&u=temple_main&v=2.1&it=r&id=GALE%7CA213033181&asid=df8 4840cd0abbf754dc1959b250e3e86.

[38] Ibid., 6.

[39] Ibid., 10.

[40] Ibid., 12.

[41] Tracy Trothen, "Hockey: A Divine Sport?—Canada's National Sport in Relation to Embodiment, Community and Hope," *Studies in Religion / Sciences Religieuses* 35, no. 2 (2006): 303.

in how the enforcer role was born, as teams sought a violent player to act aggressively against the improprieties that they were beginning to see in the sport. This supports Zakhem's arguments, which draw upon Aristotle in addressing the benefits of anger.[42] On the topic of the cross, Trothen also compares the themes of self-sacrifice between the Bible and ice hockey.[43] Self-sacrifice is an essential part of the game of hockey. Looking at the NHL, there are many examples of players admitting to playing through injuries on the ice, such as when Gregory Campbell of the Boston Bruins played for almost a minute after suffering a broken leg due to a blocked shot in the 2013 NHL playoffs.[44] Noting the similarities, Trothen states that "the blood sacrifice of Jesus traditionally has been assumed to be a moral good just as the blood sacrifice of a hockey player often is lauded as the loftiest indication of loyalty to one's team."[45] This comparison rings true in the Campbell example because coaches, fans, and other players praised him for his sacrifice for his team. These types of sacrificial plays are frequently made in hockey and are usually given significant praise, demonstrating that this violence is crucial to the game and seen as morally good. The sacrificial aspect, depicted in both Jesus' crucifixion and in the sport of hockey, shows that violence in hockey is similar to the violence depicted in the Bible.

Another example of violence and its role in the Bible appears in the Gospel of John. Many scholars have noted that while the Gospel of John is also known as the gospel of love, there is a fair amount of violence and aggression in the book. Michael Newheart uses the Gospel of John to discuss aggression and hate, introducing the idea that the aggression can be positive.[46] He proposes that people "love the hate that we find in the

---

[42] Zakhem, "The Virtues of a Good Fight," 34–35. Here, Zakhem discusses Aristotle's ideas of how anger is a natural human emotion. Zakhem mentions Aristotle's viewpoint of how in certain situations, a "good tempered" or "well-spirited" person should feel angry. Zakhem ties Aristotle's views on anger to injustice, claiming that when experiencing injustice, it is natural to be angry.

[43] Trothen, "Holy Acceptable Violence?" 37–46.

[44] Luke Fox, "Campbell Plays on Broken Leg, Done for Season," *Sportsnet*, http://www.sportsnet.ca/hockey/boston-bruins-gregory-campbell-blocks-shot-plays-on-broken-leg-done-for-season/ (last modified 6 June 2013).

[45] Trothen, "Holy Acceptable Violence?" 43.

[46] Michael Newheart, "The Transgression of Aggression: Learning to Love the Hate in the New Testament (and Ourselves!)," in *A Cry Instead of Justice: The*

text,"[47] which suggests that people should look deeper than the violence and hate in the Bible to find a more important meaning to it. Since the Bible can be read in a way where people can love violence and hatred, Christians find themselves with an opportunity to make justifications for their own violence. Zakhem supports this argument when describing how anger in moderation can be virtuous, comparing it to aggression in hockey.[48] Newheart's point on "loving the hate" is also reminiscent of Trothen's assertion of how the violence on the cross does not negate the promise of life. Both Trothen and Newheart point to specific biblical references to demonstrate how violence can be productive. Trothen then transfers these references to examples of hockey violence, further supporting Zakhem's arguments for the benefits of fighting in hockey. Seeing how the viewpoints of violence in both contexts is that violence is beneficial, the assumption that violence in hockey goes against Christianity is essentially invalid.

The Bible can be interpreted to see the positive aspects of violence because of the flexible way in which the Bible discusses the subject. Adele Reinhartz, a specialist on the Gospel of John, explains how the grammar of the violence toward the Jews in the gospel could contribute to anti-Semitism throughout history.[49] Seeing the Bible used for aggressive and hateful means is not uncommon, as much violence throughout history has been directly justified by Christianity, such as the actions of the Klu Klux Klan and the Inquisition. Reinhartz concludes her essay by saying how "the grammar of violence, and the discourses of love and hate, can leap from a literary text and into the annals of history whether they were intended to or not."[50] Reinhartz specifically discusses the differences in grammar between the violence of the Jews as perpetrators and Jews as victims.[51] She states that there is no justification mentioned in the gospel about violence perpetrated by the Jews, while there are justifications for the violence perpetrated on the Jews. While the gospel does not explicitly

---

Bible and Cultures of Violence in Psychological Perspective, ed. Dereck Daschke and Andrew Kille (New York/London: T&T Clark International, 2010), 80.

[47] Ibid.

[48] Zakhem, "The Virtues of a Good Fight," 34–35.

[49] Adele Reinhartz, "Love, Hate, and Violence in the Gospel of John," in *Violence in the New Testament*, ed. Shelly Matthews and E. Leigh Gibson (New York/London: T&T Clark International, 2005), 109.

[50] Ibid., 121–122.

[51] Ibid., 112.

state that Jews are the enemy, Reinhartz suggests that the grammar used in the Gospel of John when discussing this violence is morally subjective. She argues in this instance that readers may interpret this message in a certain way and use it to justify anti-Semitism.

This argument can also apply to the depiction of violence in hockey. The grammar surrounding competitive sport in society makes it seem as if the opposing team is an enemy who must be defeated at all costs. As Reinhartz suggests with the Gospel of John, this type of dialogue helps justify violence against the enemy, which in her example is the Jews. This translates well to hockey, as the competitiveness of most sports leads to a narrative where there is a hero and villain—a classic rivalry. In an article on the theatrics of professional wrestling, John Campbell discusses this theory with a focus on the attention drawn by prevalent hero and villain roles promoted within the sport.[52] Although wrestling is an ambiguous example, since even Campbell notes that it is more about entertainment than sport, all sports use these types of promotional tactics, including hockey.[53] Consider the famous "Miracle on Ice" game in 1980, where the "patriotic American underdogs" were trying to overthrow the powerful, "evil Soviet Union communists" on home ice in Lake Placid, New York. Campbell explains how Cold War politics enhanced these hero and villain tropes.[54] Additionally, as Thomas Mueller and John Sutherland have shown, heroes and villains are excellent marketing devices in sports.[55] Mueller and Sutherland found that marketers can effectively "utilize villains to target fans having lower involvements, while building rivalries by focusing on *heroes* for fans with higher levels of involvement." Considering this good-versus-bad dichotomy, it is logical that players are more likely to regard their own team's actions as justifiable, while regarding those same actions unjustifiable when committed by the opposing team. This is the same approach that Reinhartz suggests in relation to the Gospel of John. This constantly reinforced struggle between good and evil in both sports and in the Bible—in conjunction with the vague lan-

---

[52] John W. Campbell, "Professional Wrestling: Why the Bad Guy Wins," *Journal of American Culture* 19, no. 2 (1996): 127.

[53] Ibid., 127–128.

[54] Ibid., 128–129.

[55] Thomas S. Mueller and John C. Sutherland, "Heroes and Villains: Increasing Fan Involvement in Pursuit of 'The Elusive Fan,'" *Journal of Sport Administration and Supervision* 2, no. 1 (2010): 27–28.

guage used by the latter—encourages the justification of violence in both contexts.

Violence is also seen outside of the Gospel of John. For example, the Hebrew Bible is filled with violent acts committed by God, as seen in Genesis 19:24, Genesis 22:2, and Samuel 6:19. M. Daniel Carroll R. discusses God's violence as depicted in the Book of Amos, arguing that it "teaches that divine violence is a response to human violence."[56] Hockey violence can be seen as similar, in that violence from enforcers is a response to unwarranted violence from the opposing team. Many players believe that fighting in the game prevents more unnecessary violence and provides legitimate response for other violent plays.[57] In the latest poll of the players officially performed by the National Hockey League Players' Association (NHLPA) in 2011, 98 percent of players voted in favor of having fighting in the NHL.[58] Even as recently as 2016, the head of the NHLPA stated that they would stand firm and would only prohibit fighting in hockey if the players approved of such a decision.[59] Players witness unjust violence against their team and respond to it with violence of their own in much the same way that God does with humankind. Adrian Vasile supports this in his article discussing violence in the Hebrew Bible, saying that the text is teaching that "violence is part of our daily life and that we must know how to manage it."[60] While God's violence is not the sole reason for acting violently, as Vasile also mentions, its inclusion in the Bible makes it clear that violence is a justifiable op-

---

[56] M. Daniel Carroll R., "'I Will Send Fire': Reflections on the Violence of God in Amos," in *Wrestling with the Violence of God: Soundings in the Old Testament*, ed. M. Daniel R. Carroll and J. Blair Wilgus (University Park, PA: Penn State University Press/Eisenbrauns), 2015), 120–121.

[57] "This Week's Big Question: What Role Does Fighting Have in the Game?" *ESPN*, http://www.espn.com/nhl/story/_/id/18638712/nhl-big-question-players-see-role-fighting-game (last modified 10 February 2017).

[58] "Plenty to Chew on in NHLPA's Players Poll," *Sports Illustrated*, https://www.si.com/nhl/home-ice/2011/01/31/plenty-to-chew-on-in-nhlpas-players-poll (last modified 31 Jan. 2011).

[59] "NHLPA Head Donald Fehr on Fighting, Salary Cap, Lockouts," CBC, http://www.cbc.ca/sports/hockey/nhl/nhlpa-donald-fehr-q-and-a-1.3733844 (last modified 24 August 2016).

[60] Adrian Vasile, "Aspects of Violence in the Old Testament," *DIALOGO—The Second Virtual International Conference on the Dialogue between Science and Theology* 2, no. 1 (2015): 91–92.

tion.[61] As Reinhartz suggests, the language and grammar of the Bible, whether it intends to or not, can be read this way.

Saint Augustine's discourse on the theory of just war also demonstrates that violence in specific situations is not only justifiable, but encouraged. Augustine states that "soldiers should perform their military duties on behalf of the peace and safety of the community" and that the monarch should undertake war "if he thinks it advisable."[62] Even prominent figures within the church agree that violence can be acceptable within Christian values, since the morality of violence depends on the circumstances. Augustine's point reflects the mentality of enforcers perfectly, as they fight when the peace and safety of their team is at risk. Augustine focuses on the aspect of justice of the violent action in the same way many people view God's violence. Augustine also makes a similar point about the wars of Moses, arguing that he "acted not in cruelty, but in righteous retribution."[63] Enforcers and God both act in righteous retribution with their use of violence. Augustine's arguments echo the values seen in "the code" about fighting in hockey that hold players responsible for their actions. "The code" is how hockey players manage the violence in their sport, while those Christian leaders who support arguments about violence similar to those surrounding the code prove that Christianity can exist within ice hockey.

Saint Augustine comes to these conclusions about violence because of his view of the imperfect peace of humanity. Philosopher John Langan describes this in his piece on the elements of Augustine's just war theory.[64] He states that Augustine makes a "fundamental distinction between the ultimate peace of the heavenly city, which has an absolute value but is not directly attainable, and the partial, temporary, and imperfect peace available to sinful humanity."[65] Because the ultimate peace of the heavenly city is unattainable to humanity, the morality surrounding violence becomes ambiguous in an attempt to make the imperfect peace as perfect as it can be. Langan continues his piece by saying "the possibility of dif-

---

[61] Ibid., 92.

[62] Saint Augustine, "Contra Faustum Manichæum," trans. Richard Stothert, in *A Select Library of the Nicene and Post-Nicene Fathers of the Christian Church Vol. 4*, ed. Philip Schaff (Grand Rapids, MI: Eerdmans, 1956), 301.

[63] Ibid.

[64] John Langan, "The Elements of St. Augustine's Just War Theory," *Journal of Religious Ethics* 12, no. 1 (1984).

[65] Ibid., 29.

ferent forms of order and of peace which might differ in moral quality and which might then provide justification for wars of revolutionary change and for violent movements."[66] He is saying that because the peace is imperfect, humanity can justify wars that satisfy the criteria that Augustine outlined in *Contra Faustum*. The idea of an imperfect peace is exactly what hockey players describe when discussing the concept of natural policing. They are saying that outlawing violence will not help, because the players are imperfect and the violence will continue no matter what and will not be properly answered for. With the current system of natural policing, players "go to war" in a sense to "revolt" against the unjust actions of the opposing team. Augustine's just war theory bridges the gap between Christianity and hockey perfectly as it provides almost the same criteria for just violence as the "code," just as similar arguments supporting hockey violence do. Augustine also further proves that Christianity can be violent as well, which is one of the main reasons people assume that Christianity and hockey are not compatible.

Canada is an interesting place to analyze how hockey and Christian violence intertwine because Canada has significant influences on hockey that have given the sport many of the values that it holds. In turn, hockey has its own significant influences on Canadian society, and the way Canada interacts with Christianity in this sense is interesting because of how these influences have shaped Canadian culture. The book *Canada's Game: Hockey and Identity* describes how hockey is found in all aspects of Canadian life, adding to the idea of how hockey is a core part of being Canadian. It states that "to understand hockey in a scholarly way is to see it as a series of historical struggles that emanate from its central position in Canadian culture as national icon, as work and entertainment, as pastime, as enterprise, as privilege, and as a class-, race- and gender-based locus of identity." [67] This volume also covers the topic of violence in the essay, "'Just Part of the Game': Depictions of Violence in Hockey Prose," which analyzes violence in hockey in the context of fictional literature which sheds light on how Canadians absorb the sport outside of the are-

---

[66] Ibid., 30.

[67] Andrew C. Holman, "Canada's Game? Hockey and the Problem of Identity," in *Canada's Game: Hockey and Identity*, ed. Andrew C. Holman (Montreal and Kingston, ON: McGill-Queen's University Press, 2009), 6.

na.[68] Author Jason Blake discusses how catharsis is a major factor in supporting arguments about hockey violence and how this has penetrated much of the fictional hockey literature.[69] The fact that violence is always a prominent theme in hockey fiction shows how embedded it is in Canadian culture. This helps make people more tolerant of violence, because the more people expose themselves to violence, the more desensitized to it they become. Frequent violence in fiction only supplements this.

The arguments discussed earlier concerning biblical violence make the same points, in particular Reinhartz's argument that the grammar surrounding violence in the Gospel of John influences the interpretations of the gospel. The ingrained violence in Canadian culture also attracts more people to the sport. As previously mentioned, hockey violence is extremely popular and marketable,[70] which Blake supports with his discussion of how most hockey fiction revolves around violence. This further shows how violence is a key theme in hockey culture, as using violence to attract people feeds into the cycle of violence in the sport. While Blake provides examples of fiction that demonstrate the negative effects of violence in hockey, he also describes how the players in most stories are not to blame for involving themselves in these violent actions. Blake states "the fault lies not solely with the 'hero' but with the system as a whole."[71] This "system" creates the inevitable violence of hockey, similarly to what Vasile discusses in his piece on the Hebrew Bible. Vasile says that violence is unavoidable in daily life and that people need to manage it. Blake's argument supports this by discussing how violence is included and depicted in hockey literature. He continues by saying that somebody had to make the decision to hire the player to be a violent enforcer, which reflects how Burdekin and Morton[72] discuss the concept of hiring players as enforcers specifically to be violent and aggressive. The "system" is advertising hockey violence. For better or worse, the encouragement and depictions of violence show how this type of play is truly at the heart

---

[68] Jason F. Blake, "'Just Part of the Game': Depictions of Violence in Hockey Prose," in *Canada's Game: Hockey and Identity*, ed. Andrew C. Holman (Montreal and Kingston, ON: McGill-Queen's University Press, 2009), 66–67.

[69] Ibid., 67–69.

[70] J.C.H. Jones, "Winners, Losers and Hosers: Demand and Survival in the National Hockey League," *Atlantic Economic Journal* 12, no. 3 (1984): 54; Paul, Weinbach, and Robbins, "American Hockey League Attendance," 33.

[71] Ibid., 73.

[72] Burdekin and Morton, "Blood Money," 343–344.

of the game. This "system" of violence in hockey and hockey literature demonstrate how violence permeates hockey and Canadian culture, much like the themes and ideas about violence in Christianity.

In Canada, hockey has been elevated to the status of religion. Many observers, including Novak and Price, [73] have discussed how Canada views hockey as a religion. In 1977, author Tom Sinclair-Faulkner, following Thomas Luckmann's definitions of religion, [74] suggested that hockey is a Canadian religion—an argument supported by John Badertscher in a piece he wrote in response to Sinclair-Faulnker's "A Puckish Reflection on Religion in Canada." [75] Because of Canada's unique and arguably religious relationship with hockey, the perception of hockey violence in Canada already accepts the violence as justifiable. Factoring in how Christianity is still the dominant religion, the connection between Christianity and hockey certainly exists, as Canadians are still practicing Christianity and playing hockey, and the prevalence of violence is not preventing it. [76] Scott Schieman has argued that people take their faith into consideration when making decisions. [77] While his focus was on the level of education and how that factors into decision making based on religion, Schieman still found that those people who valued religion made decisions with their faith in mind. [78] As such, Canada has

---

[73] Joseph Price, "An American Apotheosis: Sports as Popular Religion," in *From Season to Season: Sports as American Religion*, ed. Joseph Price (Macon, GA: Mercer University Press, 2001), 216; Michael Novak, *The Joy of Sports: End Zones, Bases, Baskets, Balls, and the Consecration of the American Spirit* (Maryland: Hamilton Press, 1988), 18.

[74] Tom Sinclair-Faulkner, "A Puckish Reflection on Religion in Canada," in *Religion and Culture in Canada*, ed. Peter Slater (Waterloo, ON: Wilfrid Laurier University Press, 1977), 401; Thomas Luckmann, *The Invisible Religion* (New York: Macmillan, 1967).

[75] John Badertscher, "Response to Sinclair-Faulkner," in *Religion and Culture in Canada*, ed. Peter Slater (Waterloo, ON: Wilfrid Laurier University Press, 1977).

[76] "National Household Survey (NHS) Profile 2011," *National Household Survey, Statistics Canada*, 11 September 2013, http://www12.statcan.gc.ca/nhs-enm/2011/dp-pd/prof/index.cfm?Lang=E.

[77] Scott Schieman, "Education and the Importance of Religion in Decision Making: Do Other Dimensions of Religiousness Matter?" *Journal for the Scientific Study of Religion* 50, no. 3 (2011): 570–587.

[78] Ibid., 583–584.

actively adopted hockey and its associated violence as a religion, despite the assumption that Christianity is not compatible with hockey.

Canadian identity, along with hockey's religiousness in Canada, allow for a certain level of hockey violence despite the assumption that Christianity is incompatible with violence. In their book about the identity and politics of hockey in Canada, Richard Gruneau and David Whitson support this point when they write that boys in the United States idolize John Wayne for his masculinity and toughness, while "for generations of Canadian boys a slightly meaner version of that same image was represented by skilled but tough hockey players, the archetype of them being Gordie Howe."[79] Canadian children are conditioned to look to hockey for lessons in toughness. The extensive literature about violence in hockey helps them grow up with the idea that to be Canadian is to be a tough hockey player and that violence is just a normal aspect of the national winter sport. With this in mind, and looking at the similarities between hockey violence and Christian violence, these two seemingly incompatible entities of sport and religion can coexist, because both teach the acceptance of violence.

In their book, Gruneau and Whitson also tackle the topic of hockey violence and, specifically, its nuanced relationship with Canadian identity:

> People in and around the game view fighting and intimidation not only as good tactics but also as essential dimensions of both the hockey culture and the Canadian tradition. All professional players, and especially those developed in Canada, have come up through a system in which physical toughness is not only respected but required.[80]

To Gruneau and Wilson, Canadian identity and its justification of violence can be traced back to Aristotle's ideas about acceptable aggression, which Zakhem uses to illustrate how violence in hockey is beneficial. This complements the ideas in the Blake article about how toughness and violence penetrate hockey literature, with the literature reinforcing Gruneau and Whitson's ideas about violence in the sport— particularly in Canada where hockey is crucial to the culture. Because hockey is at the core of Canadian culture, the themes of violence and toughness translate from the sport to Canadian identity. Trothen sup-

---

[79] Richard Gruneau and David Whitson, *Hockey Night in Canada: Sport, Identities, and Cultural Politics* (Toronto: Garamond Press, 1993), 191.

[80] Ibid., 176.

ports the idea that toughness is a core aspect of being Canadian when she states that a

> fierce community approach, typified by loyalty and strength, is embedded deeply in the Canadian identity and has often served to typify what it means to be Canadian; Canadians are tougher than most, we pride ourselves on being able to survive adversity and a harsh climate, not complain, and be nice about it."[81]

Similarly, Newheart and Vasile argue that violence is a part of life and Christianity and that we need to learn to embrace it.

Despite the violence inherent in hockey, Christianity is still prevalent in the sport because there are many similarities between the interpretations of violence in both ice hockey and in the Bible. Violence itself is a difficult concept to grasp, and many debates about violence in hockey stem from ambiguity surrounding those times when violence could be considered beneficial and appropriate. These arguments demonstrate that violence is not only a core part of ice hockey but is tolerated and accepted by most Canadians. Similar arguments and discussions exist regarding violence in the Bible. As we have seen, violence does not impede Christianity from becoming a part of a sport, nor does it discourage or antagonize Christians, given that violence in the Bible has more in common with the sport of hockey than many critics of hockey violence seem to realize.

---

[81] Trothen, "Holy Acceptable Violence?" 56.

Index